THE NEW MOSES

A MATTHEAN TYPOLOGY

THE NEW MOSES
A MATTHEAN TYPOLOGY

Dale C. Allison, Jr.

FORTRESS PRESS   MINNEAPOLIS

THE NEW MOSES
A Matthean Typology

Library of Congress Cataloging-in-Publication Data

Allison, Dale C.
   The new Moses :   a Matthean typology / Dale C. Allison, Jr.
      p.   cm.
Includes bibliographical references and indexes.
ISBN 0-8006-2699-0
   1. Bible.   N.T.   Matthew—Criticism, Interpretation, etc.
2. Moses (Biblical leader) in the New Testament.   3. Typology
(Theology)   I. Title.
BS2575. 2. A55   1993
226. 2'064—dc20   93-18735
                                                  CIP

Manufactured in Great Britain   ISBN: 0-8006-2699-0
                                                  1-2699

97 96 95 94 93 1 2 3 4 5 6 7 8 9 10

IN MEMORIAM

Barbara Jean Farha
1949–1987

ἐκλαύσαμεν πικρῶς

CONTENTS ———————————————

Appendices

PREFACE

For several years now I have been writing, with W. D. Davies, a commentary on the Gospel according to Matthew. When completed the work will cover three volumes and run to approximately 2,300 pages—enough, it might seem, to say what needs to be said. In truth, however, the more one studies a book such as Matthew, so rich in ideas and so significant in influence, the more one feels that even a lifetime of research and writing would only serve as introduction. It is for this reason and others that, on p. x of the Preface to our volume l, Professor Davies and I were moved to write: "We could have wished for more expansive treatments of many aspects of the text but have had to prefer leanness to fullness both in the introductory sections and in the body of the commentary." To this one reviewer, otherwise kindly disposed to our work, responded: "They have got to be joking!" But we (who have regularly suffered the agony of cutting finished pages in order to save space) were not joking. Entire books have been written on single paragraphs of Matthew, even individual verses. How then can a commentary, an instrument of condensation, be anything other than lean and sparse? There is much of importance that even three hefty tomes must, given their nature, leave undeveloped, or out of account altogether. One could always say more, much more. Hence the present book. While working through the Gospel I have discovered that the new Moses theme, examined at length by my coauthor three decades ago, demands fresh consideration, for much of great relevance has been neglected, by him and by others; and because our commentary has not proved sufficiently spacious for the demonstration of this, the present investigation now supplies the lack.

I am happy to register the names of those who so helped with and benefitted my writing and research. W. D. Davies, whose eagle eye caught many errors, has been a constant source of stimulation and encouragement. His happy willingness to entertain objectively my criticism of his published views is proof of a character and good faith I hope always to emulate. And he has been so kind as to return the favor, so that I have profited greatly from his always-insightful criticism. Parts of the manuscript were also read by Calum Carmichael, David Daube, Craig Hinkson, Chris Kettler, Amy-Jill Levine, and Michael J. Neth: from them all I have learned much; and their observations have subtracted many errors—not all of them minuscule. Lastly, my wife, Kristine, and our three children, Emily Melissa, Andrew William, and John Matthew, have endured yet another book. They continue to requite my manifold vices with nothing but kindness and love. If God is so good we shall all fare well.

ABBREVIATIONS

AB	Anchor Bible
Adv. haer.	Irenaeus, *Adversus haereses* [*Against Heresies*]
AGJU	Arbeiten zur Geschichte des antiken Judentums und des Urchristentum
AnBib	Analecta Biblica
ANF	A. Roberts and J. Donaldson, eds., *The Ante-Nicene Fathers* (reprint, Grand Rapids: Eerdmans, 1978)
ANTJ	Arbeiten zum Neuen Testament und Judentums
Apoc.	*Apocalypse (of Moses, Zephanaiah, etc.)*
Apost. Const.	*Apostolic Constitutions*
APOT	R. H. Charles, ed., *The Apocrypha and Pseudepigrapha of the Old Testament* (Oxford: Clarendon, 1913)
ARN	*ʾAbot de Rabbi Nathan*
As. Mos.	*Assumption* (or: *Testament*) *of Moses*
Asc. Isa.	*Ascension of Isaiah*
ASOR	American Society of Oriental Research
b.	Tractates in the Babylonian Talmud (*Baba Batra, Megilla, Sanhedrin,* etc.)
BAR	*Biblical Archaeology Review*
2 Bar.	*Second Baruch*
3 Bar.	*Third Baruch*
Barn.	*Epistle of Barnabas*
BDB	F. Brown et al., *Hebrew and English Lexicon of the Old Testament* (reprint, Oxford: University Press, 1953)
BETL	Bibliotheca ephemeridum theologicarum lovaniensium
Bib	*Biblica*
BibRev	*Bible Review*
BJRL	*Bulletin of the John Rylands Library*
BTB	*Biblical Theological Bulletin*
BU	Biblische Untersuchungen
BZ	*Biblische Zeitschrift*
CMC	*Cologne Mani Codex*
CBNT	Coniectanea biblica, New Testament
CBOT	Coniectanea biblica, Old Testament
CBQ	*Catholic Biblical Quarterly*
CBQMS	Cathoilic Biblical Quarterly Monograph Series
CD	Cairo (Geneziah text of the) Damascus (Document)
EB	Etudes bibliques

EKKNT	Evangelisch-katholischer Kommentar zum Neuen Testament
1 En.	*First Enoch*
2 En.	*Second Enoch*
3 En.	*Third Enoch*
Ep. Arist.	Aristeas, *Epistle*
ETL	*Ephemerides theologicae lovanienses*
ETR	*Etudes thélogiques et religieuses*
EvT	*Evangelishce Theologie*
ExpT	*Expository Times*
FBBS	Facet Books, Biblical Series
FRLANT	Forschungen zur Religion und Literatur des Alten und Neuen Testaments
Gos.	*Gospel of (Peter, Thomas,* etc.)
HeyJ	*Heythrop Journal*
HNT	Handbuch zum Neuen Testament
HNTC	Harper's New Testament Commentary
HSM	Harvard Semitic Monographs
HTKNT	Herders Theologischer Kommentar zum Neuen Testament
HTR	*Harvard Theological Review*
HTS	Harvard Theological Studies
HUCA	*Hebrew Union College Annual*
IBS	*Irish Biblical Studies*
ICC	International Critical Commentary
IDB	*Interpreter's Dictionary of the Bible,* ed. G. A. Buttrick, 4 vols. (Nashville: Abingdon, 1962)
Int	*Interpretation*
JAAR	*Journal of the American Academy of Religion*
JBL	*Journal of Biblical Literature*
JBLMS	Journal of Biblical Literature Monograph Series
JJS	*Journal of Jewish Studies*
JNES	*Journal of Near Eastern Studies*
JQR	*Jewish Quarterly Reivew*
JSJ	*Journal for the Study of Judaism*
JSNT	*Journal for the Study of the New Testament*
JSNTSS	Journal for the Study of the New Testament Supplement Series
JSOT	*Journal for the Study of the Old Testament*
JSOTSS	Journal for the Study of the Old Testament Supplement Series
JSS	*Journal of Semitic Studies*
JTS	*Journal of Theological Studies*
LAB	*Liber Antiquitatum Biblicarum*
LD	Lectio divina
Liv. Proph.	*Lives of the Prophets* (Daniel, Habakkuk, etc.)
LXX	The Septuagint
m.	Tractates in the Mishna (*Sanhedrin, Sukka,* etc.)
Mart. Isa.	*Martyrdom of Isaiah*
Mek.	The *Mekilta of Rabbi Ishmael*

MeyerK	H. A. W. Meyer, *Kritisch-exegetischer Kommentar über das Neue Testament*
Midr.	*Midrash* (Genesis, Exodus, etc.)
MT	Masoretic text
NCB	New Century Bible
NIGTC	New International Greek Testament Commentary
NJBC	*The New Jerome Biblical Commentary,* ed. R. Brown et al. (New York: Prentice Hall, 1990)
NovT	*Novum Testamentum*
NovTSup	Novum Testamentum, Supplements
NPNF	P. Schaff, ed., *Nicene and Post-Nicene Fathers* (reprint, Grand Rapids: Eerdmans, 1978)
NRT	*La nouvelle revue théologique*
NTS	*New Testament Studies*
OBO	Orbis biblicus et orientalis
OTP	J. H. Charlesworth, *Old Testament Pseudepigrapha,* 2 vols. (New York: Doubleday, 1983, 1985)
PG	J. Migne, *Patrologia graeca*
PGM	*Papyri graecae magicae,* ed. K. Preisendanz
PL	J. Migne, *Patrologia latina*
Ps.-Clem.	*Pseudo-Clementine Homiles, Recognitions*
Ps. Sol.	*Psalms of Solomon*
Q	Qumran texts (numbered by cave)
	1QH *Thanksgiving Hymns*
	1QM *War Scroll*
	1QpHab. *The Pesher on Habukkuk*
	1QS *Rule of the Community*
	1QSa *Appendix A to Rule of the Community*
	1QSb *Appendix B to Rule of the Community*
	4QFlor *Florilegium*
QD	Quaestiones disputatae
RB	*Revue Biblique*
RBén	*Revue bénédictine*
RelSRev	*Religious Studies Review*
Rev. Thom.	*Revue thomiste*
RHPR	*Revue d histoire des religions*
RNT	Regensburger Neues Testament
RSR	*Recherches de science religieuse*
SB	H. Strack and P. Billerbeck, *Kommentar zum Neuen Testament aus Talmud und Midrash* (Münich: C. H. Beck, 1926-63).
SBLDS	Society of Biblical Literature Dissertation Series
SBS	Stuttgarter Bibelstudien
SBT	Studies in Biblical Theology
SCS	Septuagint and Cognate Studies
Sib. Or.	*Sibylline Oracles*
SJLA	Studies in Judaism in Late Antiquity
SJT	*Scottish Journal of Theology*
SNTSMS	Society for New Testament Studies Monograph Series
SPB	Studia postbiblica

SUNT	Studien zur Umwelt des Neuen Testament
T.	*Testament of (Adam, Daniel, Job,* etc.)
TDNT	G. Kittel and G. Friedrich, eds., *Theological Dictionary of the New Testament,* trans. G. W. Bromiley (Grand Rapids: Eerdmans, 1964-74)
TDOT	G. J. Botterwick and H. Ginggren, eds., *Theological Dictionary of the Old Testament,* trans. J. T. Willis (Grand Rapids: Eerdmans, 1974ff.)
TEH	Theologische Existenz heute
Tg.	Targumic materials (Isaiah, Zechariah, etc.)
TLZ	*Theologische Literaturzeitung*
TQ	*Theologische Quartalschrift*
TS	*Theological Studies*
TZ	*Theologische Zeitschrift*
VC	*Vigiliae christianae*
VT	*Vetus Testamentum*
WBC	Word Biblical Commentary
WUNT	Wissenschafliche Untersuchungen zum Neuen Testament
y.	Tractates in the Jerusalem Talmud
ZAW	*Zeitschrift für die alttestamentliche Wissenschaft*
ZKG	*Zeitschrift für Kirchengeschichte*
ZNW	*Zeitschrfit für die neutestamentlische Wissenschaft*

One

INTRODUCTION

In view of the current situation in both literary and theological circles it behooves me to begin by offering some preliminary reflections on the interpretation of texts. The first object of this work is to understand, in its original *Sitz im Leben*, an old Jewish-Christian writing and a typology it expresses. In pursuance of that object I shall be using the tools of the so-called historical-critical method, including redaction criticism. I am aware that my chosen method is now weathering much attack. Some have indeed spoken of its demise. My own conviction is that we are rather witnessing the birth of several new methods which, once refined, will, for the most, complement and correct, but not replace, the old one(s). But whether the future confirms this evaluation or proves me instead to belong to a dying breed, there is one procedure I must defend. Herein I sometimes appeal to the intentions of the author (for convenience, "Matthew"). Since the advent of the New Criticism, however, such appeal has been controversial. The so-called "intentional fallacy," defined as the reading of texts in terms of an unavailable authorial intention, is now regarded by many as frightfully naïve, altogether passé. And I concede that indeed my approach is in certain respects old-fashioned.[1] But to date a thing is not to determine its truth or falsity—otherwise the study of history would render philosophy otiose. I have not been persuaded by the New Critics, by the structuralists, or by the deconstructionists that the concept of authorial intention is either incoherent (à la Derrida) or that it stands for something we can reach for but never grasp (Wimsatt and Beardsley).[2] I remain convinced, I am intuitively certain, that

---

[1] The other side of this is that I can claim just about everyone before Heidegger as an ally.
[2] Wimsatt and Beardsley, in their famous article, "The Intentional Fallacy," *Sewanee Review* 54 (1946):568-88, did not deny that authors have intentions, only that we can know them.

1

literary texts, as the products of human beings, creatures whose public and private lives are pervaded by intentions, have the intentions of their authors encoded in them; and if we can often comprehend intentions while conversing with living human beings, we can do the same while reading the sentences on a page. There are, to be sure, great epistemological mysteries here. Nonetheless it is our common experience that, via speech, oral or written, we may gain access, however indirect, to others' purposes. To deny this is to enter the wilderness of solipsism.[3]

A book is not a relic. The latter, as a physical object without milieu, is just a piece of bone, devoid of intrinsic significance. The scientist may be able to date and classify it, but a bone alone actively conveys nothing: it is passive, uncommunicative—like a codex in an illiterate society. Hence whatever meaning a relic possesses is extraneous: it must be read in, that is, arbitrarily placed upon it. This is done (often against the facts) through a narrative which contextualizes the neutral human remain, thus turning it into a holy relic, a thing of meaning. In other words, story-tellers make a relic what it is, and exactly what it is. There is no dialectic between a bone and its interpreters, only eisegesis. Not so works of literature. To them we can listen. Of course texts cannot speak without us because without us they have no life: we must read them and so vivify them. Before Michael Ventris, the tablets of Crete were mute. But once Linear B began to be deciphered and so read, the tablets started to stammer: and now we can, in great measure, understand them—and through them the intentions of those who inscribed them. The Barthian scepticism of natural theology, according to which the created thing fails to instruct us about its Creator, does not hold for literary works and their authors. If the archaeologist can, when the data are sufficient, confidently discern purpose in an ancient, voiceless artifact ("This was an axe, made to chop wood"), how much more can readers discern purpose in verbal communications from the past, even the distant past. The dead tell tales.

That this is so follows from a conspicuous fact, one requiring no demonstration. As we all know there can be failure to read rightly, and

---

[3]Lest I be accused of being uninformed: it is sometimes implied by those enamoured of this or that trend in literary studies that others who tread a different path—especially if they are New Testament scholars—must do so in ignorance of newer knowledge. (I have recently read a book on literary criticism and the Gospels that even presumes to comment on absences from bibliographies.) But obviously it is possible to learn about a method without becoming its advocate. Absence does not prove ignorance: one can choose not to make use of something.

hence invalidity in interpretation: witness only the fundamentalist understanding of Genesis 1. But this in turn implies that there can also be right reading and so validity in interpretation (E. D. Hirsch; the Bloomian and deconstructive slogan, "all interpretation is misinterpretation," is silly if taken to mean that no interpretations are better or worse: that is exegetical evisceration).[4] Once this is conceded, once we acknowledge "the limits of interpretation" (Umberto Eco), it is all but impossible to define those limits without taking into account a work's original historical context, in which I include authorial intent. This is not to say such intent is everywhere retrievable. All too often obscurities cannot be banished (as the following pages sadly verify). Nor is it to deny that knowledge of an author's intent is ever anything other than provisional (all historical knowledge is such) or to affirm that the object of interpretation is someone else's mind, however construed. What I do maintain is that an author gives a text its "core of determinate meanings,"[5] or substantive content, that such substantive content must thus cohere with the author's intentions, and that consequently those intentions have a special claim on our attention; and by occasionally appealing to them in this study of a complex book written by a first-century Jew, I am reminding myself and my readers that while the text is still with us, it comes to us from another time and place, a time and place in many respects unimaginably different from our own, and that unless we permit it to speak in the idiom of its defunct world, unless we, to the best of our ability, firmly place it in the historical context of its author, whose ways were not our ways, we can never approximate what it was intended to communicate.

I must add that the words, "intended to communicate," do not imply simplicity, or reduction to one thing. The search for *the* meaning of a work (as opposed to the meaning of its individual sentences) is problematic.[6] What, for instance, could be the answer to the question—I think it a very strange question—What is the meaning of the First Gospel? Works of literature are inevitably constituted by a complexity of meanings. In fact, the potential meaning of a text is no

---

[4]Useful here is Robert Alter, *The Pleasures of Reading in an Ideological Age* (New York: Simon and Schuster, 1989), 206-38.

[5]The phrase is that of M. H. Abrams, "History and Criticism and the Plurality of Histories," in Wayne C. Booth, *Critical Understanding: The Powers and Limits of Pluralism* (Chicago: University Press, 1979), 187.

[6]See further Stein Haugorn Olsen, *The End of Literary Theory* (Cambridge: University Press, 1987). Also quite instructive, although from a different perspective, is Booth, *Critical Understanding.*

less expansive than its significance (= what a text has come to mean)—
not because the two are identical but because anything, including a
text, can be viewed from any number of perspectives and because,
following Gadamer, words always possess an infinite horizon of
unspoken meaning, if only in the sense that every statement contains
unlimited submeaning.[7] Textual meaning is for all practical purposes
inexhaustible, a sort of infinity. But it is not Derrida's infinity, an
ahistorical, unbounded play of nonsignifying signs. Rather is it a
bounded infinity: not the unlimited number of points on a plane but
the infinity of points between two parallel lines, one line representing
an author's intention, the other the conventions of language. To erase
either line is to abandon the idea of stable and statable meaning and
to replace the author with the reader, to substitute speaking for
listening.

Much can often be learned about men and women from knowledge
of their parents. The circumstance instances a fundamental principle:
to understand the present we need to know the past, and to understand a thing before us, including a text, we need to know, as Aristotle
explained, who or what brought it into being and to what end.[8]
Pedigrees illuminate, and we often "get the best view of the matter if
we learn of the natural growth of things at the beginning" (Aristotle,
Polit. I.ii 1252a24). C. S. Lewis rightly inveighed against "the Personal
Heresy," and the New Criticism understandably protested the excessive employment of works as transparencies for historical circumstances. But their redress of excess was one thing, the new excess,
which emphasizes a text—the so-called "autonomous text"—or its
readers to the utter depredation of the author, another. To grant (as I
freely do) that the text, not an author's biography, should be, if the goal
is appreciation or understanding of a literary work, the interpreter's
focus, does not entail authorial irrelevance. Would any interpretation
of a book long endure if some new discovery (for example, of the
author's diaries) showed it blatantly to contradict the author's inten-

---

[7] A very simple example: "I love you, Kristine, most of all," implies "I love you more
than Nancy," "I love you more than Mary," and as many sentences as there are names.

[8] We need also to know when. To illustrate: J. R. R. Tolkien's *Lord of the Rings* is not
(as some early reviewers suggested) an allegory about the atomic bomb because,
although the trilogy was published after Hiroshima and Nagasaki, Tolkien's friends
have informed us that the main elements of the plot were in place in the 1930's, when the
author was in no position to know about the splitting of atoms—a biographical fact
interpretation cannot ignore. Similarly, if archaeology could prove, by the discovery of
a manuscript, that 4 *Ezra* circulated in its present form before the destruction of the
Jerusalem temple, interpreters would have to start over again.

tion? Again, would an interpretation not be dismissed if it were determined to be based upon an inferior manuscript and so upon what was never planned by the author (the actual author, that is, not the so-called "implied author")? Where is the commentator who regards Mark 16:9-20 as secondary and yet still employs it to interpret Mark?[9] Textual criticism, as G. Thomas Tanselle has steadfastly argued, is firstly recovery of what an author purposed to appear in print.[10] This is assumed by all of us when, while reading, we correct for ourselves obvious misprints. The so-called Freudian slip can, to be sure, be instructive; but typically we seek what was intended, knowing that it is sometimes only imperfectly signified. We are not, after all, if I may so put it, interested in understanding texts but the works or verbal statements that somehow subsist behind them. The former, made of paper and ink, are vessels, the latter the treasures of meaning they carry; and while a work thus defined (which, as Bradbury's *Fahrenheit 451* vividly portrays, can exist in someone's memory even after all physical representations of it have been lost or destroyed) possesses an enigmatic ontology (does it belong to Karl Popper's World 3?), it was indubitably intended and generated by an author. "Whether one is listening to a friend, a radio announcer, or a poet, or reading a postcard, a newspaper, or a novel, one transforms the seemingly erroneous and nonsensical into the seemingly correct and meaning-ful—and thus implies that the verbal statement is not coequal with its oral or written presentation. Not only philosophers but all who use language have at times concluded, in one way or another, that verbal constructions are abstractions, not bound by the shortcomings of their spoken or inscribed texts" (Tanselle). Are not even first editions corrected when determined to be inaccurate representations of autho-rial design? And as in textual criticism, so too in hermeneutics: there remains a place for authors and their aims. To illustrate the point yet again: if one of T. H. Huxley's simians, in its undirected attempt to type Hamlet, ever did unwittingly manage to punch out a coherent line of English, we could list the dictionary meanings for the individual words; but could we interpret the line as we do other lines? Would it

---

[9]This is not to deny that one could interpret Mark with the longer ending in mind, only that such an interpretation might not be congruent with the original core of determinate meanings.

[10]See esp. *A Rationale of Textual Criticism* (Philadelphia: University of Pennsylvania, 1989). This should be supplemented by the evaluation of Tanselle in Steven Mailloux, *Interpretive Conventions: The Reader in the Study of American Fiction* (Ithaca: Cornell, 1982), 93-125.

make sense to ask whether the chimp's sentence contains irony, or if it alludes to another text? Just like the charge of plagiarism, questions such as these assume the existence of and our access to authorial activities and intentions.[11]

I so stress the point because this essay might be regarded as an exercise in what is now called intertextuality, but if so, it is intertextuality of a particular kind only, one which presupposes our ability to recover an author's intentions.[12] Every text is a mosaic of previously formed words and phrases and therefore a mosaic of conscious and unconscious borrowing. The generalization embraces Matthew, who, unlike Shakespeare and Coleridge, had no fondness for coining new words. Further, as perusal of the critical commentaries reveals, almost every construction and phrase in Matthew had a pre-Matthean history. The First Gospel, like all literary texts, is consequently a new whole made out of old pieces. Often the provenience of an old piece matters: it was chosen precisely because it was already charged with meaning and carried useful connotations. But of course it is also often otherwise. In 2.11 we read of the magi "opening their treasures." Now the construction, *anoigō + thēsauros*, is not uncommon in Greek literature, and it is attested in the Septuagint. So Matthew did not first bring it into the world: he rather borrowed it. But it makes no difference to the reader, just as it made no difference to Matthew, from whence he borrowed or learned it, for no subtext is being alluded to. Contrast the situation in 2.1: "Now when Jesus was born in Bethlehem of Judea in the days of Herod the king...." Although the expression, "in the days of X the king," does not direct us to any one subtext, it is notably a biblicism, one quite common in the Septuagint. We thus have here not an allusion to a particular text but—assuming the idiom was not dead— the utilization of what we may call biblical-sounding language. Readers familiar with the Greek Bible—and Matthew wrote with such in mind—would presumably have intuited a continuity between the story of Israel's sacred history and Jesus' story and hence would have read with solemnity, in anticipation of profound significance.

Neither 2.1 nor 2.11 alludes to any one text. 2.19-20, however, does: "But when Herod died, behold, an angel of the Lord appeared in a

---

[11]For additional considerations see Denis Dutton, "Why Intentionalism Won't Go Away," in *Literature and the Question of Philosophy,* ed. Anthony J. Cascardi (Baltimore: Johns Hopkins, 1987), 194-209.

[12]On the necessary connection between allusions and authorial intention see P. D. Juhl, *Interpretation: An Essay in the Philosophy of Literary Criticism* (Princeton: Princeton University Press, 1980), 58-62; and for critical comment, Olsen, *End,* 47-49.

dream to Joseph in Egypt, saying, 'Rise, take the child and his mother, and go to the land of Israel, for those who sought the child's life are dead.'" The informed reader is to recall a subtext, one from the Bible, Exod. 4.19-20: "And the Lord said to Moses in Midian, 'Go back to Egypt; for all the men who were seeking your life are dead.' So Moses took his wife and his sons and set them on an ass, and went back to the land of Egypt." This recollection of the story of Moses is, as we shall have occasion to see, just one in a series of recollections of that story in Matthew's first chapters. Its purpose is to intimate not that there was, happily, some vague or coincidental connection between Moses, the first deliverer, and Jesus, the messianic deliverer, but rather that the histories of those two men were, in the mysterious providence of a consistent God, and according to the principle that the last things are as the first, strikingly similar even down to details.

It follows from our brief examination of Matt. 2.1, 11, and 19-20 that there are at least three types of intertextuality: borrowing which alludes to no subtext, borrowing which alludes to a series of subtexts, and borrowing which alludes to or cites a specific subtext.[13] The second and third types of borrowing, which concern us because they are the basis of all the Moses typologies to be examined herein, involve the conscious intention of an author and were designed to be perceived by others. That they still can be perceived by us is due to their primary source, Scripture, a collection of texts to which we maintain complete access. To sum up, then, the first task of this study is to search for subtexts, mostly scriptural, beneath old Jewish and Christian works; and the supposition is that, when intertextual fusions satisfy certain criteria designed to prevent the misreading of coincidence for purpose,[14] we may behold an author's intention, which was to create a series of hermeneutical events in a community of readers, events which together add up to a typological conclusion: this person is like that person because their two stories have so much in common.

I shall muster my arguments as an historian, and that is as far as the present investigation dares go: I shall not be doing theology. I am fully cognizant, however, that study of Matthew's new Moses theme raises a very difficult issue. We may—I certainly do—admire the aesthetics of Matthew's literary art. For most of us, however, there is no longer

---

[13]I leave aside as of no account for our study of Matthew conscious borrowing of insignificance—as when a playwright fills a work with names known from childhood. Likewise irrelevant is plagiarism, a conscious borrowing one hopes is never detected.

[14]See below, pp. 21-23.

anything mysterious or profound about his Moses typology. Since John Toland and the eighteenth-century rationalists, and especially since David Friedrich Strauss and the rise of nineteenth-century biblical criticism, typology has shown itself to be merely a literary device. Its rather common appearance in the secular fiction of the last two centuries only confirms this. Matthew, on the other hand, like the Church Fathers, medieval theologians, and pre-liberal Protestants, almost certainly believed that typological correlations have some deep meaning, that they hold important clues for fathoming God's obscure intentions. Was our evangelist in this particular simply deluded? Must we now dismiss his typological method as without doctrinal relevance? My own thoughts on the matter are sufficiently diffuse and complex as to exceed my powers of condensation, and this book is long enough already. For what it is worth, I am not convinced that Matthew and his typology necessarily belong to what Jaroslav Pelikan has called "the cemetery where history has buried tradition." But my reasons must await another day.

PART I
MOSES AS A TYPE OUTSIDE MATTHEW

Two ─────────────────────────────────

JEWISH FIGURES

INTRODUCTION

Arrian's *Anabasis* of Alexander the Great contains these two passages:

> Once ashore [in Asia], he [Alexander] travelled inland to Troy and offered sacrifice to Athena, patron goddess of the city; here he made a gift of his armour to the temple, and took in exchange, from where they hung on the temple walls, some weapons which were still preserved from the Trojan war. These are supposed to have been carried before him by his bodyguard when he went into battle. He is also said to have offered sacrifice to Priam on the altar of Zeus Herceius, to avert his anger against the family of Neoptolemus [son of Achilles], whose blood [through his mother, Olympias] still ran in his own veins (1.12).
>
> I do not... think it unlikely that Alexander cut his hair short in mourning for his friend, for he might well have done so, if only in emulation of Achilles, whose rival he had always felt himself to be, ever since he was a boy (7.l4).[1]

Whether or not the historical Alexander sought to emulate Achilles — a thing not impossible: famous people have often imitated other famous people[2]—there was a tradition which held the two heroes up for comparison. Now such comparison of two subjects is a commonplace of all biography. Just as analogies and similes are endemic to all literature, so too, when human beings are the subjects, is it natural for one person to be measured by another already known. For learning is always *anamnesis*, recollection—if not exactly in the sense Plato taught,

---

[1] Arrian, *The Campaigns of Alexander*, trans. A. de Selincourt (New York: Penguin, l958), 66-67, 372.

[2] In time Alexander himself became a model for later military conquerors, including Julius Caesar and Napoleon I; and Napoleon in turn became a model for others (Antonio Lopez de Santa Anna, commander of the Mexican forces at the Alamo, called himself "the Napoleon of the West"). —D. Daube, "Typology in Josephus," *JJS* 31 (1980):18-36, argues that Josephus understood himself to be like, among others, Jacob and Jeremiah.

then at least in the sense that the new is invariably apprehended through the old.

Sometimes biographical comparison, for which the Greek rhetoricians had a technical term, *sygkrisis*,[3] is obvious and explicit. Plutarch's parallel lives, which set famous Greeks beside famous Romans, are prime instances. Sometimes such comparison is inexplicit and far from manifest. The phrases in Porphyry's *Vita Phythagorae* which seemingly glorify Pythagoras by likening him to Odysseus and Socrates scarcely jump out at the contemporary reader;[4] and Aeneas' likeness to Augustus became obvious to moderns only after D. L. M. Drew's famous study.[5] But whether explicit or implicit, the biographical analogy is a relatively easy way of saying much—which is why it has been and remains so prevalent a device of public discourse. To praise the genius of a young scientist one speaks of another Einstein. To condemn a national leader any insinuation of a likeness to Hitler will do. To characterize an acerbic journalist one mentions H. L. Mencken. An exceptionally kind and caring nurse is still sometimes called Florence Nightingale, while a detective who solves a particularly complex crime by dint of wit will hear the name Sherlock Holmes. A traitor is a Benedict Arnold or a Quisling. And so it goes. Famous (and infamous) people become types and as such the standards for other people. In other words, they are turned into adjectives.

This generalization holds for the Jewish Bible, where the comparison of one figure with another is common enough.[6] Some examples: (i) in 1 and 2 Kings David is often the paradigm by which kings are evaluated. A king "like David his father" is a good king. A king "not like David his father" is a bad king.[7] (ii) In 1 Macc. 2:23-26 Mattathias' murder of a fellow Jew is justified by precedent: "He burned with zeal for the law, as Phinehas did against Zimri, the son of Salu." (iii) In the Elijah and Elisha cycles of Kings, the narrator often characterizes his

---

[3]See for example Menander Rhetor, *Treatise II* 372, 377 (ed. D. A. Russell and N. G. Wilson, 1981, pp. 84, 92).

[4]See P. Cox, *Biography in Late Antiquity* (Berkeley: University of California Press, 1983), 102-33.

[5]*The Allegory of the Aeneid* (Oxford: University Press, 1927).

[6]Note Michael Fishbane, *Biblical Interpretation in Ancient Israel* (Oxford: University Press, 1985), 372-79; also Y. Zakovitch, "Assimilation in Biblical Narratives," in *Empirical Models for Biblical Criticism*, ed. J. H. Tigay (Philadelphia: University of Pennsylvania, 1985), 176-96.

[7]See 1 Kings 3:14; 9:4; 11:4, 6, 38; 15:11; 2 Kings 14:3; 16:2; 18:3; 22:2. —Cf. Eutropius, *Brev.* 8:5.3: in the fourth century the emperor was praised as "more successful than Augustus, better than Trajan."

two prophetic heroes by assimilating them to one another.[8] (iv) In 2 Chronicles king Hezekiah acts like Solomon (cf. 31:3 with 8:12-13) and produces similar effects: "So there was great joy in Jerusalem, for since the time of Solomon the son of David king of Israel there had been nothing like this in Jerusalem" (30:26).[9] Aside from such obvious examples, the Bible also contains many subtle biographical comparisons which emerge only upon close examination. Thus if one compares Gen. 1:26-31 with 9:1-7 and 3:17 with 5:29, Noah appears to be another Adam, the second father of the human race.[10] And, as ensuing pages will show, in 1 Chronicles 22 and 28 David in some particulars simulates Moses, even though the lawgiver is not mentioned.

Both in the Bible and out the assimilation of one thing to another, including one person to another, is not always profoundly meaningful. Many of the textual harmonizations in the synoptic manuscript tradition must be the result of unconscious alteration; and there are biblical stories which resemble each other simply because they utilize common folk-tale motifs (for example, Genesis 12, 20, and 26 all tell of a man passing his wife off as his sister).[11] Aesthetic sensibilities may also lend a hand in making two things alike. To take an example from art history: if one sets depictions of the holy family's entrance into Egypt beside renditions of the palm-Sunday entry into Jerusalem, their ever growing proclivity to mirror each other is patent.

In the biblical tradition, however, assimilation, along with typology, which is extended assimilation (of characters and events), can convey much meaning. Aside from the obvious services of characterizing, praising, and blaming individuals, there is the effect generated by employing language traditionally associated with a holy figure or

---

[8]Cf. 1 Kings 17:8-16 with 2 Kings 4:1-7; 1 Kings 17:17-24 with 2 Kings 4:32-37; 2 Kings 2:8 with 2:14. Each prophet purportedly performed altogether eight great miracles.

[9]See further H. G. M. Williamson, *Israel in the Book of Chronicles* (Cambridge: University Press, 1977), 119-225.

[10]See Fishbane, *Interpretation,* 33-34.

[11]Given my task, the point requires expanding. The prize example of a cluster of wandering motifs may be the one-time well-known Christian myth of Barlaam and Josaphat. The latter was an Indian prince who, converted by the former, became an ascetic. The story is essentially that of the Buddha, and it can be traced through Georgian sources to Islam, thence to the Manicheans, who got it from Buddhists of Central Asia; and the Buddhists may themselves have derived the tale, their foundational myth, from the Jainsenists or Hindus. In any case we now have many texts which feature the same story line and similar motifs. Nonetheless we can nowhere speak of typology. This last, which involves either a retrospective or a presaging story, requires knowledge of two different people or series of events as well as their juxtaposition. But parallelism, even extensive parallelism which is not coincidental, may exist without such knowledge or juxtaposition.

the sacred past. Commenting on the use of biblical language in monastic literature, J. Leclercq has written:

> It is often poetic in essence. Sometimes it has greater value because of its power of suggestion than because of its clarity or precision; it hints at much more than it says. But for that very reason it is the better suited to express spiritual experience which is completely impregnated with a mysterious light impossible to analyze. Furthermore, though lacking in precision, this vocabulary is endowed with a great wealth of content...".[12]

Leclercq's words hold equally for many early Christian writings: these frequently feature "Septuagintalisms" and biblical forms (recall the scriptural language of the *Protevangelium of James*). But, as we shall see, in this respect primitive Christian literature simply follows the Jewish Bible, which already imitates itself.

Perhaps we can better appreciate the intended impact of sacred assimilation in the Bible by citing a modern parallel, one which happily has to do with Moses. Consider Martin Luther King's 1968 speech at the Memphis Mason Temple. In this the Reverend King said that he had "been to the mountaintop" and that he had "seen the Promised Land." He also stated, in the event prophetically, "I may not get there with you." King did not name Moses. But who would deny his allusion to the lawgiver? King was implicitly likening himself to Moses on Pisgah. In doing so he was characterizing himself as well as the circumstances of his audience. He could instead have dully declared: "I have seen a better day, although it may be further off than hoped." But the implicit yet crystal clear allusions to a shared world of religious ideas cast upon his words an emotional aura not soon forgotten. By evoking the rich tradition which likens the experience of American blacks to the experience of Israel in Egypt,[13] King summoned the ghosts of a sacred history and struck distinct cords in the caves of memory, thus stirring souls. Assimilation through allusion can have such power.

But the emotional effects of assimilation should not blind us to its possible theological dimension. One God stands behind history in the monotheistic tradition, and because like events hint at like causes, the mysterious homology of events or persons can be taken as testimony to divine activity within history. Put otherwise, when history's tumult throws up two things alike, they intimate a third thing, the cause of

---

[12]*The Love of Learning and the Desire for God: A Study of Monastic Culture* (New York: Fordham, 1982), 75-76.

[13]See E. D. Genovese, *Roll, Jordan, Roll: The World the Slaves Made* (New York: Random House, 1974). On pp. 252-56 Genovese observes, what is of interest to us, that the slaves merged Moses and Jesus into the image of a single deliverer.

their likeness—for the believer, God. There is of course in the Bible itself no cloning of old events, and the mythological identification of beginning and end is foreign to Scripture: there is no cyclical return to what once was. In the Bible history moves forward. But if there is not repetition, there is resemblance. We can indeed speak of the "general biblical disposition to see history as a chain of duplicating patterns,"[14] which patterns testify to the one faithful God and his role in human events.[15] Fishbane is correct:

> The fact that a particular event [I would add: or person] is not rendered solely in its own terms, but is rather reimagined in terms of another—a prototype—is not due to its paucity of religious significance but rather to its abundance. By means of retrojective typologies, events are removed from the neutral cascade of historical occurrences and embellished as modalities of foundational moments in Israel's history.[16]

In his book on Arshile Gorky, H. Rosenberg wrote this:

> In this century, every major work of art, whether pictorial or not, is charged—the word is Ezra Pound's—with allusion: to things or events, read, dreamed or half-remembered, but, above all, to high points in the history of its medium.[17]

We can adapt these words for our own purposes: in the Bible, almost every book is charged with allusion: to things and events, above all to the high points in salvation-history. From at least the Babylonian exile on, Jewish literary history—this includes the New Testament—is to significant degree a chain of responses to foundational traditions (especially those preserved in the Pentateuch). Thus the biblical books are all "fraught with background,"[18] and their meaning largely depends upon knowing that background. I think it was wholly appropriate that "ancient exegetes tended to view the Bible as fundamentally elliptical," that they believed "it said much in a few words and often

---

[14]Alter, *Pleasures of Reading*, 117.

[15]Cf. N. Frye, *The Great Code: The Bible and Literature* (San Diego: HBJ, 1981), 80-81: "What typology really is as a mode of thought, what it both assumes and leads to, is a theory of history, or more accurately of historical process: an assumption that there is some meaning and point to history, and that sooner or later some event or events will occur which will indicate what that meaning or point is, and so become an antitype of what has happened previously. Our modern confidence in historical process, our belief that despite apparent confusion, even chaos, in human events, nevertheless those events are going somewhere and indicating something, is probably a legacy of Biblical typology: at least I can think of no other source for its tradition."

[16]Fishbane, *Interpretation*, 360.

[17]H. Rosenberg, *Arshile Gorky: The Man, the Time, the Idea* (New York: Grove, 1962), 56.

[18]The phrase in from E. Auerbach, *Mimesis* (Princeton: University Press, 1953), 12.

omitted essentials, leaving the full meaning to be figured out by readers alert to the tiniest irregularities in the text."[19] The canonical writings, literature of inheritance, are deliberately interactive and full of allusive reciprocal discourse; hence much like modern poetry, when we listen closely we can hear them talking to themselves. By "modern poetry" I refer not to the so-called post-moderns, with their extraordinarily obscure allusions and subtle word games. Certainly the Bible "is not written in Balthazar's character, in a Mene, Tekel, Upharsim, that we must call in Astrologers, and Chaldeans, and Soothsayers, to interpret it" (John Donne, *XXVI Sermons* (1660), p. 47). Rather, my analogy is with poets such as Shelley and Eliot, who consciously made themselves members of the Western literary tradition through regular allusion to it.[20] In like manner, resonances in Scripture are there neither for erudite display nor for the playing of sophisticated hide and seek. Inexplicit biblical parallelism is instead a natural, if eloquent, method of communication: "this is like that" means, if the latter is sacred, that so is the former: both belong to holy history.[21]

There is, however, a problem. Ovid imitated Virgil, *non subripiend, causa sed palam mutuandi, hoc animo ut uellet agnosci*: not to steal, but to borrow openly, with the intention of being recognized (Seneca the Elder, *Suasoriae* 3.7).[22] But how does the contemporary reader of an ancient work recognize such intention? When is an allusion an allusion?[23] Anyone familiar with the critical literature on the New Testament knows that the hunting of allusions is an uncertain enterprise. Surely John 1.51 ("you will see heaven opened, and the angels of God ascending and descending upon the Son of man") adverts to Jacob's ladder and Gen. 28:12. But does Mark 10:45 ("to give his life as a ransom

---

[19]James L. Kugel, *In Potiphar's House: The Interpretive Life of Biblical Texts* (San Francisco: Harper & Row, 1990), 3.

[20]Cf. I. A. Richards, *Principles of Literary Criticism* (reprint ed.; San Diego: HBJ, 1985), 217-18.

[21]There is a close parallel in Renaissance writers such as Petrarch and Poliziano. Their frequent use of *contaminatio*, or conventional allusions and phrases, was part of an attempt to unite themselves with an admired and authoritative past; see T. M. Greene, *The Light in Troy: Imitation and Discovery in Renaissance Poetry* (New Haven: Yale, 1982), passim.

[22]There is always pleasure in such recognition: those "who make a complete demonstration of the object thereby lack mystery; they deprive the mind of that delicious joy of imagining that it creates. To name the thing means forsaking three quarters of a poem's enjoyment" (Mallarmé).

[23]An allusion is to be distinguished from repetition: in the latter case the past is repeated but the fact is irrelevant for the act of interpretation. With an allusion the author's intent is to lead the reader back to a subtext. Cf. the discussion on pp. 6-7.

for many") draw upon MT Isaiah 53? And is Rom. 8:32 (God "did not spare his own Son but gave him up for us all") a reminiscence of Genesis 22 and the *Akedah*, of the offering up by Abraham of his son Isaac? The texts are silent, and scholars disagree. How then does one decide? All concur that the New Testament books, not unlike "The Waste Land" of T. S. Eliot, constantly elicit tradition through the device of allusion. But whereas Eliot condescended to footnote his poem, the New Testament writers did not add scholia. As modern readers of the Bible are we not in the position of the college student struggling to understand Dante or Milton in an old edition, one without annotations? Every phrase has something in it, much more than initially perceived; but how to perceive it? Time removes us from all texts and subtexts (as well as from their earlier interpretations) and so cripples our ability to detect tacit references—which is why, as history marches on, annotated editions of the classics become longer and longer.[24] The exoteric always, with time, becomes the esoteric. How many twentieth-century readers of Milton's famous sonnet XVI would, unaided, grasp the meaning of "that one talent which is death to hide" (cf. Matt. 25:14-30)? Commentary is now required.[25] With age,

---

[24]Cf. G. Steiner, *In Bluebeard's Castle* (New Haven: Yale, 1971), 99ff. —In this connection we do well, in a book on Moses, to remember that much both about and allegedly by Moses has irretrievably perished. The *Assumption of Moses* cited in Jude 9 and by several Church Fathers is no longer extant. The same is true of the *Apocryphon of Moses* named by Euthalius and Photius as well as of the *Book of Mystical Words of Moses* mentioned by Gelasius Cyzicenus. The *Testament of Moses* as it has come down to us, in one very poor Latin manuscript, ends in the middle of a sentence. The Moses apocryphon from Qumran (*1QDM* = *1Q22*) is fragmentary, as is *2QapMoses* (= *2Q21*), which may be another apocryphon of Moses; so too the Moses pseudepigrapha published by John Strugnell, *4Q375* and *4Q376*. See further James H. Charlesworth, *The Pseudepigrapha and Modern Research* (Missoula: Scholars Press, 1976), 160-63. In certain respects rabbinic literature displays a tendency to play down Moses rather than exalt him, from which it follows that the rabbis undoubtedly let much fall away.

[25]Cf. John Hollander, *The Figure of an Echo: A Mode of Allusion in Milton and After* (Berkeley: University of California, 1981), 65, on the need of commentary for recovering lost allusions. I note that there now exists something called *The Facts on File Dictionary of Classical, Biblical, and Literary Allusions*, ed. Abraham H. Lass et al. (New York: Facts on File, 1987), a work which tells us the meanings of words and phrases once well known but apparently now recondite to many, words and phrases such as "Doubting Thomas," "Golden Calf," "Pandora's Box," "Rubicon," "Scylla and Charybdis." The existence of this book, which serves a real need, as anyone who has recently taught undergraduates can sadly testify, is as good a witness as any to our society's ever-increasing collective amnesia. Moreover, as more and more biblical scholars who have had little or no religious training, by which I mean intensive exposure to the Bible as children and young adults, enter our field, we will, I think, see less interest in and more scepticism toward internal biblical allusions and typologies. There will be a generation who knew not Joseph.

transparent allusions become "delicate cross-references that are now the discoveries of the learned."[26]

Our historically conditioned deafness to oblique allusions in the Bible can sometimes lead us to doubt their very existence.[27]But a contemporary analogy may give us pause, the more so as ancient "readers" were in fact always "listeners."[28] Those who habitually listen to music over the radio can often identify a popular song after hearing just the smallest portion of it. There are in fact contests—I have heard them—which require people to name a musical piece after hearing only a slight excerpt from it, one lasting no more than a second or two, and consisting of no more than two or three notes or cords. The uninitiated will discern only noise. But to those with the requisite musical knowledge (gained, be it noted, not through arduous study but through effortless listening), the briefest extract can conjure up a world: a song, an album, a musical group. Was it maybe not similar with those Jews who first heard the Gospel of Matthew? Are we not sometimes forced to pick up a concordance in order to perceive connections which were once immediately grasped by trained ears with unconscious sureness?

On the other hand, if we are sometimes hard of hearing, we must beware of auditory hallucinations. The biblical studies sections of seminary libraries are filled to overflowing with books and articles urging dubious typologies and strained parallels, upon which the dust of time is rightly settling. We may have eradicated the excesses of medieval allegory, but the impulse behind it lives on. It is all too easy to fall prey to the common infirmity Samuel Sandmel dubbed Parallelomania, as well as to what I may call Typologicalmania (a

---

[26]William Empson, *Seven Types of Ambiguity* (3rd ed.; Norfolk: New Directions, 1953), 47.

[27]The present book is about a typology whose very existence can be doubted. According to T. Saito, *Die Mosevorstellungen im Neuen Testament* (Europäische Hochschulschriften Series 23, Theology, vol. 100; Bern: Peter Lang, 1977), the First Gospel contains a Moses typology only in 1:18-2:23—but that section derives largely from "Palestinian Jewish Christianity," and the interest in Moses must be reckoned pre-Matthean; see pp. 51-72. Furthermore, the new Moses motif evaporates entirely in A. Sand's commentary, *Das Evangelium nach Matthäus* (Regensburger Neues Testament; Regensburg: Friedrich Pustet, 1986). See also Sand's *Das Gesetz und Propheten, Untersuchungen zur Theologie des Evangeliums nach Matthäus* (Regensburg: Friedrich Pustet, 1974), 101-103. Cf. Ulrich Luz, *Matthew 1-7* (Minneapolis: Augsburg, 1989), 186, n. 18 (citing Saito): "Elsewhere also, the Gospel of Matthew does not emphasize, I think, any personal correspondence between Jesus and Moses."

[28]Instructive here is Paul J. Achtemeier, "*Omne verbum sonat*: The New Testament and the Oral Environment of Late Western Antiquity," *JBL* 109 (1990):3-27.

malady which often afflicted the late, brilliant Austin Farrer). Given the excesses of the past, one understands why it has been said that "the ability to declare typology absent is a kind of proof of sound modern critical method."[29]

In order to gain, in our present circumstances, so far removed from those of ancient Jews and Christians, some way of measuring the probability or improbability of a proposed allusion in the Bible, we must begin by asking in what ways one text may be linked to another. There are at least six.

1. Explicit statement. An author can circumvent ambiguity by straightforward comparison, as in John 3:14 ("And as Moses lifted up the serpent in the wilderness, so must the Son of man be lifted up") or Milton, *Paradise Lost* 1:6-10 ("Sing, heavenly Muse, that on the secret top of Oreb or of Sinai didst inspire that shepherd who first taught the chosen seed in the beginning how the heavens and earth rose out of chaos").[30]

2. Inexplicit citation or borrowing. Texts can be dug up and transplanted without acknowledgment. This has happened in Matt. 2:20, which reproduces part of LXX Exod. 4:19 (see p. 142). Note also how Mark's Gospel assimilates John the Baptist to Elijah:

LXX 2 Kings 1:8	Mark 1:6
kai zōnēn dermatinēn	*kai zōnēn dermatinēn*
periezōsmenos	*peri*
tēn osphyn autou	*tēn osphyn autou*

The text might just as well say: John was like Elijah.

3. Similar circumstances. An event may be intended to recall another circumstantially like it. Joshua's crossing of the Jordan, patterned as it is after Moses' crossing of the Red Sea, is a case in point. Less obvious is the modelling of Hanina ben Dosa upon Elijah in *b. Ber.* 34b: "He put his head between his knees and prayed." That this is an allusion to 1 Kings 18:42 ("Elijah... bowed himself down upon the earth, and put his face between his knees") follows from the fact that

---

[29]So E. Miner, "Afterword," in *Literary Uses of Typology*, ed. E. Miner (Princeton: University Press, 1977), 377.

[30]A caveat: what is straightforward in one context may become indistinct in another. When Aristotle said that he did not want to give Athens a second opportunity to sin against philosophy, he was not being cryptic, even though he did not mention Socrates by name. But a modern student unfamiliar with what happened to Socrates would not understand Aristotle's words.

other rabbinic texts undoubtedly compare Hanina and Elijah (*b. Ber.* 61b for instance).

4. Key words or phrases. One may dress up a story with the words of another that is like it and well known. Both the synoptic and Johannine accounts of the feeding of the five thousand share words with 2 Kings 4:42-44, the tale of Elisha miraculously feeding a hundred men with twenty loaves of barley (see the commentaries). That is not coincidence. Compare, in an instance more obscure, how the Chronicler, by changing the wording of 2 Sam. 24:24 (*mĕhîr* has become *kesep mālē' qānâ* has become *nātan*), assimilated the story of David buying a threshing floor from a foreigner (2 Samuel 24) to that of Abraham buying a burial place from the Hittites (Genesis 23).[31]

5. Similar narrative structure. The structure of a text can itself be allusive. Were B. W. Bacon correct concerning the pentateuchal structure of Matthew,[32] the First Gospel as a whole would evoke the Pentateuch (cf. how Joyce's *Ulysses* in its entirety recalls the Odyssey). On a smaller scale, both Mark 1:16-20 (Jesus' calling of four disciples) and 1 Kings 19:19-21 (Elijah's calling of Elisha) have the same form:

1 Kings 19	Mark 1
Elijah appears	Jesus appears
Elisha is at work	The disciples are at work
The call to discipleship	The call to discipleship
Elisha follows Elijah	The disciples follow Jesus

6. Word order, syllabic sequence, poetic resonance. The rhythm or meter of sentences as well as the patterns of words and syllables can be imitative in order to allude. There are examples in Milton's poetry, where a change in meter and/or rhythm serves to declare a debt to Spenser,[33] and, in a lighter vein, poetic parodies offer countless examples, such as Lewis Carroll's take-off on Longfellow's "Hiawatha." John 1:1 supplies a New Testament illustration. It is not just the shared phrase, *en archē*, that sends one back to Gen. 1:1. There is additionally a deeper parallel of sound and order: *en archē* prefacing a sentence at the beginning of a book + verb (*epoiēsen*/*ēn:ē* and *n* are common) + *ho* + two-syllable subject with two vowels ending in *-os* (*the-os* in Genesis, *log-os* in John). Clearly the new beginning is like the old beginning.

---

[31]Details in Zakovitch, "Assimilation," 181. See 2 Chron. 21:24f.
[32]See appendix I, pp. 293-98.
[33]J. Hollander, *Melodious Guile: Fictive Pattern in Poetic Language* (New Haven: Yale, 1988), 166-70.

The preceding points are easy enough to understand. All uncertainty, however, is not thereby exorcised. While devices (l) and (2) are readily perceived and allow no argument, the others often remain indistinct. Consider device (4), key words or phrases. Any two texts of significant length written in the same language share common vocabulary; so how does one judge when that fact is meaningful? When a foreign king declares, in *T. Job* 34:3, *dio anachōrēsōmen eis tas idias chōras*, that is not an allusion to Matt. 2:12; nor is the editorial comment in Matt. 2:12, that the foreign wise men *di allēs hodou anechōrēsan eis tēn chōran auton*, designed to recall *T. Job* 34:3. Similarity in vocabulary does not always betray dependence or imply deliberate allusion. So too with similar circumstances, narrative structures, and syllabic sequences. A likeness can be a simulacrum, a semblance without substance. Is Kafka's Joseph K., who dies with hands outstretched after having been stripped of his clothing, a Christ figure or not? Some think so. Others think not. Using the talent we have to discover animal shapes in clouds, diligent searching can always unearth resemblances between two texts—most of them comparatively meaningless. Of the drawing of many parallels there is no end—for "the mind... can connect any two things in an indefinitely large number of different ways."[34] How then do we sort out the meaningful? Again, when is an allusion an allusion?

In the end, there is no simple answer. Only a delicate and mature judgment bred of familiarity with a tradition will be able to feel whether a suggested allusion or typology is solid or insubstantial: the truth must be divined, groped for by "taste, tact, and intuition rather than a controlling method."[35] Nonetheless, if the boundaries of the objectively certain are severely constricted, a few broad guidelines for our task do exist, and these I now list before examining Moses typologies in Jewish literature.

l. One text can only allude to or intentionally recall another prior to it in time. (Although not a problem for evaluating the New Testament's use of the Jewish Bible, the Jewish Bible's use of its own traditions is another matter: chronological relationships are all too often disputed.)

2. Probability will be enhanced if it can be shown (on other grounds) that a passage's proposed subtext belongs to a book or tradition which

---

[34] I. A. Richards, *The Philosophy of Rhetoric* (London: Oxford, 1976), 125.

[35] M. H. Abrams, "Rationality and Imagination in Cultural History," in Booth, *Critical Understanding*, 176.

held some significance for its author. (Milton criticism has been beset by studies which unearth allusions to works which the poet may not even have known.)

3. In the absence of explicit citation or clear unacknowledged borrowing, a typology will not be credible without some combination of devices (3) - (6); see above. Without similar circumstances, for example, similar vocabulary will not suffice, and vice versa. To illustrate: in Mark 6 the mention of "green grass" (v. 39) alone would not constitute a strong allusion to Psalm 23 ("He makes me lie down in green pastures"). But because "green grass" occurs after the word "shepherd" (Mark 6:34; cf. Ps. 23:1: "The Lord is my shepherd") and in a context of want being met (cf. Ps. 23:1: "I shall not want;" 23:5: "Thou preparest a table before me"), and that beside the waters (Mark 6:32, 34; cf. Ps. 23:2: "He leads me beside still waters"), we begin to wonder.[36] On the other hand, we must deem fanciful Clement of Alexandria's association of the burning thorn bush of Exodus 3 (MT: *seneh*; LXX: *batos*; Philo, *Mos.* 1:65: *batos en akanthōdes*) with Christ's crown of thorns; for nothing more than a single word (*akantha*—Matt. 27:29; John 19:2) joins the Gospels to the Moses traditions at this point.

4. A type should be prominent. A proposed typology based on Moses and the exodus owns an initial plausibility, whereas one requiring knowledge of Ittai, the Philistine commander (2 Samuel 15), does not. Obscurity does not commend itself. As Joseph Addison wrote: "The chief Design of an Allusion being to illustrate and explain the Passages of an Author, it should always be borrowed from what is more known and common than the Passages which are to be explained."[37]

5. An alleged typology has a better chance of gaining our confidence if its constituent elements have been used for typological construction in more than one writing. When, for instance, it is offered that Matthew's references to Jesus fasting for forty days and forty nights (4:2) and to Jesus going up on a mountain (5:1-2) allude to Moses, one should inquire: are there non-Matthean typologies in which people, in imitation of Moses, fast for forty days and forty nights and climb a mountain? Precedent enhances probability.[38]

---

[36]See my article, "Psalm 23 in Early Christianity: A Suggestion," *IBS* 5 (1983):132-37.

[37]*Spectator* July 3, 1712, essay 421.

[38]Yet caution is in order: there is obviously a first time for everything. In Bede's *Life of St. Cuthbert*, set in Scotland, only foods found in the Jewish Bible are eaten. This assimilation of past to present is obscure and, I have read, has no precedent; and yet the correlation is manifestly purposeful.

6. Unusual imagery and uncommon motifs. Two texts are more plausibly related if what they share is out of the ordinary. Petrarch, *Canzoniere* 23, has this:

What I became, when I first grew aware
of my person being transformed
and saw my hairs turning into those leaves
which I had formerly hoped would be my crown,
and my feet, on which I stood and moved and ran,
as every member answers to the soul,
becoming two roots beside the waves
not of Peneus but of a producer river,
and my arms changing into two branches.[39]

The allusion to Ovid, *Metamorphoses* 1:550-51, is guaranteed not only by the mention of the Peneus but by the exotic nature of the shared elements. Contrast the situation regarding Otto Betz's claim that Matt. 7:13-14 directly refers to the two-way theme in Deuteronomy: as it stands, the suggestion is less than compelling because that theme, occurring as it does so often in so many Jewish texts, cannot in itself be a pointer to any one of them.[40]

With these prefatory observations in mind we may now examine the use of Moses as a type in old Jewish literature. For our first purposes, which have to do with Matthew, it is vital to establish the general fact that the lawgiver was, before, during, and after Matthew's age, commonly made a type for important religious figures. Beyond that, we must in particular explore both how and why authors reactivated Mosaic memories and superimposed them on others, for only then can we gain the historical knowledge requisite for evaluating the many proposals that have been made about Matthew's Jesus as a new Moses.

JOSHUA

The Book of Joshua opens by subordinating the conqueror of Canaan to the leader of the exodus: "After the death of Moses the servant of the Lord, the Lord said to Joshua the son of Nun, Moses' minister"

---

[39]I quote from the trans. and ed. of R. M. Durling, *Petrarch's Lyric Poems* (Cambridge: Harvard, 1976), 62.
[40]See appendix VIII, pp. 325-28

(*mĕšārēt-Mōšeh*, 1:1); and throughout the work Joshua follows commands given earlier by the lawgiver.[41] In this way the normative character of the Mosaic law, which law Joshua faithfully obeys, is reinforced. But Joshua's subordination to Moses coexists with a well-developed parallelism. In 1:5 the Lord says to Joshua: "As I was with Moses, so I will be with you;" and in 1:17 the Reubenites, the Gadites, and the half-tribe of Manasseh declare to their new leader: "Just as we obeyed Moses in all things, so we will obey you." This setting of Joshua beside Moses in chapter 1 prepares for chapters 3-4, where Israel, under Joshua's command, crosses the Jordan river—a miracle which puts one in mind of Moses leading the children of Israel through the Red Sea. The text,[42] using certain loaded words and phrases, makes the recall inescapable. "Dry ground" (Josh. 3:17; 4:18, 22: *hārābâ* and *yabbāšâ*), harks back to Exod. 14:16, 21, and 29 (again, *hārābâ* and *yabbāšâ*), while the words "haste" (Josh. 4:10, *māher*) and "heap" (*nēd*, 3:16) have their parallels in Exod. 12:33 (*māher*; cf. Isa. 52:12) and 15:8 (*nēd*) respectively. After the Jordan is crossed we are told: "on that day the Lord exalted Joshua in the sight of all Israel; and they stood in awe of him, as they had stood in awe of Moses" (4:14). There is also this: "The Lord dried up the waters of the Jordan for you until you passed over, as the Lord your God did to the Red Sea, which he dried up for us until we passed over" (4:23). From the duplicating pattern thus explicitly noted the reader infers: the God of the exodus is also the God of the promised land. The point is continuity in salvation-history (cf. Psalm 114). God did not lead his people into the wilderness and there perform miracles for them and then guide them to the border of Canaan, only to forsake them when Moses died. Rather, Joshua, functioning, to quote Ecclus. 46:1, as Moses' *diadochos*, his successor,[43] completed what Moses began. In this way two stories or cycles of tradition—those about the exodus and those about the conquest—become united.

In addition to the parallels between the stories of Moses and Joshua already cited, several others deserve notice:

[41]Cf. Josh. 1:12-18 with Numbers 32 and Deuteronomy 3; Josh. 8:30-35 with Deuteronomy 27; Josh. 11:10-15 with Deut. 20:16; Josh. 11:21-23 with Deut. 9:1-3; Josh. 14:2 = Num. 34:13; Joshua 20 with Num. 35:9-15 and Deut. 19:1-10; Josh. 21:1-42 with Num. 35:1-8.

[42]For our purposes the extremely involved problems surrounding Joshua's sources are of little concern. We are only interested in the canonical shape of the work. But for the evidence that the final redactor of Joshua made additions to underline the new exodus motif see B. Peckham, "The Composition of Joshua 3-4," *CBQ* 46 (1984):413-31.

[43]Cf. the rabbinic claim that Moses handed the Torah to Joshua: *m. ʾAbot* 1:1.

Numbers 13: Moses sends spies into the land	Joshua 2: Joshua sends spies into the land
Exodus 15: the Song of the Sea contains this: "All the inhabitants of Canaan have melted away, terror and dread fall upon them."	Joshua 2: Rahab says: "the fear of you has fallen upon us, and… and all the inhabitants of the land melt away before you"[44]
Exodus 12: under Moses Israel celebrates the passover and shortly thereafter eats manna	Joshua 5:10-13: under Joshua Israel celebrates the passover and shortly thereafter the manna dries up
Exodus 3: Moses has a vision and is told: "Put off your shoes from your feet, for the place on which you are standing is holy ground" (v. 5)	Joshua 5: Joshua has a vision and is told: "Put off your shoes from your feet, for the place where you stand is holy" (v. 15)
Deuteronomy 9: Moses successfully intercedes for a sinful Israel[45]	Joshua 7: Joshua successfully intercedes for a sinful Israel (cf. 4 Ezra 7:106-107)

[44]Additional possible reminiscences of the exodus story in Joshua 2 are forwarded by Alter, *Reading*, 118: "Is the hiding of the spies in the thatch a reminiscence of the hiding of the infant Moses, who is afterward placed in an ark among the bulrushes? A lexical similarity and a grammatical peculiarity may provide clues here. Of four or more biblical terms for 'hide,' the same verb, *ts-p-n*, is used in both texts (Exodus 2:2; Joshua 2:4), and oddly, even though she is hiding 'them,' as all the translators plausibly say, the received Hebrew text actually has a singular object of the verb, 'him,' which could be either an authorial choice to make us think of Moses or a scribal error caused by the recollection of Exodus 2:2 that the language of the verse triggered. Finally, when Rahab gives the spies instructions for safe flight, she tells them, 'get you to the mountain' (v. 16). Though in context 'mountain,' *har*, may mean hill country, it is lexically identical with the often stated goal of the flight from Egypt, and the two men wait there three days— admittedly, a formulaic number in biblical narrative, but also the number of days that the Israelites are enjoined to wait at the foot of the mountain before the giving of the law."

[45]On Moses as intercessor see E. Aurelius, *Der Fürbitter Israels: Eine Studie zum Mosebild im Alten Testament* (CBOT; Stockholm: Almquist & Wicksell, 1988). Cf. Exod. 8:8, 30; 9:33; 10:18; 17:11; 32:11-13, 30-33; 34:9; Num. 11:2; 12:11-14; 16:20-24; 21:7; Jer. 15:1; Ps. 99:6; 106:23; *Jub.* 1:19-21; *As. Mos.* 11:11, 14, 17; 12:6; *LAB* 19:3. Was Psalm 70 attributed to Moses because it contains an intercessory prayer for Israel?

Exodus 17: when Moses, with the staff of God, holds up his hands, the battle goes to Israel	Joshua 8: when Joshua stretches out his hand with its sword, the victory goes to Israel
Deuteronomy 1-34: Moses delivers a farewell speech which includes reference to his old age (31:2), promises future victory over peoples of the land (31:3-5), calls for obedience to the Torah (31:12-13) and sets forth the alternative of serving God or other gods and the consequent blessings and curses (11:26-28; 30:15-20)	Joshua 23-24: Joshua delivers a farewell speech[46] which includes reference to his old age (23:2), promises future victory over peoples of the land (23:4-5), calls for obedience to the Torah (23:6), and sets forth the alternative of serving God or the gods and the consequent blessings and curses (23:6-16)
Exodus 24: Moses mediates a covenant; the people say: "All that the Lord has spoken we will do, and we will be obedient" (v. 7)	Joshua 24: Joshua mediates a covenant; the people say: "The Lord our God we will serve and him we will obey" (v. 24)[47]

Surely it would be a dull or uninformed reader who does not recognize that the life of Joshua is to significant degree a replay of the life of Moses. Joshua completed the work left undone by his predecessor, with the result that the conquest of Canaan fulfilled the promise of the exodus from Egypt.[48] We may say that the conqueror of the land is "almost a second Moses."[49]

Over and above multiplying the connections between the conquest and the exodus and so making their relationship seem almost organic,

[46]Characterized by J. Blenkinsopp, *Prophecy and Canon: A Contribution to the Study of Jewish Origins* (Notre Dame: University Press, 1977), 48, as "a sort of precis of the contents of Deuteronomy."

[47]Two additional parallels (which take us outside Joshua): both Moses and Joshua are said to "go out and come in" (Num. 27:17-18; Deut. 31:2) and both, in their capacity as leaders, are implicitly likened to shepherds (Num. 27:17-18).

[48]Fishbane, *Interpretation*, 359, labels Joshua a "new Moses." On the same page he notes that Ps. 114:1-3 fuses the exodus and the crossing of the Jordan, which "makes sense only in the light of a typological identification ...of two historical events separate in time but comparable in the religious-historical imagination."

[49]So E. M. Good, "Joshua, Son of Nun," in *IDB* 2:996.

the assimilation of Joshua to Moses may have served two other interests. To begin with, if the book of Joshua, as most now suppose, was composed during or near the time of Josiah (640/39-609 B.C.E.), and if, as appears, Joshua himself is intended to be "the prototype of the ideal king of Israel,"[50] modelled upon Josiah and the model for him,[51] it follows that Moses is, so to speak, the model for the model of the king. That is, Moses, as Joshua's type, is implicitly the prototype of Israel's (or Judah's) ruler. Perhaps in this fact we have early evidence for the tradition, so well-attested in later times, despite the biblical testimony that kingship was a subsequent development (1 Samuel 8, etc.), that Moses was Israel's king before David.[52] And maybe the Deuteronomistic school understood Deut. 33:5 ("and he became king in Jeshurun") to refer to Moses, as did the rabbis.[53] However that may be, when *LAB* 20:5 names Joshua, in his capacity as Moses' successor, "ruler in Israel," this would seem to be correct interpretation of the biblical text. The author of Joshua made his hero the standard of kingship by, among other things, indelibly stamping Moses' shape upon him.

Also of likely relevance for evaluating Joshua's resemblance to Moses is Deut. 18:15-18, which contains the promise of a future prophet like Moses. The Deuteronomists probably took the text to envisage a succession of prophets with Mosaic features, that is, a line of prophets

---

[50]So M. D. Coogan, "Joshua," in *NJBC*, 111a.

[51]See R. D. Nelson, "Josiah in the Book of Joshua," *JBL* 100 (1981):531-40; also G. Widengren, "King and Covenant," *JSS* 2 (1957):1-32.

[52]Cf. Ezekiel the Tragedian, in Eusebius, *Praep. ev.* 9:28-29; Philo, *Mos.* 1:148-49, 158, etc.; *Sib. Orac.* 1:435; *Ps.-J. Tg.* on Deut. 33:5; *Mek.* on Exod. 18:14; *Sipre Num.* § 78; *Sipre Deut.* § 357; *b. Zeb.* 102a; *Exod. Rab.* 15:13; *Midr. Ps.* 1:2. Pompeius Trogus (36:2:16) made Moses' son, Arruas (= Aaron?), a king; and both Eupolemus and Justus of Tiberius wrote books on the Jewish kings which began with Moses. *11QTemple*, in its law of the king, borrows material from the career of Moses; see M. O. Wise, *A Critical Study of the Temple Scroll from Qumran Cave 11* (Studies in Ancient Oriental Civilization 49; Chicago: Oriental Institute, 1990), 102-110. Christian texts include Clement of Alexandria, *Strom.* 1:24 (on this see R. Mortley, "The Past in Clement of Alexandria," in *Jewish and Christian Self-Definition*, vol. 1, ed. E. P. Sanders (Philadelphia: Fortress, 1980), 192-94); *Apost. Const.* 2:29; 6:19; Eusebius, *Dem. ev.* 3:2; Gregory the Great, *Reg. Past.* 2:5. For the argument that Moses was already understood in early times to be the prototypical Davidic king, and that this view of him has affected many Pentateuchal texts, see J. R. Porter, *Moses and Monarchy* (Oxford: Basil Blackwell, 1963). (He also urges that Joshua is presented as a king; cf. E. M. Good, *IDB* 2, s.v., "Joshua," and R. D. Nelson, "Josiah in the Book of Joshua," 531-34.) Much of Porter's case is convincing. See also his article, "The Succession of Joshua," in *Proclamation and Presence*, ed. J. I. Durham and J. R. Porter (London: SPCK, 1970), 102-32, and Erwin R. Goodenough, "Kingship in Early Israel," *JBL* 48 (1929):169-205.

[53]W. A. Meeks, *The Prophet-King: Moses Traditions and the Johannine Christology* (NovTSup 14; Leiden: E. J. Brill, 1967), 186-92.

with Moses as the prototype (see p. 74). That being so, Joshua's
likeness to his predecessor could have been understood as confirmation of Deut. 18:15 and 18: Joshua was the first prophet like Moses.[54] This
was the view of Jesus ben Sirach, according to whom "Joshua... was
the successor of Moses in prophesying" (Ecclus. 46:1). R. H. Charles
believed that the author of the *Testament of Moses* had the same
thought.[55] Compare Clement of Alexandria, *Paed.* 1:7(60): "Moses
made way for the perfect Educator, the Word, prophesying both His
name and His method of educating, and placed Him in charge of the
people with the command to obey Him. He said: 'God will raise up to
thee a prophet of thy brethren like unto me,' meaning Jesus, son of
Nun, but implying Jesus, the Son of God."[56]

GIDEON

Judges 6 introduces the story of Gideon by recounting Israel's harsh
oppression under Midian (vv. 1-6), noting that "the people of Israel
cried for help to the Lord" (v. 6), and recording these words from a
prophet: "Thus says the Lord, the God of Israel: I led you up from
Egypt, and brought you out of the house of bondage; and I delivered
you from the hand of the Egyptians, and from the hand of all who
oppressed you, and drove them out before you, and gave you their
land; and I said to you, 'I am the Lord your God; you shall not pay
reverence to the gods of the Amorites, in whose land you dwell.' But
you have not given heed to my voice" (vv. 8-10). There follows
Gideon's call (vv. 11-18). Gideon, a man in hiding from his enemies, is
at work (in the pay of his father, a pagan priest) when the angel of the
Lord appears to him and promises Israel's deliverance. The angel
opens with, "the Lord is with you," to which Gideon protests: "If the
Lord is with us, why then has all this befallen us? And where are all
his wonderful deeds which our fathers recounted to us, saying, 'Did
not the Lord bring us up from Egypt?'" Next comes this: "And the
Lord turned to him [Gideon] and said, 'Go in this might of yours and
deliver Israel from the hand of Midian; do not I send you?'" When
Gideon objects that he is weak and the least in his family, the Lord
simply declares: "But I will be with you, and you shall smite the

---

[54]Cf. Blenkinsopp, *Prophecy and Canon*, 48.
[55]See *APOT* 2:412.
[56]For an example of post-biblical assimilation of Joshua to Moses see p. 94, n.214.

Midianites as one man." Even this does not satisfy Gideon, who subsequently asks for a sign. God obliges, and in the event there is a fire theophany which frightens the judge to be (vv. 21-22), who then declares he has seen the Lord "face to face."[57]

Has Judges 6 been influenced by the story of Moses and the exodus from Egypt? At the time of Moses (who, incidentally, is associated with Midian: Exod. 2:15; 4:19) Israel suffered under foreign oppression and cried out to God for help (*zāʿaq* appears in Judg. 6:6 and Exod. 2:23). The answer to Israel's prayer was Moses, a man in hiding from his enemies. To him appeared the angel of the Lord in a fire—while he was working for his father-in-law, a pagan priest. Through Moses, who came to know God "face to face," the deliverance of Israel was promised. But after learning of his rôle Moses protested: "Who am I?" (Exod. 3:11). When God then promised, "I will be with you" (Exod. 3:12), Moses first asked about God's name and then about his own credibility before the people. In response God gave him miracles or signs (his staff became a serpent, his hand became leprous: Exod. 3:13-19). As in Judges 6, "a vastly disproportionate space is given to the eliciting of the dutiful response."[58]

Four observations move us to discern in the kindred images and parallel circumstances of Judges 6 and the well-known, foundational story in Exodus 3 not coincidence but "calculated reminiscence."[59] Consider first the fact that Judges 6 twice explicitly refers to the exodus from Egypt; see vv. 7-10 and 13. These verses raise the issue of why God once delivered his people yet has now seemingly abandoned them; and as the story continues, it becomes manifest that what God once did he is about to do again, this time by the hand of Gideon. That is, the references to the exodus function precisely to imply that the coming act of liberation will be like that of old: the deliverance from Egyptian bondage under the leadership of Moses will have its analogue in the deliverance from Midian under the leadership of Gideon.

There is, in the second place, common vocabulary. Judg. 6:16 and Exod. 3:12 share the formula, "because I will be with you;" and the introductory notice, "and there appeared (*wayyērāʾ*) to him the angel of the Lord" appears only three times in the Jewish Bible, in Exod. 3:2; Judg. 6:12; and 13:3.

---

[57]To no other judge does God speak directly.
[58]So R. G. Boilng, *Judges* (AB; Garden City: Doubleday, 1975), 132.
[59]So Bolilng, ibid.

Thirdly, the Gideon narrative in its entirety has a structural parallel in Exodus: oppression of Israel, call of deliverer, ruin of foreign deities, holy war.[60] There is cause to suppose that, whatever the tradition-history may be,[61] the final form of Judges makes the story of Gideon a typical instance of salvation history after the exodus model.[62]

Fourthly, the *Liber Antiquitatum Biblicarum*, in retelling the call of Gideon, has the judge emulate Moses: "And Gideon said to him, 'May my Lord not be angry that I should say a word. Behold Moses the first of all the prophets asked the Lord for a sign, and it was given to him. But who am I, unless perhaps the Lord has chosen me?" (*LAB* 35:6). Beyond this explicit recollection, three additional alterations attest Gideon's assimilation to Moses: (i) Gideon's call now takes place on a mountain (*LAB* 35:1; cf. Exod. 3:1); (ii) Gideon now asks, "Who am I?" (*LAB* 35:5; cf. Exod. 3:11); (iii) God now tells Gideon he is looking for the virtue "meekness" (*LAB* 35:5; cf. Num. 12:3). Clearly the author of the *Liber Antiquitatum Biblicarum* perceived the similarities between Judges 6 and Exodus 2-3 and was in fact intent on adding to them.

What is the significance of the parallels, confessedly rather quiescent, between Gideon and Moses, of Gideon being "a model of Mosaic piety," or a "Moses figure"?[63] It would appear to lie in an understanding of sacred history, according to which God's mighty acts repeat themselves. They do so because (i) God's people time and time again find themselves in similar circumstances, and (ii) God's character is constant. With regard to Judges 6 and Exodus 3 in particular, the common circumstance is foreign domination, the common divine remedy a commissioned liberator. As it was in Egypt, so in the land. As God sent Moses, the first deliverer, so he sent Gideon, a second deliverer. The link between Moses and Gideon is therefore deliverance. The former, being the greatest example of a human instrument through whom God saves, is the natural model for the latter, which is to say: the Moses typology depends upon Moses' status as exemplary deliverer or savior.

---

[60]Cf. B. G. Webb, *The Book of Judges: An Integrated Reading* (JSOTSS 46; Sheffield: JSOT, 1987), 149.

[61]For the argument that the Gideon story is "an example of late biblical narrative" which presupposes the Moses materials see A. Graeme Auld, "Gideon: Hacking at the Heart of the Old Testament," *VT* 39 (1989):257-67.

[62]So W. Beyerlin, "Geschichte und heilsgeschichte Traditionsbildung im Alten Testament: ein Beitrag zur Traditionsgeschichte von Richter vi-viii," *VT* 13 (1963):1-25.

[63]So Webb, *Judges*, 153. Webb suggests additional possible parallels between Moses and Gideon: Gideon was in the wilderness (8:16) and made an ephod which became an idolatrous cult object (8:24-27; cf. 2 Kings 18:4).

SAMUEL

More than one scholar has suggested that the biblical Samuel is a "new Moses."[64] Samuel, labelled, like Moses, both "prophet" (1 Sam. 3:20) and "man of God" (1 Sam. 9:6),[65] was given up by his parents not long after birth (1 Sam. 1:21-28; cf. Exodus 2). He grew up to be an intercessor for Israel (1 Sam. 7:5, 8-9; 12:19-25; 15:10-31).[66] When God first spoke to him, with the words, "Samuel, Samuel," his response was, "Here I am" (1 Sam. 3:4; cf. Exod. 3:4). Samuel also called Israel away from its idolatry (1 Sam. 7:3-4; cf. Exodus 32) and anointed others (1 Sam. 10:1 [Saul]; 16:13 [David]; cf. Lev. 8:1-13 [Moses anoints Aaron]); he was a holy war leader (1 Sam. 7:7-14; cf. Deut. 2:33-36) and renewed the covenant (1 Sam. 7:3-6; cf. Deut. 31:9-13); he also wrote legislation for the king (1 Sam. 10:25; cf. Deuteronomy 17) and, in a farewell speech, set before the people the two ways of obedience and disobedience (1 Samuel 12; cf. Deuteronomy 28-30).

The parallels just listed are not numerous. Nor do they share significant vocabulary. And several carry little weight because they are not unique to Moses and Samuel. Thus the call narrative in 1 Samuel 3, with its use of the double vocative and "Here I am," also resembles Gen. 22:9-14 (God calls to Abraham, "Abraham, Abraham," and the patriarch answers, "Here I am"). Further, Moses and Samuel were not, to state the obvious, the only intercessors for Israel; and Samuel's farewell address is closer to Joshua 24 than Deuteronomy 28-30. Nonetheless, such vitiating considerations do not exclude the possibility of a Moses typology in 1 Samuel. For one thing, 1 Sam. 9:16 ("I have seen the affliction of my people, because their cry has come up to me") does clearly call to mind the situation before the exodus (Exod. 3:9: "the cry of the people of Israel has come to me, and I have seen the oppression with which the Egyptians oppress them"). For another, 1

---

[64]So e.g. E. Jacob, "Prophètes et Intercessors," in *De la Tôrah au Messie: Mélanges Henri Cazelles*, ed. M. Carrez, J. Doré, and P. Grelot (Paris: Desclée, 1981), 209. Several times, in his deconstructive reading of 1 Samuel, P. D. Miscall notes parallels between Moses and Samuel; see *1 Samuel: A Literary Reading* (Bloomington: Indiana University Press, 1986), 1-3, 42-46. And more than once he asks whether Samuel should not be identified with the prophet like Moses of Deut. 18:15, 18 (as on pp. 3, 44-46, and 50-51). On p. 79 he calls Samuel "a delayed successor of Moses." Cf. James Muilenburg, "The 'Office' of Prophet in Ancient Israel," in *The Bible and Modern Scholarship*, ed. J. Philip Hyatt (Nashville: Abingdon, 1965), 91-93; he notes the parallels between Samuel and Moses and uses the expression, "the second Moses."

[65]For Moses as prophet see n. 135; for the title, "man of God," see n. 69.

[66]On Moses as intercessor see n. 45.

Samuel plainly refers to the exodus from Egypt (2:27), while 1 Sam. 12:6-11 invites us to set the time of Samuel beside the time of Moses:

> And Samuel said to the people, "The Lord is witness, who appointed Moses and Aaron and brought your fathers up out of the land of Egypt. Now therefore stand still, that I may plead with you before the Lord concerning all the saving deeds of the Lord which he performed for you and for your fathers. When Jacob went into Egypt and the Egyptians oppressed them, then your fathers cried to the Lord and the Lord sent Moses and Aaron, who brought forth your fathers out of Egypt, and made them dwell in this place. But they forgot the Lord their God; and he sold them into the hand of Sisera, commander of the army of Jabin king of Hazor, and into the hand of the Philistines, and into the hand of the king of Moab; and they fought against them. And they cried to the Lord, and said, 'We have sinned, because we have forsaken the Lord, and have served the Baals and the Ashtaroth; but now deliver us out of the hand of our enemies, and we will serve thee.' And the Lord sent Jerubbaal and Barak, and Jephthah, and Samuel, and delivered you out of the hand of your enemies on every side; and you dwelt in safety."

Here Moses and Aaron are the first deliverers, to whom other deliverers may be likened, and Samuel is among their number.

Also favoring the existence of a Moses typology in 1 Samuel is the circumstance that sandwiched between the Samuel materials collected in 1:1-4:1 and 7:2ff. is the account of the capture of the ark by the Philistines. According to this "the hand of the Lord [cf. Exod. 9:3, etc.] was heavy upon the Philistines because of the ark of God" (5:6, 9, 11). Initially the inhabitants of Ashdod were afflicted with tumors, then the inhabitants of Gath, and when the holy thing came to Ekron, "there was a deathly panic throughout the whole city," and "the men who did not die were stricken with tumors" (5:11-12), for a plague brought by mice was "destroying (*mashîtim*, cf. Exod. 12:23) the land" (6:5). Finally, after seven (cf. Exod. 7:25) months of "plague" (*maggēpâ*, 6:4; cf. Exod. 9:14), the Philistines, having belatedly recognized the ark as the cause of their tribulations, called "the priests and diviners" and inquired of them what to do (6:1-2). The answer came: "send away the ark of the God of Israel," and inside it place, as a guilt offering, objects (*kělî*, cf. Exod. 12:35) of gold (6:3-8; cf. Exod. 3:21; 11:2, etc.). There can be no doubt that in all this the intelligent reader should perceive a parallel with the exodus traditions, to wit:

Israel in captivity	The ark in captivity
Plagues	Plagues
Release of Israel	Release of the ark
The Egyptians despoiled	Gold guilt offering sent

Near the beginning of our narrative the Philistines, before they capture the ark, declare: "Woe to us! Who can deliver us from the power of these angry gods? These are the gods who smote the Egyptians with every sort of plague in the wilderness" (4:8). And in 6:6, in the speech of the priests and diviners, there is this: "Why should you harden your hearts as the Egyptians and Pharaoh hardened their hearts? After he made sport of them, did not they let the people go, and they departed?" These two verses make manifest that the narrative of Samuel's call prefaces three chapters which, in their present form, tell of "a kind of second Exodus."[67] One can indeed ask whether the juxtaposition of the traditions about Saul and those about the ark was not fostered by the desire to reproduce the fundamental pattern of the Moses traditions, this being: (i) call of Israel's deliverer (Moses, Samuel), (ii) plagues upon foreign power that wrongly holds God's property ("my people," "the ark of God"), (iii) release of God's property (Israel, the ark).

Although I am inclined to believe that one or more contributors to 1 Samuel sought to assimilate Samuel to Moses, many modern commentators have nothing to say on the subject, which implies that they have not perceived such assimilation. Perhaps, however, we should in this be directed not by the moderns but by the ancients, who often associated Samuel and Moses—so often in fact that we may justly speak of a well-established tradition. Jer. 15:1 supplies the earliest instance. Here the two men are together remembered as the great intercessors for Israel: "Then the Lord said to me, 'Though Moses and Samuel stood before me, yet my heart would not turn toward this people.'" Compare Ps. 99:6: "Moses and Aaron were among his priests, Samuel also was among those who called on his name. They cried to the Lord, and he answered them." Later Eupolemus (*apud* Eusebius, *Praep. ev.* 9:30) presented Samuel as the direct successor of Moses and Joshua while Philo, for his part, adverted to Samuel as "the greatest of kings and prophets" (*Ebr. 143*), a title which makes him resemble Philos' Moses. According to *Midr. Rab.* on Ps. 1:3, Samuel fulfilled the promise of a prophet like Moses given in Deut. 18:15, 18:

> The verse "Moses and Samuel stood before Me" (Jer. 15:1) suggests a likeness between Moses and Samuel. For you find that what is said of the one is said of the other. The one was a Levite, and the other was a

[67]Ralph W. Klein, *1 Samuel* (WBC; Waco: Word, 1983), 61. Cf. Patrick D. Miller and J. J. M. Roberts, *The Hand of the Lord: A Reassessment of the "Ark Narrative" of 1 Samuel* (Baltimore: Johns Hopkins, 1977), 48, 55, 67, 103, n. 11.

Levite. The one built an altar, and the other built an altar. The one brought offerings, and the other brought offerings. The one became king, and the other became king. The one was summoned by a call from God, and the other summoned by a call from God. Indeed, Scripture alludes to this likeness in the verse: "A prophet will the Lord thy God raise up unto thee, from the midst of thee, of thy brethren, like unto me" (Deut. 18:15).

Other late texts make Samuel's conception occur when his mother is one hundred and thirty years old—the same age tradition gave to Jochebed at her conceiving of Moses.[68] Comparison of Samuel and Moses appears also in the *Liber Antiquitatum Biblicarum*. In the section on Samuel, not only is Ps. 99:6 expressly quoted (51:6), but twice Samuel is related to Moses:

And Samuel was sleeping in the temple of the Lord. And when God called to him, he gave it consideration first, saying, "Behold now Samuel is young so as to be beloved before me. In spite of the fact that he has not heard the voice of the Lord or has been confirmed with the word of the Most High, nevertheless he is like my servant Moses. To an eighty-year old I spoke, but Samuel is eight years old. And Moses saw the fire first, and his heart was very much afraid. And if Samuel should see fire now, how will he survive? (53:2).

And Samuel sent and gathered all the people and said to them, "Behold you and your king. But I am in your midst as God has commanded me. And so before your king I say to you as my lord Moses the servant of God said to your fathers in the wilderness when the company of Korah rose up against him… (57:1-2).

Moreover, we are told that Samuel was a "handsome child" (51:1; cf. Philo, *Mos.* l:9, 15; Acts 7:20; Josephus, *Ant.* 2:224, 231-32), that he was raised up when "God remembered Israel" (53:2; cf. Exod. 2:24; 6:5), and that he "show[ed] to the nations the statutes" (*LAB* 51:3).

A last illustration of Moses/Samuel parallelism occurs in 2 *En.* 48 A 5. It deserves to be quoted nearly in full:

But when the Holy One, blessed be He, shall see that there is none righteous in that generation, none pious on the earth, no righteousness in men's hands, no one like Moses, no intercessor like Samuel, who could entreat the Omnipresent One for salvation, for redemption… then the Holy One, blessed be he, will at once remember his own righteousness, merit, mercy, and grace, and for his own sake, will deliver his great arm, and his own righteousness will support him, as it

---

[68]L. Ginzberg, *The Legends of the Jews* (Philadelphia: Jewish Publication Society, 1942), 4:59.

is written, "He saw that there was no one"—like Moses, who sought mercy many times for Israel in the wilderness and annulled the decree against them—"and he was astonished that there was no intercessor"—like Samuel, who interceded with the Hold One, blessed be he, and cried to him; and the Holy One answered him, and did what he wanted, even what was not foreordained, as it is written, "It is now wheat harvest, is it not? I will call on the Lord and he shall send thunder and rain." Moreover, Samuel is linked with Moses, as it is written, "Moses and Aaron among his priests, and Samuel among those who invoke his name," moreover, Scripture says, "Even if Moses and Samuel were standing in my presence."

Leaving aside 1 Samuel itself, where the evidence for a Moses typology is somewhat feeble, what accounts for the common association of Samuel and Moses? Determinative for Jer. 15:1 and Ps. 99:6 was the two men's status as pre-eminent intercessors. In later literature, such the *Liber Antiquitatum Biblicarum* and *2 Enoch*, Scripture itself, that is, Jer. 15:1 and Ps. 99:6, may well have been the major impetus. One additionally suspects that Samuel's status as a great prophet—so emphasized in Ecclus. 46:13-20—played its rôle, for Moses was the prophet *par excellence* (Deut. 34:10).

But a factor more subtle may also have been at work in several sources. God, we read, raised up Samuel at a decisive time in Israel's history, the transition from a theocracy with judges to a kingdom with monarchs. And as Ecclus. 46:13 has it, Samuel, by anointing Saul and then David, "established the kingdom." Hence Samuel closed one era and ushered in another. In that crucial respect he was very much like Moses, who broke the Egyptian bondage and inaugurated the age of Torah. This fact is so suggestive because the transition under Moses became paradigmatic: it was the prime example of history changing course, of one dispensation giving way to another. So just as it was natural to comprehend any great historical transition as another exodus, so too was it natural to liken to Moses men who altered the seasons and straddled epochs.

DAVID

Two figures dominate the Jewish Bible: Moses and David. Both were shepherds before leading Israel and both were given the appellation, "man of God;"[69] and whereas Moses was thought to have failed in only

---

[69]Moses: Deut. 33:1; Josh. 14:6; Ps. 90:1; Ezra 3:2; 1 Chron. 23:14; 2 Chron. 30:16. David: Neh. 12:24, 36; 2 Chron. 8:14.

one particular, by striking twice a rock at Meribah (Numbers 20), so David was remembered as doing what was right in the eyes of the Lord, not turning aside from anything He commanded him all the days of his life, "except in the matter of Uriah the Hittite" (1 Kgs. 15:5). One might therefore have anticipated that Jewish tradition, which assigned to Moses the Pentateuch and to David the five books of Psalms, would relate the two men to each other. And so it does. *Midr. Ps.* 1:1 contains this:

> "For this is the law of man:" Scripture does not say here "for this is the law of Abraham, of Isaac, or of Jacob," but "for this is the law of man." But what man? He who is foremost among the prophets; he who is foremost among kings. The foremost among prophets—he is Moses, of whom it is said "And Moses went up unto God" (Exod. 19:3); the foremost among kings—he is David. You find that whatever Moses did, David did. As Moses led Israel out of Egypt, so David led Israel out of servitude to Goliath. As Moses fought the battles of the Lord against Sihon and Og, so David fought the battles of the Lord in all the regions around him, as Abigail said: "My lord fighteth the battles of the Lord" (1 Sam. 25:28). As Moses became king in Israel and in Judah, for it is said "And he became king in Jeshurun, when the heads of the people... were gathered together" (Deut. 33:5), so David became king in Israel and in Judah. As Moses divided the Red Sea for Israel, so David divided the rivers of Aram for Israel, as it is said "David... divided the rivers of Aram" (Ps. 60:1, 2). As Moses built an altar, so David built an altar. As the one brought offerings, so the other brought offerings. As Moses gave five books of laws to Israel, so David gave five Books of Psalms to Israel.... Finally, as Moses blessed Israel with the words "Blessed art thou, O Israel" (Deut. 33:29), so David blessed Israel with the words "Blessed is the man."

Aside from this passage, rabbinic literature supplies, surprisingly, very few instances of the comparison of Moses and David (one example, *Midr. Ps.* 24:5). These do not suffice to establish a genuine tradition. There is also, to judge from my researches, no genuine tradition outside the rabbinic corpus. The Hebrew Bible, however, does contain one book in which David plays the part of Moses. I refer to 1 Chronicles. Consider 1 Chron. 22:6-13:

> Then he called for Solomon his son, and charged him to build a house for the Lord, the God of Israel. David said to Solomon, "My son, I had it in my heart to build a house to the name of the Lord my God. But the word of the Lord came to me, saying, 'You have shed much blood and have waged great wars; you shall not build a house to my name, because you have shed so much blood before me upon the earth. Behold, a son shall be born to you; he shall be a man of peace. I will give him peace from all his enemies round about; for his name shall be Solomon, and I will give peace and quiet to Israel in his days. He shall build a house for

my name. He shall be my son, and I will be his father, and I will establish his royal throne for ever.' Now, my son, the Lord be with you, so that you may succeed in building the house of the Lord your God, as he has spoken concerning you. Only, may the Lord grant you discretion and understanding, that when he gives you charge over Israel you may keep the law of the Lord your God. Then you will prosper if you are careful to observe the statutes and ordinances which the Lord commanded Moses for Israel. Be strong, and of good courage. Fear not; be not dismayed."

Against his will, David, because of bloodshed, did not, in accordance with the word of the Lord, live to complete the temple. This reminds one of Moses who, because of sin, had his desire to enter the land thwarted by God. Further, just as Moses commissioned a successor, Joshua, to complete his labors and lead Israel into the land, so David commissioned a successor, Solomon, to complete the task of building the temple. That these parallels are not fortuitous is demonstrated by David's words to his son, delivered near his death. The venerable king told Solomon that God would be with him (v. 11), enjoined him to keep the law (v. 12), reminded him that keeping the law would bring prosperity (v. 13), and entreated him to be strong and of good courage, and not to be afraid or dismayed (v. 13). All this irresistibly recalls the commissioning stories in Deuteronomy 31 and Joshua 1. According to these, Moses, near the end of his days, along with God told Joshua that God would be with him (Deut. 31:8, 23; Josh. 1:5), enjoined him to keep the law (Josh. 1:7-8), reminded him that keeping the law would bring prosperity (Josh. 1:8), and entreated him to be strong and of good courage, and not be afraid or dismayed (Deut. 31:7-8, 23; Josh. 1:9).

In 1962 N. Lohfink construed the parallels between 1 Chronicles 22 on the one hand and Deuteronomy 34 and Joshua 1 on the other as evidence for the existence of an old *Gattung* of installation.[70] The evidence for this is less than overwhelming. What appears more probable, or is perhaps true at the same time, is the straightforward literary dependence of 1 Chronicles 22 upon Deuteronomy 34 and Joshua 1.[71] In addition to the similarities already observed, "Be strong, and of good courage. Fear not; be not dismayed" has, besides 2 Chron. 32:7, its only close parallel in the four-fold formula of Josh. 1:9 and

---

[70]"Die deuteronomistische Darstellung des Übergangs der Führung Israels von Moses auf Josue. Ein Beitrag zur altestamentliche Theologie des Amtes," *Scholastik* 37 (1962):32-44. Cf. D. J. McCarthy, "An Installation Genre?," *JBL* 90 (1971):31-41.

[71]See Roddy Braun, *1 Chronicles* (WBC 14; Waco: Word, 1986), 222-23, and H. G. M. Williamson, "The Accession of Solomon in the Books of Chronicles," *VT* 26 (1976):351-61.

Deut. 31:6. Moreover, the sequence of a private commissioning of Solomon followed by a public commissioning, found in 1 Chronicles 22 and 28, appears also when Deuteronomy and Joshua are juxtaposed (Deut. 31:14-15 records a private commissioning, Joshua 1 a public commissioning).[72] Lastly, the association of the concept of rest with Solomon and the building of the temple (1 Chron. 22:9) depends upon the Book of Joshua, where rest is the prerequisite for the assembling of the tent of meeting at Shiloh (see esp. Josh. 11:23 and 18:1).[73]

Granted the literary relationship between 1 Chronicles 22 and the Hexateuch's two stories of Joshua's commissioning, the chapter might be thought to contain a typology: when David commissioned Solomon, he was doing what Moses did when Moses commissioned Joshua; or, as one commentator has put it, "the succession of Moses and Joshua [served] as a paradigm for that of David and Solomon."[74] In explanation for this, Roddy Braun has urged that "the Chronicler's primary objective... [was] to portray Solomon as the divinely chosen temple builder."[75] In this there must be some truth. The Chronicler manifestly purposed to improve upon the picture of Solomon in the Deuteronomistic history, and an implicit likening of his beloved king with the divinely commissioned Joshua must have been congenial. But is there not more?

The question is not idle, because there is a second text in 1 Chronicles which features a Mosaic David. 1 Chron. 28:11-19, an insertion between David's speech to the princes of Israel (vv. 1-10) and his exhortation to Solomon (vv. 20-21), says that

> David gave Solomon his son the pattern (*tabnît, paradeigma*, cf. Exod. 25:9, 40) of the temple and its rooms, its treasuries, its upper chambers, its inner chambers, and the room for the mercy seat, the pattern (*tabnît, paradeigma*) of all that he had in mind concerning the courts of the house of Yahweh and concerning all of the chambers round about.... All he (David) made plain to him (Solomon) in a writing from the hand of Yahweh (cf. Exod. 31:18), including all the details of the pattern (*tabnît, paradeigma*).

These lines, like Ezekiel 40 and 42, obviously depend upon the tabernacle narrative in Exodus 25ff., where Moses is shown the

[72]Cf. McCarthy, "An Installation Genre?," 35-36.
[73]Roddy Braun, "Solomon, the Chosen Temple Builder: The Significance of 1 Chronicles 22, 28, and 29 for the Theology of Chronicles," *JBL* 95 (1976):582-86.
[74]So Raymond B. Dillard, *2 Chronicles* (WBC 15; Waco: Word, 1987), 3.
[75]"Solomon," 590.

"pattern" (*tabnît, paradeigma*) of the tabernacle and all its furniture.[76] Just as Moses was directly given by God the plans for the tabernacle, so too David; and just as Moses handed on the plans to Bezalel (Exod. 31:3; 35:30-35), similarly did David hand on the plans he received to Solomon.[77] Did David then not have a Mosaic type authority?[78]

It is difficult to know what one should make of the Moses-David parallelism in 1 Chronicles 22 and 28. More than the enhancement of Solomon's reputation by way of favorable comparison with Joshua, Moses' divinely appointed successor, must have been involved, for in 1 Chronincles 28 Solomon's type is Bezalel, not Joshua. My own suspicion—it can be no more—is that the Chronicler was eager to prove David nobody's inferior. The genealogy in 1 Chronicles 6 manages to introduce Moses without citing one of his exploits or even bestowing upon him an adjective: "The children of Amram: Aaron, Moses, and Miriam" (v. 6).[79] Further, the reduction to genealogy of all history prior to David leaves the definite impression that such history was perhaps unimportant, at least comparatively. The Chronicler seems to have believed, and then set out to show, that the Davidic covenant, not the Mosaic, was definite.[80] If so, this would explain why his work mentions Moses only in passing, why it exalts David and Solomon, and why it models David upon Moses in chapters 22 and 29: the former was made like the latter in order to be his equal, perhaps even his superior.

ELIJAH

Many have remarked that 1 Kings 17-19 and 2 Kings 1-2 have a "Mosaic atmosphere"[81] and that they present Elijah as "a second Moses"[82] or "a new Moses."[83] What is the evidence for so thinking, that is, for

---

[76]For the evidence of direct literary borrowing see Braun, *1 Chronicles*, 272.

[77]For the argument that Solomon is "the new Bezalel" see Dillard, *2 Chronicles*, 4.

[78]See Simon J. De Vries, "Moses and David as Cult Founders in Chronicles," *JBL* 107 (1988):119-39, urging that the chronicler used David to legitimate the Levites.

[79]In 1 Chron. 23:14 and 2 Chron. 30:16, however, he is called "the man of God," and in 1 Chron. 6:49 and 2 Chron. 24:6 "the servant of God." The main impression of Moses one receives from 1 and 2 Chronicles is that God through him gave commandments which are written in a book: 1 Chron. 15:15; 22:13; 2 Chron. 8:13; 33:8; 34:14; 35:12.

[80]For this position see R. North, in the new *JBC*, 362-83.

[81]R. A. Carlson, "Élie à l'Horeb," *VT* 19 (1969):432.

[82]Kastner, *Moses*, 30.

[83]E.g. F. M. Cross, *Canaanite Myth and Hebrew Epoch* (Cambridge, Mass.: Harvard, 1973), 192; G. W. Coats, "Healing and the Moses Traditions," in *Canon, Theology, and Old Testament Interpretation*, ed. G. M. Tucker et al. (Philadelphia: Fortress, 1988), 136; R. P.

supposing that 1-2 Kings offers "an intentional comparison between Elijah and Moses"?[84] Elijah, whose mission was to uphold the Mosaic tradition and covenant against the idolatrous religion of Baal, confronted King Ahab and then went into exile (1 Kgs. 17:1-7). Moses, afraid of Pharaoh, also went into exile, into Midian (Exod. 2:11-15). Elijah was miraculously fed "bread and meat in the morning and bread and meat in the evening" (*lehem ûbāśār baboqer welehem ûbāśār bā'āreb*, 1 Kgs. 17:6). Moses and the Israelites in the wilderness were given "in the evening meat to eat and in the morning bread" (*bā'ereb bāśār le'ĕkol welehem baboqer*, Exod. 16:8; cf. v. 12). Elijah spoke in his own name (1 Kings 17:1: "As the Lord the God of Israel lives, before whom I stand, there shall be neither dew nor rain these years, except by my word"). Moses spoke in his own name (Deut. 5:1: "Hear, O Israel, the statutes and the ordinances which I speak in your hearing this day…"). Elijah gathered Israel at Mount Carmel (1 Kgs. 18:19). Moses gathered all Israel at the foot of Mount Sinai (Exod. 19:17). Elijah combatted the prophets of Baal (1 Kgs. 18:20-40). Moses combatted the magicians of Pharaoh (Exod. 7:8-13, 20-22; 8:1-7). Elijah successfully interceded for an idolatrous Israel by praying to the God of Abraham, Isaac, and Israel (1 Kgs. 18:36-39). So too Moses (Exod. 32:11-14).[85] On Carmel Elijah repaired the altar of the Lord, taking twelve stones "according to the number of the tribes of the sons of Jacob" (1 Kgs. 18:30-32). At the foot of Sinai Moses built an altar with twelve pillars "according to the twelve tribes of Israel" (Exod. 24:4). Elijah, who "came near" (*yiggaš*) to God (cf. Exod. 24:2), offered an oblation upon which "the fire (*'ēš*) of the Lord fell, and consumed the burnt offering (*tō'kal 'et-hā'ōlâ*), and the wood, and the stones, and the dust, and licked up the water that was in the trench. And when all the people saw it (*wayyar' kol-hā'ām*), they fell on their faces ('*al-pĕnêhem*)…" (1 Kgs 18:36-39). Moses and Aaron also made an offering upon which "fire" (*'ēš*) came forth from before the Lord… [it] consumed the burnt offering (*wattōkal… 'et-hā'ōlâ*) and the fat upon the altar; and when all the people saw it (*wayyar' kol-hā'ām*), they shouted and fell on their faces ('*al-pĕnêhem*)" (Lev. 9:22-24). By Elijah's authority the idolatrous prophets of Baal were slain (1 Kgs.

Carroll, "The Elijah-Elisha Sagas: Some Remarks on Prophetic Succession in Ancient Israel," *VT* 19 (1969):411. G. Fohrer, *Elia*, ATANT 53 (Zürich: Zwingli, 1957), 57, calls Elijah "a second and new Moses."

    [84]R. D. Nelson, *First and Second Kings* (Atlanta: John Knox, 1987), 128.

    [85]"Abraham, Isaac, and Israel" is rare in the Jewish Bible: Exod. 32:13; 1 Kgs. 18:36; 1 Chron. 29:18; 2 Chron. 30:6.

18:40).[86] By Moses' authority three thousand idolaters were slain (Exod. 32:25-29). Elijah, after the killing of the prophets of Baal, climbed Carmel to have his prayer heard (1 Kgs. 18:42). Moses, after the slaying of the worshippers of the golden calf, went up to Sinai to have his prayer heard (Exod. 32:30, etc.). Elijah, on his way to Horeb, went "forty days and forty nights" without food (1 Kgs. 19:8). Moses on Sinai went without food "forty days and forty nights" (Exod. 34:28; Deut. 9:9). Elijah was commissioned, or rather recommissioned, on Horeb (= Sinai) (1 Kings 19). Moses received his divine call and commission on Sinai (Exodus 3). Elijah was in "the cave"[87] on Horeb = Sinai when the Lord "passed by" (1 Kgs. 19:9-11). Moses on Sinai was hid "in a cleft of the rock" when the Lord "passed by" (Exod. 33:21-23). Elijah was on Horeb = Sinai when a theophany brought storm, wind, an earthquake, and fire (1 Kgs. 19:11-12). Moses was on Sinai when a theophany brought wind, earthquake, and fire (Exod. 19:16-20; 20:18; Deut. 4:11; 5:22-27).[88] Elijah, despite his victory over the prophets of Baal, became so depressed that he "asked that he might die" (1 Kgs. 19:1-4). Moses was so despondent that he prayed for death to end his misery (Num. 11:10-15). Elijah called down fire from heaven to consume his enemies (2 Kgs. 1:9-12). When men assembled against Moses in the wilderness, fire fell from the Lord and consumed them (Numbers 16; cf. Lev. 10:1-3). At the Jordan river Elijah "took his mantle and rolled it up, and struck the water; the water was parted to the one side and to the other, till the two of them could go over on dry ground" (2 Kgs. 2:8). At the Red Sea Moses stretched out his hands and the waters were divided,

---

[86]"Though the reading *wayyaśhitem* might be strictly correct in sense—the Qal of the MT is not unintelligible, signifying that what was done was by Elijah's authority, he remaining on the mountain, as the sequel demands, while the massacre took place in the plain below;" so J. Gray, *I and II Kings* (2nd ed.; Philadelphia: Westminster, 1970), 403.

[87]Gray, ibid., 409: "The definite article with the singular *hammĕ'ārā* ('cave') is explained by Montgomery (ICC, p. 317) as the generic article ('the cave region'), as in 18.4. Here, however, it seems rather to point to the tradition of a definite cave on the holy mountain, possibly that from which Moses saw the back of Yahweh…". Cf. R. L. Cohn, "The Literary Logic of 1 Kings 17-19," *JBL* 101 (1982):342; Cross, *Canaanite Myth*, 193; and *b. Meg.* 19b ("the cave in which Moses and Elijah stood").

[88]The "silent sound" or "still small voice" of 1 Kgs. 19:12 may also be associated with the Moses traditions. According to R. B. Coote, "Yahweh recalls Elijah," in *Traditions in Transformation*, ed. B. Halpern and J. D. Levenson (Winona Lake: Eisenbrauns, 1981), 119, "the silent sound is said to be 'thin' (*daqqâ*). This description recalls to the ear of the hearer the description of manna as a 'flaky thin thing (*daq*), a thin thing (*daq*) like hoarfrost' (Exod. 16:14), and as the 'insubstantial, or perhaps contemptible (*qĕlōqēl*), food' (Num. 21:5). Why this allusion to manna? Because there was a tradition in Israel that God's intelligible word, by which one lives, was food, like manna;" cf. Deut. 8:3; Amos 8:11.

and the Israelites passed through "as on dry land," the waters forming a wall on the right and on the left (Exod. 14:16, 21-22). Elijah appointed as his successor a man who served him as minister and came to resemble him in many ways—Elisha, who, like Elijah, split the Jordan and walked across (2 Kings 2). Moses appointed as his successor a man who served him as minister and came to resemble him in many ways—Joshua, who, like Moses at the Red Sea, split the Jordan and walked across. Elijah was mysteriously translated to heaven, but people thought that he might still be alive, cast "upon some mountain or into some valley" (2 Kgs. 2:9-18). Moses died mysteriously and was buried in a valley, but no one knew the precise location (Deut. 34:6).[89]

We cannot know exactly what percentage of the suggested similarities—many of which were observed by the author of *Pesiq. R.* 4:2[90]—

---

[89]It is not impossible that one or more contributors to Kings knew the tradition, to which Deuteronomy may already be a counter, that Moses never died.

[90]"R. Tanhuma Berabbi began his discourse as follows: 'And by a prophet the Lord brought Israel out of Egypt' (Hos. 12:14), that prophet being Moses; 'and by a prophet was he preserved' (*ibid.*)—that is, by Elijah. You find that two Prophets rose up for Israel out of the Tribe of Levi; one the first of all the Prophets, and the other the last of all the Prophets: Moses first and Elijah last, and both with a commission from God to redeem Israel: Moses, with his commission, redeemed them from Egypt, as is said 'Come now, therefore, and I will send thee unto Pharaoh' (Exod. 3:10). And in the time-to-come, Elijah, with his commission, will redeem them, as is said 'Behold, I will send you Elijah the prophet' (Mal. 3:23). As with Moses, who in the beginning redeemed them out of Egypt, they did not return to slavery again in Egypt; so with Elijah, after he will have redeemed them out of the fourth exile, out of Edom, they will not return and again be enslaved—theirs will be an eternal deliverance. You find that Moses and Elijah were alike in every respect: Moses was a prophet; Elijah was a prophet. Moses was called 'man of God' (Deut. 33:1) and Elijah was called 'man of God' (1 Kgs. 17:18). Moses went up to heaven: 'And Moses went up unto God' (Exod. 19:3); and Elijah went up to heaven, as is said, 'And it came to pass when Elijah would go up... into heaven' (2 Kgs. 2:1). Moses slew the Egyptian; and Elijah slew Hiel, as is said, 'But when [Hiel] became guilty through Baal, he died' (Hos. 13:1). Moses was sustained by a woman, by the daughter of Jethro: 'Call him, that he may eat bread' (Exod. 2:20); and Elijah was sustained by the woman of Zarephath in Zidon: 'Bring me, I pray thee, a morsel of bread' (1 Kgs. 17:11). Moses fled from the presence of Pharaoh; and Elijah fled from the presence of Jezebel. Moses fled and came to a well; and Elijah fled and came to a well, as is written 'He arose, and went... and came to Beer-sheba' [the well of Sheba] (1 Kgs. 19:3). Moses: 'And the cloud covered him six days' (Exod. 24:16); and Elijah went up in a whirlwind: 'And it came to pass, when the Lord would take up Elijah by a whirlwind' (2 Kgs. 2:1). The power of Moses: 'If these men die the common death of all men' (Num. 16:29); and the power of Elijah: 'As the Lord, the God of Israel, liveth, before whom I stand, there shall not be dew nor rain these years, but according to my word' (1 Kgs. 17:1). Of Moses: 'And the Lord passed by before him' (Exod. 34:6); and of Elijah: 'And, behold, the Lord passed by' (1 Kgs. 19:11). Of Moses: 'Then he heard the Voice' (Num. 7:89); and of Elijah: 'And, behold, there came a Voice unto him' (1 Kgs. 19:13). Moses gathered Israel about Mount Sinai; and Elijah gathered them about Mount Carmel. Moses exterminated idolaters: 'Put ye every man his sword upon his thigh' (Exod. 32:27); and Elijah exterminated

were intended by the author(s) or editor(s) of l and 2 Kings.[91] But their

idolatry, when he seized the prophets of Baal and slew them. Moses was zealous for the Lord: 'Whoso is on the Lord's side, let him come unto me' (Exod. 32:26); and Elijah was zealous for the Lord: 'Elijah said unto all the people: "Come near, I pray ye, unto me…"' And he repaired the altar of the Lord that was thrown down' (l Kgs. l8:30). Moses hid in a cave: 'I will put thee in a cleft of the rock' (Exod 33:22); and Elijah hid in a cave, spending a night there: 'And he came unto a cave, and lodged there' (l Kgs. 19:9). Of Moses: 'He… came to the mountain of God' (Exod. 3:1); and of Elijah: 'And came… to the mount of God' (l Kgs. l9:8). Moses went to Horeb, and Elijah went to Horeb. Moses went into the wilderness: 'He led the flock to the farthest end of the wilderness' (Exod. 3:1); and Elijah went into the wilderness: 'But he himself went into the wilderness' (l Kgs. 19:4). Moses—God spoke to him through an angel: 'And the angel of the Lord appeared to him' (Exod. 3:2); and Elijah—also through an angel: 'And, behold, an angel' (l Kgs. l9:5). Moses spent forty days and forty nights, during which he did not eat and did not drink; so, too, Elijah, 'went in the strength of that meat forty days' (l Kgs. l9:8). Moses made the orb of the sun stand still: 'By means of this day will I begin to put the dread of thee… upon the peoples that are under the heaven' (Deut. 2:25); and Elijah made the orb of the sun stand still: 'By means of this day let it be known that Thou art God in Israel' (l Kgs. l8:36). Moses prayed in behalf of Israel: 'Destroy not thy people and Thine inheritance' (Deut. 9:26); and Elijah prayed in behalf of Israel: 'Hear me, O Lord, hear me… for Thou didst turn their heart backward' (l Kgs. l8:37). Moses, when he prayed on behalf of Israel, seized upon the merit of the Fathers: 'Remember Abraham, Isaac, and Israel' (Exod. 32:13); so, too, Elijah: 'O Lord, the God of Abraham, Isaac, and Israel' (l Kgs. l8:36). Moses—through him Israel accepted love for God: 'All that the Lord hath spoken we will do, and obey' (Exod. 24:7); and Elijah—through him they accepted love for God, saying, 'The Lord, He is God' (l Kgs. l8:39). Moses made the Tabernacle in an area in which two *sĕʾâ* of seed might be sown; and Elijah made a trench about the altar in an area in which a two *sĕʾâ* measure of seed might be sown…. Moses brought down fire; and Elijah brought down fire. Moses—when he brought down fire, all Israel stood by and saw it, as is said: 'There came a fire from before the Lord… which, when all the people saw, they shouted' (Lev. 9:24); and Elijah, when he brought down fire, all Israel stood by and saw it: 'When all the people saw it, they fell on their faces' (l Kgs. l8:39). Moses built an altar; and Elijah built an altar. Moses called the altar by the name of the lord: 'Moses… called the name of it Adonai-nissi' (Exod. l7:l5); and Elijah—the name of his altar was the Lord: 'And with the stones he built an altar in the name of the Lord' (l Kgs. l8:32). Moses, when he built the altar, built it with twelve stones, according to the number of the children of Israel; and Elijah, when he built the altar, built it according to the number of the Tribes of Israel, as is said, 'And Elijah took twelve stones' (l Kgs. l8:32)."

[91]Others have also suggested that the mantle over Elijah's face (l Kgs. l9:13) is reminiscent of the veil over Moses' face (Exod. 34:33), and that Elijah's ability to produce food for the widow at Zarephath (l Kings l7) recalls Moses' miraculous provisions for Israel in the desert. Note also Cohn, "Literary Logic," 341: "Ahab, the chief apostate, having witnessed offstage Baal's demise and Yahweh's power, submits to the prophet's order to ascend the mountain and to eat and drink. These motifs… appear to allude to the ancient covenant making treaty on Mount Sinai (Exod. 24:3-ll). There, after the burnt and peace offerings are made and the people swear allegiance to Yahweh, the leaders ascend the mountain and eat and drink. The author here suggests that through his silent compliance the apostate king participates in the ratification of the covenant renewal." For the suggestion that the entire collection of Elijah narratives is similar in structure to the Yahwist's tradition about Moses see S. J. DeVries, *l Kings* (WBC 12; Waco: Word, l985), 209-l0. —I have ignored the problem of the literary evolution of l and 2 Kings; but one could make the case that the parallels between Elijah and Moses were multiplied by later hands.

great number, especially given the relatively short scope of the Elijah traditions, is startling. Further, the verbal parallels between l Kgs. 17:6 and Exod. 16:8, between l Kgs. 18:36-39 and Lev. 9:22-24, and between l Kgs. 19:9-11 and Exod. 33:21-23 are not easily put down to happenstance. The same holds for the forty day fasts, the similar theophanies on Horeb = Sinai, and the partings of the two rivers. Therefore if we presume, with the majority, that most of the relevant traditions about Moses were in circulation before most of the relevant traditions about Elijah, we may fairly conclude that certain stories about the Tishbite— who, like Moses, was known both as "man of God" (2 Kgs. 1:9) and "servant" (1 Kgs. 18:36)—were composed or recast so as to make the prophet like the lawgiver.

Following scriptural precedent, such recasting continued in the post-biblical tradition. *LAB* 48 tells us that Phineas, who is equated with Elijah,[92] is to die after reaching one hundred and twenty years of age (cf. Deut. 34:7), and that he should go and "dwell in Danaben on the mountain"—"Daneben" being, one suspects, a mistranslation of the Aramaic *tûrā dinbô* (as in *Tg. Onq.* on Deut. 32:49), that is, "Mount of Nebo."[93] And *b. Sota* 13a says that Elijah was the disciple of Moses just as Elisha was the disciple of Elijah. It is also worth observing that Moses and Elijah, who, be it remembered, appear together at the transfiguration of Jesus, came to have similar eschatological functions in Jewish and Christian circles. Some have even suggested that Mal. 4:5 assumes the equation, Elijah = the prophet like Moses (see n. 180). We can moreover wonder whether the tradition that Moses miracu- lously disappeared from the kin of his contemporaries (see p. 266, n. 320) was not stimulated largely by the conviction that if Elijah, who in so many other ways emulated Moses, went up bodily to heaven, then Moses, inferior to none, must have also.

J. T. Walsh, after remarking, in his commentary on 1 Kings, that "Elijah is a new Moses," continues: "the events on Mt. Carmel are a new beginning for the Sinai covenant."[94] R. L. Cohn has commented to similar effect: "The author has patterned the Carmel narrative upon the Sinai covenant story. In so doing, he assigns overwhelming significance to the event. He claims that at Carmel Elijah, a 'prophet like Moses,' remade the covenant with the people of Israel who 'put

---

[92]Cf. Origen, *In Jn.* 6:7; *Tg. Yerus.* on Exod. 6:18; Ps.-Jerome, *Quaest. Heb. in Lib. Regum* 15. See further A. Zeron, "The Martyrdom of Phineas-Elijah," *JBL* 98 (1979):99-100.

[93]See A. Zeron, "Einige Bemerkungen zu M. F. Collins 'The Hidden Vessels in Samaritan Tradition," *JSJ* 4 (1974):165-68.

[94]J. T. Walsh and C. T. Begg, "1-2 Kings," in *NJBC*, 171.

away' the baalim."[95] This is one way of explaining the presence in 1 and 2 Kings of parallels between Elijah and Moses. If Elijah renewed what Moses inaugurated, the point would be reinforced through semblances in their two stories.[96] Another possible motive is mentioned by R. D. Nelson, who labels Elijah "the comic foil of Moses."[97] The observation unhappily goes undeveloped. Yet one can readily see how the numerous parallels with Moses accentuate the surprising weaknesses of Elijah, who, with God on his side, and in the wake of victory, only feels sorry for himself.[98] But the parallels could also, in view of the thrice-repeated "The Lord was not in the wind/the earthquake/the fire," serve to emphasize something else again, namely, that Yahweh now refuses to appear as he did on Sinai, in the traditional manifestations of the storm god. So F. M. Cross, who discerns in this "a polemic against Ba⟨al and the language of his storm theophany."[99]

Perhaps the most satisfactory accounting of the Mosaic mask worn by Elijah, an accounting not inconsistent with those already mentioned, has come from R. P. Carroll.[100] He first urges that "the compilers of the books of Kings were interested in the Elijah-Elisha sagas because they gave weight to the Deuteronomistic thesis of a Mosaic prophetic succession" (p. 403). It is but a small step to infer that either "the Deuteronomists were demanding an ideological conformity in their legislation for the prophet, or were trying to describe the authentic prophet in the light of Israel's prophetism" (p. 414). Carroll himself thinks both probably true at once, a reasonable surmise. My conclusion, then, is that Elijah was overlaid with Moses' features largely because his life and ministry were understood to correspond to Deut. 18:15 and 18: he was in the line of the prophets like Moses.[101]

[95]"Literary Logic," 341.

[96]Gray, I and II Kings, 376, seems to suggest that the historical Elijah himself gave birth to the comparison: "the parallels... [are] likely to reflect a real aspect of the mission of Elijah as a new Moses" (cf. p. 409).

[97]First and Second Kings (Atlanta: John Knox, 1987), 124.

[98]Cf. B. P. Robinson, "Elijah at Horeb, 1 Kings 19:1-18: A Coherent Narrative," RB 98 (1991), esp. pp. 528-30.

[99]Canaanite Myth, 194.

[100]"The Elijah-Elisha Sagas."

[101]When people were later compared to Elijah, it was usually to support their prophetic status; cf. Mark 8:28; Luke 9:8, 19.

JOSIAH

In his fascinating book, *Who wrote the Bible?*,[102] R. E. Friedman, on pp. 111-13, lists several parallels between the Moses of Deuteronomy on the one hand and the figure of King Josiah as found in 2 Kings on the other, as well as texts where Josiah fulfills the law of Moses:

Moses	Josiah
Deut. 34:10: "There has not arisen since in Israel a prophet like Moses, whom the Lord knew face to face"	2 Kgs. 23:25: "Before him there was no king like him… nor did any like him arise after him"
Deut. 6:5: the Lord gave this command to Moses: "You shall love the Lord your God with all your heart, and with all your soul, and with all your might"	2 Kgs. 23:25: Josiah "turned to the Lord with all his heart and with all his soul and with all his might, according to the law of Moses" (the triadic expression occurs only two places in the Hebrew Bible)
Deut. 17:8-13: through Moses God commands that in reaching certain decisions the levitical priests should be consulted	2 Kgs. 22:11-13: Josiah the king instructs the priests: "Go, inquire of the Lord for me" (the Deuteronomist depicts no other king doing this)
Deut. 17:11: "According to the decision which they pronounce to you, you shall do; you shall not turn aside from the verdict which they declare to you, either to the right hand or to the left" (cf. v. 20—of the king)	2 Kgs. 22:2: Josiah "did what was right in the eyes of the Lord, and walked in all the way of David his father; he did not turn aside to the right hand or to the left" (the warning about turning to the right or left occurs only here[103] after the Hexateuch)
Deut. 31:26: Moses to the Levites: "Take this book of the	After the Book of Joshua "the book of the law" is not

---

[102]New York: Summit, 1987.
[103]On this parallel see Thomas W. Mann, "Theological Reflections on the Denial of Moses," *JBL* 98 (1979):492-93.

law, and put it by the ark of the covenant of the Lord your God, that it may be there for a witness against you;" and again, Deut. 31:11: "When all Israel comes to appear before the Lord your God at the place which he will choose, you shall read this law... in their hearing"

mentioned again until 2 Kgs. 22:8ff.; then "the book of the law" is discovered, it is "read in their hearing" to Josiah and all the people, and it is obeyed

Deut. 9:21: Moses took "the [golden] calf" and "burned it with fire" and crushed it, until it was reduced "thin as dust"

2 Kgs. 23:6: Josiah, fulfilling Deut. 12:3, brings out the image of Asherah from the temple, burns it, and beats it "thin as dust"

Deut. 5:8: Moses prohibits "statues" (cf. 4:16, 23, 25; 27:15) and requires their burning

2 Kgs. 23:15: Josiah removes and burns the two "statues" of Asherah placed there by King Manasseh

What do these parallels mean, or do they mean at all? Friedman raises "the possibility that the wording of Deuteronomy and 2 Kings are so similar because these were the natural words to describe these acts" (p. 113). But he discounts this explanation. Why? "Just a few chapters before Josiah in 2 Kings is the story of Hezekiah's reform. Yet Hezekiah performs many of the same acts that Josiah does, or similar acts. Yet Hezekiah and his activities are described in different language—language that does not repeat the expressions of Moses' words and actions" (p. 113). Friedman's judgment is that "the Deuteronomic historian paints Josiah in special colors—Mosaic colors. He is a culmination of that which began with Moses. His actions in his day emulate Moses' actions in his own day. He is the hope that the covenant that began with Moses will be fulfilled as never before" (pp. 113-14).

Friedman's interest in Josiah's likeness and obedience to Moses is not our pursuit. He makes his case in order to contend that the original Deuteronomist (he thinks of Jeremiah and/or Baruch) lived in Josiah's time and sought to glorify that monarch's reign.[104] That issue I need

---

[104]Following Cross, he thinks the first edition of the Deuteronomic history culminated in Josiah.

not decide. The important point for us is another, namely: someone it seems sought to relate Josiah to Moses and his laws. This fact is doubly intriguing given that so many scholars now believe that the author of Joshua saw his Moses-like hero as a model for or reflection of Josiah. We appear to have the Moses-Josiah link in two different places, in Joshua and 2 Kings. Whereas the Josiah of 2 Kings recalls the lawgiver, the figure of Joshua simultaneously resembles Moses and anticipates Josiah. As explanation it may be that Joshua and 2 Kings passed through the same hands, those of the Deuteronomist and his school, and they, perceiving Moses to be the prototypical leader or king, naturally lent Joshua and Josiah, two esteemed leaders, Mosaic traits. But whether that be so or not, 2 Kings, like Joshua, testifies that Mosaic characteristics sometimes served to depict an ideal king.

But there is more. 2 Kings 22-23 and 2 Chronicles 34-35, which report on Josiah's reforms, disagree on certain particulars, and certain historical matters are open for debate; but few would question that Josiah sought to purge the state of foreign cults and practices, and that he did so in part because he was, as Jerome already recognized, under the spell of Deuteronomy,[105] with its contingent promises and threats of judgment, promises and threats which stripped Israel of her robe of security, the unconditional Davidic covenant. All this was done in the midst of a resurgent nationalism, with its nostalgia for olden times; and Josiah himself, by making a covenant with Yahweh, took up "a role similar to that of Moses in Deuteronomy (and Joshua in Josh., ch. 24)."[106] The fact is crucial, for it may elucidate more than just the parallels between Moses and Josiah in Kings.

The new always calls the old to witness to it, and given that the original Deuteronomist (or his school) supported Josiah's reforms, which were perceived as a recovery of the Mosaic past, it was incumbent to demonstrate (i) congruity between the age of Moses and the age of Josiah and (ii) the efficacy of the Mosaic covenant in between the two ages. The first point was made by having Josiah act the part of Moses. The second was made by mechanically correlating Israel's sin with Israel's doom, in accord with the theology, or theodicy, of Deuteronomy 28—and also by regularly inserting into Israel's story episodes in which God raises up prophets like Moses to speak to and lead his people.

---

[105]Or rather some early form of it, perhaps chapters 5-28, minus some later additions. See B. Oded, "Judah and the Exile," in *Israelite and Judaean History*, ed. John H. Hayes and J. Maxwell Miller (Philadelphia: Westminster, 1977), 460-69.

[106]John Bright, *A History of Israel* (3rd ed.; Philadelphia: Westminster, 1981), 322.

It is perhaps impossible to know at what stage or point in time Deut. 18:15-18 was added to the Deuteronomistic corpus. But even if the passage was a tardy addition it is not likely to have been a *theologoumenon de novo*. For we have discovered many texts which make Joshua and Gideon and Samuel and Elijah and Josiah like Moses—and all of these figures belonged to the Deuteronomistic history, whose first edition, as Cross showed, probably saw the light of day during Josiah's regency.[107] I cannot, to be sure, prove that all of the verses I have called upon when discussing Joshua and the others belonged to the first or Josianic edition. Still, it is more than hypothetical to suppose that the pre-exilic form of the Deuteronomic history included several Moses typologies whose common purpose was to exhibit the constant and consistent presence of the Mosaic tradition in Israel's history. Such continuity would have served as royal propaganda because it would have lent authority to Josiah's Mosaic reforms by establishing his faithfulness to the authoritative past.

If this thesis can be maintained it is well worth observing that the Moses typologies of Joshua - Kings are evenly scattered[108] and tend to appear at crucial transitions. After the first section of the Deuteronomic history (Deuteronomy), which of course Moses himself dominates, the second section (the Book of Joshua) is dominated by the Mosaic Joshua, who directs the conquest of the land, a conquest presented as a second exodus. The third major section (Judges) tells the history of the period of the judges and its numerous crises, during one of which God raised up Gideon. The fourth part (1 Samuel - 1 Kings 8) recounts the rise of the monarchy under the ministry of Samuel and its early glories under David and Solomon. Finally, the fifth part (1 Kings 9 - 2 Kings 23), which chronicles the progressive decline of the monarchy, has two climaxes—Elijah's ministry and Josiah's reforms, which ministry and which reforms both renew the Mosaic covenant. It appears, then, that the Moses typologies in the Deuteronomic history were strategically placed for the greatest effect: no period failed to see God raise up a prophet like Moses, and each time he did so, the nation was guided through a time of crisis. In this way then was demonstrated the existence of a line of prophets like Moses, a line that culminated in Josiah, to his greater glory. Whether or not the Deuteronomic history first issued from Josiah's court or from some

---

[107]*Canaanite Myth*, 274-89; cf. Friedman, *Who wrote the Bible?*, 101-16.
[108]One occurs in Joshua, one in Judges, one in 1 Samuel, one in 1 Kings, one in 2 Kings.

outside admirer(s), the various Moses typologies implied the king's status as the faithful heir of an old and ever-renewed tradition.

EZEKIEL

In summarizing the main thrust of Ezek. 43:l8-27, in which Ezekiel receives instructions for consecrating the altar of the new temple, Walter Zimmerli wrote: "The prophet himself, the charismatic addressed by God, becomes the new Moses who is permitted to inaugurate the new sacrificial cult."[109] 43:l8-27 is not the only passage in Ezekiel which turns thoughts to Moses. In fact, J. D. Levenson, in his *Theology of the Program of Restoration of Ezekiel 40-48*,[110] has maintained that in the closing chapters of Ezekiel[111] "the role of Moses falls upon the prophet Ezekiel" (p. 39). Given our interests his case invites review.

Levenson commences by observing that "Ezek. 40-48 stands in a peculiar rivalry to the Mosaic documents" (p. 38). Num. 28:ll directs that the new moon offering is to be two bulls, one ram, and seven yearling sheep, whereas Ezek. 46:6-7 directs that the same offering be one bull, six sheep, and one ram. There are similar contradictions between Ezek. 44:ll and Exod. 22:30, between Ezek. 45:l8 and Num. 28:ll = Deut. l4:21, and between Ezek. 45:20 and Lev. 7:25. These differences much exercised the rabbis (cf. *b. Menaḥ.* 45a; *b. Mak.* 24a; *b. Šabb.* 13b). But Levenson relates them to Ezekiel's status as "a 'new Moses'" (p. 38) and adds that Ezek. 20:33-44[112] exhibits the new exodus theme:

> As I live, says the Lord God, surely with a mighty hand and an outstretched arm, and with wrath poured out, I will be king over you.

---

[109]*Ezekiel 2* (Hermeneia; Philadelphia: Fortress, l983), 436.

[110]HSM l0; Missoula: Scholars Press, l976.

[111]Many believe that Ezekiel 40-48 (marked by a change of style) is secondary (cf. perhaps Josephus, *Ant.* l0:79, a reference to Ezekiel's two books), or is more heavily indebted to an editor than other parts of Ezekiel. Beyond doubt there are interpolations (e.g. 40:46; 44:6-31; 43:l9a; 48:llb), but the present form of Ezekiel as a whole, which is probably the product of a school close in time to the prophet himself, is not an uneven compilation of disparate sources; rather, it displays an integrity which allows us to treat it as a unity, whatever the course of its literary evolution may have been (cf. the situation with the canonical gospels). And we cannot exclude the possibility that most of Ezek. 40-48 derives from the prophet himself; cf. S. Niditch, "Ezekiel 40-48 in a Visionary Context," *CBQ* 48 (l986):208-24.

[112]Which contains clear allusions to Exod. 6:6-8; see M. Fishbane, *Text and Texture: Close Readings of Selected Biblical Texts* (New York: Schocken, l979), l3l-32.

> I will bring you out from the peoples and gather you out of the countries where you are scattered, with a mighty hand and an outstretched arm, and with wrath poured out; and I will bring you into the wilderness of the peoples, and there I will enter into judgment with you face to face. As I entered into judgment with your fathers in the wilderness of the land of Egypt, so I will enter into judgment with you, says the Lord God. I will make you pass under the rod, and I will let you go in by number. I will purge out the rebels from among you, and those who transgress against me; I will bring them out of the land where they sojourn, but they shall not enter the land of Israel. Then you will know that I am the Lord.

This idea of a new exodus, with its correlation between the time of Moses and the time of the exile, has its boldest expression, or so it would seem, in 20:25-26: "Moreover I gave them statutes that were not good and ordinances by which they could not have life; and I defiled them through their very gifts in making them offer by fire all their firstborn, that I might horrify them; I did it that they might know that I am the Lord."[113] Levenson comments: "Underlying this is probably the old prophetic idea of a new, or at least a dramatically renewed, covenant, attested in Ho. 2:18-23 and Jer. 31:31-34" (p. 39). The old can be criticized because the new is coming.

With this as background Levenson returns to Ezek. 40-48. These chapters constitute "the only corpus of legislation of the Hebrew Bible which is not placed in the mouth of Moses" (p. 39). Further, just as Moses received revelation on a mountain, so too Ezekiel (40:2). Even more notably, the temple vision in Ezekiel 40-42 has a close parallel in Exodus 25: "According to all that I show you [Moses] concerning the pattern of the tabernacle, and of all its furniture, so you shall make it" (v. 9); "and see that you make them after the pattern for them, which is being shown you on the mountain" (v. 40). Moses, like Ezekiel after him, gazed upon the heavenly blueprints for the earthly temple. As J. Blenkinsopp has stated, there is "a remarkably close parallelism… [between Ezekiel 40-42 and] the Priestly version of the Sinai event, according to which Moses saw a vision of the divine effulgence and received detailed specifications for the construction of the tent (tabernacle) and ark together with their furnishings…".[114]The strong parallel was already noted long ago by the author of *Liv. Proph. Ezek.* 15: "Like Moses, this man [Ezekiel] saw the pattern of the Temple, with its wail and broad outer wall."

---

[113]Ezekiel appears to have had in mind the law of the first-born in Exod. 22:29 and 34:19-20, and he understood it to command human sacrifice; see W. Eichrodt, *Ezekiel: A Commentary* (Philadelphia: Westminster, 1970), 270-72. He probably knew of Jews who participated in the cult of Molech.

[114]*Ezekiel* (Louisville: John Knox, 1990), 194.

Levenson goes on to argue that Ezekiel's mountain, which is literally Zion, is typologically Sinai. In addition to the preceding parallels, there is the circumstance that both Ps. 50:1-3 and Isa. 2:2-4 move Sinai motifs to Zion (cf. p. 325). Levenson also detects a connection with Mount Abarim, or Nebo, the summit of Pisgah, from which Moses was permitted to see the promised land (Num. 27:12-13; Deut. 32:48-52; 34:1). On his mount of revelation "Ezekiel is allowed to see the Land about which all his preaching has centered, but only in an inspired vision. He is not allowed to settle there, but must instead return to Babylon to tell the exiles of his vision and to communicate to them the laws revealed to him" (p. 42). That there is substance in the parallel follows from this, that "the P material between the command to Moses to ascend the mountain and his death bears a not incidental similarity to the material of Ezek. 40-48" (p. 43). Consider this chart:

Numbers		Ezekiel
28-29	liturgical calendar, sacrifice rules	45:18-25; etc.
32; 33:50-56	allocation of the land	47:13-48:29
34:1-15	boundaries	47:13-20
35	Levitical lands and cities	45:1-6; 48:13-14
36	right of inheritance	46:16-18

According to Levenson, "from the time Moses is commanded to climb Abarim until his death, the only P material unparalleled in Ezek. 40-48 is Nu. 30 (laws about vows), Nu. 31 (the raid on Midian, in which the theme of allocation of booty among the clans is paramount), and Nu. 33:1-50 (stations of the Exodus)" (pp. 43-44). Hence there is a close resemblance between Nu. 27-36 in its entirety and Ezek. 40-48, and Levenson plausibly concludes that just as there is a typological relationship between Ezekiel's "very high mountain" and Sinai, so also is there such a relationship between that "very high mountain" and Abarim/Nebo.[115]

If, as I do, one concedes that the result of Levenson's several observations is Levenson's conclusion, if, in several respects, "Ezekiel is a new Moses,"[116] the question of motive remains to be raised. Why does Ezekiel 40-48 relate Ezekiel to Moses and the eschatological mount of Zion to Sinai? The answer lies in Jewish conceptions about the source of Torah. All biblical collections of law (except that found

---

[115]The tendency of recent scholarship is perhaps to date P before Ezekiel; see Friedman, *Who wrote the Bible?*, 161-73, referring to the works of A. R. Guenther, A. Hurvitz, J. Milgrom, R. Polzin, G. Rendsburg, and Z. Zevit.

[116]Fishbane, *Interpretation*, 371.

in Ezekiel) are traced to Moses on Sinai. That is, the Bible places all legislation of significant length in the mouth of Moses. This is so despite the fact that the many laws gathered in the Pentateuch are of various proveniences. Why the artificial and transparent fiction? The compilers of the biblical laws apparently undertook their work persuaded, as *m.)Abot* l:l has it, that "Moses received (all) the Torah from Sinai." Jewish tradition did not, to be sure, restrict *revelation* to Moses and Sinai. The prophets uttered and wrote down revelation, as did the apocalyptic seers. But they were not lawgivers. The one lawgiver was Moses, and all Torah was *missinay*, from Sinai. If then someone other than Moses, in our case Ezekiel, made so bold as to hand down new Torah, the problem of his relationship to Sinai must have arisen. Ezekiel 40-48 confirms this and likewise shows us the course adopted. The chapters were not retrojected onto the Pentateuch or assigned to Moses (contrast *Jubilees*, which ascribes non-Pentateuchal legislation to Moses). The chapters were rather assigned to one *like* Moses, whose circumstances were reminiscent of Sinai. All this was assisted by the ideas of a new exodus and a new covenant (cf. 20:25-26, 32-44; 36:8-l5). These attenuated the difficulty of imagining that God had given additional Torah to another prophet. Still, it was necessary for that prophet to simulate Moses, for Torah unrelated to the revelation of Sinai was simply unthinkable.

JEREMIAH

On the mosaic in the Basilica of San Vitale, Ravenna (9th cent.), Moses appears in the upper right hand corner, receiving the law. In the upper left hand corner, as the complement, there appears Jeremiah, reading the law. This visual association of Moses and Jeremiah reflects a very rich literary tradition.[117] To illustrate:

>—In *The Legends of the Jews*, vol. 6, on pp. 385-86, Louis Ginzberg offered this partial summary of the rabbinic evidence: "The Haggadah maintains that Jeremiah was meant in the promise made by God to Moses that He will raise up a prophet 'like unto thee' (Deut. l8.l8), and although

---

[117]In addition to what follows see esp. C. Wolff, *Jeremia im Frühjudentum und Urchristentum* (Berlin: Akademie-Verlag, l976), 79-83. —I note that the tradition I am here reviewing apparently lived on past antiquity. One example: in John Donne's *First Anniversary* the poet imitates the Lamentations of Jeremiah while he simultaneously lays claim to the office of Moses; see B. K. Lewalski, *Donne's Anniversaries and the Poetry of Praise* (Princeton: University Press, l973), 236-40, 275-79.

there 'hath not arisen a prophet in Israel like Moses' (Deut. 34.l0), the lives of these two prophets show so many striking resemblances, that the description of Jeremiah as 'a prophet like unto Moses' is well justified. Moses prophesied for forty years, so did Jeremiah; Moses prophesied concerning Judah and Israel, so did Jeremiah; Moses was attacked by members of his own tribe (i.e., the Levite Korah), so was Jeremiah (comp. Jer. 20.l); Moses was thrown into the water, and Jeremiah into a pit; Moses was saved from death by a bondwoman (Exod. 2.5), and Jeremiah by a slave (comp. Jer. 38.9...); Moses addressed words of exhortation to the people, so did Jeremiah. See PK 13,112a; Ekah Z. 75; Midrash Tannaim lll; a quotation from an unknown Pesikta in Midrash Aggada, 160, on Num. 30.ll, where many more parallels are drawn between the life of Moses and that of Jeremiah... . In his modesty and humility Jeremiah declined the honor to be compared with Moses. When God told him to take the place once occupied by Moses and to become the leader and guide of the people, he rejoined: 'Who am I to take the place of Moses? May it be granted to me to be like his pupil.' See the Midrash quoted by Shu'aib, Mattot, 9ld." To Ginzberg's references add *Midr. Ps.* 1:3: "So, too, you find of [Moses and] Jeremiah, that what is said of the one is said of the other."

—The *Jeremiah Apocryphon* is a little known book of uncertain date, written in Arabic characters. In its present form it is transparently Christian.[118] The work tells the story of the deportation to Babylon and the return to Palestine in such a way that the exodus is frequently recalled and Jeremiah made the leader after the example of Moses. Among the numerous parallels, which are about as extensive as those between Joshua and Moses in the Hexateuch, the following may be cited:

P. 157, lines 5ff.: "Listen to what the Lord Omnipotent says: 'I protected your fathers when I took them out of the Land of Egypt, but because you have forgotten the great goodness I did to your fathers in the desert, you shall be requited with a much greater evil'" (for example, that generation's clothes did not wear out, this generation's clothes will, and instead of a column of light there will be a column of darkness).

P. l6l, 6ff.: Jeremiah prays to God, that he not destroy the people (cf. Exodus 32).

P. l75, 21ff.: The Israelites in Babylon are made to do forced labor, including brickwork. They constructed "many villages, towers, houses, granaries, and forts" (cf. Exodus l)

P. l76, 21ff.: The Jews' fortunes become frightfully worse upon the accession of a new king (cf. Exodus 1).

[118]I have used for what follows the edition of A. Mingana, in *Woodbrooke Studies*, vol. l (Cambridge: W. Heffer & Sons, l927), 125-233. This includes an introduction (by J. Rendel Harris) and a translation (by Mingana) along with two facsimiles of two manuscripts.

P. l82, 28ff.: "If the kings of Babylon do not allow them [the Jews] to go, I shall wax angry with them and destroy their land, in order to force them to send them back, and if in spite of this they refuse I shall do with them what I did with Pharaoh, the king of Egypt" (so God, through Jeremiah).

P. l83, 13ff.: The king and his general respond to Jeremiah's plea to let the people go with this: "And who is the God of Israel? You, O Hebrews, return to your work, and throw such words away from you" (cf. Exod. 5:2, 4).

P. l83, 25ff.: "The earth shook, a big earthquake occurred, wind became fierce, the sun suffered eclipse in the middle of the day, and darkness covered the earth. The inhabitants of the earth mixed pell-mell, horse-men with the crowds, and the feet of the horses that were ridden sunk deep into the earth like pegs; until all the Chaldeans cried to King Cyrus and to Emesis [Cyrus' general] and said to them: 'Is not this sufficient for you?'"; the king then repents and lets the people go (cf. the plagues upon Egypt and their issue).

P. l84, 14ff.: The Jews leave Babylon with much gold and silver (cf. Exod. 12:35-36).

P. l84, l6ff.: Jeremiah is the leader of the new exodus.

—In *Paraleipomena Jeremiou*, or *4 Baruch* (2nd cent. C.E.?), Baruch sends an epistle to Jeremiah. It contains this: "Now, these are the words that the Lord God of Israel, who led us from the land of Egypt, out of the great furnace, spoke: 'Because you didn't keep my commandments, but your heart was lifted up and you stiffened your neck (cf. Exod. 32:9, etc.) before me, in wrath and anger I delivered you to the furnace of Babylon. However, if you will listen to my voice,' says the Lord, 'from the mouth of Jeremiah my servant, whoever listens I will bring back from Babylon, and whoever does not listen will become a stranger to Jerusalem and Babylon. And you will prove them with the water of the Jordan'" (6:23-25). The "you" in this last sentence is Jeremiah, and the implication is that he will lead the new exodus through the waters. A few verses later, after an eagle has raised a dead man, the people exclaim: "Is this the God who appeared to our fathers in the wilderness through Moses who has now appeared to us through this eagle?" (7:20). Then in chapter 8 "the day came in which the Lord led the people out of Babylon. And the Lord said to Jeremiah, 'Get up, you and the people, and come to the Jordan'" (vv. 1-2). Jeremiah obeys and leads the people over the Jordan (8:6). Should we not infer that Jeremiah's role is analogous to that of Moses, that he is "the Moses of the exile period"?[119] The case that *4 Baruch*

---

[119]So Wolff, *Jeremia*, 80. Cf. G. W. E. Nickelsburg, *Jewish Literature between the Bible and the Mishnah* (Philadelphia: Fortress, l981), 316. For full discussion see J. Riaud, "La figure de Jérémie dans les Paralipomena Jeremiae," in *Mélanges bibliques et orientaux en l' honneur de M. Henri Cazelles*, ed. A. Caquot and M. Delcor (Neukirchen-Vluyn: Neukirchener, l981), 373-85.

presents Jeremiah as "the new Moses of the new exodus" (Riaud) could in truth scarcely be greater. Jeremiah proclaims the law of God (5:19, *ton logon*, cf. Deut. 30:14) and, after petitioning the king (Nebuchadnezzar), he leads his people to a desert place (*topon eremon*) outside the city (7:12); also Babylon,from which the people are departing, is called a furnace, as is Egypt (6:23-24), and it is said that God, "who led us out of Egypt" (6:23), will deliver his people because he remembers the covenant he made with Abraham, Isaac, and Jacob (6:21)—the same motivation behind the Egyptian exodus according to Exod. 2:24 (cf. 6:5). In addition, God, who is spoken of in very anthropomorphic terms (after speaking with Moses "the Lord went up into heaven," 3:17), speaks directly with Jeremiah, without an intermediary, and Jeremiah speaks directly to him in his presence (3:6, *enopion sou*)—all of which was, according to Num. 12:8, characteristic of God's communication with Moses. Finally, Jeremiah is called "the elect (*eklektos*) of God"[120] and "the servant of God",[121] and the people, in words reminiscent of Deut. 18:15 and 18, which anticipate a prophet like Moses, are commanded, as the condition of their return to Jerusalem, to "hear" Jeremiah (*ean oun akousete*, 6:24, cf. LXX Deut. 18:19), who is the mediator between them and God.

—In the *Life of the Prophet Jeremiah* (first cent. C.E.?), Jeremiah gives "a sign to the priests of Egypt" (v. 8; cf. Exodus 7), he prays for and delivers the Egyptians from vipers (cf. Num 21:4-9), and he hides the ark in a rock, where it will remain until Moses fetches it, "so that he [Jeremiah] might become a partner (*sunkoinonos*) of Moses, and they are together to this day" (v. 19).

—Eupolemus, frag. 4 (= Alexander Polyhistor, *On the Jews*, *apud* Eusebius, *Praep. ev.* 9:39:2), relates that, during the reign of Jonachim (?), Jeremiah "caught the Jews sacrificing to a golden idol." This fictional incident was presumably inspired by Exodus 32, where Moses, upon descent of Sinai, discovers the Israelites sacrificing to the golden calf. In other words, a circumstance from Moses' life was evidently grafted on to that of Jeremiah.

Why, we must now ask, do so many different texts from various times and places liken and assimilate Jeremiah to Moses? The book of

---

[120]1:1, 5, 8. For Moses see Ps. 106:23 (LXX: *eklektos*); *Liv. Proph. Jer.* 14. Of course, the title was also bestowed upon other worthies, including Jacob (Isa. 45:4) and David (Ecclus. 47:22).

[121]1:4; 6:24; For this title applied to Moses see Exod. 14:31; Num. 12:7-8; Deut. 34:5; Josh. 1:1, 2, 7; 1 Kgs. 8:56; 2 Kgs. 18:12; 1 Chron. 6:49; 2 Chron. 1:3; Ps. 105:26; Dan. 9:11; Mal. 4:4; Bar. 1:20; 2:28; Heb. 3:5; Rev. 15:3; Josephus, *Ant.* 5:39; *LAB* 20:2; *1 Clem.* 4:12; 51:3, 5; *Barn.* 14:4; *Apoc. Moses* preface; Clement of Alexandria, *Paed.* 1:7.59; *Apost. Const.* 7:33.6; *Acts Pilate* 16:8; *m. Yoma* 3:8; 4:2; 6:2; *Sipre Deut.* § 357; *Tg. Ps-Jn.* on Num. 16:34; *b.Sabb.* 89a; etc. "Servant" is the most common title for Moses in the Jewish Bible, occurring there forty times.

the prophet himself holds the solution. The call narrative in Jeremiah
1 has the same form as the call narrative in Exodus 3:[122]

commission	Jer. 1:5	Exod. 3:10
objection	1:6	3:11
reassurance	1:7-8	3:12
sign(s)	1:9(11-16)	3:12(4:1-19)

Related forms appear also in Isaiah 6 and Ezekiel 1-3,[123] but the closest
formal parallel to Jeremiah 1 appears in Judges 6, which records the call
of Gideon; and there, as we have seen, Moses and his call are being
imitated. Beyond that, Jeremiah's objection, that he does not know
how to speak (v. 6), is identical with Moses' objection in Exod. 4:10;
6:12, and 30; and the combination of "send" and "go" in Jer. 1:7 has its
parallel in Exod. 3:10-13. Further, "you shall speak all that I command
you" is common to Jer. 1:7 and Exod. 7:2 (cf. Deut. 18:18); the encouragement of Jer. 1:8 ("I am with you") echoes Exod. 3:12 ("I will be with
you"); and Jer. 1:6 ("Ah, Lord God! Behold, I do not know how to speak,
for I am only a youth") resembles Exod. 4:10 ("Oh, my Lord, I am not a
man of words"): "both responses begin with a precative interjection
followed by *)dny* both have a form of the root *dbr* preceded by *l)*, [and]
both end with *)nky)*."[124] No less significantly, Jer. 1:9 ("Behold, I have put
my words in your mouth," cf. 5:14) is close to Deut. 18:18[125] ("I will put

---

[122]Cf. W. L. Holladay, *Jeremiah 1* (Hermeneia; Philadelphia: Fortress, 1986), 27.

[123]See B. S. Childs, *The Book of Exodus: A Critical, Theological Commentary* (Philadelphia: Westminster, 1974), 53-56.

[124]W. L. Holladay, "The Background of Jeremiah's Self-Understanding. Moses,
Samuel, and Psalm 22," in *A Prophet to the Nations: Essays in Jeremiah Studies*, ed. L. G.
Perdue and B. W. Kovacs (Winona Lake: Eisenbrauns, 1984), 315. Ambrose, *De off. min.*
1:66, wrote: "Moses and Jeremiah, chosen by the Lord to declare the words of God to the
people, were for avoiding, through modesty, that which through grace they could do."

[125]For the priority of Deut. 18:18 over Jer. 1:9—a disputed issue— see Holladay, "Background"; contrast R. P. Carroll, *Jeremiah: A Commentary* (Philadelphia: Westminster, 1986),
99: "The extent to which Jeremiah may be considered the prophet of Deut. 18.15, 18 or an
instantiation of it is difficult to determine because Deut. 18.15-18 are a late addition to the
Deuteronomistic law on the prophet.... The influence could be the other way and the
producers of 1.7,9 might have belonged to the circles which contributed to the formulations
of Deut. 18.9-22." For the general question of whether the book of Jeremiah presupposes
Exodus and Deuteronomy, and a positive answer, see Holladay, *Jeremiah 2* (Hermeneia;
Philadelphia: Fortress, 1989), 38-39, 53-63. According to E. K. Holt, "The Chicken or the
Egg—Or: Was Jeremiah a Member of the Deuteronomist Party?," *JSOT* 44 (1989):109-22,
Moses was modelled on Jeremiah in order to bolster Moses' authority. The more usual and
more plausible view is that both Jeremiah himself and the traditions about him were
influenced by the Deuteronomic tradition. For the argument that Jeremiah and/or Baruch
drew up an edition of the Deuteronomic history see Friedman, *Who wrote the Bible?*

my words in his mouth"—of a coming prophet like Moses). Concerning this it has been remarked: "Though the phrase 'put (God's) words in the mouth (of a prophet)' is rather common in the OT, the verb usually is *šûm* (ten times), while the verb in Jer. 1:9 is *ntn*, a verb occurring in this phrase only twice otherwise in the OT: Jer. 5:14... and Deut. 18:18."[126]

The evidence, whether explained in terms of Jeremiah's self-conception or the Deuteronomistic redaction, does seem to force the conclusion that Jeremiah 1 assimilates the call of Jeremiah to the call of Moses.[127] But it is not only the call narrative which stirs memories of the lawgiver. Throughout Jeremiah, whose alternation of poetic oracles and paraenetic prose so resembles the end of Deuteronomy, there are more than just dim adumbrations of the exodus story. Moses is in fact named in 15:1: "Then the Lord said to me, 'Though Moses and Samuel stood before me, yet my heart would not turn toward this people. Send them out of my sight, and let them go (*yēṣēʾû*)!'" A recent commentator has observed: "Moses' task was to get the people out of Egypt; Jeremiah's task is to get the people out of Yahweh's presence. And the verb *yṣʾ* 'go out, away,' is equally a verb of the exodus."[128] In other words, Jeremiah leads another exodus, albeit one rather different from the first. Consistent with this interpretation is 7:26-27, where the divine oracle through Jeremiah mourns that those of the prophet's generation are like those who disobeyed Moses in the wilderness: "They did not listen to me, or incline their ear, but stiffened their neck. They did worse than their fathers. So you shall speak all these words to them, but they will not listen to you [Jeremiah]" (cf. Exod. 32:9; Deut. 9:6, 13). Additional passages which *may* extend the similitude between Jeremiah and Moses and their two generations include the following:

Jeremiah	Moses
Jeremiah "speak(s) in his name"	The prophet like Moses will

[126]Holladay, "Jeremiah's Self-Understanding," 315. Further discussion in P. E. Broughton, "The Call of Jeremiah: The Relation of Deut. 18:9-22 to the Call and Life of Jeremiah," *AusBR* 6 (1958):37-46.

[127]Cf. K. M. O'Connor, *The Confessions of Jeremiah: Their Interpretation and Role in Chapters 1-25* (SBLDS 94; Atlanta: Scholars' Press, 1988), 121; also G. P. Couturier, "Jeremiah," in *NJBC*, 271: "There is no doubt that Jeremiah is related to Moses in this call narrative, as his true successor in the delivery of the word of God." See further W. Theil, *Die deuteronomistische Redaktion von Jeremia 1-25* (WMANT 41; Neukirchen-Vluyn: Neukirchener, 1973), 66-72. In this connection one should recall that Moses was remembered as a prophet: see below, n.135.

[128]Holladay, *Jeremiah I*, 440.

(20:9)	"speak in my name" (Deut. 18:19)
Jeremiah was called when a "youth" (*na'ar*, 1:6)	Moses was already chosen by God when a "youth" (*na'ar*, see Exodus 2.6)
The Babylonians "refuse[d] to let them [Jeremiah's people] go" (50:33)	The Egyptians "refuse[d] to let them [Moses' people] go" (Exod. 8:2; cf. 4:23; 7:14; 9:2)
"Now, after the king had burned the scroll with the words which Baruch wrote at Jeremiah's dictation, the word of the Lord came to Jeremiah: 'Take another scroll and write on it all the former words that were in the first scroll...'" (Jer. 36: 27-28)	"The Lord said to Moses, 'Cut two tables of stone like the first; and I will write upon the tables the words that were on the first tables, which you broke'" (Exod. 34:1)
In Jer. 23:16-32 Jeremiah polemicizes against false prophets whose supposed revelation is given in dreams or visions; Jeremiah himself has stood in the council of the Lord and has heard God's word;	In Num. 12:6-8 we learn that God did not speak to Moses in a dream or in a vision: "With him I speak mouth to mouth, clearly, and not in dark speech; and he beholds the form of the Lord"

"Jeremiah sees the difference between his mission and those of
...[other] prophets in the fact
that he has received his messages direct
from Yahweh—he does not say this, but it
is clearly meant—whereas the...
[others] have received their message from
dreams"[129]

---

[129]H.-J. Kraus, *Worship in Israel: A Cultic History of the Old Testament* (trans. G. Buswell; Oxford: Basil Blackwell, 1966), 106.

Jeremiah's generation "offended me [the Lord] with their idols, their alien nothings" (8:19)	Moses' generation "offended me [the Lord] with their nothings" (Deut. 32:31)
Jeremiah proclaims a new covenant "not like the covenant which I made with their fathers when I took them out of the land of Egypt, my covenant which they broke" (31:32)[130]	Moses made the first covenant with Israel

In view of all the above, it is more probable than not that Jeremiah considered himself "the legitimate successor to Moses," that is, "understood himself to be a prophet like Moses,"[131]—or at least that such was the view of those responsible for shaping canonical Jeremiah.[132] Alonso Schökel, however, prefers to express matters thus: Jeremiah perceived himself, or was perceived as, an "anti-Moses."[133] Moses was a great intercessor (see n. 45). Jeremiah, on the contrary, was bade not to intercede for Israel: Jer. 15:1. To Moses was revealed the name of God, and Moses led the people out of Egypt. But Jeremiah and his people, in apparent violation of Deut. 17:16 ("he [the king] must not... cause the people to return to Egypt to multiply horses, since the Lord has said to you, 'You shall never return that way again'") returned to Egypt,

---

[130]It has also been suggested that "the early prophetic oracles of Jeremiah contain... many reminiscences to Deut. xxxii, the so-called 'Song of Moses," and that we should entertain "the possibility that Deut. xxxii was known to Jeremiah and understood by him as a poem sung by Moses: thus when Jeremiah wished to offer prophetic oracles in his role of the prophet like Moses, he had a model already before him of what he took to be Mosaic piety;" so Holladay, "A Fresh Look at 'Source B' and 'Source C' in Jeremiah," *VT* 25 (1975):410. See further the first volume of his commentary.

[131]So Holladay, *Jeremiah 1*, 46, and *Jeremiah 2*, 56 respectively. For the possibility that Jeremiah could have thought himself the physical descendant of Moses see J. Bright, *Covenant and Promise* (Philadelphia: Westminster, 1976), 144-45. Strangely enough, while Friedman, *Who wrote the Bible?*, has recently urged that Jeremiah himself may have been the Deuteronomist, R. Polzin, *Moses and the Deuteronomist: A Literary Study of the Deuteronomic History. Part One* (New York: Seabury, 1980), has argued that the Deuteronomist considered himself to be the prophet like Moses.

[132]J. Muilenburg, "Baruch the Scribe," in *Proclamation and Presence*, 221, refers to Jeremiah as "a second Moses," one who "performs the functions of the Mosaic office." *Sipre Deut.* § 175 asks how Jer. 1:5 can make Jeremiah "a prophet to the nations" when Deut. 18:15 says the prophet like Moses will be "from your [= the Jews'] midst." The difficulty obviously presupposes that Jeremiah is the or a prophet like Moses according to Deut. 18:15, 18. Cf. *Pesiq. R.* 112a.

[133]"Jeremías como anti-Moses," in *De la Tôrah au Messie*, ed. M. Carrez, J. Doré, and P. Grelot (Paris: Desclée, 1981), 245-54.

where God's name would be erased: Jeremiah 42-44. Moses established a covenant with Israel. Jeremiah, however, with words which "must have been shocking in Jerm's day and thereafter; after all, the passage implies that Yahweh will draw up a fresh contract without the defects of the old, implying in turn that he could improve on the old one, that he had learned something from the failure of the old,"[134] spoke of a new covenant (31:31-34).

Despite these observations, one may doubt whether "anti-Moses" is just the right expression. Does it not wrongly imply opposition to Moses himself, whereas the point seems instead to have been the exceeding sinfulness of Jeremiah's generation, which sinfulness undid past blessings? Sad experience appears to have led the lonely prophet or his disciples to interpret Jeremiah's Mosaic likeness in ironic terms: the exodus was being inverted.

Leaving for others the difficult biographical problems, I am content to affirm that the present form of Jeremiah, by way of echoic phrases and analogous episodes, compares and contrasts the prophet Moses[135] and his generation with the prophet Jeremiah and his generation. But why? What generated the typology, which was carried on in so many later sources? The answer has already been anticipated: the construction of a Moses-like Jeremiah was a rhetorically effective means of condemning Jeremiah's contemporaries. One of the outstanding features of the Pentateuch is the interminable opposition to Moses by those he unselfishly serves. Moses' generation was obduracy and ingratitude incarnate. At every turn the stiff-necked people rebelled

---

[134]Holladay, *Jeremiah 2*, 197. Further discussion in Davies, *Setting*, 122-30.

[135]While moderns do not usually think of Moses as a prophet, it was otherwise with the ancients. In the Pentateuch Moses has the Spirit of God (Num. 11:17), receives a divine calling (Exodus 2-3), and speaks God's word. For explicit references to Moses as a prophet see Deut. 18:15, 18; 34:10; Hos. 12:13; Ecclus. 46:1; Wisd. 11:1; discussion in E. Fascher, Προφήτης: *Eine sprach- und religionsgeschichtliche Untersuchung* (Giessen: Alfred Töpelmann, 1927), 110-14; also G. von Rad, *Old Testament Theology, volume I* (New York: Harper & Row, 1962), 289-96. Post-biblical references include *T. Mos.* 1:5; 3:11; 11:16; 12:7; *Asc. Isa.* 3:8; Aristobulus, frag. 2, *apud* Eusebius, *Praep. ev.* 8:10:4; Justus of Tiberius *apud* Eusebius, *Chron.*, *apud* George Syncellus, *Chronicle*, p. 122 (ed. Dindorf); Philo, *Quaest. in Gen.* 1:86; 4:29; *De virt.* 5:1, and often (see the full listing in the Loeb edition of Philo, vol. 10, p. 387, n. b); Josephus, *Ant.* 2:327; 4:165, 329; 2 *Bar.* 59:4-11; *m. Sota* 1:9; *Deut. Rab.* 1:10; *Tg.* on Cant. 1:8. Additional references in Ginzberg, *Legends*, 5:404, 6:125. For the Samaritan evidence see Meeks, *Prophet-King*, 220-27. Moses was also remembered as a prophet in early Christianity: *Barn.* 6.8; *1 Clem.* 43:6; Justin, *1 Apol.* 32:1; 54; Ps.-Justin, *Coh. ad Gent.* 9; *T. Jacob* 7:3; Irenaeus, *Dem. Apost. Teach.* 43; Athenagoras, *Leg.* 9; Clement of Alexandria, *Paed.* 1:11:96; Eusebius, *H.E.* 1:2:4; *Dem. ev.* 3:2(90a); Ambrose, *De mysteriis* 3:14; Chrysostom, *Hom. in Gen.* 2:2. Cf. Strabo, *Geog.* 16:2:39; *PGM* 5:108-18.

against God and his servant. Further, spectacular miracles and providential protection availed nothing: hearts remained hardened to the very end. God accordingly consigned that generation to the wilderness, and it was not permitted to enter the land flowing with milk and honey. Rather were the exiles from Egypt fated to perish in the wilderness—a memorable fact indeed, and one with great polemical potential. What could be more damning than the likening of a generation to the generation of Moses, one which, blind and unsatisfied, was forced to wander in a desert for forty years? The New Testament shows us that such polemical potential did not go unnoticed: there is clearly implicit in the synoptics a likening of Jesus' contemporaries to those who resisted Moses.[136] Matters are much the same in Jeremiah. Further, I strongly suspect that we should find in this the primary stimulus behind the creation of parallels and contrasts between Jeremiah and Moses. Rejected by an evil generation, Jeremiah, prophet of exile, came to be viewed as the counterpart of the suffering Moses.

EZRA

In *4 Ezra* 14 a voice from a bush cries out to Ezra as he is sitting under an oak: "Ezra, Ezra" (v. 1). One cannot but recollect Exodus 3, where a voice from a bush calls out, "Moses, Moses." Moreover, just as Moses responded, "Here I am" (Exod. 3:4), so too Ezra: "Here I am, Lord" (v. 2). The voice addressing Ezra then continues: "I revealed myself in a bush and spoke to Moses, when my people were in bondage in Egypt; and I sent him and led my people out of Egypt; and I led him up on Mount Sinai, where I kept him with me many days; and I told him many wondrous things.... And now I say to you [Ezra]: Lay up in your heart the signs that I have shown you, the dreams that you have seen, and the interpretations that you have learned; for you shall be taken up from among men..." (vv. 3-9). This last—"you shall be taken up from among men" (cf. 14:48 v.l.)—further adds to the Moses schematic, for some Jews, despite Deut. 34:5-6, believed that Moses did not taste death but rather ascended to heaven.[137] Likewise typological is the mention of "wondrous things," for "this is hardly a summary of the

---

[136]E. Lövestam, "The ἡ γενεὰ αὕτη Eschatology in Mk 13,30 parr.," in *L'Apocalypse johannique et l'Apocalyptique dans le Nouveau Testament*, ed. J. Lambrecht (BETL 53; Gembloux: J. Duculot; Leuven: University Press, 1980), 403-13.

[137]See below, p. 265, n. 320.

legislation in the Pentateuch given at Mount Sinai; rather it presents Moses as a recipient of apocalyptic visions."[138] So just as Moses received esoteric, apocalyptic revelation, so too Ezra.

The parallels between Ezra and Moses continue to add up in vv. 23ff. Ezra is told that revelations will be granted to him over a forty day period,[139] and he is instructed to procure writing tablets and five rapidly writing scribes. He subsequently quaffs an angelic concoction which brings enlightenment, whereupon he dictates to his scribes, who sit for forty days and nights (see v. 43), writing down inspired oracles. The parallels with the Sinai traditions, although not exact, are nonetheless unmistakable. On Sinai the divine revelation was written on tablets (Exod. 34:1). On Sinai Moses remained for forty days and nights. And on Sinai, according to a well-attested tradition to be considered later, Moses sat. It is therefore transparently obvious that *4 Ezra* 14 depicts Ezra's experience as a conflated replay of Moses' calling and the giving of Torah on Sinai—hence the regularity with which commentators refer to Ezra as a "second Moses."[140]

In order to clarify why *4 Ezra* recreated Ezra the scribe in the image of Moses the lawgiver, we need to turn to vv. 45-47: "And when the forty days were ended, the Most High spoke to me, saying, 'Make public the twenty-four books that you wrote first and let the worthy and the unworthy read them; but keep the seventy that were written last, in order to give them to the wise among your people. For in them is the spring of understanding, the fountain of wisdom, and the river of knowledge.'" The twenty-four books are those of the Tanak (cf. *b. B. Bat.* 14b-15a). That leaves an additional seventy esoteric or hidden works also inscribed by Ezra—a convenient fiction designed to lend authority to disputed or little known texts. Thus *4 Ezra* functions as an apology of sorts for pseudepigrapha, including *4 Ezra* itself. In this connection the parallels between Moses and Ezra exert their force. Moses was *the* channel of Torah and revelation. As for Ezra, tradition made him, like Moses (Exod. 24:7), a reader of the law (Nehemiah 8) and, more importantly, one who restored the Scriptures after they had

---

[138]M. A. Knibb, in *The First and Second Books of Esdras*, by R. J. Coggins and M. A. Knibb (Cambridge: University Press, 1979), 274.

[139]For the argument that there are actually *two* forty day periods in *4 Ezra*, in recollection of the two forty day periods of Moses, see M. P. Knowles, "Moses, the Law, and the Unity of IV Ezra," *NovT* 31 (1989):257-74.

[140]E.g. G. H. Box, in *APOT* 2:620; J. M. Myers, *I and II Esdras*, AB 42 (Garden City: Doubleday, 1974), 322; Nickelsburg, *Jewish Literature*, 292; M. Stone, *Fourth Ezra*, Hermeneia (Minneapolis: Fortress, 1991), 410-13, 416-17, 419, 426.

purportedly been destroyed in 568 B.C.E. (*4 Ezra* 14:21; cf. 2 Kgs. 25:8-9; *b. Sukka* 20a). So what Moses delivered at the beginning, Ezra gave a second time. Both were accordingly lawgivers, indeed givers of the very same law. And in *4 Ezra* 14, where the concern is the authenticity of revelation, Ezra's likeness to Moses makes him an authoritative dispenser of such. As Michael Stone has put it, "the typology of Moses" establishes "Ezra's activity as revealer."[141] One is reminded of John's Gospel, where Jesus reveals that he is the revealer (Bultmann). That by itself inevitably raises the issue of the relationship between the Son of God and the first revealer, Moses—an issue which the Gospel explores by drawing, explicitly and implicitly, parallels and contrasts between Jesus and Moses. The difference between *4 Ezra* and John lies in this, that whereas in the former the one like Moses only relives the experience of the lawgiver, in the Gospel the new revealer supersedes and replaces the old one.

The likeness of Ezra to Moses is not confined to *4 Ezra*. In *t. Sanh.* 4:7 we find this: "Ezra was worthy that the Torah be given by him, had Moses not preceded him. Of Moses the term 'ascent' is used and of Ezra the term 'ascent' is used. Of Moses, as it is said, 'And Moses ascended to God' (Exod. 19:3); of Ezra—'He, Ezra, ascended from Babylon' (Ezra 7:6)." Compare *b. Sanh.* 21b-22a, where we also read: "Concerning Moses, it is stated: 'And the Lord commanded me at that time to teach you statutes and judgments' (Deut. 4:14); and concerning Ezra, it is stated, 'For Ezra had prepared his heart to expound the law of the Lord to do it and to teach Israel statutes and judgments' (Ezra 7:10)." Outside rabbinic sources, *Gk. Apoc. Ezra* (of uncertain date and place of origin) merits special examination. Here the voice is the voice of Ezra, but the facts are the facts of Moses. In chapter 6 a voice comes to "the prophet"[142] and announces his death. Like Moses in *Sipre Deut.* § 305, Ezra resists.[143] When the angels thereafter announce that they

---

[141]"Apocalyptic Literature," in *Jewish Writings of the Second Temple Period: Apocrypha, Pseudepigrapha, Qumran Sectarian Writings, Philo, Josephus,* ed. M. E. Stone, Compendia Rerum Iudaicarum ad Novum Testamentum (Assen/Philadelphia: Vam Gorcum and Fortress, 1984), 414.

[142]This, a title of Moses, and not the expected "the scribe," is Ezra's title throughout the book.

[143]For the tradition of Moses resisting death see M. R. James, *The Testament of Abraham* (Cambridge: University Press, 1892), 64-70; also S. E. Loewenstamm, "The Death of Moses," in *Studies on the Testament of Abraham,* ed. G. W. E. Nickelsburg (Missoula, Montana: Scholars Press, 1976), 185-217; idem, "The Testament of Abraham and the Texts Concerning Moses' Death," in *ibid.,* 219-25. Loewenstamm establishes that the tradition about Moses predates the similar tradition about Abraham, as found, for example, in the *Testament of Abraham.* Cf. E. P. Sanders, in *OTP* 1:879.

will bereave Ezra of his soul through the mouth, Ezra responds: "I spoke mouth to mouth with God and it will not go forth there" (v. 6). This is a clear borrowing from Num. 12:8 ("with him [Moses] I speak mouth to mouth"). When the angels next propose to rid the scribe of his soul via the nostrils, he answers them: "My nostrils smelled the glory of God." This too may have been taken over from the Moses traditions, for in the Armenian *Life of Moses* the lawgiver speaks thus: "My nostrils smelt the fragrance of sweetness."[144] However that may be, when the angels next affirm, "We can bring it forth through your eyes" (v. 9), and when Ezra retorts, "My eyes have seen the back of God" (v. 10), the dependence upon Moses' encounter with God in Exodus 33 is indisputable. Finally, when the angels decide to draw Ezra's soul through his feet, he replies with this: "I walked with Moses on the mountain, and it will not come forth there" (v. 12). The ease with which the *Greek Apocalypse of Ezra* fills out Ezra's life with incidents from Moses' career is clear indication that the assimilation of the two figures was firmly established.[145]

BARUCH

2 Baruch 76, in which Baruch is bidden to exhort to good works what is left of the Jewish nation, is a short chapter composed mostly of Mosaic pieces. The scribe, near the end of his days, is informed that he will "depart from this world" and not taste death, so that he might be kept for the end of times (v. 2); he is commanded to go to the top of a mountain (v. 3); he is advised that "all countries of this earth will [there] pass before you, as well as the likeness of the inhabited world, and the top of the mountains, and the depths of the valleys, and the depths of the seas, and the number of rivers, so that you may see that which you leave and whither you go" (v. 3); and he is told that all this will befall him "after forty days" (v. 4). Anyone alive to the Jewish

---

[144]See M. E. Stone, "Three Armenian Accounts of the Death of Moses," in *Studies on the Testament of Moses*, ed. G. W. E. Nickelsburg (Cambridge, Mass.: Society of Biblical Literature, 1973), 118.

[145]James, *Testament of Abraham*, 66-68, also suggests parallels between the *Greek Apocalypse of Ezra* and the two *De Morte Mosis* printed by Fabricius (1840). For later, Armenian texts which carry forward the parallels between Moses and Ezra see M. E. Stone, "The Apocryphal Literature in the Armenian Tradition," *Proceedings of the Israel Academy of Sciences and Humanities* 4 (1971):67. —It is just possible that the historical Ezra thought himself to be inaugurating a new exodus when he led Jews back to the land; see K. Koch, "Ezra and the Origins of Judaism," *JSS* 19 (1974):173-97. Cf. Fishbane, *Interpretation*, 363.

traditions about Moses cannot but in all this recognize the familiar. Moses spent forty days on Sinai (Exod. 34:28; Deut. 9:9; etc.). At the end of his earthly course, and on a mountain, whither he was bade to go by God himself (Deut. 32:49), the lawgiver saw all the world (see p. 171). And, according to some, Moses was translated to heaven, not buried in the ground (see p. 265, n. 320). That *2 Baruch* 76 depicts Baruch as very much like Moses is inescapable.

The parallelism between Baruch and Moses is far from being a central feature of *2 Baruch*: its disappearance from the book's narrative flow would leave few ripples on the surface. 84:1-8 does, however, offer more of the same:

> Now, I [Baruch] gave you knowledge, while I still live. For I have said that you should particularly learn my mighty commandments which he has instructed you. And I shall set before you some of the command-ments of his judgment before I die. Remember that once Moses called heaven and earth to witness against you and said, "If you trespass the law, you shall be dispersed. And if you shall keep it, you shall be planted" (Deut. 33:19-20). And also other things he said to you when you were in the desert as twelve tribes together. And after his death you cast it away from you and, therefore, that which has been said before has come upon you. And now, Moses spoke to you before it befell you and, behold, it has befallen you for you have forsaken the Law. Also I, behold, I say to you after you suffered that if you obey the things which I have said to you, you shall receive from the Mighty One everything which has been prepared for you. Therefore, let this letter be a witness between me and you that you may remember the commandments of the Mighty One, and that it also may serve as my defense in the presence of him who has sent me. And remember Zion and the Law and the holy land and your brothers and the covenant and your fathers, and do not forget the festivals and the sabbaths.

All this is quite reminiscent of the end of Deuteronomy; and of the author's intention to leave that impression there is no doubt: "Moses spoke to you.... Also I, behold, I say to you...".[146]

Chapter 84 holds the key to understanding *2 Baruch*'s minor Moses typology. The book as a whole is a sort of theodicy, an attempt to come to terms with the questions and disillusionment of post-70 Judaism. The temple was in ruins, the land was trampled under foot by foreigners, and the Day of the Lord tarried as ever. The author of our apocalypse attempted intellectual and spiritual solace by maintaining

---

[146]Consult also 59:4: "For he [God] showed him [Moses] many warnings together with the ways of the law and the ends of times, as also to you" [Baruch].

the nearness of a judgement to right all wrong and by reiterating a deuteronomic-like philosophy of history, according to which collective evil is the effect of collective sin. See, for instance, 85:10 ("For the youth of the world has passed away, and the power of creation is already exhausted, and the coming of the times is very near") and 79:1-2 ("Nebucadnezzar, the king of Babylon, came up against us. For we had sinned against him who created us, and had not observed the commandments which he ordered us"). Now one way of defending a deuteronomic theodicy would be to go back to the two ways of Deuteronomy 30 and show how following the way of death did in fact lead to catastrophe; and this is what we indeed have in 2 *Baruch*: the generation of the exile brought doom upon itself. The argument was made rhetorically more effective by likening Moses and Baruch, both of whom set before the people the contingent future: prosperity will follow good deeds, ills will trail evil works. Of course Baruch and his generation stand for the troubled Judaism of the Jamnian period, and the implication is that they have suffered for their wrongful acts, but if they turn again, God will have abundant mercy, and they will enter the eschatological land of promise. In other words, with the end at hand, they are at the border of the eschatological inheritance, and faced with the same momentous decision Moses left his contemporaries, to choose between life and good and death and evil:

> When we… subject ourselves to him who brought us out of Egypt, we shall come again [at the resurrection] and remember those things which have passed away, and rejoice with regard to the things which have been. But if we… do not recognize the sovereignty of him who brought us up from Egypt, we will come again and ask for that which has now occurred, and shall be severely grieved because of that which has happened (75:7-8; cf. the way of death imagery in 85:13).

As in Jeremiah, then, the Moses typology is, so to speak, almost an epiphenomenon: the focus is on the character of the generation living after Titus' destruction of the temple.

There is perhaps one additional thought to register. Many have suspected, with some justice, that, in part, 2 *Baruch* was originally a response to the disturbing and much more profound 4 *Ezra*, a book which exhibits genuine disquiet with traditional Jewish solutions to the problem of evil. On this reading, 2 *Baruch* was someone's attempt to recommend a more conventional and reassuring understanding of the world's perplexities. If so, then our author must have known that the apocalypse he was attempting to better clearly claimed to be written by one like Moses, than whom no authority could be greater (see pp. 62-65). Is it not then likely that he needed to make manifest that his own apocalyptic seer and hero, Baruch the scribe, was, no less than Ezra, a man of Mosaic stature?

THE SUFFERING SERVANT

Attempts to interpret Deutero-Isaiah's servant songs (42:1-4[7 or 9]; 49:1-6[7-13]; 50:4-9[11]; 52:13-53:12) and to make out the identity of the so-called suffering servant have proliferated with time's passage and generated seemingly insoluble conundrums.[147] Fortunately it is unnecessary here to add my own feeble voice to the interminable discussion, except to observe, what is incontrovertible, that many have traced connections between the servant and Moses. Already rabbinic texts, which sometimes associate the servant with the righteous generally (as in *b. Ber.* 5a; cf. Dan. 12:3), at other times single out Moses for mention. *b. Sota* 14a quotes Isa. 53:12 ("Therefore I will divide him a portion with the great, and he shall divide the spoil with the strong; because he poured out his soul to death") and explains that Moses offered himself unto death (Exod. 32:32) and will enter the promised land in the future (cf. *Sipre Deut.* § 355).[148] Much later, in the sixteenth century, Moses el-Shaikh referred Isa. 53:9-12 (but not the surrounding verses) to Moses. In our own century, E. Sellin once urged (he later changed his mind) that the suffering servant is Moses come to life,[149] while A. Bentzen argued that the suffering servant (of the songs only) should be identified with the author, who perceived himself to be a prophet like Moses, indeed "the new Moses."[150] Similarly, Gerhard von Rad, expressing doubt about the common distributive interpretation of Deut. 18:18 ("a prophet on and on forever"), gave it as his judgment that, "as with Deuteronomy, Deutero-

---

[147]Reviews of the critical literature are cited by L. W. Wilshire, "The Servant-City: A New Interpretation of the 'Servant of the Lord' in the Servant-Songs of Deutero-Isaiah," *JBL* 94 (1975):356, n. 1.

[148]There are *perhaps* even earlier traces of an interpretation of the suffering servant as Moses. *T. Mos.* 3:11 refers to "Moses, who suffered many things (*multa passus est*) in Egypt and at the Red Sea and in the wilderness for forty years." One might think this reminiscent of Isaiah 53. And in Acts 3, Jesus is simultaneously God's servant (*pais*) and one like Moses; see R. F. Zehnle, *Peter's Pentecost Discourse: Tradition and Lukan Reinterpretation in Peter's Speeches of Acts 2 and 3* (SBLMS 15; Nashville: Abingdon, 1971), 48-49, 75-89.

[149]See C. R. North, *The Suffering Servant in Deutero-Isaiah* (2nd ed.; Oxford: University Press, 1956), 53-55.

[150]*King and Messiah* (London: Lutterworth, 1955); see North, *Suffering Servant*, 233-39.

Isaiah stood with a tradition which looked for a prophet like Moses." He fortified his position by asking: "Does not this message [of the new exodus] actually demand the foretelling—as antitype—of a prophetic mediator who is to be greater than Moses in the same degree as the new Exodus is to outdo the old?"[151] Others have been content simply to affirm that the Moses traditions constituted one of several streams which flowed into the servant songs.[152]

What features of the servant have been considered Mosaic?[153] The servant is a prophet,[154] as was Moses (see n. 135). His chief title is "servant," one shared with the lawgiver (n. 121). God's Spirit is upon him (Isa. 42:l), just as it was upon his predecessor (Num. ll:17). The servant, again like Moses, brings "torah" (Isa. 40:4).[155] He is in addition chosen from birth (Isa. 49:l, 5; cf. Exodus l-2); he is exceedingly meek (Isa. 42:2-3; 50:5-6; 53.3-4; cf. Num. 12:3: Moses was "the meekest man upon the earth"); he is a mediator (53:12; cf. n. 45); he teaches the words of Yahweh (Isa. 50:4); he raises up and restores the people, returning them from exile (Isa. 49:6);[156] he is God's elect one (42:l; cf. Ps. l06:23); he suffers for others (Isa. 53:4-12; cf. Exod. l7:4; 32:30-34; Numbers 11-14; Deut. 1:37-40; 3:26; 4:21-22); and, as the old tradition of a leprous Messiah[157] attests, he appears to be a leper (see the commentaries on 53:1-3; for Moses' temporary leprosy see Exod. 4:6-7). Lastly, if the meaning of 52:l5 is that the servant will "splatter (with blood)" many nations (so BDB, s.v. *nzh*), then one should perhaps find an allusion to

---

[151]*Old Testament Theology*, 2:26l.

[152]E.g. P. R. Ackroyd, *Exile and Restoration* (London: SCM, l968), 126-28; G. W. Coats, "Healing and the Moses Traditions," 132-33; A. Gelin, "Moïse dans l'ancien testament," in *Moïse: L'Homme de L'Alliance* (Paris: Desclée, l955), 50-51. Cf. C. R. North, *The Second Isaiah* (Oxford: Clarendon, 1964), 21-22: "We need not doubt that there are features of Moses, of Jeremiah, and indeed of DI himself, in the portrait of the servant."

[153]In addition to what follows see C. Charasse, "The Suffering Servant and Moses," *Church Quarterly Review* 165 (1964):152-63.

[154]See esp. S. Mowinckel, *He That Cometh* (New York: Abingdon, n.d.), 213-33. Even Mowinckel, who denies that the servant is a "new Moses," deems it quite plausible that "the meaning" of Moses "helped to form the portrait of the Servant in the mind of the poet-prophet" (p. 232).

[155]Discussion in W. D. Davies, *The Setting of the Sermon on the Mount* (Cambridge: University Press, l963), 130-37. The *mišpāṭ* of 42:2 may also imply that the servant is a teacher of the law.

[156]If one translates 49:6 as does John D. W. Watts, *Isaiah 34-66* (WBC; Waco: Word, l987), 182—"I appoint you a light to Nations, to be my salvation to the border of the land"—one could conceivably think of the circumstance that Moses brought the people to the border of the promised land.

[157]*b. Sanh.* 98a, 98b; see also *SB* 2:29l. According to Jerome, *In Isa. ad loc.*, at Isa. 53:4 Aquila translated *nāgûaʿ* with *aphemenon*, "leprous." The Vulgate has *quasi leprosum*.

Exod. 24:8, where Moses throws the blood of the covenant upon the people.

It is, *pace* von Rad, probably going too far to see in Deutero-Isaiah's servant the fulfiller of Deut. 18:15 and 18, interpreted eschatologically: the verbal connections between the songs and the two verses from Deuteronomy are insufficient. Still less should one identify the servant with Moses himself. But it is a possibility, bordering on probability, that Moses served the author of the songs as a type—one of several—for the suffering servant. The constant reiteration of the new exodus theme in Deutero-Isaiah[158]—it is the controlling motif—does, with von Rad, raise the question of Israel's future deliverer. And what would have been more natural than to model the central figure of a second exodus upon the famous leader of the first? Furthermore, the servant, while pre-eminently a prophet, also bears certain royal traits[159], and, as already indicated, Moses was both a prophet and a king. This too could have fostered the attribution of Mosaic characteristics to an eschatological prophet/king.[160] We are not obliged, let me emphasize, to contend that the servant is a "new Moses"[161] or a "second Moses." I suspect those expressions imply too much. Although traditions about Moses seemingly fed into the servant songs, they certainly do not dominate them. For the same reason, the servant is not really a "new" or "second Jeremiah," even though a definite resemblance to Jeremiah does obtain.[162] The fact is, the servant reminds one most of a composite photographic face, one produced by the superimposition

---

[158]Not in the songs themselves; but even if the songs were inserted later, that does not demand another author, especially for the first three; cf. C. Westermann, *Isaiah 40-66: A Commentary* (London: SCM, 1969). For the argument that the songs are an integral part of Deutero-Isaiah see T. N. D. Mettinger, *A Farewell to the Servant Songs: A Critical Examination of an Exegetical Axiom* (Lund: Gleerup, 1983), and, for a survey of research through 1979, C. Westermann, *Sprache und Struktur der Prophetie Deuterojesajas* (CTM; Stuttgart: Calwer, 1981), 89-123.

[159]H. H. Rowley, *The Servant of the Lord and other Essays on the Old Testament* (Oxford: Basil Blackwell, 1965), 46-48.

[160]Cf. Westermann, *Isaiah 40-66*, 97: "The two lines of mediation [kingship and prophecy] which had parted company during the course of Israel's history are reunited in the servant. Perhaps this is also implied in the designation 'servant,' for the Old Testament very often uses it of Moses, in whose person the two lines were still one."

[161]So Kraus, *Worship*, 231, and G. Vermes, "La figure de Moïse au des deux testaments," in *Moïse: L'Homme de L'Alliance, Cahiers Sioniens* 8 (1954), 80.

[162]Cf. Isa. 50:4-11 with Jeremiah's so-called confessions (Jer. 11:18-23; 12:1-6; 15:10-21; 17:[9-10]14-18; 18:18-23; 20:7-13, 14-18); Isa. 53:6 with Jer. 15:11, etc.; Isa. 53:7 with Jer. 11:19; Isa. 53:8 with Jer. 11:19 and 15:15. For additional parallels and discussion (but unjustified conclusions) see F. A. Farley, "Jeremiah and 'The Suffering Servant of Jehovah' in Deutero-Isaiah," *ExpT* 38 (1927):521-24.

of several negatives, the result of which is likeness to several, identity with none. Hence it behooves prudence to affirm no more than that Moses may well have served the author of Deutero-Isaiah as a type of the suffering servant, insofar as the lawgiver, in conjunction with others, contributed several features to the prophet's enigmatic portrait.

HILLEL

We regrettably know far too little about the historical Hillel. Most of the sayings attributed to him in *Mishnah ʾAbot* are perhaps authentic, and Jewish tradition is presumably correct in assigning to him a significant role in the evolution of rabbinic hermeneutics (cf. the seven rules of Hillel) and in remembering that he implemented several emergency ordinances or *taqqanot* (such as the *pĕrôzbôl: b. Giṭ.* 36b). Our immediate concern, however, is not the truth about Hillel the man but certain details from the often legendary tradition about him.

According to *Sipre* on Deuteronomy § 357, Hillel died when one hundred and twenty years of age, and his life may be divided into three parts: he arrived in Jerusalem when forty, he studied for the next forty years, and he was leader of the rabbis for forty years. This tripartite scheme, which is also applied to Johanan ben Zakki and Akiba, goes back to and was intended to evoke Deut. 34:7 ("Moses was a hundred and twenty years old when he died") and the tradition that Moses' life could be divided into three equal parts (Acts 7:23, 30; *Sipre Deut.* § 357; SB 2:679-80). So the chronological circumstances of Hillel's life were similar to those of Moses' life.[163]

Hillel was reckoned by the rabbis to be like Moses in other ways, too. Consider the tradition in *b. Sanh.* 11a:

> Once when the Rabbis were met in the upper chamber of Gurya's house at Jericho, a *Bath-kol* was heard from Heaven, saying: "There is one among you who is worthy that the *Shekinah* should rest on him as it did on Moses, but his generation did not merit it." The Sages present set their eyes on Hillel the elder.

One strongly suspects that Hillel's "gentleness," which became proverbial,[164] may have been emphasized precisely because it was Mosaic. Recall the following famous story preserved in *b. Šabb.* 30b-31a:

---

[163]Cf. A. Kaminka, "Hillel's Life and Work," *JQR* 30 (1939):83.
[164]Cf. *Sipre Num.* 101; *ARN* A 15; *t. Sota* 13:3; *y. Sota* 9:13; *b. Sanh.* 11a.

> Our Rabbis taught: A man should always be gentle like Hillel, and not impatient like Shammai. It once happened that two men made a wager with each other, saying, He who goes and makes Hillel angry shall receive four hundred *zuz*. Said one, "I will go and incense him." That day was the Sabbath eve, and Hillel was washing his head. He went, passed by the door of his house, and called out, "Is Hillel here, is Hillel here?" Thereupon he robed and went out to him, saying, "My son, what do you require?" "I have a question to ask," said he. "Ask, my son," he prompted. Thereupon he asked: "Why are the heads of the Babylonians round?" "My son, you have asked a great question," replied he: "because they have no skilful midwives." He departed, tarried a while, returned, and called out, "Is Hillel here; is Hillel here?" He robed and went out to him, saying, "My son, what do you require?" "I have a question to ask," said he. "Ask, my son," he prompted. Thereupon he asked: "Why are the eyes of the Palmyreans bleared?" "My son, you have asked a great question," replied he: "because they live in sandy places." He departed, tarried a while, returned, and called out, "Is Hillel here; is Hillel here?" He robed and went out to him, saying, "My son, what do you require?" "I have a question to ask," said he. "Ask, my son," he prompted. He asked, "Why are the feet of the Africans wide?" "My son, you have asked a great question," said he; "because they live in watery marshes." "I have many questions to ask," said he, "but fear that you may become angry." Thereupon he robed, sat before him and said, "Ask all the questions you have to ask." "Are you the Hillel who is called the nasi of Israel?" "Yes," he replied. "If that is you," he retorted, "may there not be many like you in Israel." "Why, my son?" queried he. "Because I have lost four hundred *zuz* through you," complained he. "Be careful of your moods," he answered. "Hillel is worth it that you should lose four hundred *zuz* and yet another four hundred *zuz* through him, yet Hillel shall not lose his temper."

The word here used of Hillel's humility is the Aramaic equivalent of the Hebrew in Num. 12:3: "the man Moses was very meek."[165] Now this verse played a key role in later depictions of Moses, with the result that his meekness, like Hillel's, became proverbial. Hence, whatever virtues the historical Hillel may in fact have exhibited, the rabbinic emphasis upon his "gentleness" or "meekness" conformed him further to Moses.

One may venture that other features of the Hillel tradition were cast by Moses' shadow. For example, Hillel's universal knowledge is sometimes recorded (*Mas. Sophrim* 16:9; cf. the implications of *b. Sabb.* 30b-31a), and this is comparable to the traditions which have Moses,

---

[165]See further A. Büchler, *Types of Jewish-Palestinian Piety from 70 B.C.E. to 70 C.E.* (New York: KTAV, 1968), 9-15, with additional references to Hillel's meekness.

on Sinai and Pisgah, becoming nearly omniscient (see pp. 171, 222-25). Again, the strange tale that Moses temporarily forgot everything he had learned on Sinai[166] has a parallel of sorts in *b. Pesah.* 66a-b, where, on several occasions, Hillel declares, "I have heard this halachah but have forgotten it." That this put rabbis in mind of Moses is made explicit in *b. Pesah.* 66b, which follows upon examples of Hillel's forgetfulness:

> Resh Lakish said: As to every man who becomes angry, if he is a Sage, his wisdom departs from him; if he is a prophet, his prophecy departs from him. If he is a Sage, his wisdom departs from him: [we learn this] from Moses. For it is written, "And Moses was wroth with the officers of the host," etc. (Num. 31:14); and it is written, "And Eleazar the priest said unto the men of war that went to the battle: This is the statute of the law which the Lord hath commanded Moses," etc. (Num. 31:21), whence it follows that it had been forgotten by Moses.

The occasional assimilation of Hillel to Moses is easily understood. The rabbis, who perceived Hillel to be their spiritual forebear, believed that his function was that of Ezra: he restored the law. As *b. Sukk.* 20a has it: "In ancient times when the Torah was forgotten from Israel, Ezra came up from Babylon and established it. [Some of] it was again forgotten and Hillel the Babylonian came up and established it." Hence Mosaic traits were naturally fabricated for Hillel just as they were naturally fabricated for Ezra, whose "disciple" Hillel was taken to be (*t. Sota* 4:8; *b. Sanh.* 11a). [167] In this way the essential unity of the tradition was established. Moreover, Hillel's Mosaic features elevated his person and helped vindicate, in retrospect at least, the triumph of his disciples, the Hillelites, over the followers of Shammai: Hillel, not Shammai, had the greater affinity with the lawgiver.

THE PROPHET LIKE MOSES

"The Lord your God will raise up (*yāqîm*) for you a prophet like me from among you, from your brethren—him you shall heed." So Moses, in Deut. 18:15. Similar is Deut. 18:18: "I [God] will raise up (*ʾāqîm*) for them a prophet like you from among their brethren; and I will put my words in his mouth, and he shall speak to them all that I command

---

[166]*3 Enoch* 48D:4; *b. Ned.* 38a; *Exod. Rab.* 12:6; *Pesiq. R.* 20; Ginzberg, *Legends*, 6:47, n. 248.

[167]Hillel was, it may be added, sometimes assimilated to Ezra, which partly explains the frequent mention of Hillel's Babylonian origin.

him." Exegetical history has attached at least four different interpretations to these verses.

(i) Most modern scholars, presuming a distributive sense for *yāqîm* and *ʾāqîm* ("from time to time"), have thought of a series or even institution of prophets:

> The "prophet" contemplated is not a simple individual, belonging to a distant future, but *Moses' representative for the time being*, whose office it would be to supply Israel, whenever in its history occasion should arise, with needful guidance and advice: in other words... the reference is not to an individual but to a prophetical order.[168]

According to this understanding, which seems to have been that of the Deuteronomist and his school, there will be a number of prophets like Moses.

(ii) A second interpretation, attested in both Palestinian and diaspora materials, has been unearthed by Wayne A. Meeks: "In some circles there was a persistent notion of a *succession of prophetic rulers* over Israel, beginning with Moses, passed on to Joshua, continuing in Samuel and, presumably, also found in the remaining great prophets of Israel, especially Jeremiah."[169] The difference from the first interpretation lies in this, that Deut. 18:15 and 18 are taken to refer not to a series of prophets but to a series of prophet-kings. Compare perhaps Eupolemus, *apud* Eusebius, *Praep. ev.* 9:30:1-3:

> Moses prophesied forty years; then Joshua, the son of Nun, prophesied thirty years. Joshua lived one hundred and ten years and pitched the holy tabernacle in Shiloh. After that, Samuel become a prophet. Then, by the will of God, Saul was chosen by Samuel to be king, and he died after ruling twenty one years. Then David his son ruled... .[170]

iii) The Dead Sea Scrolls, referring Deut. 18:18 to an individual, preserve an eschatological interpretation of the prophet like Moses expectation. In *lQS* 9:ll we read of "the prophet and the anointed ones of Aaron and Israel." This is to be construed in the light of *4QTestimonia*, which quotes Deut. 5:28-29 followed by Deut. 18:18-20; Num. 24:15-17; and Deut. 33:8-11. These last three Scriptures serve to ground expecta-

---

[168]So S. R. Driver, *A Critical and Exegetical Commentary on Deuteronomy* (ICC; Edinburgh: T& T Clark, 1916), 229. See further Kraus, *Worship*, 105-12, and J. Coppens, *Le Messianisme et sa rèleve prophétique* (BETL 34; Gembloux: Duculot, 1974), 36-40.

[169]*The Prophet-King*, 189.

[170]Trans. of C. R. Holladay, *Fragments from Hellenistic Jewish Authors, Volume 1: Historians* (SBL Texts and Translations 20, Pseudepigrapha Number 10; Chico: Scholars Press, 1983), 115. See Meeks, *Prophet-King*, 142-44.

tion of, respectively, a prophet like Moses, a Davidic Messiah, and a priestly Messiah.[171] There is a related expectation in John 1:20-21, 25; and 7:40. In these verses "*the* prophet," obviously the one like Moses, and "the (one) Messiah," are two different figures.

(iv) A fourth interpretation is met with in early Christianity and was not, in my judgement, invented by the church: the prophet like Moses is the Messiah. See especially Acts 3:17-26. This view, as we shall see later, was that of Matthew.

Unhappily, the neat distinctions just drawn would have been blurred in antiquity. There is, to begin with, evidence not only for an eschatological prophet like Moses but also for the eschatological return of Moses himself. The Jewish sources are abundant and reach back to the first century C.E.[172] The New Testament also seemingly contributes testimony. The story of the transfiguration of Jesus (Mark 9:2-8 par.) records the appearance of Moses as well as Elijah, and their joint manifestation could originally have had eschatological sense: Moses and Elijah have come, therefore the end is at hand. Revelation 11, which foretells the advent of two prophets who can shut the sky so that no rain falls (cf. 2 Kgs. 1:10) and smite the earth with every plague (cf. Exod. 7:17, 19), may likewise take up the same expectation of a return of Moses,[173] albeit, if so, to rather different ends. Here fulfillment has reverted to expectation: the two eschatological prophets are yet to come.

How might the expectations of Moses and of the prophet like Moses have been related to each other? Later Samaritan theology may well have merged the two.[174] Perhaps the *Life of the Prophet Jeremiah* (first century C.E.?) already presupposes the identification.[175] But that is most uncertain, and Jewish sources are silent on the matter. Were there people who identified Moses and the prophet like Moses? Were there

[171]Discussion in A. S. van der Woude, *Die Messianischen Vorstellungen der Gemeinde von Qumran* (Assen: Van Gorcum & Co., 1957), 75-89.

[172]See *4 Ezra* 6:26(?); 7:28(?); *Liv. Proph. Jer.* 14; *Frag. Tg.* on Exod. 12:42; *Pal. Tg.* on Deut. 33:21(?); *Deut. Rab.* 3:17; the Slavonic Josephus after *Bell.* 2:174 ("Our first lawmaker is risen from the dead, and he has displayed signs and wonders"). For the Samaritan evidence see Meeks, *Prophet-King*, 246-50, and in general R. Le Déaut, *La nuit pascale* (Rome: Biblical Institute, 1965), 298-303.

[173]It is usually assumed that the two figures are Elijah and Moses, but they could be Elijah and the prophet like Moses.

[174]See Teeple, *Prophet*, 43-48. Cf. how the Christian form of the *Testaments of the Twelve Patriarchs* melts together the Messiahs of Levi and Judah.

[175]So apparently D. R. A. Hare, in *OTP* 2:383, noting that Moses is called "God's chosen one" (14), a title elsewhere used of the Messiah (e.g. Luke 23:35).

others who expected them both?[176] Barring the unforeseen discovery
of long-lost texts, we can only wonder. We might also wonder about
the extent of the belief in a coming prophet like Moses. Such belief
appears in the Dead Sea Scrolls and in early Christian literature. But
was an eschatological expectation founded upon Deut. 18:15 and 18
well-known and wide-spread,[177] or, as its absence from the rabbinic
corpus might suggest, was it something marginal?[178] It is noteworthy
that while there is in the canonical gospels a discussion of how it can
be that the Messiah has come but Elijah has not (Mark 9:9-13 par.), no
one ever objects that the prophet like Moses has failed to appear. This,
however, could have several explanations, in addition to the obvious
one, that the prophet like Moses was not much on people's minds.
Perchance the gospels preserve not extra-mural polemics but only
objections that occurred to Christians, and because they operated with
the equation, the Messiah = the prophet like Moses, no difficulty was
sensed. Alternatively, perhaps the same equation was already made
by pre-Christian Jews, with the same result. Or maybe Elijah was
regularly identified with the prophet like Moses,[179] so that a remark

---

[176]Cf. how some Christians, by combining the expectation of Revelation 11 with the
belief that John the Baptist had fulfilled Mal. 4:5 ("Behold, I will send you Elijah the
prophet before the great and terrible day of the Lord comes"), came to believe in the
advent of one like Elijah (= John the Baptist) as well as in the future, eschatological
advent of Elijah himself.

[177]So D. M. Frankfurter, "The Origin of the Miracle-List Tradition and Its Medium of
Circulation," in *Society of Biblical Literature 1990 Seminar Papers*, ed. D. J. Lull (Atlanta:
Scholars Press, 1990), 349: "There is considerable evidence that a popular folklore of the
Mosaic prophet and his signs played a large part in Palestinian Jewish belief...".

[178]So R. A. Horsley, "'Like One of the Prophets of Old': Two Types of Popular
Prophets at the Time of Jesus," *CBQ* 47 (1985):441-43.

[179]Blenkinsopp, *Prophecy and Canon*, 87, thinks the author of the late Mal. 4:4-5
("Remember the law of my servant Moses, the statutes and ordinances that I commanded him at Horeb for all Israel. Behold, I will send you Elijah the prophet before the
great and terrible day of the Lord comes") had Deut. 18:15-18 in mind. Malachi does
mention Elijah and Moses in close connection, and if, as is widely assumed, the
"messenger of the covenant" in 3:1 was identified by the author of 4:4-5 with Elijah, then
Elijah would be like Moses, for presumably the messenger is to renew the Mosaic
covenant. (In support of combining 3:1 with 4:4-5 is this: "the words of Malachi (2:4-7)
on God's covenant with the priestly messenger recall to memory His covenant with
Phinehas [= Elijah in Jewish tradition] and his seed in Num 25:12-13. Accordingly it
seems natural to identify this priestly messenger (Mal 3:1) with Elijah (Mal 3:23 [= 4:4]).
Kimchi (on Mal 3:1) refers to this interpretation and obviously Ps-Philo (28:3) knew it,
for he describes Phinehas in phrases taken from Mal 2:4-7 (*Dicito Finees. Numquid aliquis
loquitur prior sacerdote qui custodit mandata Domini Dei nostri, presertim cum exeat de ore eius
veritas*, etc.);" so A. Zeron, "The Martyrdom of Phinehas-Elijah," 99. See further Beth
Glazier-McDonald, *Malachi: The Divine Messenger*, SBLDS 98 (Atlanta: Scholars Press,
1987), 263-64, on the links between 3:1 and 4:4-5. Note also that Matt. 11:10 and Mark 1:12

about Elijah was, for some, simultaneously a remark about the prophet like Moses. Already, as we have seen, the Jewish Bible models Elijah on Moses. And yet the evidence that the early Christians identified the prophet like Moses with Elijah is vanishingly small.[180] Matthew and Mark plainly identify John the Baptist with Elijah, Jesus with the prophet like Moses, while in John 1:21 the Baptist is asked first whether he is Elijah and next whether he is "the prophet," thus clearly implying that an answer to the first question is no answer to the second question: John might have been "the prophet [like Moses]" without being Elijah. Also, Revelation distinguishes between Elijah and Moses or the prophet like Moses (see chapter 11).

While uncertainty abounds, one guess seems more probable than not: the expectation of an eschatological prophet like Moses was not held just by Qumran sectaries and early Christians. 1 Macc. 4:46 and 14:41 are, admittedly, defective argument for this, because the verses are too cryptic, their ramifications uncertain.[181] Also less than helpful is the expectation of "the unique prophet" in *T. Benj.* 9:2-3, although his being the instrument of "salvation" (*sōtērion*) as well as his "meek-

---

apply Mal. 3:1 to John the Baptist, who in Matthew and Mark is the eschatological Elijah.) However one interprets Malachi, according to John Strugnell, "Moses-Pseudepigrapha at Qumran: 4Q375, 4Q376, and Similar Works," in *Archaeology and History in the Dead Sea Scrolls*, ed. L. Schiffmann, JSOT/ASOR Monographs 2 (Sheffield: JSOT, 1990), 234, "in all probability the Mosaic eschatological prophet was, in the thought of Qumran... identical with Elijah *redivivus*...". He does not explain. There is no trace of Elijah expectation in 1QS IX:11 or 4QTestimonia or in 11QMelchizedek, where "the herald" = "the anointed one of the Spirit" is probably the prophet like Moses (cf. A. S. van der Woude and M. de Jonge, "11QMelchizedek and the New Testament," *NTS* 12 (1966):306-308). On the other hand, 4Q375, which refers to "the prophet" (the eschatological prophet?) "is clearly inspired by the discussion of false prophets in Deuteronomy 13 and 18" (Strugnell), and there may be allusions to Mal 4:5 (*šbth, lb, gdl*; the averting of wrath through obedience to the prophet also recalls Mal. 4:5). Any definite verdict is unwarranted. —If one could, with reference to Mal. 4:5, translate the Samaritan "Taheb" as "restorer" (transitive), then, as Taheb was (although we do not know precisely when) identified with Moses, one might infer that Malachi's prophecy of Elijah was understood by the Samaritans to pertain to Moses. But is use of Malachi by the Samaritans likely? And "returning one" (intransitive) is the usual translation of "Taheb." —I fail to find documentary support for the assertion of A. R. C. Leaney, *The Rule of Qumran and Its Meaning* (Philadelphia: Westminster, 1966), 225, that "the prophet promised in Deuteronomy 18.15,18f was often identified with Elijah *redivivus*."

[180]The evidence is gathered by J. Louis Martyn, "We have found Elijah," in *Jews, Greeks and Christians: Religious Cultures in Late Antiquity, Essays in Honor of William David Davies*, ed. R. Hamerton-Kelly and Robin Scroggs (SJLA 21; Leiden: Brill, 1976), 181-219.

[181]See Davies, *Setting*, 143-45. 1 Macc. 4:45-46: "So they tore down the altar, and stored the stones in a convenient place on the temple hill until there should come a prophet to tell what to do with them." 14:41: "And the Jews and their priests decided that Simon should be their leader and high priest for ever, until a trustworthy prophet should arise...".

ness" (*tapeinos*) might remind one of the Moses traditions.[182] Many would moreover regard the purport of the canonical Gospels[183] as less than compelling because reflective only of the church's own convictions. Josephus, however, more than makes up the lack, so that we need not be restricted to vague surmises. The following texts are usually considered together:[184]

> 1)*Ant.* 20:97-99: During the period when Fadus was procurator of Judaea, a certain imposter (*goēs*) named Theudas persuaded the majority of the masses to take up their possessions and to follow him to the Jordan River. He stated that he was a prophet and that at his command the river would be parted (*schisas*) and would provide them an easy passage. With this talk he deceived many. Fadus, however, did not permit them to reap the fruit of their folly, but sent against them a squadron of cavalry. These fell upon them unexpectedly, slew many of them and took many prisoners. Theudas himself was captured, whereupon they cut off his head and brought it to Jerusalem. These, then, are the events that befell the Jews during the time that Cuspius Fadus was procurator.

Comment: During Cuspius Fadus' much-troubled procuratorship (C.E. 44-46), which commenced when the Jewish kingship, upon the death of Herod Agrippa I, became extinct, there appeared Theudas, a man who claimed, so Josephus says, to be a *prophētēs*. Acts 5:36, although at odds chronologically with Josephus, also names Theudas, and it has Gamaliel I report that the man claimed to be somebody (*legōn einai tina heauton*). We are thus informed, and we may believe, that Theudas himself, his person, was significant for his followers. Was he imagined to be the prophet like Moses, interpreted eschatologically? That is possible, even probable. That he sought, like Joshua, to cross the Jordan and not, like Moses, the Red Sea, is no compelling counter for, beyond the evident fact that it was the Jordan, not the Red Sea, that was in the neighborhood, the biblical narrative of Joshua's crossing of the Jordan develops, as we have seen, an

---

[182]See pp. 180-81 and 222. The extent to which *T. Benj.* is to be regarded as Jewish is problematic: there are at the very least clear Christian interpolations.

[183]For "the prophet" see Matt. 21:l0-ll; Luke 7:39 B; 9:8; John 6:l4; 7:52 v.l. Sometimes the references to "a prophet" have been thought to have definite sense; thus Alan Richardson, *An Introduction to the Theology of the New Testament* (London: SCM, l958), l67. The *prophētēs hōs* of Mark 6:l5 does resemble LXX Deut. l8:l5: *prophētēn… hōs*; and note that in 1QS IX:ll "prophet" is anarthrous, as it is in Deut. l8:l5 and l8. For the intriguing suggestion that the seemingly redundant phrase in Mark 6:l5 ("a prophet like one of the prophets") is to be explained by the use of the cardinal for the ordinal in Aramaic and at one time meant "a prophet like the first of the prophets [= Moses]" see C. Perrot, "'Un prophète comme l'un des Prophètes' (Mc 6,l5)," in *De la Tôrah au Messie*, 417-23.

[184]See also *Bell.* 6:284-87.

extended Moses typology—as, incidentally, does the related narrative of Elijah's similar water miracle. To cross the Jordan once again was to repeat the exodus again, and to be like Joshua was to be like Moses. Moreover, the unexpected note that Theudas persuaded "the majority of the masses"—this was not done in a corner—to take up their possessions reminds one of nothing so much as Exodus 12, where the Israelites pack their possessions for the wilderness (vv. 32-36). Note also that *schisas* harks back to LXX Exod. 14:21 but has no parallel in Joshua.

> 2)*Bell*. 2:261-63 (= *Ant*. 20:169-72): A still worse blow was dealt at the Jews by the Egyptian false prophet. A charlatan, who had gained for himself the reputation of a prophet, this man appeared in the country, collected a following of about thirty thousand dupes, and led them by a circuitous route from the desert to the mount called the mount of Olives. From there he proposed to force an entrance into Jerusalem and, after over-powering the Roman garrison, to set himself up as tyrant of the people, employing those who poured in with him as his bodyguard. [*Ant*. 20:170 specifies: at his command Jerusalem's walls would fall down.] His attack was anticipated by Felix [procuratorship: C.E. 52-60], who went to meet him with the Roman heavy infantry, the whole population joining him in the defence. The outcome of the ensuing engagement was that the Egyptian escaped with a few of his followers; most of his force were killed or taken prisoners; the remainder dispersed and stealthily escaped to their several homes.

Comment: The Egyptian, like Theudas, hoped to emulate the achievements of Joshua, who made the walls of a city come tumbling down (Joshua 6). This, as already indicated, is consonant with his having conceived of himself as a new Moses. But that is not all. The man was known as "the Egyptian" (*ho Aigyptios*), led a crowd into "the desert" (*tēn erēmon*), and set as his goal the Mount of Olives, a locale owning strong eschtological reverberations.[185] Compare the passing notice in Acts 21:38: "Are you [Paul] not the Egyptian, then, who recently stirred up a revolt and led the four thousand men of the Assassins out into the wilderness?" Now a man who came from Egypt (cf. *Ant*. 20:169), who led the people in the desert, who made himself out to be a prophet, and who sought to rule Israel (*tou demou tyrannein*)—how could such a one not have been perceived as another prophet-king like Moses? The seemingly otherwise unmotivated circumstance that the Egyptian's desert route was circuitous (*periagagon*) is confirmatory, for according to Exod. 13:18, "God led the people by the roundabout

---

[185]John B. Curtis, "An Investigation of the Mount of Olives in the Judaeo-Christian Tradition," *HUCA* 28 (1957):137-80.

way of the wilderness toward the Red Sea." The Egyptian, it seems, did his futile best to replay the liberating past.[186]

> 3)*Ant*. 20:167-68 (cf. *Bell*. 2:258-60): Impostors and deceivers called upon the mob to follow them into the desert. For they said that they would show them unmistakable marvels and signs that would be wrought in harmony with God's design. [*Bell*. 2:259 adds: "...God would there give them tokens of freedom."] Many were, in fact, persuaded and paid the penalty of their folly; for they were brought before Felix and he punished them.

Comment: Not only does the wilderness motif again appear, but, as P. W. Barnett has remarked, the expression, "tokens of freedom" (*sēmeia eleutherias*), is used in Josephus' exodus narrative, *Ant*. 2:327.[187] Barnett has further observed that "marvels and signs that would be wrought in harmony with God's design" (*terata kai sēmeia kata tēn tou theou pronoian ginomena*) is close to a phrase elsewhere used by Josephus to describe what Moses, in contrast to Pharaoh's magicians, wrought in the Egyptian court (*Ant*. 2:286). Josephus, one suspects, believed that the unnamed *goētes* futilely sought to produce Mosaic *sēmeia*.

> 4)*Ant*. 20:188: Festus also sent a force of cavalry and infantry against the dupes of a certain imposter who had promised them salvation and rest from troubles, if they chose to follow him into the wilderness. The force which Festus dispatched destroyed both the deceiver himself and those who had followed him.

Comment: Notwithstanding the fateful aftermath, the promises of "salvation" (*sotērian*) and of "rest" (*paulan kakōn*) may, for Josephus, have been reverberant of the exodus, as was, presumably, "the wilderness." See *Ant*. 2:276 (*sōsein*, of God delivering his people from bondage, *kakois*, of God bringing disaster upon the Egyptians) and 3:64 (the *sotēria* of the exodus); also LXX Deut. 3:20 and 12:9-10 ("rest" in the land beyond the Jordan).

> 5)*Ant*. 18:85-87: The Samaritan nation too was not exempt from disturbance. For a man who made light of mendacity and in all his designs catered to the mob, rallied them, bidding them go in a body with him to Mount Gerizim, which in their belief is the most sacred of mountains. He assured them that on their arrival he would show them the sacred vessels which were buried there, where Moses had deposited them. His hearers, viewing this tale as plausible, appeared in arms. They posted themselves in a certain village named Tirathanan, and, as they planned

---

[186]Cf. Tg. Onk. on Gen 49.11, where the Messiah leads his people *around* Jerusalem.
[187]"The Jewish Sign Prophets—A.D. 40-70—Their Intentions and Origin," *NTS* 27 (1981):682-83. I am much indebted to this article in the following pages.

to climb the mountain in a great multitude, they welcomed to their ranks the new arrivals who kept coming. But before they could ascend, Pilate blocked their projected route up the mountain with a detachment of cavalry and heavy-armed infantry, who in an encounter with the firstcomers in the village slew some in a pitched battle and put the others to flight. Many prisoners were taken, of whom Pilate put to death the principal leaders and those who were most influential among the fugitives.

Comment: Early Jewish tradition made Jeremiah (2 Macc. 2:4- 8[188]) or Jeremiah and Baruch (*Liv. Proph. Jer.* 11; *4 Bar.* 3:1-22) or angles (in the sight of Baruch: *2 Bar.* 6:1-9; 80:1-2; cf. Bar. 1:8-10) responsible for secreting the things of the tabernacle. If, however, we may trust Josephus, among at least some Samaritans the task had been transferred to Moses (cf. *b. Sota* 9a?)—just as in rabbinic literature it came to be transferred to Josiah (*b. Yoma* 52b). Regarding responsibility for restoration, Jewish tradition variously nominated God (2 Macc. 2:7-8), Elijah (*Mek.* on Exod. 16:33-34; *y. Seq.* 6.49c), and Moses and Aaron (*Liv. Proph. Jer.* 14-15). Now it seems a safe bet that Josephus' Samaritan, operating with the belief that Moses had hidden the vessels, also operated with the belief that Moses (cf. *Liv. Proph. Jer.* 14-15) or someone like him (cf. *Mek.* on Exod. 16:33-34; *y. Seq.* 6.49c: Elijah was remembered as a prophet like Moses) would reveal them. Perhaps indeed Josephus, *Ant.* 18:85-87 is, as Marilyn F. Collins has urged, evidence for Samaritan expectation of an eschatological prophet like Moses.[189]

Because fortune, proving them false, frowned upon Josephus' self-proclaimed prophets, the extant accounts are neither sympathetic nor full: we have instead of eulogies little more than damning epitaphs. How we should like to know more about those enthusiasts to whom Providence must have appeared tardy. What is known, however, may be enough, at least for this chapter. In first-century Palestine there were ostensible prophets who, following a more or less fixed scenario, led people into the desert, where miracles of deliverance like those of Moses and his imitator, Joshua, were to be enacted. In view of the clear application of Deut. 18:15 and 18 to an eschatological prophet like Moses in the Dead Sea Scrolls and the New Testament, in view of the evident prominence of the *goētes* themselves (they were prophets and

---

[188]According to this, Jeremiah "went out to the mountain where Moses had gone up and had seen the inheritance of God."

[189]"The Hidden Vessels in Samaritan Traditions," *JJS* 3 (1972):97-116.

leaders who had not only great popular appeal but the authority to command their followers at risk of death), and in view of the New Testament's testimony that popular opinion often settled upon "prophet" or "the (Mosaic) prophet" as explanation for out-of-the-ordinary religious activity,[190] why resist the inference that Theudas, the Egyptian, and the hapless others like them provoked speculation regarding the fulfillment of Deut. 18:15 and 18?[191] It is no effective retort that the works of Josephus never say as much. Had Deut. 18:15 and 18 indeed helped precipitate revolutionary movements, Josephus' apologetical interests would have led him to feign of the fact ignorance.

Three observations take us further in the same direction. First, Origen closely associated Theudas and Judas the Galilean with a certain Dositheus, and this last purportedly "wished to persuade the Samaritans that he was the Christ predicted by Moses"—a likely reference to Deut. 18:15, 18 (see C. Cels. 1:57). Secondly, Josephus called more than one false prophet a *goēs*, or deceiver: *Ant.* 20:97, 167, 188; *Bell.* 2:261. Now the word, *goēs*, means, in classical Greek texts, "sorcerer" or "wizard." In 2 Tim. 3:13 the meaning is slightly different: "imposter," while in Philo, *Spec. leg.* 1:315, *goēs* is a name for a false prophet. But what were the noun's precise connotations for Josephus? Interestingly enough, he used it several times in retelling the story of Moses. See *Ant.* 2:286, 302, 332, 336. In these places the *goētes* are the Egyptian magicians of the exodus, that is, people who sought, effectively and ineffectively, to imitate the miracles of Moses. Perhaps, then, Josephus found *goēs* so congenial for characterizing Theudas and his ilk because, in the right context, it connoted for him not charlatan in general but Mosaic charlatan in particular.

Thirdly, and more significantly, Barnett has ascertained a common pattern in the narratives about sign prophets. In each instance we have to do with a prophet, a crowd, a miraculous sign, and a significant location (mountain or wilderness). Burnett has also recognized that the feeding of the five thousand in John 6 exhibits the same pattern: in the wilderness and before a crowd Jesus performs a great exodus sign (he produces bread miraculously), whereupon (*idontes ho epoiēsen sēmeion*) he is hailed prophet. I should like to underline what Burnett has not, namely, that the declaration called forth by the Mosaic

[190]Mark 6:15; 8:28; John 6:14. See also n. 183.
[191]See further Otto Betz, "Miracles in the Writings of Flavius Josephus," in *Josephus, Judaism, and Christianity*, ed. L. H. Feldman and Goher Hata (Detroit: Wayne State University, 1987), 212-35.

miracle—"This is truly the prophet who is coming into the world"—is, to judge from the near consensus of the modern commentators, a claim that the prophet like Moses, the prophet of Deut. 18:15 and 18, has appeared.[192] Whether or not we are dealing in John 6:14-15 with historical tradition is in this context moot. The pertinent fact is another: if the author of John or the source of his tradition found it appropriate for Jesus to be heralded as the prophet like Moses because he performed, before a multitude and in the wilderness, a Mosaic miracle, so too may others, confronted by like circumstances in real life, have thought it appropriate so to hail the sign prophets.[193]

The outcome of this discussion is that the expectation of an eschatological prophet like Moses, founded upon Deut. 18:15 and 18, was not little known, or just the esoteric property of the Qumran coventile and Jewish-Christian churches.[194] It was instead very much in the air in first-century Palestine and helped to instigate several short-lived revolutionary movements. Jesus was far from being the only individual thought of as the eschatological fulfillment of Deut. 18:15 and 18. Indeed, there were several men who bravely, if in the event foolishly, set out to hasten divine intervention by imitating Moses in their deeds. Which is to say: emulation of the lawgiver was not limited to literature: it was also a fact of extratextual experience.[195] I note that Peter, in *Ps.-Clem. Rec.* 1:43, reports that the Jews often wished to talk

---

[192]Cf. most recently R. F. Collins, *These Things have been written: Studies on the Fourth Gospel* (Louvain Theological and Pastoral Monographs 2; Louvain: Peeters, 1990), 194. See further C. H. Dodd, *According to the Scriptures: The Sub-structure of New Testament Theology* (London: Fontana, 1965), 56.

[193]Worth comparing is the narrative in Socrates, *H.E.* 7:38: On fifth century Crete there was "a certain Jewish imposter" who "pretended that he was Moses, and had been sent from heaven to lead out the Jews inhabiting that island, and conduct them through the sea…" (NPNF 2:174-75). While one must allow for distortion in Socrates' account, the "imposter," if he did not make himself out to be Moses reincarnate, probably did apply Deut. 18:15 and 18 to himself.

[194]As is well known, Philo, *Spec. leg.* 1:65, might also attest to the expectation under discussion: "A prophet possessed by God will suddenly appear and give prophetic oracles. Nothing of what he says will be his own, for he that is truly under divine inspiration has no power of apprehension when he speaks…". This probably depends upon Deut. 18:15-18. Unfortunately, however, Philo's words do not clarify if he knew or accepted an eschatological interpretation of that passage.

[195]Perhaps that is one reason why "the prophet" is, in the New Testament, overshadowed by other christological titles, and also why Deut. 18:15 and 18 are so seldom cited in rabbinic literature: the title and the texts behind it were too much associated with failed imitators of Moses. Cf. G. Vermes, *Jesus the Jew* (London: William Collins Sons, 1973), 97-99.

about the prophet like Moses. The notice, I believe, is not without
historical verisimilitude.[196]

[196]The proposition that the Teacher of Righteousness known from the Dead Sea
Scrolls was identified with the eschatological prophet of Deuteronomy 18, or that he was
at least reckoned a second Moses, is often met in the literature. See e.g. W. H. Brownlee,
"Messianic Motifs of Qumran and the New Testament," *NTS* 3 (1956):17; Philip R.
Davies, "The Teacher of Righteousness and the 'End of Days,'" *RevQ* 49-52 (1988):313-
17; R. H. Fuller, *The Foundations of New Testament Christology* (London: Lutterworth,
1965), 50-53; M. Giblet, "Prophétisme et attente d'un messie-prophète dans l'ancien
Judaïsme," in *L'Venue du Messie*, 127-28; Hahn, *Christology*, 363; Leaney, *The Rule of
Qumran and Its Meaning*, 228; Teeple, *Prophet*, 51-56; G. Vermes, *Scripture and Tradition in
Judaism* (Leiden: Brill, 1961), 59-66; N. Wieder, "The 'Law-Interpreter' of the Sect of the
Dead Sea Scrolls: The Second Moses," *JJS* 4 (1953):158-75. Contrast Raymond E. Brown,
"The Messianism of Qumran," *CBQ* 19 (1957):73-75, and Gert Jeremias, *Der Lehrer der
Gerechtigkeit* (SUNT 2; Göttingen: Vandenhoeck & Ruprecht, 1963), 295-98. Brown's
argument, that "since 1QS 9,11 places the coming of the prophet in the same future
expectations as that of the messiahs, we must conclude that the Teacher was not the
prophet who would come at the end" (pp. 72-73), is bereft of compulsion, for it simply
presupposes that *1QS* IX:11 was composed after the advent of the Teacher of Righteousness; but recent literary criticism suggests otherwise. For the strong argument that *1QS*
VIII:1-16a + IX:3-X:8a represents the earliest literary stage of *1QS* and indeed reflects the
ideology of a sect before the establishment at Qumran see J. Murphy O'Connor, "Le
genese litteraire de la Regle de la Communaute," *RB* 76 (1969):528-49. And for the same
argument concerning *CD* VI:9-11 (which refers to one "who shall teach righteousness at
the end of days") see P. R. Davies, *The Damascus Covenant* (Sheffield: JSOT, 1983). It is
quite possible, and I am inclined to think, on the basis of the work of O'Connor and
Davies, that a pre-Qumran group expected a righteous teacher according to an
eschatological interpretation of Deut. 18:15 and 18, and that subsequently one arose who
was held to fulfill that expectation; see Davies, "Teacher of Righteousness," and cf.
Leaney, *Rule*, 227-28. There is no denying a certain resemblance between the Teacher of
Righteousness and Moses. The former, leader of a desert community that had experienced a new exodus, was a teacher and interpreter of the law. He was "raised up" (*CD*
I:6), just as Deut. 18:15, 18 and *4Q175* foretell that God will "raise up" the prophet like
Moses (in each case the verb is *qûm*). He was in addition known as the "faithful
shepherd" (*1Q34* bis ii 8), a title the rabbis gave to Moses (*Mek.* on Exod. 14:31, etc.), and
he was believed to be a prophet at the end of days, who spoke from "the mouth of God"
(*1QpHab.* II:2-3; cf. Num. 12:6-8; *4Q175* 5-6) and who had come to guide a people who
were theretofore wandering "in a pathless wilderness" (*CD* I:13ff.). He had a special
understanding, greater than the writing prophets themselves (*1QpHab.* II:9; VII:3-5). He
was an object of faith, as was Moses (*1QpHab.* II:7-8; cf. below, p. 303), and people were
to listen to him (*1QpHab.* II:7-9; *CD* XX:28-34; cf. Deut. 18:15-18). It may further be
observed that the Teacher of Righteousness drew to himself the title "vessel," just as did
Moses in the targumim and rabbinic texts; references in Wieder, "Second Moses," 161.
Of even more interest is *1QH* IV:5 ("Thou hast illumined my face by Thy Covenant"; cf.
IV:27-29). There are good reasons for assigning *1QH* IV:5, 27-29 to the Teacher of
Righteousness himself; see Jeremias, *Der Lehrer der Gerechtigkeit*; also P. Schulz, *Der
Autoritätsanspruch des Lehrers der Gerechtigkeit in Qumran* (Meisenheim am Glan: Anton
Hein, 1974). This matters because the author of *1QH* IV:5-V:4 may well have been
likening himself to Moses. The hymnist's *face* has been illumined by God's covenant (cf.
Exodus 24, 34); God has appeared to him (IV:6; cf. Exodus 33); he is the mediator of the
law, which is written on his heart (IV:10); and the faithful hearken (*šāma'*, IV:25) to him
(cf. Deut. 18:15, 18). No less suggestive is the circumstance that the closest extant parallel

THE MESSIAH

Rabbi Berekiah said in the name of Rabbi Isaac: "As the first redeemer was, so shall the latter Redeemer be. What is stated of the former redeemer? And Moses took his wife and his sons, and set them upon an ass (Exod. 4:20). Similarly will it be with the latter Redeemer, as it is stated, Lowly and riding upon an ass (Zech. 9:9). As the former redeemer caused manna to descend, as it is stated, Behold, I will cause to rain bread from heaven for you (Exod. 16:4), so will the latter Redeemer cause manna to descend, as it is stated, May he be as a rich cornfield in the land (Ps. 72:16). As the former redeemer made a well to rise, so will the latter Redeemer bring up water, as it is stated, And a fountain shall come forth of the house of the Lord, and shall water the valley of Shittim (Joel 4:18)" (*Eccl. Rab.* 1:28).

This passage, well known to students of the New Testament, is not isolated. Other rabbinic texts make the latter redeemer, the Messiah, like the former redeemer, Moses. Some examples:

—*Exod. Rab.* 1:26: "The daughter of Pharaoh… [brought] up him who was destined to exact retribution from her father. The messianic king, too, who will one day punish Edom, dwells with them in that province…".

—*Ruth Rab.* 5:6: "Just as the former redeemer revealed himself and later was hidden from them… so the future redeemer will be revealed to them, and then be hidden from them" (cf. *Pesiq. R.* 15:10).

---

is to be found in 2 Cor. 3:7-4:6, where Moses is indisputably in view; see J. A. Fitzmyer, "Glory Reflected on the Face of Christ (2 Cor 3:7-4:6) and a Palestinian Jewish Motif," *TS* 42 (1981):630-44, although Fitzmyer does not consider the obvious Moses connection; contrast W. H. Brownlee, *The Meaning of the Qumran Scrolls for the Bible* (New York: Oxford, 1964), 139-40, and Linda L. Belleville, *Reflections of Glory: Paul's Use of the Moses-Doxa Tradition in 2 Corinthians 3.1-18* (JSNTSS 52; Sheffield: JSOT, 1991), 45-46. One last point: *11QTemple* must be brought into the discussion. If the document was written or redacted by the Teacher of Righteousness (so Wacholder and Wise), that would certainly bear on our subject. The scroll, according to some, is an eschatological law for the land (cf. p. 188), and while it could be a Moses pseudepigraphon (so Yadin and Wacholder), Moses' name has consistently been stricken from the Biblical sources, so *11QTemle* may instead be a direct revelation to a new Moses. See Wise, *Temple Scroll*, 155-94. I refrain from coming to any definite conclusion on whether the Teacher of Righteousness was thought of as the prophet like Moses. Although that is a real possibility, the issue cannot at this point in time be settled. Perhaps texts yet to be published will remove our uncertainty.

—*Tg. Cant.* on 4:5: "Your two deliverers who are destined to deliver you, the Messiah the Son of David and the Messiah the son of Ephraim, are like Moses and Aaron..." (cf. *Tg. Lamen.* on 2:22).

Expectation of a Mosaic Messiah is abundantly attested in Jewish literature.[197]

The sources just cited, however, are all of uncertain or late date, and one may ask how early the Messiah donned his Mosaic dress.[198] At Qumran, Deut. 18:18 was understood to promise an eschatological prophet like Moses, a figure independent of the Messiahs of Aaron and Israel: so the one like Moses was not Messiah but another. Clearly the later rabbinic teaching was not always held by pre-Christian Jews looking for a Messiah.

J. Jeremias imagined that the several popular prophets mentioned by Josephus, the prophets with whom we have just finished, constitute "impressive testimony to the strength with which the idea that the Messiah would be a second Moses was anchored in popular expectation."[199] He simply assumed, without argument, and despite the silence of the sources, that those individuals considered themselves, or were considered by others to be, properly messianic. This begs the question. Josephus called the men "prophets." He did not use the word, "Messiah." In this connection one should recall that John the Baptist was dubbed a "prophet" (Matt. 11:9, etc.) and drew many people to the wilderness but was not, as far as we know, called by his contemporaries "Messiah." This is not to say that Jeremias must have been wrong. Matt. 24:23-26 does hint that some of the prophet pretenders may have been known as "Messiah:" "Then if any one says to you, 'Lo, here is the Christ!' or 'There he is!' do not believe it. For false Christs and false prophets will arise and show great signs and wonders, so as to lead astray, if possible, even the elect... . So, if they say to you, 'Lo, he is in the wilderness,' do not go out..." (cf. Mark 13:21-23). Moreover, Josephus reports that the so-called Egyptian sought to set himself up as a ruler or king (see p. 79). This is surely suggestive.

The one piece of clear evidence Jeremias could and did cite is *Tanhuma ʿEkeb* 7b: "How long do the days of the Messiah last? R. Akiba

---

[197]See further R. Bloch, "Moïse dans la tradition rabbinique," in *Moïse*, 149-61.

[198]The evidence from Samaritan sources concerning Taheb is too problematic to add anything but confusion; and in any case use of the title "Messiah" by Samaritans seems to have been quite a late development.

[199]*TDNT* 4:862.

said: Forty years. Just as the Israelites spent forty years in the wilderness, so will he [Messiah] draw them forth and cause them to go in the wilderness and will make them eat loaves and straw." The attribution of this to Akiba, were it correct, would supply evidence from the early second century. But is it correct? The accuracy of rabbinic attributions has become, in the light of recent critical inquiry, notorious.

A few remarks are in order before proceeding further. It is imprecise to refer, without qualification, to "Jewish messianic expectation." In the post-exilic period there were various Jewish groups holding variegated beliefs about the fullness of time. It has even been proposed that we should, in deference to the manifold facts, speak no longer of ancient "Judaism" but of "Judaisms." However that may be, "the Messiah" was not, before Christian times, a well-defined conception; and some groups even appear to have had little or no use for it. Hence one should not talk about what Jews in general, or of a particular period, thought about "the Messiah." If it is, notwithstanding comparatively abundant materials, extremely difficult to make generalizations just about the eschatological teachings of the Dead Sea Scrolls, how much more the fragmented, many-pieced puzzle known as "Judaism."

Another point to consider: while certain rabbinic texts explicitly compare Moses and the Messiah, there is a near dearth of earlier materials. Indeed, the (non-Christian) Jewish texts from the pre-Mishnaic period which refer to a Messiah or anointed one are few and far between. This may be a misleading fact, an unfortunate gap in our historical knowledge. Or we may have here a just proportion, instructing us that "the Messiah" was not of pressing import for many Jews, and that therefore relatively little thought, systematic or otherwise, was given to him.

We also do well to acknowledge that our modern rationalistic habits are likely to mislead us, just as they misled scholars earlier in this century, when so many pseudepigraphical texts, because thought incoherent, were mutilated by source criticism. Our quest for consistency and precision may demand too much of the extant documents, with their all-too-frequent eschatological vagaries, and we may often be attempting to bring order out of what was only chaos. It is unjustified to approach antique Jewish documents with the presupposition that behind each one was a systematic theologian. With respect to our immediate concerns, it might just have been the case that Jews who hoped for an anointed one did not much dwell on his character and functions or on his relationship to Moses or the prophet like Moses.

Having said that, and having given caution its due, there are perhaps reasons for supposing that, at least by the close of Matthew's century, some Jews expected a Messiah with Mosaic lineaments.[201] The first reason lies implicit in Acts 3:17-26:

> And now, brethren, I know that you acted in ignorance, as did also your rulers. But what God foretold by the mouth of all the prophets, that his Christ should suffer, he thus fulfilled. Repent therefore, and turn again, that your sins may be blotted out, that times of refreshing may come from the presence of the Lord, and that he may send the Christ appointed for you, Jesus, whom heaven must receive until the time for establishing all that God spoke by the mouth of his holy prophets from of old. Moses said, "The Lord your God will raise up for you a prophet from your brethren as he raised me up. You shall listen to him in whatever he tells you. And it shall be that every soul that does not listen to that prophet shall be destroyed from the people." And all the prophets who have spoken, from Samuel and those who came afterwards, also proclaimed these days. You are the sons of the prophets and of the covenant which God gave to your fathers, saying to Abraham, 'And in your posterity shall all the families of the earth be blessed.' God, having raised up his servant, sent him to you first, to bless you in turning every one of you from your wickedness.

In these words attributed to Peter, which are usually thought to depend upon old sources,[202] Jesus' status as the Messiah is upheld by appeal to Deut. 18:15-18. If—this is a big if—such an argument was ever made, as Acts supposes it was, by early Jewish Christians in an evangelistic or apologetical setting, would its force not have been empty without prior speculation that the prophet like Moses and the Messiah might be one and the same? In other words, does Acts 3 not presuppose that Peter's Jewish audience knew the oracle in Deuter-

---

[200]I pass by *T. Levi* 8:15, where the Messiah is "the prophet of the Most High." This may equate the Messiah with the prophet like Moses, but that is not a certainty. I also cannot put much weight upon Revelation 11, but it does give one pause. If the two figures there spoken of are not Elijah and Moses (as is usually assumed) or Enoch and Elijah (some have thought this) or Peter and Paul (so Johannes Munck) but rather Elijah and the prophet like Moses, then we could have here indirect evidence for the messianic interpretation of Deut. 18:15 and 18; for the two figures are identified with the two olive trees of Zechariah 4, a text which encouraged, if it did not engender, the expectation, attested in the Dead Sea Scrolls and the Testaments of the Twelve Patriarchs, of two anointed ones, one priestly, one Davidic. There is every reason to believe that Rev. 11:1(3)-13 largely reproduces a Jewish source, and in that source the two prophets need not have been forerunners.

[201]F. Hahn, "Das Problem alter christologischer Überlieferungen in der Apostelgeschichte unter besonderer Berücksichtigung von Act 3, 19-21," in *Les Actes des Apôtres: Tradition, rédaction, théologie*, ed. J. Kremer (BETL 48; Gembloux/Leuven: J. Duculot/Leuven, 1979), 129-54; also Zehnle, *Pentecost Discourse*.

onomy 18 and reckoned with the possibility of its messianic application?[203] If one were to come to Acts 3 fully persuaded that the prophet
like Moses and the Messiah were distinct figures, the argument would
collapse. Surely early Christian rhetoricians were not so foolish as to
add difficulty to difficulty: they already had more than enough
obstacles to overcome. Still, Acts 3:17-26 may not be what it purports
to be, that is, apologetic for non-Christian Jews, in which case my
inference would be nullified.

A second, and much more considerable reason for supposing a first-
century identification of the Messiah with the prophet like Moses emerges
from John's Gospel, which implies that while some Jews differentiated
between the Messiah and the prophet like Moses (see 1:20-21, 25; 7:40-43),
others, including the evangelist, did not. John 1:43-51 equates Jesus with
the prophet promised by Deut. 18:15 and 18 (v. 45, Philip to Nathanael: "we
have found him of whom Moses in the law ... wrote") and simultaneously
identifies him with the Messiah (v. 49, Nathanael to Jesus: "You are the
king of Israel;" cf. v. 41).[204] The same link holds in 6:14-15. After Jesus
multiplies bread, thus reproducing the miracle of the manna, the crowds,
alluding to Deut. 18:15-18, call him *the* prophet who is to come into the
world"—and then seek to make him "king" (= Messiah). Shortly thereafter Jesus is asked, "[W]hat sign do you do, that we may see, and believe
you? What work do you perform? Our fathers ate the manna in the
wilderness; as it is written, 'He gave them bread from heaven to eat'"
(6:30-31). According to this, Jesus, as Messiah and king of Israel, was
expected by outsiders to do what Moses did.[205]

Chapter 4 of John might also be relevant. Here the Samaritan
woman perceives Jesus to be a prophet (v. 19) and then wonders
whether he is not "Messiah" (v. 29—an unexpected expression for a
first-century Samaritan). Given that first-century Samaritans presumably looked for the fulfillment of Deut. 18:15 and 18 (see pp. 80-81) but
did not esteem the biblical prophets generally, may we not suppose
that John assumed that Samaritans identified their redeemer (Taheb)
with the prophet like Moses?[206] While we cannot answer with full

---

[202]The argument of B. Lindars, *New Testament Apologetic* (London: SCM, 1961), 207-
10, that "the implicit identification of Jesus with the Prophet in Acts does not mean a
theory of christology in terms of this figure," does not convince.

[203]Discussion see J. Louis Martyn, *History and Theology in the Fourth Gospel*, rev. ed.
(Nashville: Abingdon, 1979), 104-106.

[204]See further Martyn, ibid., 123-28.

[205]So Martyn, ibid., 120; cf. Oscar Cullmann, *The Christology of the New Testament* (2nd
ed.; Philadelphia: Westminster, 1963), 19. Further discussion in M. de Jonge, *Jesus:
Stranger from Heaven and Son of God* (Missoula: Scholars Press, 1977), 102-106.

conviction, the evidence from the Gospel as a whole, if taken to reflect a dialogue with the Judaism of John's day, does suffice for Martyn's conclusion: "In the theological treasury of the Jewish community in John's city was the hope for the Mosaic prophet. Alongside it, or developing from it, was the expectation of the Mosaic Prophet-Messiah."[206]

Aside from when the expectation of a Mosaic Messiah first arose, what was its probable cause? The eschatological redemption, as we shall have occasion to see, came to be imagined as another exodus. But to contemplate the exodus was also to reckon with Moses: the two were inextricably intertwined. So to think of the one was to think of the other; and therefore the further one carried the eschatological exodus theme, the more inescapable thought of another Moses would have become. Put simply, to bring the exodus complex into connection with eschatology was to bring eschatology very near to Moses. Deutero-Isaiah, with its recurrent exodus theme, is probable evidence for this, for the servant, who exhibits eschatological features, has a Mosaic mien. Later on, this may not have gone unnoticed; and we should not forget the fact that the servant songs were sometimes given a messianic interpretation.[207] Above all, however, Moses was a deliverer or redeemer: he broke the Egyptian bondage. So too the Messiah: he would liberate Israel from all foreign oppression (cf. the *Psalms of Solomon*). In all likelihood, then, the common theme of deliverance forged the linkage of Messiah and Moses, as indeed the rabbinic formula indicates: "as the first *redeemer* was, so shall the latter *redeemer* be."[208]

---

[206]Martyn, *History*, 117.

[207]H. Hegermann, *Jesaja 53 in Hexapla, Targum und Peschita* (Gütersloh: Bertelsmann, 1954); also S. H. T. Page, "The Suffering Servant beteen the Testaments," *NTS* 31 (1985):481-497.

[208]Scripture may also have stimulated such thought. (i) Ps. 105:15 = 1 Chron. 16:22 sets "anointed ones" and "prophets" in parallel. (ii) The "he" of Deut. 33:5 ("thus he became king in Jeshurum") is usually equated with God (so RSV) or Moses (e.g. the *Fragment Targums*); but *Pseudo-Jonathan* on Deut. 35:5 has "and there will be a king from the house of Jacob." Would some not have been aware that the one clause was applied by some to Moses, by others to the Messiah? (iii) Moses is called "the man" in Deut. 33:1 and elsewhere (see n. 69), and he was so remembered by the Samaritans. But "the man" also had messianic associations: LXX Num. 24:17; Zech. 6:12; *T. Jud.* 24:1; John 19:5; see further W. Horbury, "The Messianic Associations of 'The Son of Man,'" *JTS* 36 (1985):34-55.

CONCLUDING OBSERVATIONS

Although the pertinent material is not exhausted,[209] I shall at this point cease cataloging Jewish figures who were likened to Moses. What has been learned? Several results merit pondering. (i) To begin with, Moses served as a well-used type because he was many things, an occupier of several offices. Joshua and Josiah were likened to Moses because they, like he, were leaders or kings. Gideon and the Messiah became Mosaic because of their character as saviors or deliverers. Ezra, Ezekiel, and Hillel had the lawgiver as their type because they were teachers or revealers. And Jeremiah and the servant of Deutero-Isaiah naturally came to be stamped with Mosaic features because they were intercessors and suffering prophets. When evaluating the First Gospel it will prove prudent to recall that the Matthean Jesus is leader and king, savior and deliverer, teacher and revealer, and intercessor and suffering prophet all at once. Would it not therefore be simplistic to suppose that the extensive parallelism hereafter to be

---

[209]There is an embarrassment of riches. The late Abraham traditions show assimilation to the Moses traditions, a subject worthy of extended investigation. For the stories of Abraham's infancy, so reminiscent of Exodus 1-2, see Ginzberg, *Legends*, 1:186-93, and the notes to these pages in volume 5; also C. Perrot, "Les récits d'enfance dans la haggada antérieure au II siècle de notre ère," *RSR* 55 (1967):485-88. In *Apoc. Abr.* 12:l, Abraham fasts forty days and nights on Horeb. According to several sources Abraham's face was transfigured by light (cf. p. 246). *Mek.* on Exod. 17:14 relates that God showed Abraham the holy land just as he showed it to Moses. For the tradition of Abraham's refusal to die and its secondary character *vis-à-vis* the similar tradition about Moses see n. 143. Additional parallels between Moses and Abraham may be found in Ginzberg, *Legends*, 6:47. Note that Acts 7:7 moves Exod. 3:12 to the story of Abraham. Already the Bible itself may liken Abraham to Moses, or liken his experience to that of the exodus; cf. Fishbane, *Interpretation*, 375-76; also U. Cassuto, *A Commentary on the Book of Genesis*, 2 vols. (Jerusalem: Magnes, 1961, 1964), 2:334-35. The patriarch—a prophet according to Gen. 20:7—went to Egypt. After his wife was taken by Pharaoh, a plague came against the king and his household, after which Abraham and Sarah were permitted to leave. See further J. Weingreen, "'*hws' tyk* in Genesis 15:7," in *Words and Meanings*, ed. P. R. Ackroyd and B. Lindars (Cambridge: University Press, 1968), 209-15. Aaron's death in Num 20:22-29 appears to be modelled upon that of Moses (see the commentaries). There may be a weak Moses typology in 1 Maccabees: Judas' order in 3:55 parallels that of Moses in Exod. 18:25, his encouragement of his men in 4:9 includes remembrance of God's victory at the Red Sea, and his request of Ephron in 5:48, "Let us pass through your land to get to our land. No one will do you harm; we will simply pass by on foot," recalls Moses' request in Num. 20:14-21; cf. also 1 Macc. 5:45 with Exod. 12:37-42. Just as Christian tradition has constantly sought and found and created parallels between Jesus Christ and the saints, so too has Judaism assimilated many of its heroes to Moses. Examples are interminable. For Sabbatai Sevi see below, p. 272, n. 3. —Lest I be accused of never meeting a Moses typology I did not like, I record my verdict that G. S. Ogden, "Moses and Cyrus," *VT* 28 (1978):195-203, is mistaken in proposing that Deutero-Isaiah implicitly likens Cyrus to Moses.

observed between Jesus and Moses is nothing more than the expected correlation between the Messiah and Moses,[210] or merely the fruit of the fulfillment of Deut. 18:15 and 18? Certainly such considerations do not suffice to explain the Jewish materials. Moses was a multifaceted figure with rich associations, and Matthew's motives for assimilating his hero to such a one may have been, or rather probably were, multiple.[211]

(ii) Next, most of the Jewish texts reviewed do not make explicit the typological relationship between type and antitype. *4 Ezra* 14 is here the exception. The usual method in narrative is to recount events reminiscent of passages in Exodus or Deuteronomy and to use key words or phrases taken therefrom. In this connection Egypt and the exodus and Moses may sometimes be mentioned, but most of the typological features remain covert and so the reader is expected to perform what has been called "subreading." We are a great distance from the pedagogical method found in Melito of Sardis, who, in his *Peri Pascha*, explained the meaning of every type and antitype in detail. The Jewish sources, by contrast, tend to assume a far-reaching knowledge of Scripture or tradition and so leave it to us to descry the implicit: there is no exhibition of the obvious. What one commentator has said of Deutero-Isaiah in particular seems to hold equally for the other Jewish sources we have examined: "throughout his whole work… [he] is concerned with the Mosaic tradition, though nowhere does he make any direct quotation from the Pentateuch. He seems to take for granted that his hearers know the traditions as well as he does."[212] While the pervasion of our sources by the implicit is a stubborn fact which makes contemporary interpretation difficult, it is useless to complain about improbable literary complexity or subtly encoded messages. Why expect an ancient Jew to have floated everything with meaning to the surface of his text, so that its contents should be as visible to us, bad readers with poor memories, as to those who shared his small literary canon and memorization skills? We, who are temporally estranged from the biblical writers, must not confuse our eyes and ears with the eyes and ears of those who first read, let us say, Isaiah or Matthew. If there is always the danger of thinking we can see the grass grow, that is, of overinterpreting texts, we must equally beware

---

[210]This is all the more true as the evidence that the Messiah was Mosaic by Matthew's time is, if adequate, still meager.

[211]Contrast the impression left by Davies and Allison, *Matthew* 2:296-97.

[212]G. A. F. Knight, *Isaiah 40-55* (Edinburgh: Handsel, 1984), 12.

of underinterpreting texts. Much of what was once unconcealed has become, with time's passage, hidden. That is why there are historians: they recover what has been lost. Even so, an adult learner of a second language never quite catches all the nuances; and such are we. I think T. L. Donaldson, when discounting a Sinai background for Matt. 5:1-2, misses the mark with his comment that "an allusion to Moses and Sinai [in Matt. 5:1-2] could easily have been made more explicit, if this had been Matthew's intention."[213] That is true. But it is also well-nigh irrelevant. As the preceding pages have abundantly shown, the same objection, which is in effect an attack against the imagination in reading, could be lodged against almost all of the Moses typologies in the Jewish Bible. For in ancient Jewish narratives typology consists, as a general rule, of references that are almost always implicit. Said allusions could regularly have been made less cryptic—as Jesus' parables could have come with neat explanations. That, however, would have deprived the informed Jewish imagination of its native function, and to what end? Why demand the superfluous? Allusiveness is in the eye of the beholder.

(iii) Another result of our investigation is this: comparison with Moses, in the texts so far examined, serves to exalt a man and make him like the ideal king, savior, prophet, lawgiver, or intercessor. It is true that Gideon, in the end, proves to be an ambiguous figure, and likewise true that Jeremiah sees Moses' work undone. Yet the point stands, and it is relevant for New Testament exegesis. Early Christian texts which liken Jesus to Moses are often, as a matter of course, taken to exalt the former at the expense of the latter. Sometimes such interpretation is justified. In John 6 Moses undeniably suffers by comparison with Jesus, and in 2 Corinthians 6 he suffers by comparison with Paul. But does he always suffer so? What about Matthew 2, or Acts 7? Was it not possible, Moses' stature being what it was— "Whom can we find greater and more honored than Moses? (*Mek.* on Exod. 13:19)—for glory to pass from him to Jesus, and possible that the parallels between the two were not always there for the sake of the differences? Moses was a colossus. Should we not then entertain the possibility that comparison of Jesus with such a one was sometimes in continuity with the Jewish texts we have reviewed, that is, that such comparison sometimes honored Jesus, even though he was held to be Messiah, Lord, and Son of God? The Chronicler may well have

---

[213]Donaldson, *Mountain*, 113. P. Nepper-Christensen's entire discussion of typology in Matthew is marred by his incessant demand for the explicit: *Das Matthäusevangelium: ein judenchristliches Evangelium?* (Aarhus: Universitetsforlaget, 1958).

implied the supremacy of David to Moses, and yet his modeling of the former upon the latter served to exalt David, not to shorn Moses of his former glory: the lawgiver remained of pious memory.[214]

(iv) The parallels between Moses and later figures and between the exodus and subsequent events always appear amidst multitudinous differences, and there is always matter—much matter—extraneous to a typology. This should come as no surprise. Typology is not the gray uniformity of events. Apart from the fact that typology does not so much generate traditions as superimpose itself upon them, history, with its vicissitudes and labyrinths, does not precisely repeat itself, a circumstance understood no less by our ancestors than by us. Hence whatever resemblances may obtain between two narratives, we never behold mirror images. It is accordingly invalid, despite common custom, to dismiss a typology solely on the grounds that type and antitype are dissimilar. Consider P. Nepper-Christensen's case against a typological correspondence between Matt. 2:20 and Exod. 4:19: Moses fled from Egypt, Jesus to Egypt; Moses was an adult when he escaped, Jesus a child; Moses himself decided to flee, and whereto, while Joseph, Jesus' father, followed the instructions of an angel.[215] This sort of argument entirely fails to establish what it purports to establish, the reason being that, carried to its logical conclusion, it would establish the elimination of all typologies. Because no two events or narratives are alike in every particular, one can always observe differences. The truth is, typology requires only a few signifi-cant points of agreement (Matthew 2 certainly satisfies on that score), not perfect *mimesis* or one-to-one correspondence. Here I may call upon Chrysostom: "The type must not have nothing in common with the antitype, for then there would be nothing typical. Nor on the other hand must it [the type] be identical with the other [the antitype], or it would be the reality itself" (PG 51:248).[216] Nepper-Christensen might

---

[214]The "greater than Moses" theme (cf. *Mart. Isa.* 3:6-10—an accusation against Isaiah; *Yalkut Shimeoni* to Isa. 52:13—of the Messiah) has not really appeared in the preceding pages. We may suspect that the Enoch traditions, which eventually enthroned Enoch in heaven, evolved in constant competition with the Moses traditions; but this had little or nothing to do with typology (although note Nickelsburg, *Literature*, 151; he posits a testament behind portions of *1 Enoch* that was modeled on the end of Deuteronomy). — Sometimes in later Christian tradition Joshua, who made the sun stand still, is a greater miracle worker than Moses (e.g. George Hamartolus, in PG 110:193-94); but that has as its explanation Joshua's typological equation with his namesake, Jesus.

[215]*Das Matthäusevangelium*, 165.

[216]Cf., in quite a different context, the words of Petrarch: "A proper imitator should take care that what he writes resembles the original without reproducing it" (*Fam.* 23:19).

just as well have urged that there can be no typological correlation between Joshua 3 and Exodus 14 because while under Moses the Israelites were entering the desert, under Joshua they were exiting it; and whereas in the one case Israel crossed the Red Sea, the other time she passed over the Jordan; and if, at the time of Moses, Israel moved with an army waxing hot at her heels, in Joshua's time she was at leisure. Such an argument would, of course, be hopeless: the book of Joshua more than once makes the typological equation explicit. But if such an argument is void of substance in Joshua, what force should be reckoned to Nepper-Christensen's short catalogue of differences between Exodus 4 and Matthew 2, or to T. L. Donaldson's true but indecisive comment, that "the parallel between [Matt.] 5.1 and Ex 19-20 or Ex 34 is by no means exact"?[217] In my judgement, none whatsoever.[218]

(v) Finally, the many Jewish texts I have cited were written at various times and span more than a millennium. But it should be kept in mind that I have focused firstly on the Moses typologies in the Jewish Bible, and that all the books in that collection were known to Matthew. It follows that not only did Jewish tradition supply precedent for Matthew's execution of a Moses typology, but such precedent was to hand in documents the evangelist studied, treasured, and probably knew by heart.

---

[217]*Jesus on the Mountain: A Study in Matthean Theology* (JSNTSS 8; Sheffield: JSOT, 1985), 113. He continues: "In Exodus, Moses ascends the mountain alone to receive the Torah from Yahweh, and then descends to communicate it to the people." But one can always complain that parallelism could be more exact.

[218]The typologies in the miracle stories of Gregory the Great's *Dialogues* usually display important differences between type and antitype, as Gregory himself on occasion noted (e.g. *Dial.* 3:37). For discussion see J. M. Petersen, *The "Dialogues" of Gregory the Great in their Late Antique Cultural Background* (Rome: Pontifical Institute of Mediaeval Studies, 1984), 29-32.

Three _____

CHRISTIAN FIGURES

INTRODUCTION

In Matthew, as in Luke, traditions about John the Baptist and Jesus have been reworked so as to increase their resemblance to each other;[1] and in Acts, narratives about both Stephen and Paul strongly recall narratives about Jesus in Luke.[2] In ancient martyrological literature, moreover, heroes and their circumstances often mimic Jesus in his passion. Clearly the assimilation of saints to Jesus, that is, the use of Jesus as a type, was common in early Christianity.[3] No less common, however, was the custom of comparing or assimilating Jesus (as antitype) to ancient Jewish worthies (his types).[4] In Q material, for instance, Jesus compares himself with both Jonah and Solomon (Luke 11:30-32 par.). And in Mark and Luke the savior performs deeds which mimic those of Elijah and Elisha.[5] In 1 Cor. 15:42-49, Jesus is the last Adam (cf. Rom. 5:12-21), while in Hebrews he is likened to Melchizedek (chapters 5-7). But of all the Jewish figures with whom Jesus is implicitly or explicitly compared in Christian literature of the first few centuries, Moses, both in terms of frequency and significance, holds pride of place. The pertinent material is in fact so copious that herein all I can do is offer the essential facts in minimum compass.

[1]W. D. Davies and Dale C. Allison, Jr., *A Critical and Exegetical Commentary on the Gospel according to Matthew* (ICC; Edinburgh: T& T Clark, 1988, 1991) 1:289-90; 2:475-76; Charles H. Talbert, *Literary Patterns, Theological Themes, and the Genre of Luke-Acts* (Missoula: Scholars Press, 1974), 44-48; below, pp. 137-38.

[2]Talbert, ibid., 15-23; Gerd Lüdemann, *Early Christianity according to the Traditions in Acts* (Philadelphia: Fortress, 1989), 90-92.

[3]Useful here is Peter Brown, "The Saint as Exemplar in Antiquity," in *Saints and Virtues*, ed. John Stratton Hawley (Berkeley: University of California, 1987), 3-14.

[4]Cf. David Daube, *The New Testament and Rabbinic Judaism* (London: Athlone, 1956), 3-26, and R. T. France, *Jesus and the Old Testament* (London: Tyndale, 1971), 38-82.

[5]See the commentaries on Mark 1:16-20 par.; 6:32-44 par.; Luke 4:25-27; 7:11-17; also Raymond E. Brown, "Jesus and Elisha," *Perspective* 12 (1971):85-104, and Martyn, "We have found Elijah."

JESUS

Whether Jesus, as some have supposed of Jeremiah, ever likened himself to Moses, or whether he intimated that he was either the eschatological prophet of Deut. 18:15, 18 or one of several prophets like Moses, is, although uncertain, far from unthinkable.[6] He did, it appears, claim to cast out demons by "the finger of God," by which "finger" Moses likewise performed his miracles.[7] Jesus further, maybe in imitation of the lawgiver, who elected the twelve phylarchs, chose twelve men for evangelistic ministry, and he probably set his word beside that of Moses as an equal or perhaps greater authority (Matt. 5:21-48).[8] He is even purported to have retired into the wilderness, there to perform a feeding miracle, one strongly reminiscent of Moses' provision of manna.[9] Without pursuing further what the historical Jesus made himself out to be, a vexed subject on which we are not permitted to know enough, it is unquestionable that early Christians regularly compared Jesus and Moses. In addition to the aforementioned items from the Jesus tradition, evidence is supplied by the speeches of Acts 3 and 7, speeches which probably preserve pieces of old Christian apologetic.[10] In these two speeches Jesus is the prophet

[6]Cf. C. Chavasse, "Jesus: Christ and Moses," *Theology* 54 (1951):244-50, 289-96. Undecided is A. Descamps, "Moïse dans les évangiles et dans la tradition apostolique," in *Moïse*, 178. For demurral see J. Coppens, *Le Messianisme et sa Relève prophétique* (BETL 34; Gembloux: Duculot, 1974), 179-80.

[7]Luke 11:20; Exod. 8:15; see T. W. Manson, *The Teaching of Jesus* (Cambridge: University Press, 1935), 82-83. Eusebius, *Dem. ev.* 3:2, wrote: "And in Exodus: 'The magicians therefore said to Pharaoh, It is the finger of God.' In like manner Jesus, the Christ of God, said to the Pharisees: 'If I by the finger of God cast out devils.'" Cf. Augustine, *Civ. Dei* 16:43: Jesus "is called in the gospel the Finger of God because He recalls to our remembrance the things done before by way of types." Instead of "finger of God" Matt. 12:28 has "the Spirit of God," which is probably secondary; see below, p. 237. Curiously enough, Matt. 12:28 = Luke 11:20 is followed by mention of the "strong man," a phrase which is often taken to derive from Isa. 49:24, whose context concerns a new exodus.

[8]Cf. Luz, *Matthew* 1:279, accepting the authenticity of the so-called "antithetical" formulations in 5:21-2 and 27-28.

[9]For the possibility of an historical event behind the various feeding accounts see Ernst Bammel, "The Feeding of the Multitude," in *Jesus and the Politics of His Day*, ed. Ernst Bammel and C. F. D. Moule (Cambridge: University Press, 1984), 211-40.

[10]Although some would now assign the Moses typology in Acts 7 to Luke himself. For traditions in Acts 3 see p. 88, n. 201. For Acts 7 see Charles H. H. Scobie, "The Use of Source Material in the Speeches of Acts III and VII," *NTS* 25 (1979):399-421; Zehnle, *Discourse*, 75-89. The recent tendency, altogether justified, to attribute to Lukan redaction more and more in the speeches of Acts, goes too far when it denies that Acts 3 and 7 were based on pre-Lukan speeches.

like Moses (3:22; 7:37), he bears Mosaic titles,[11] and his experience is parallel to that of Moses: both worked miracles and were rejected by Israel (7:35-40).

The conviction that Jesus was like Moses, and indeed the eschatological fulfillment of Deut. 18:15 and 18, was not just part of Christian proclamation: it also helped shape portions of the Jesus tradition during its oral stage. The traditions behind Matthew 1-2, to be reviewed in the next chapter, told the tale of Jesus' infancy as though it were the tale of Moses.[12] A Moses typology also informed the story of Jesus' transfiguration, with its many parallels to Exodus 24 and 34 (see pp. 243-48); and the pre-Matthean complex now preserved, with additions, in Matt. 11:25-30, was, as we shall determine later, largely put together in order to compare and contrast the Son of God and the lawgiver. Another example: although the synoptic stories of Jesus feeding five thousand and then four thousand share few significant verbal links with the pentateuchal miracle of the manna, John 6, where Jesus plainly relates his miracle to that of olden times, suggests that the connection was obvious to many.[13]

When we move from stage II of the Jesus tradition (the stage between Jesus and the evangelists) to stage III, we continue to encounter Moses. While Mark did not obviously increase the semblances between the first redeemer and the last, Matthew, as I shall read the facts, certainly did. So did Luke. Even if one does not concur (I have my doubts) that Luke's central section (9:51-19:44) is a Christian Deuteronomy,[14] the remarkable parallels throughout Luke-Acts between Jesus and Moses, an abridgement of which follows, are plain enough:[15]

Moses	Jesus
Moses determined to "visit"	In Jesus God "visited"

---

[11](i) 3:15: *archēgos*, cf. 7:35, citing Exod. 2:14; (ii) 3:14: *dikaios*, cf. Acts 7:35; (iii) 3:13, 26: *pais*, see p. 121, n. 56; (iv) 3:14: *hagios*, a possible Mosaic background for which is urged by Zehnle, ibid., 51-52.

[12]For the argument, not to my mind entirely persuasive, that assimilation to Moses was also a factor in the development of the Lukan infancy traditions, see Roger D. Aus, *Weihnachtsgeschichte, Barmherziger Samariter, Verlornener Sohn* (Berlin: Institut Kirche und Judentum, 1988), 11-58.

[13]See further below, pp. 238-42. For the proposal that lists of Jesus' miracles functioned in early Christianity to vindicate Jesus' status as the eschatological prophet like Moses see Frankfurter, "Miracle List Tradition," 344-76.

[14]Originally forwarded by Evans, "Central Section," and now defended at length by D. P. Moessner, *The Lord of the Banquet: The Literary and Theological Significance of the Lukan Travel Narrative* (Minneapolis: Fortress, 1989).

[15]Cf. R. T. O'Toole, "The Parallels between Jesus and Moses," *BTB* 20 (1990):22-29; also J. Mánek, "The New Exodus in the Books of Luke," *NovT* 2 (1955):8-23.

(*episepsasthai*) his people,
Acts 7:23

(*epeskepsato*) the people of
Israel, Luke 1:68; 7:16

Moses was "instructed"
(*epaideuthē*) in all the
"wisdom" (*sophia*) of the
Egyptians, Acts 7:22

Jesus the *paidion* grew in
"wisdom" (*sophia*), Luke
2:40, 52

Moses was transfigured on a
mountain as God spoke from
a cloud, Exodus 24, 34

Jesus was transfigured on a
mountain as God spoke from
a cloud, Luke 9:28-36

Moses led the *exodus* from
Egypt, Exod. 19:1, etc.

Jesus experienced an *exodus*,
Luke 9:31[16]

Moses belonged a generation
that was "perverse"
(*diestrammenē*) and "without
faith" (*ouk estin pistis*),
Deut. 32:5, 20

Jesus belonged to a generation
that was "perverse"
(*diestrammenē*) and "without
faith" (*apistos*), Luke 9:41

Moses chose seventy men to
"share the burden of the
people" (Num. 11:16-17,24-25)

Jesus chose seventy men to
go before him in missionary
activity (Luke 10:1-17; cf.
Eusebius, *Dem. ev.* 3:2; but
the correct reading may be
"seventy-two")

Moses was "sent" (*aposteilō*)
by God, Acts 7:34-35

Jesus was sent by God (*ton
aposteilanta me*), Luke 10:16

Moses did his miracles by "the
finger of God," Exod. 8:19

Jesus cast out demons by "the
finger of God," Luke 11:20

Pharaoh spoke to Moses and Aaron:
"Why do you take the people

Jesus' opponents accused him,
saying, "We found this man

---

[16]On how Luke conceived of Jesus' "exodus" see Susan R. Garrett, "Exodus from
Bondage: Luke 9:31 and Acts 12:1-24," *CBQ* 52 (1990):656-80. Garrett reviews the
opinions of others and then argues that Jesus led his people out of bondage to Satan.

away (*diastrephete*) from their work," Exod. 5:4

perverting (*diastrephonta*) our nation," Luke 23:2

Moses was the "redeemer," Acts 7:35 (*lutrōtēn*)

Jesus came to "redeem" (*lutrousthai*) Israel, Luke 24:21

"These are the words that Moses spoke to all Israel beyond the Jordan…", Deut. 1:1

"These are my words which I spoke to you, while I was still with you, that everything written about me in the law of Moses and the prophets and the psalms must be fulfilled," Luke 24:44

Forty years passed between the exodus from Egypt and Moses' death, after which Israel entered the promised land, Deut. 29:5, etc.

Forty days passed between Jesus' exodus in Jerusalem and his departure, which inaugurated the new age of the church, Acts 1:3

Moses did "wonders and signs" (*terata kai sēmeia*), Acts 7:36

Jesus did "signs and wonders" (*sēmeia kai terata*), Luke 2:22; 4:30

Moses was "denied" (*ērnēsanto*) by his own people, Acts 7:35

Jesus was "denied" (*ērnēsasthe*) by his own people, Acts 3:13-14

Moses was *archōn* and *dikastēs*, Acts 7:27, 35

Jesus was *dikaios* and *archēgos*, Acts 3:14-15

Moses said: "The Lord your God will raise up for you a prophet like me from among your brethren," Deut. 18:15

Peter said: "Moses said: 'The Lord your God will raise up for you a prophet like me from among your brethren;'" that prophet is Jesus, Acts 7:37-38

Comment is needless: the columns speak for themselves.

Turning from the synoptics to John, more than one writer has emphasized the many exodus and Mosaic motifs in this last.[17] Jesus is

---

[17]For a brief survey of research see Robert Kysar, *The Fourth Evangelist and His Gospel* (Minneapolis: Augsburg, 1975), 137-44.

"the lamb of God" (1:29),[18] a passover victim, killed at the hour of the paschal slaughter (19:14). Like the paschal sacrifice he pours out his blood (19:34), although no bone is broken (19:33, 36; cf. Exod. 12:46; Num. 9:12); and he is, unrealistically, sprinkled with vinegar "on hyssop" (19:29; cf. Exod. 12:22). Jesus is also typologically equated with the gifts Israel received in the wilderness: he is manna, water, and guiding light; for in chapter 6 the Johannine Son of God is the bread from heaven, in chapter 7 the living water, and in chapter 8 the light of the world.[19] Even more, however, is Jesus, who is the true shepherd (10:1-18) and king of Israel (1:49, etc.), Mosaic, as well as—the polemical edge is undeniable—more than Mosaic. "The law was given through Moses, grace and truth through Jesus Christ" (1:17). "No one [not even Moses in Exodus 33] has ever seen God; the only Son, who is in the bosom of the Father, he has made him known" (1:18). "Moses in the law wrote" of a coming prophet (Deut. 18:15, 18), and Jesus, as even the crowd recognizes (6:14-15), is that "prophet who is to come into the world" (1:45; cf. 5:46; 7:40).[20] "As Moses lifted up the serpent in the wilderness, so must the Son of man be lifted up" (3:14). "It was not Moses who gave you bread from heaven. For the bread of God is that which comes down from heaven, and gives life to the world" (6:32-33). If Moses, according to LXX Num. 16:28, said, "By this will you know that (gnōsesthe hoti) the Lord has sent me to perform all these works, that not of myself (ap emautou) have I done them," then Jesus similarly said: "When you have lifted up the Son of man, then you will know that (gnōsesthe hoti) I am he, and that I do nothing of myself (ap emautou) but speak as the Father thus taught me" (8:28-29; cf. 7:16-17; 14:10).[21]

The likening of Jesus to Moses is encountered much less frequently when one leaves the canonical Gospels and Acts to look at the remainder of the New Testament. This is in part because that remainder is dominated by Paul, and in his extant correspondence Jesus is not presented as the prophet like Moses. It is true that the apostle to the

[18]For the probable paschal background of this expression see Raymond E. Brown, *The Gospel according to John (i-xii)* (AB 29; Garden City: Doubleday, 1966), 58-63.

[19]See Glasson, *Moses*, 60-64. The manna, water from the rock, and the fiery pillar are grouped together in Neh. 9:12, 15; and Ps. 105:39-41.

[20]Echoes of Deut. 18:15-18 may be found in 12:49-50; 14:10; and 17:8. The interesting case that Johannine Christology developed in four major stages, the first of which identified Jesus with the prophet like Moses, is made by M.-E. Boismard, *Moise ou Jesus. Essai de christologie johannique* (BETL 84; Leuven: Leuven University, 1988).

[21]For the evidence that John's farewell discourses are structurally and thematically reflective of Deuteronomy, a collection of Moses' closing addresses, see Aelred Lacomara, "Deuteronomy and the Farewell Discourse (Jn 13:31-16:33)," *CBQ* 36 (1974):65-84.

Gentiles thought of the Christian dispensation as a new exodus (1 Cor. 10:1-4), and also true that he could speak of being *ennomos Christou* and refer to the *nomos Christou*, expressions which, for a former Pharisee, could not but have recalled analogous phrases formulated with *Mouseōs* (see p. 187). But given that Paul's polemical defense of justification by faith involved sharp contrasts between the old and the new, and given further that some of Paul's opponents may very well have likened not only Jesus but themselves to the lawgiver,[22] the ranking of Jesus beside Moses would have been counterproductive. In addition, Paul had his reasons, if I may here anticipate, for comparing not Jesus' ministry but his own with that of Moses (see pp. 109-12).

Hebrews is another story. Chapter 3 commences with this:

> Therefore, holy brethren, who share in a heavenly call, consider Jesus, the apostle and high priest of our confession. He was faithful to him who appointed him, just as Moses also was faithful in God's house. Yet Jesus has been counted worthy of as much more glory than Moses as the builder of a house has more honor than the house. (For every house is built by some one, but the builder of all things is God.) Now Moses was faithful in all God's house as a servant, to testify to the things that were to be spoken later, but Christ was faithful over God's house as a son.

For us the exegetical conundrums of these verses are subsidiary.[23] All that matters is the two-fold comparison: Jesus is like Moses, Jesus is greater than Moses. Such comparison also appears in 8:5-7, where Jesus mediates a new covenant. And there may well be implicit parallelism elsewhere. 13:20-21 contains this benediction: "Now may the God of peace who brought again from the dead our Lord Jesus, the great shepherd of the sheep, by the blood of the eternal covenant, equip you with everything good that you may do his will...". Westcott commented: "The old commentators saw rightly in the words here a reference to Is. lxiii. ll (LXX.) *pou ho anabibasas ek tēs thalassēs ton poimena tōn probatōn;* The work of Moses was a shadow of that of Christ: the leading up of him with his people out of the sea was a shadow of Christ's ascent from the grave."[24]

1 Peter and Revelation also fall to be considered. In 1 Pet. 1:13-20 and 2:1-10, "all the themes of the Exodus," to quote Jean Daniélou, "reappear:" the "girding of the loins ([Exod.] 12:ll), the rejection of the

[22]Dieter Georgi, *The Opponents of Paul in Second Corinthians* (Philadelphia: Fortress, 1976).

[23]See Mary Rose D'Angelo, *Moses in the Letter to the Hebrews* (SBLDS 42; Missoula: Scholars Press, 1979)—an unjustly neglected contribution.

[24]B. F. Westcott, *The Epistle to the Hebrews* (Grand Rapids: Eerdmans, 1973), 448.

flesh pots of Egypt (16:3), the dwelling in the desert among the heathen, the feedom from bondage (15:13),[25] the blood of the Lamb without spot or blemish (12:5), the rock of living water," as also "the people of God designated as a 'priestly kingdom, a holy nation, an acquired possession' (19:5-6; Isa 43:20)." With respect to Revelation, "the whole story is," to quote Daniélou again, "dominated by the sacrifice of the Lamb," and the church is represented by the twelve tribes (7:4-8) "while their deliverance is explicitly compared to the crossing of the Red Sea..." (see 15:2-3: standing by a sea of glass the victorious sing the song of Moses). Beyond that, the signs of Sinai appear—the noise of trumpets (8:7) and thunders and lightnings (8:5)—and the punishments repeat the plagues of Egypt: hail (8:7), the sea turned into blood (8:8; 16:3), darkness (8:12; 16:10), locusts (9:3). We have here "an Apocalyptic version of the Exodus... ."[26]

When we pass from the New Testament to Christian literature of the second, third, and later centuries, there are many texts which represent Jesus as the fulfillment of Deut. 18:15 and 18,[27] and the use of Moses as a type for Jesus continues (although he is eventually superseded by Joshua, Jesus' namesake).[28] As an exhaustive review of the mass of evidence would cover too many pages with only repetitive results, suffice it to cite merely seven representative texts:

> *Sib. Orac.* 8:251-54: "Moses prefigured him [Christ], stretching out his holy arms, conquering Amalek by faith so that the people might know that he is elect and precious with God his father..."[29]

> *Acts of Pilate* 5:1: "Nicodemus said: '...This man does many signs and wonders, which no one has done nor will do. Let him alone and contrive no evil against him. If the signs which he does are from God, they will

---

[25]There is here a footnote: "The word used to indicate this feedom is *lytroō* which is the same as that in Exodus 15:13 when speaking of the liberation. E. G. Selwyn (*The First Epistle of St. Peter*, London, 1947) remarks: 'It is reasonable to see here a reference to Christian baptism as a new Exodus' (p. 144)."

[26]See *From Shadow to Reality* (London: Burnes & Oates, 1960), 163-165. —Cf. *Apoc. Abr.* 30-31, where God's eschatological wrath takes the form of ten plagues.

[27]A sampling: Clement of Alexandria, *Paed.* 1:7; *Ps.-Clem.Rec.* 1:36, 40, 43, 56, 57; Origen, *Exod. Hom.* 12:3;Eusebius, *Dem. ev.* 3:2; 9:11; *Apost. Const.* 5:20; Athanasius, *Ep. Fest.* 14:4; idem, *Ar.* 1:13(55); Novatian, *De trin.* 9; Lactantius, *Div. inst.* 4:17. Cf. Julian, *Adv. Galil.* 253c.

[28]There is much useful material in Daniélou, *ibid.*, part IV, and in H. J. Schoeps, *Theologie und Geschichte des Judenchristentums* (Tübingen: J. C. B. Mohr (Paul Siebeck), 1949), 87-116.

[29]This comparison is frequent in patristic texts; cf. *Barn.* 12:2; Justin, *Dial.* 97; 111; 112; Tertullian, *Adv. Marc.* 3:18; Cyprian, *Exh. mart.* 8; *Test. II* 20-22; Augustine, *C. Faust.* 12:30; Aphraates, *Dem. 21,* 10.

stand; if they are from men, they will come to nothing (Acts 5:38f.). For
Moses also, when he was sent by God into Egypt, did many signs which
God commanded him to do before Pharaoh, king of Egypt. And there
were there servants of Pharaoh, Jannes and Jambres, and they also did
signs not a few which Moses did, and the Egyptians held them as gods,
Jannes and Jambres. And since the signs which they did were not from
God, they perished themselves and those who believed them. And now
let this man go, for he does not deserve death.'"

Eusebius, *Dem. ev.* 3:2: "Moses was the first leader of the Jewish race. He
found them attached to the deceitful polytheism of Egypt, and was the
first to turn them from it, by enacting the severest punishment for
idolatry. He was the first also to publish the theology of the one God,
bidding them worship only the Creator and Maker of all things. He was
the first to draw up for the same hearers a scheme of religious life, and
is acknowledged to have been the first and only lawgiver of their
religious polity. But Jesus Christ too, like Moses, only on a grander
stage, was the first to originate the teaching according to holiness for the
other nations, and first accomplished the rout of the idolatry that
embraced the whole world. He was the first to introduce to all men the
knowledge and religion of the one Almighty God. And He is proved to
be the first Author and Lawgiver of a new life and of a system adapted
to the holy."[30]

Ps. Clem. Rec. 1:57: "John showed them that if they would abandon the
error of Mount Gerizim, they should consequently acknowledge that
Jesus was indeed He who, according to the prophecy of Moses, was
expected to come; since, indeed, as Moses wrought signs and miracles,
so also did Jesus. And there is no doubt but that the likeness of the signs
proves Him to be that prophet of whom he said that He should come,
'like himself.'"

Cyril of Jerusalem, *Cat. illum.* 13:21: "The beginning of signs under
Moses was blood and water; and the last of all Jesus' signs was the same.
First, Moses changed the river into blood; and Jesus at the last gave forth
from His side water with blood."

Aphraates, *Dem. 21* 10: "Moses also was persecuted, as Jesus was
persecuted. When Moses was born, they concealed him that he might
not be slain by his persecutors. When Jesus was born they carried Him
off in flight into Egypt that Herod, His persecutor, might not slay Him.
In the days when Moses was born, children used to be drowned in the
river; and at the birth of Jesus the children of Bethlehem and in its border
were slain. To Moses God said: 'The men are dead who were seeking
your life'; and to Joseph the angel said in Egypt: 'Arise, take up the child,
and go into the land of Israel, for they are dead who were seeking the life

---

[30]I should like to continue this quotation, but space prohibits. Eusebius, after setting
many miracles of Moses and Jesus side by side, commented: "Moses and Jesus acted in
closely similar ways," so that "any one... can gather instances at leisure."

of the child to take it away.' Moses brought out his people from the service of Pharaoh; and Jesus delivered all nations from the service of Satan. Moses grew up in Pharaoh's house; and Jesus grew up in Egypt when Joseph brought Him there in flight. Miriam stood on the edge of the river when Moses was floating in the water; and Mary bare Jesus, after the Angel Gabriel had made the annunciation to her. When Moses sacrificed the lamb, the firstborn of Egypt were slain; and when they crucified Jesus the true Lamb, the people who slew him perished through his slaying.... Moses laid his hands upon his messengers and they received priesthood; and Jesus laid his hand upon his apostles and they received the Holy Spirit. Moses ascended the mountain and died there; and Jesus ascended into heaven and took his seat at the right hand of the Father."

Niceta of Remesiana, *De symbolo* 1: "A believer in Christ is one who follows Him as a leader toward the true life, much as the people of Israel followed Moses and entered the land of promise."

The belief that Moses "foreshadowed the Mediator between God and man" (Basil the Great, *Spir.* 33) is, I should subjoin at this point, reflected not only in the literature of the ancient church but also in its art. Jesus holds the rod of Moses on several bas reliefs, and there are any number of plastic art objects which make visible the comparisons drawn by Aphraates and other church Fathers. One example: carved on the sculptured wood door of S. Sabina in Rome (probably 5th cent.), on the left side, are miracles of Moses: the sweetening of the waters of Marah, the coming of the quails, the providing of the manna, and the flowing of the water from the rock; while on the right are miracles of Jesus: the cure of a blindman, the multiplication of loaves, the turning of water into wine.[31] It should also be registered that early depictions of Jesus' ascent into heaven appear to have been influenced by the tradition of Moses' ascent to reveal the law.[32]

The preceding review, while necessarily cursory, is sufficient for several generalizations. (i) For its early adherents, Christianity eventually became a substitute for Judaism, and Jesus, as prophet, deliverer, king, and lawgiver, accordingly took the place of Moses, a fact which expressed itself through the attributing of Mosaic qualities to Jesus.

(ii) The similarities between Jesus and Moses were sometimes collected so that the entire careers of the two men became catenas of

[31]See A. Grabar, *Christian Iconography* (Princeton: University Press, 1968), 142-44 and plates 338-39.
[32]G. Kretschmar, "Himmelfahrt und Pfingsten," *ZKG* 66 (1954/55):217-22.

parallels (cf. the quotations from Eusebius and Aphraates); also—
what is of pertinence to the analysis of Matthew—comparison and
contrast sometimes ran throughout a literary work (as in Luke-Acts
and John).[33]

(iii) Jesus' Mosaicity did not always entail criticism of Moses; that
is, parallelism did not, in itself, always communicate subordination.
The traditions behind Acts 3 and 7, the typology in Luke-Acts, and the
proclamation of the Pseudo-Clementines, not to mention many of the
incidental comparisons found in patristic literature, betray little or no
anxiety about Moses' status *vis-à-vis* Jesus. Only sometimes, as in John
and Hebrews, was Moses introduced for the primary purpose of
putting him in his place, beneath Jesus.

(iv) Because we cannot believe that one author, then another, and
then another, just happened upon the idea that Jesus' significance
should be gauged by placing him beside Moses, we may justly speak
of a tradition: Moses' utility as a type was an item of *paradosis*. Further,
that item clearly entered the tradition very near the birth of the church,
perhaps even in the pre-Easter period. In any case we must believe,
given the copiousness of the evidence in general, as well as the
presence in particular of Mosaic elements in portions of Mark (especially 9:1-8) and in traditions behind Matthew 1-2, that Matthew and
his community were, before the publication of the First Gospel, quite
familiar with a Jesus of Mosaic mien.

PETER

From the fourth century on Christian art closely associated Peter and
Moses. There are the gold glass medallions which depict "a person
striking a rock, where the person in question is not, in fact, described
as Moses but carries above it the name of Peter, indicating that the
traditional gesture of Moses making the water gush from the rock
symbolizes the action of Peter considered as mediator of the Grace
whose source is Christ."[34] There are the numerous interior church

---

[33]It is in fact possible that the lost book written by Ammonius of Egypt, entitled *On
the Agreement between Jesus and Moses*, largely consisted of an extensive list of parallels
between Jesus and Moses. See J. E. Bruns, "The 'Agreement of Moses and Jesus' in
Eusebius," *VC* 31 (1977), pp. 117-25.

[34]Pierre du Bourguet, *Early Christian Painting* (New York: Viking, 1966), 29. See
further E. Becker, *Das Quellwunder des Moses in der altchristlichen Kunst* (Strassburg:
Heitz and Mündel, 1909), 67-68. Becker's entire book is a goldmine for our present topic.

paintings of Peter receiving a new law, paintings clearly modelled on the iconographic tradition of Moses receiving the Torah from Christ.[35] There are sarcophagi (Vatican 161 for instance) which depict episodes from the life of Peter, among which episodes is one just like that on the gold glass medallions—as well as other sarcophagi and artifacts, such as the Podgoritza Cup, which feature a figure who is *either* Peter or Moses: the experts cannot tell us which, so much was Moses Peter's type.[36]

The extant literary evidence, although not abundant, suffices to confirm that the association of Peter with Moses was widespread and popular no later than C.E. 300. Again I choose seven texts, from various times and places:[37]

Aphraates, *Dem. 21* 10: "Moses brought out water from the rock for his people; and Jesus sent Simon Cephas (the rock) to carry his doctrine among the nations."

Macarius of Egypt, *Hom.* 26: "In the Old Testament, Moses and Aaron, when they held the Priesthood, had much to suffer. Caiaphas, when he occupied their seat, himself persecuted and condemned the Lord... . Peter was the successor of Moses, entrusted with Christ's revelation and the true priesthood."

(Ps.-)Ephrem the Syrian, in P. Mobarek and S. E. Assemani, *Opp. Graec.* (Rome, 1743), 44: at the transfiguration there appeared "the leader of the old covenant and the leader of the new... the steward of the Father and the guardian of the Son, the one split the Red Sea, so that the people walked in the midst of the flood, but the other set up a camp to rebuild the Church."

Augustine, *Cont. Faust.* 22:70: "The Lord, indeed, had told his disciples to carry a sword; but He did not tell them to use it. But that after this sin [the cutting off of Malchus' ear, John 18:10] Peter should become a pastor of the church was no more improper than that Moses, after smiting the Egyptian, should become the leader of the congregation."

Maximus of Turin, *Serm.* 49: "He therefore chooses Peter's boat and forsakes Moses'; that is to say, He spurns the faithless synagogue and takes the faithful Church. For the two were appointed by God as boats, so to speak, which would fish for the salvation of humankind."

---

[35]See Louis Réau, *Iconographie de l'art chrétien*, vol. 2, part 2 (Paris: Presses Universitaires de France, 1957), 315-16.

[36]Cf. P. Levi, "The Podgoritza Cup," *HeyJ* 4 (1963):55-60. —Attention may also be directed to the icon of St. Peter from Sinai (5th cent.?); this has above it three smaller icons—Christ in the center, Mary on the right, and, on the left, a man who is probably to be identified with Moses.

[37]For what follows I am greatly indebted to C. A. Krieller, "Moses und Petros," *Stimmen aus Maria Laach* 60 (1901):237-57.

Idem, *Hom.* 68: "Just as God in the desert brought forth for the people, because they thirsted, water out of the rock [by the hand of Moses], so too has flowed for the whole world, which languished from the thirst of unbelief, the spring of saving knowledge from the mouth of Peter."

Paulinus of Nola, *Natalilcium* 8 (= *Poem* 26): "Note how the teachers of the Old and New Testaments differ in their deeds but are paired in glory, for the one Wisdom issued twin laws in the two testaments, so equal distinction gives the same weight to differing pairs. Peter did not divide the sea with a rod, but then Moses did not walk on the waters. However, both have the same bright glory, for the one Creator inspired both the cleavage of the waters with a rod and the treading of the waves underfoot."

The primary causes of Peter becoming the antitype of Moses were two in number and are sufficiently clear. First there was word-association exegesis. If Paul identified the rock of the wilderness with Christ (1 Cor. 10:1-4), later Christians, not surprisingly, associated the rock of Massah with *Petros*, the rock of Matt. 16:17 (cf. already Origen, *Comm. on Mt.* 12:11). The two rocks were naturally linked because from each flowed life (cf. Maximus' second quotation). Secondly, as the power and prestige of the Roman bishop waxed, it became possible to interpret Peter, misremembered as the first Roman bishop, as the leader of the new people of God—which made him one like Moses, who was the leader of the old people of God. Moreover, although it was common, in the third century, to depict the salvation of God by means of a picture of Moses bringing forth water from the rock, subsequent to Cyprian, the view that the Church alone is authorized to dispense salvation prevailed, so that it became less congenial to see Moses as a channel of saving grace, more congenial to represent Peter, head of the church, as such.[38]

Of what interest is all this to the student of Matthew and the New Testament? The lesson for us emerges from the circumstance that the relating of Peter to Moses is attested in the visual arts, not in written texts alone. This demonstrates that the comparison, proved to have been traditional by the literary evidence, was not esoteric at all. The typology was rather popular and had an existence outside the writings of church leaders and theologians. One suspects that an analogous situation obtained in Matthew's environment. Given the many independent textual witnesses from the first century which liken Jesus and Moses, such likening must have been extra-textual, that is, part of oral teaching, and popular as opposed to esoteric. This in turn implies that Matthew's first Christian readers may have been, and I think probably were, prepared for or even predisposed to find a Moses typology in the story of Jesus. In other words, just as the ancient reader of Augustine or Maximus was already familiar with the idea of Peter as a new Moses, so probably was it with Matthew's intended audience: the comparison of Jesus to Moses, being conventional, was the more easily perceived.

One final point about Peter: attention may be directed to an apocryphal story about him. In the *Acts of Processus and Martinian* (6th cent.?), Peter baptizes Processus and Martinian, his warders in prison, with water miraculously sprung from a rock. It has occasionally been maintained that the plastic representations of Peter striking a rock were based on this legend. The truth is almost certainly the other way around: the art of the catacombs gave birth to the tale.[39] But however brought about, the apocryphal story reinforces my earlier conclusion that ancient typologies did not necessarily involve the exact replication of some past event but only a point or points of significant likeness amidst diversity; and that conclusion merits reiteration. In the present instance, while the *Acts of Processus and Martinian* has Peter playing the part of Moses, the differences between the story in the *Acts* and its ancient model could scarcely be greater. There are different settings (a prison instead of the desert), different purposes for the water (baptism instead of the quenching of thirst), and different benefactors (two Gentile jail keepers instead of the wandering Hebrew people). So I say again: a suggested typology cannot be discredited just by adding up obvious differences between type and antitype.

PAUL

Eustratius Constantinopolitanus, in the sixth century, labelled Paul a "new Moses" (*Stat. anim.* 5). This typological equation was perhaps already made long before, by the Pauline school, for in 2 Tim. 3:8-9 the opponents of Paul are characterized as the opponents of Moses: "As Jannes and Jambres[40] opposed Moses, so these men also oppose the

---

[39]Discussion in G. Stuhlfauth, *Die apokryphen Petrusgeschichten in der altchristlichen Kirche* (Berlin: de Gruyter, 1925), 50-71.

[40]On these two figures see M. R. James, *The Lost Apocrypha of the Old Testament* (London: SPCK, 1920), 31-38, and A. Pietersma and R. T. Lutz, in *OTP* 2:427-30.

truth, men of corrupt mind and counterfeit faith; but they will not get very far, for their folly will be plain to all, as was that of those two men." Even more notable, given our interests, is Rom. 9:1-3, composed by the apostle himself. Here we read: "For I could wish that I myself were accursed and cut off from Christ for the sake of my brethren, my kinsmen by race." The commentators are nearly unanimous in citing for illustration Exod. 32:31-32, where Moses entreats God: "Alas, this people have sinned a great sin; they have made for themselves gods of gold. But now, if thou wilt forgive their sin—and if not, blot me, I pray thee, out of thy book which thou hast written." Just as Moses pleaded to be cut off for the sake of Israel, so similarly Paul wrote that he too would pray for such if it were permissible and if it would be of benefit.[41] We have here "the consciousness of playing a role of decisive salvation-history significance, like Moses."[42]

The same consciousness emerges in 2 Cor. 3:1-4:6, whose centre-piece is this:[43]

> Now if the ministry that leads to death, engraved in letters of stone, appeared with [such] glory, although it was transient, how much more glorious will be the ministry of the Spirit! For if the ministry that leads to condemnation was glorious, how much more will the ministry that leads to righteousness abound in glory! Indeed, that which had partial glory has really lost whatever glory it had, compared with surpassing glory [of the new covenant]. For if the transient [ministry] had its moments of glory, how much is the enduring ministry filled with glory!

> Since, then, we really do have such a hope, we speak with great freedom born of confidence. We are not like Moses who was in the habit of putting a veil over his face to prevent the Israelites from fixing their eyes [to see] the significance of what was about to be done away. But [this happened because] their minds were obtuse; for until the present day, the same veil remains at the reading of the old covenant, and since the veil is not lifted, it is not evident that [only] in Christ is the glory done away. But until today, as often as Moses is read, a veil lies over their mind; yet "whenever there is a turning to the Lord, the veil is removed." "The Lord" represents the Spirit; and wherever the Spirit of the Lord is, there is freedom. And we, all of us, with faces uncovered, beholding as in a mirror the glory of the Lord are being transformed into the same image [of God] from one degree of glory to another; this is the work of the Lord, who is the Spirit.

---

[41]C. E. B. Cranfield, *A Critical and Exegetical Commentary on the Epistle to the Romans* (ICC; Edinburgh: T& T Clark, 1979), 454-59.

[42]J. D. G. Dunn, *Romans 9-16* (WBC; Waco: Word, 1988), 525.

[43]I reproduce the translation of R. P. Martin, *2 Corinthians* (WBC; Waco: Word, 1986), 57.

Perhaps, as others have remarked, when the author of 2 Peter wrote, regarding Paul's epistles, that there are in them some things hard to understand, he had this passage in mind: it is in several respects one of the most perplexing in the New Testament. Nonetheless, not all is opaque, and the work of C. K. Stockhausen[44] has made clearer still, what was clear enough before, namely, that in 2 Corinthians 3-4 Paul "describe[d] himself as a true Christian apostle on the model of Moses."[45] In defining and defending the nature of his apostleship, Paul had recourse to an extended comparison with Moses, a comparison implying that "Judaism and Christianity... [are] personified in the figures of Moses and Paul respectively."[46]

Moses was a servant and a covenant minister. So too Paul. And Moses had a *doxa*, a glory, again like Paul. But whereas the Mosaic covenant was carved on stone (Exod. 34:1, 27-28), the new covenant (cf. Jer. 31:31-34) is "in the Spirit" (3:6; cf. Ezek. 11:19; 36:26). Further, if the old covenant exhibited a transient splendor (Exod. 34:29-35), the new covenant owns a surpassing, abiding splendor (3:7-11); and while the *doxa* of the old *diathēkē* was hidden by Moses' veil (Exod. 34:34-35), Paul's face is unveiled (3.12-18). In fine, although "Moses is Paul's primary model for the proper conduct of a minister (*diakonos*) or servant (*doulos*) of God," and although "Paul's authentic apostleship [is] in conformance to a Mosaic paradigm,"[47] the newcomer is not, strictly speaking, really a second Moses[48] but one greater than Moses. Compare the verdict of a recent commentator: Paul set his "calling side by side with Israel's great leader, both positively and negatively," and in doing so dared to assert that he had *"parrēsia* to challenge Moses as the last word in God's salvation-history."[49]

The motivation behind Paul's comparison of himself with Moses can be plausibly divined. 2 Corinthians 3-7 and 10-13 record that Paul's credentials as an apostle had been questioned, or rather dismissed. And those who diminished Paul in front of the Corinthians

[44]*Moses' Veil and the Glory of the New Covenant. The Exegetical Substructure of II Cor 3, 1-4, 6* (AnBib 116; Rome: Pontifical Biblical Institute, 1988).

[45]Ibid., 41; cf. P. Jones, "L'Apôtre Paul: Un second Moïse par là Communaté de la nouvelle Alliance: Une Étude sur l'Autoritié apostolique paulinienne," *Foi et Vie* 75 (1976):36-58.

[46]Johannes Munck, *Paul and the Salvation of Mankind* (London: SCM, 1959), 58.

[47]Stockhausen, *Veil and Glory*, 154 and 175 respectively.

[48]Cf. 2 Cor. 3:13 (*ou kathaper Mōusēs*—"not like Moses") and A. T. Hanson, "The Midrash in II Corinthians 3: A Reconsideration," *JSNT* 9 (1980):16. Contrast Jones, as in n. 45.

[49]Martin, *2 Corinthians*, 67.

evidently modelled their own ministry on Moses, who performed signs and wonders and handed down the Torah.[50] On their view, Paul was not *hikanos*, competent (2 Cor. 2:17; cf. 3:5-6). He did not, in contrast to themselves, perform signs and wonders, and he did not uphold the Mosaic Torah.[51] In responding to such criticism, Paul in effect conceded that Moses may stand as the model minister of a covenant. That explains why certain similarities between Paul and Moses, both covenant ministers, emerge from the text. But the apostle also contended that the lawgiver's covenant, as Jeremiah and Ezekiel prophesied, had been superseded. Thus Paul, minister of the new covenant, could present himself as Moses' superior[52]—and as the superior of all who made Moses their spiritual model or ideal.

The main moral of 2 Corinthians 3-4 for our concerns is straightforward and obvious: Paul's claim to be greater than Moses was generated by a polemical situation. This is typical. It is true that all Christian typology, ancient and modern, has taken for granted the superiority of the new covenant over the old, and thus the new Moses theme, whether attached to Jesus or some other, regularly implies the greater-than-Moses theme. But when the latter is, as in 2 Corinthians, explicitly emphasized, one must postulate a polemical[53] or apologetical[54] occasion.

GREGORY THAUMATURGIS

Gregory was born ca. 213, at Neocaesarea in Pontus. At the approximate age of twenty he travelled to Palestine, there to commence studies under the great Origen, who received from him the greatest compliment ever given a teacher by his pupil: to leave the Alexandrian philosopher, Gregory wrote, was to re-enact the fall of Adam. After

---

[50]Georgi, *Opponents*. Cf. David L. Balch, "Backgrounds of 1 Cor. VII: Sayings of the Lord in Q; Moses as an Ascetic *Theios Anēr* in II Cor. III," *NTS* 18 (1972):351-64.

[51]See further Jerome Murphy O'Connor, *The Theology of the Second Letter to the Corinthians* (Cambridge: University Press, 1991), 12-13, 32-35.

[52]Cf. Munck, *Paul*, 60-61: "Moses and Paul are compared here with each other. The service of the former cannot in any way be matched in glory with the service of the latter. Of Paul's many new and startling utterances, this is perhaps the most surprising. The greatest man in the history of Israel is put beneath the travelling tentmaker, a man who is at the same time contending for the church at Corinth, so that it may submit to him. No stronger proof can be produced that as a figure in redemptive history in the age of the Messiah Paul far surpasses even the greatest of the great figures of Israel."

[53]Cf. the Moses typology in the Gospel of John.

[54]As with Eusebius' Moses typology; see *Dem. ev.* 3:2.

successful completion of Origen's curriculum, a task of five years, Gregory was consecrated, perhaps reluctantly, bishop of his home town. His evangelistic success there and in the surrounding region was extraordinary, and by his death, ca. 274, there were, so the records relate, few pagans left in all Pontus.

Gregory was a real man of flesh and blood from whom we have at least five documents. He can be linked to known persons, places, and dates. It was not long, however, before popular tradition obscured the facts of the man with legends of the saint, not long before Gregory, bishop of Neocaesarea, become Gregory Thaumaturgis, Wonderworker. Besides Gregory of Nyssa's *Vita* (see below), three other lives of Gregory, all biographically worthless, survive.[55] In these we read that Gregory became invisible and commanded evil spirits, altered rivers and dried up lakes, read minds and moved literal mountains, healed multitudes and saw the future.

In his treatise, *Liber de Spiritu sancto*, Basil the Great, in citing Gregory Thaumaturgis as an authority for naming the Holy Spirit in doxologies, had this to say: "By the working of the Spirit he was filled with a superabundance of grace, which manifested itself in such powerful signs and wonders that he was called a second Moses, even by enemies of the church" (*Spir.* 74(29)). This comment, designed to bolster Gregory's authority, is annexed to a brief resume of the saint's feats, in which it is claimed, among other stupendous things, that "by Christ's mighty name he even commanded rivers to change their courses; and once, when some brothers were quarreling over a lake, each wishing to possess it for his own, he caused it to dry up."

As might be gathered from Basil, the Cappadocian was not the first to call Gregory "a second Moses." There was, it would seem, a tradition to that effect. Thus it is that, in *De Vita Beati Gregorii Thaumaturgi*, written by Basil's younger brother, Gregory of Nyssa, the Moses parallels become a significant theme. We are told that Gregory Thaumaturgis was a teacher, that his life fell into three stages (see p. 71), that he fled into the desert, and that he died humbly, without pomp—all of which proved him to be like Moses.

Gregory of Nyssa's *Vita* extended a comparison already to hand in the oral tradition of the Wonderworker's deeds. But what originated that comparison in the first place? We may guess that the miracle stories about Gregory reminded people of stories in the Pentateuch

---

[55]In Syriac, Georgian, and Latin; see Johannes Quaesten, *Patrology, Volume II* (Utrecht: Spectrum, 1950), 124.

(recall the water miracles mentioned above). According to Basil, whom we may trust on the matter, Gregory "was called a second Moses" precisely because he performed "such powerful signs and wonders." As *The Prologue from Ochrid*, a Russian Orthodox annotated calendar, or Synaxarion, has it, Gregory was "a mighty wonderworker who was called a second Moses."[56]

The likening of a man to Moses primarily because that man worked Mosaic wonders has a parallel of sorts in the careers of the Jewish sign prophets known through Josephus. As argued on pp. 78-82, they set about imitating Moses' miracles as part of the end-time scenario. For them, to be like Moses, or specifically the prophet like Moses of Deut. 18:15, 18, meant the reproduction of signs done by the lawgiver. The eschatological dimension is, admittedly, absent from the traditions about Gregory, and I know of no real evidence that saint himself sought to imitate Moses, so the suggested parallel is imperfect. Still, a typology based upon Mosaic miracles does appear in more than one place, in Josephus and early Christian hagiography. Such also informs John 6 (see p. 89), and one further recalls the parallelism of Luke 2:22; 4:40 and Acts 7:36: the circumstance that Jesus worked "signs and wonders" makes him like Moses. We shall need to keep all this in mind when evaluating the proposal that the collection of miracle stories in Matthew 8-9 paints Jesus as a wonderworker like Moses.

ANTHONY THE GREAT

Near the conclusion of Athanasius' *Vita Antonii*, two of Anthony's companions seek, in accordance with the holy man's wishes, to bury him in secret (91). We are subsequently told that they were successful and that "to this day no one knows where it [Anthony's body] has been hidden (*kai oudeis oide teōs pou kekruptai*), except these two" (92). This is quite like LXX Deut. 34:6b: *kai ouk oiden oudeis tēn taphēn autou heōs tēs hēmeras tautēs*. In this respect, then, Anthony was like Moses.

There are manifold reasons to suspect that the apparent assimilation of Anthony to Moses in *Vit. Ant.* 91-92 is not isolated, that rather a developed Moses typology is diffused throughout Athanasius' narrative. Anthony bore titles Moses bore: "God's friend,"[57] "the man

---

[56]Ed. Bishop Nikolai Velimirovic (Birmingham: Lazarica, 1986), Part 4, 208 (Nov. 17).
[57]*Theophilēs*: 4; cf. 85, 93; for Moses see Exod. 33:11; Philo, *Sac.* 130; *Mos.* l:156, etc.; *Sib. Or.* 2:245; *Apost. Const.* 6:l9.4; Aphraates, *Dem. 17* 3.

of God,"[58] "servant of God."[59] And, like Moses, he was born in Egypt
(1), ventured forth into the Egyptian desert (ll, etc.), and spent vast
lengths of time on a mountain, there communing with God and
receiving revelations (llff., 49ff.). Indeed, the remark that Anthony
"sat (alone) on the mountain" comes close to being a refrain in the last
half of the book,[60] and we shall see later that Jewish tradition similarly
spoke of Moses sitting on Sinai (pp. 172-80). Also, the comment that
Anthony came forth from the mountain, having been initiated into
divine mysteries and inspired by God (14: *memustagōgēmenos kai
theophoroumenos*), sounds as though it might have been lifted straight
from Philo's *Vita Mosis*; and when we read, in *Vit. Ant.* 49, of Anthony
"journeying three days and three nights" (*hodeusas treis hēmeras kai
treis nuktas*) into the "desert" (*erēmon*), until he came to "a very high
place" (*oros hupsēlon lian*), we are reminded both of verses in Exodus[61]
and of the tradition that Sinai was "very high" (see p. 243). Likewise
suggestive are (i) the locality of Anthony's "inner mountain:" it[62] was
not far from the Red Sea; (ii) the notice of Anthony's "meekness"[63] (67);
and (iii) the miracle in chapter 54:

> One time the monks requested that he return to them, and oversee them
> and their places for a short time. He traveled with the monks who had
> come up to him, and a camel carried their loaves and water—for that
> whole desert is arid, and there is no water except in that mountain
> where his cell is, and they drew their water there. Now when the heat
> became oppressive and the water ran out along the way, they all were
> in peril. Having gone around to several places and finding no water,
> they were unable to travel any farther, but lay instead on the ground,
> and released the camel, despairing for their lives. But the old man,
> seeing everyone in peril, being greatly distressed and sighing deeply,
> departed from them a short distance. And bending his knees and
> stretching out his hands, he offered a prayer. Immediately the Lord
> made water gush forth from where he was praying. And after everyone
> drank his fill, they were revived.

Despite their number, it is difficult to come to a fair and just estimate
of the parallels just cited, for there is a regrettable absence of explicit
controls, and so a non-disclosure of authorial intent. Nowhere is

---

[58]*Ho tou theou anthrōpos*: 70, 71, 93; for this title of Moses see p. 35, n. 69, to which add
Philo, *Mut.* 125, 128.
[59]*Doulos tou theou*: 85; for this of Moses see p. 56, n. 121.
[60]59 (bis), 60, 66, 82, 93.
[61]3:18; 5:3; 8:27: Moses asked Pharaoh to let Israel make a three days journey into the
wilderness.
[62]Presumably Mount Colzim = Dêr Mar Antonios.
[63]But whereas Num. 12:3 has *praus*, here the Greek is, *tēn psychēn tapeinophrōn*.

Moses or the exodus from Egypt mentioned. The one clear comparison drawn with a pre-Christian personality is with Elijah: the Tishbite is a mirror for the ascetic, and one should, as did Anthony, imitate him (7).[64] Furthermore, one hesitates, given its commonality, to put much weight on the appellation, "servant of God;" and "the man of God" became a standard title for Christian miracle workers.[65] Even the supernatural bringing forth of water in the desert may not have been consciously Mosaic: this wonder became, in Christian tradition, one of many perambulating wonders, performed by several individuals,[66] so one may doubt that its tellers were always put in mind of Moses. Perhaps in fact Anthony did not set out to invest his hero with Mosaic traits. Do the parallels indicated truly add up to a Moses typology? or are they instead evanescent, the product of an overactive imagination?

The same problem of unfolding the genuinely implicit confronts impartial readers of Matthew; for, as my following chapter shows, scholars have often disputed whether or not a particular text has Mosaic reverberations. Sometimes a firm conclusion cannot be summoned. So too with Anthony's *Vita Antonii*. Nonetheless, I believe, albeit with equivocation, that the document does at least probably close by likening the pioneer monk to the lawgiver. The allusion to Deut. 34:6 in *Vit. Ant.* 91-92 seems solid, and it may not stand alone. According to Deut. 34:7, when Moses expired, his eyes were not dimmed (LXX: *ouk ēmaurōthēsan hoi ophthalmoi autou*).[67] Compare *Vit. Ant.* 93: at the end Anthony's "eyes were undimmed and sound, and he saw clearly" (*tous ophthalmos asineis kai holoklērous eiche, blepōn kalōs*). The wording may not be the same, but the sense is. Moreover, Athanasius' remark that Anthony had lost none of his teeth (93) has its parallel in LXX Deut. 34:7 (*ephtharesan ta chelōnia autou*) and in *Tg. Ps.-J.* on that verse: Moses' teeth did not decay. Even more striking is the apparent reference to a light perceived to be emanating from Anthony's face as death drew near: "as he lay there, his face seemed bright" (92:

---

[64]Cf. *Sancti Pachomii Vitae Graecae, Vita Prima* 2: "The life of our truly virtuous and most ascetic father Anthony was like the lives of the great Elijah, Elisha, and John the Baptist."

[65]B. Steidle, "Homo Dei Antonius: zum Bild des 'Mannes Gottes' im alten Mönchtum," *Studia Anselmiana* 38 (1956):148-200.

[66]Theodoret of Cyrrhus, *Rel. Hist.* 2:7-8; 10:7; Cyril of Scythopolis, *Lives of the Monks of Palestine* 56-57, 94; Gregory the Great, *Dial.* 2:8; Bede, *Life of Cuthbert* 18. I note, however, that in more than one of these texts the parallel with Moses is explicitly observed.

[67]Contrast the notices in Gen. 27:1; 48:10; 1 Sam. 3:2; 4:15.

ephaineto gar anakeimenos ilarō tō prosōpō).[68] Coming upon the heels of other circumstances reminiscent of Moses,[69] one may opine that Athanasius was indeed thinking of Moses, especially as Jewish tradition had, long before the fourth century, transfigured into light not only the face of Moses on Sinai but the appearance of Moses at his departure from this world.[70]

One readily understands why Athanasius might have been moved to model Anthony on Moses. The latter was, partly because of his forty days fast, partly because of his sexual abstinence in Exod. l8:2,[71] and partly because of his philosophic self-control in Philo's biography, sometimes held up as an example of asceticism.[72] Furthermore, Athanasius conceived of Anthony as the first of his kind, the hero who led the Egyptian monks into the desert, and precisely in the same general area that Moses had led the children of Israel out of Egypt and into the wilderness. Hence the drawing of parallels between Moses and Anthony would have been natural. Still, one cannot plausibly maintain that such parallels dominate the *Vita Antonii* or are even conspicuous. Although not negligible, they protrude themselves only occasionally and so constitute nothing more than a relatively quiescent motif.[73] Their purpose was no more than to color the background

---

[68]This is the translation of Robert C. Gregg, *Athanasius: The Life of Anthony and the Letter to Marcellinus* (New York: Paulist, l980), 98. —Cf. the event recorded in PG 65, Sisoes 14, where Antony is named.

[69]Cf. also perhaps *Vit. Ant.* 89 ("This is the last visitation I shall make to you, and I wonder if we shall see each other again in this life. Now it is time for me to perish, for I am nearly a hundred and five years old") with Deut. 31:3 ("I am a hundred and twenty years old this day; I am no longer able to go out and come in").

[70]This is implicit in LXX Num. 27:20 and the targumim on that verse; it is explicit in *LAB* 19:l6; *Pesiq. R.* 21:6 (contrast 21:4); and in Targums Onkelos, Neofiti, and Fragmentary on Deut. 34:7. See further Ginzburg, *Legends* 3:93, 119, 44l; 6:164. Note also the selection from the Armenian *History of Moses*, translated by M. E. Stone, "Three Armenian Accounts of the Death of Moses," in *Studies on the Testament of Moses* (SBLSCS 4, ed. G. W. E. Nickelsburg, Jr.; Cambridge: Society of Biblical Literature, l973), 120. For Samaritan sources see J. D. Purvis, "Samaritan Traditions on the Death of Moses," in ibid., 97, 108; see esp. *Memar Marqah* 5:4. Exod. 34:35 was widely taken to imply that Moses' glorification lasted until his death, and even beyond.

[71]Much was made of this; see e.g. Philo, *Mos.* 2:68; *ARN* A 2; *Deut. Rab.* ll:l0; *Cant. Rab.* 4:4; Ginzburg, *Legends* 2:316; 3:107, 258; 6:90 (with additional references).

[72]Cf. Clement of Alexandria, *Strom.* 3:7:57; Gregory of Nyssa, *De anima et resurrectione;* idem, *Virg.* 23; Theodoret of Cyrrhus, *Rel. Hist.* 2:4; 26:7; 29:7; epilogue; Aphraates, *Dem.* l8 3; Isaac the Syrian, *Asc. Hom.* 25; Gregory the Great, *XL Hom. ev.* 2:34.11-12. —It is worth observing that Sinai was a place of pilgrimage for monks already by the fourth century: Ephrem the Syrian, *Hymni de Juliano Saba* 19, 20; Theodoret of Cyrrhus, *Rel. Hist.* 2:6; *Itineranium Aethenae* 1-5.

[73]Those who discern the new Moses theme in Matthew but think it relatively unimportant might cite the *Vita Antonii* as a parallel.

scenery; that is, they were intended to lend the narrative a biblical atmosphere, thereby linking Anthony to the authoritative past—a boon for Athanasius, with his abiding concern to co-opt the famous holy man for orthodoxy in the combat with Arianism. The implicit likeness to Moses, then, functioned as did the explicit references to Elijah and Paul: Anthony, opponent of Arius and model monastic, stood in true continuity with the received tradition, so his spiritual lineage was that of the saints, including Moses.

CONSTANTINE

In telling the story of Constantine's momentous victory over Maxentius at the battle of the Milvian bridge, Eusebius turned to Exodus 15 and its account of Moses and Pharaoh at the Red Sea (*H.E.* 9:9). Maxentius and his guard had drowned when a pontoon bridge collapsed. What was this but a second instance of God throwing horse and rider into the sea?

> In the time of Moses himself and the godfearing nation of the ancient Hebrews, "The chariots of Pharaoh and his host He hurled into the sea; his picked horsemen, his captains, He swallowed up in the Red Sea; with the deep He covered them" (Exod. 15:4-5). In just the same way Maxentius and his bodyguard of infantry and pikemen "went down into the depths like a stone" (Exod. 15:5).... [T]hrough the breaking of the floating bridge, the crossing collapsed, and in a moment the boats, men and all, went to the bottom, and first the prime villain, then his bodyguard of picked men, in the way foretold by the inspired sayings, "sank like lead in the mighty waters" (Exod 15:10). Thus, if not in words at any rate in deeds, like the great servant Moses and his companions, the men who with God's help had won the victory might well sing the same hymn as was sung about the villainous tyrant of old: "Let us sing to the Lord, for gloriously has He been glorified: horse and rider He threw into the Sea. The Lord became my helper and protector, to my salvation" (Exod. 15:1-2). And "who is like Thee among the gods, Lord? Who is like Thee? Glorified among the saints, marvelous in praises, doing wonders?" (Exod. 15:11). These things and many others akin to them and just like them, Constantine by his very deeds sang as a hymn to the universal Lord the author of his triumph, God.

When narrating the same event in his *Life of Constantine*, Eusebius cited the very same Scriptures (*Vit. C.* 1:38-39). Here, however, the parallelism between Constantine and Moses is further developed and yields even greater impact. *Vit. C.* 1.12 relates how Moses was raised in the palaces of the kings he overthrew and how the same was true of Constantine:

But now the same God has given to us to be eye-witnesses of miracles more wonderful than fables, and, from their recent appearance, more authentic than any report. For the tyrants of our day have ventured to war against the supreme God, and have sorely afflicted His church. And in the midst of these, Constantine, who was shortly to become their destroyer, but at that time of tender age, and blooming with the down of early youth, dwelt, as that other servant of God had done, in the very home of the tyrants, but young as he was he did not share the manner of the life of the ungodly (cf. 1:19).

Note also 1:20:

The emperors then in power, observing his [Constantine's] manly and vigorous figure and superior mind, were moved with feelings of jealousy and fear, and thenceforth carefully watched for an opportunity of inflicting some brand of disgrace on his character. But the young man, being aware of their designs, the details of which, through the providence of God, more than once came to him, sought safety in flight; in this respect again keeping up his resemblance to the great prophet Moses.

We may wonder whether Eusebius wanted his readers to think of Moses at other junctures as well. Constantine was "meek," indeed "the meekest" (just like Moses; 1:45, 46).[74] He was known as "servant" (1:6, etc.) and as "the friend of God" (1:3), and Eusebius' use of the phrase, *pistos kai agathos therapōn* (1:6), strongly recalls LXX Num. 12:7 and Heb. 3:5.[75] Furthermore, and again like Moses, Constantine delivered laws (2:21; 5:27; etc.) and forbade idolatrous worship (3:48, 54-55; 4:23). Lastly, the very Divine Presence, Eusebius informs us, in words that might recall Exodus 33, appeared to the emperor "in a most marvelous manner" (1:47).

How should we evaluate these possible parallels? Before dismissing them as random trifles, we would do well to remember that the comparison between Moses and Constantine was probably not invented by Eusebius but by imperial propaganda. Not only does the motif appear also in Gelasius Cyzicus, *Hist. conc. Nic.* 6, but the immense popularity, in the plastic arts of the fourth century, of Pharaoh drowning in the Red Sea, has as its most likely explanation its conventional and typological equation with Constantine's victory.[76]

---

[74]I note that while "meekness" was a standard virtue of Hellenistic kings (cf. Stobaeus 14:7.24, 25, 62; Isocrates, *Ad Nic.* 23; Plutarch, *Mor.* 781A; etc.), Socrates, *H.E.* 7:42, was still able to associate the meekness of Theodosius the Younger with Num. 12:3 and Moses in particular.

[75]Cf. E. Becker, "Konstantin der Grosse, der 'neue Moses.' Die Schlact am Pons Milvius und die Katastrophe am Schilfmeer," *Zeitschrift für Kirchengeschichte* 31 (1910):167.

[76]So also Meyer Schapiro, *Late Antique, Early Christian and Mediaeval Art* (New York: George Braziller, 1979), 59.

For all we know, Constantine himself promoted the idea.[77] In the light of this, then, the first Christian readers of Eusebius' *Life of Constantine* would have been predisposed to read therein of a Mosaic emperor.

In the judgement of Glen F. Chestnut,

> When Eusebius portrayed Constantine in one of his most important images as the New Moses, this may possibly have been due to the influence of Philo, who... treated Moses in his *Life of Moses* as the ideal philosophic ruler of Hellenistic kingship. This seems one possible way of explaining why it was Mosaic imagery... that was chosen in the most important linkages of Constantine with Old Testament political leaders, even though David, to modern eyes at any rate, seems much more kingly than Moses.[78]

With this one may concur, without thinking it quite the whole story. For not only should we reckon with the likelihood that the paralleling of Constantine with Moses was conventional, not Eusebius' *novum*, but two additional considerations suggest themselves. First, "the Hellenistic definition of royalty included sacerdotal functions, so that, once the Christians had accepted the *basileus* as God's unique creation... they could not deny him some right to approach God on behalf of his subjects. This implied on the part of the Church the recognition of some vague imperial priesthood."[79] But how could such a recognition be harmonized with the exclusivity of the Christian priesthood? No layperson, not even the emperor, could undertake priestly functions. A compromise had to be reached. And that compromise, at least in Eusebius' mind, was made under the influence of Philo (cf. Chestnut); for Philo united the royal, the prophetic, and the priestly offices in his Jewish heroes, above all in Moses. Thus, to one under the influence of Philo, Constantine's religious activities as king would have appeared to own good precedent. If Moses, whose status and piety were not subject to question, was both king and priest, why not Constantine, who in other important respects was like Moses? Such a line of reasoning would have encouraged and made valuable Eusebius' Moses typology.

[77]Discussion in Becker, "Konstantin der Grosse;" idem, "Protest gegen den Kaiserkult und Verherrlichung des Sieges am Pons Milvius in der christlichen Kunst der Konstantinischen Zeit," in *Konstantin der Grosse und seine Zeit*, ed. F. J. Dölger (Freiburg i. Br.: Herders, l913), 155-90. Becker even finds evidence associating Constantine with a Mosaic relic, the *rabdos Mōuseōs*.

[78]*The First Christian Historians* (2nd ed.; Macon: Mercer, l986), 162-63.

[79]F. Dvornik, *Early Christian and Byzantine Political Philosophy*, vol 2 (Washington: Dunbarton Oaks Center for Byzantine Studies, l966), 643.

Secondly, Eusebius found in history a "sequence of stages," behind which stood the one true God, working out his saving purpose.[80] This explains the appearance in *Vit. Const.* l:12 of the phrase, "the same God." The father of church history was prodding his readers to set the present beside the past. To what end? So that those, such as certain educated pagans, who judged Exodus to be unbelievable because "fabulous,"[81] would, in view of what had undeniably happened in their own time, reconsider their opinion, and so that those Christians who already believed the Scriptures but were unsure of Constantine would come to acknowledge that the God of Moses had shown himself to be no less the God of the new emperor. In other words, depending upon one's point of view, Eusebius' apologetic, which underlined the continuity between the hoary past and recent events, either bore witness to Moses or enhanced Constantine's Christian reputation.[82]

EPHREM THE SYRIAN

Ephraem Syrus (ca. 306-73), born in Nisibis, spent the closing decade of his life as a deacon in Edessa, where he composed, in Syriac, numerous hymns, verse homilies, commentaries, and polemical treatises. These, filled with striking, extended metaphors and splendid oratory, made him famous, as did his life of piety and acts of charity.

There exists, from the hand of Jacob of Serugh (ca. 451-521), known in the Syriac-speaking world as "the Flute of the Holy Ghost," a panegyric on Ephrem. In this the saint is likened to Moses:

> The wise Moses made the virgins
> not to refrain from requisite praise;
> so too Ephraem, proving to be a second Moses to women,
> taught them to sing praise with the sweetest songs.
>
> ...The blessed Ephraem saw that the
> women were silent in praise
> and so decided in his wisdom that they should sing;

---

[80]Chestnut, *Historians*, 66.

[81]M.J. Hollerich, "Myth and History in Eusebius' *De Vita Constantini*: *Vit. Const.* 1:12 in Its Contemporary Setting," *HTR* 82 (1989):421-45, suggests that Eusebius had especially Porphyry in mind.

[82]Constantine, along with certain later emperors, was also sometimes known as a "new David" or a "new Solomon." See e.g. Athanasius, *Apol. ad Const.* 5:12, 20; Ambrose, *De off. min.* 2:7, 31-34. Justinian was another Melchizedek. I also note that Eusebius compared Constantine with Cyrus and Alexander: *Vit. C.* 1:7-8. —For earlier examples of Moses as a type in royal propaganda see pp. 48-51.

> so just as Moses gave timbrels to the young girls,
> so did this discerning man compose hymns for virgins.[83]

In these lines the analogy with Moses depends upon Exod. l5:20-21, where we read that Miriam, the prophetess, and "all the women," following upon Moses' praise at the Sea, themselves broke forth: "Sing to the Lord, for he has triumphed gloriously; the horse and his rider he has thrown into the sea." Ephrem was therefore like Moses not because he worked miracles or exhibited Mosaic virtues but because he enjoined women to sing praises.

Such an unusual comparison must, one suspects, have grown out of a traditional likening of Ephrem to Moses, and for this there is evidence. PG 46:819-50 preserves a sermon on Ephrem, a sermon traditionally, but incorrectly, ascribed to Gregory of Nyssa. It extols Ephrem by likening him to fourteen different biblical figures, as well as to Basil the Great. Of the biblical models cited, Moses, who receives by far the most attention, is clearly the most important. We read that Ephrem lived a life of three parts (cf. p. 71), that he grew up in two cultures, and that he desired no particular tomb (PG 46:837, 840, 845). Further, sentences traditionally associated with Moses are rehearsed with the Syrian saint as subject: Ephrem

> fled from the demonic Pharaoh, camped in the desert and saw God (as far as that is possible through contemplation). He performed miracles and, bearing the name "teacher," led the people. He triumphed over the Egyptians by cunning, and despoiled them of their treasure, taking into servitude their heretical books and triumphing over them. He split in two the sea, that is, ignorance, salty and undrinkable. He made the people, the orthodox assembly, cross over. He triumphed over Amalek, if one does well to give that name to the first of heretics. From God he received the orthodox law and passed it on to us (PG 46:844-45).

We need not concern ourselves with the interpretation of these sentences, that is, with the events in Ephrem's career which are here typologically presented. More needful is the observation that the *sygkrisis* is thoroughly conventional. To my knowledge there were in fact no events in Ephrem's life that would have readily reminded people of Moses. In fact, most of the parallels between Ephrem and Moses appear also in Gregory of Nyssa's *In laudem Basilii fratris*, to which we shall turn shortly: there is nothing unique about them. In the circles from which our *encomium* emanated, circles very close to the Cappadocian Fathers, comparison to Moses had become a rhetorical

---

[83]*Acta Martyrum et Sanctorum 3*, ed. P. Bedjan (Paris, l892), 668, 672.

device for praising outstanding Christian figures, especially bishops (cf. *Apost. Const.* 2:26). In addition to Gregory's laudation of his older brother, examples of such comparisons in the writings of the Cappadocians include Gregory of Nyssa, *Laudatio Meletii episcopi* (Melitius, like Moses, had the virtue of goodness, *agathotēs*); Gregory Nazianzen, *Orat. 7* 3 (Gregory's father, Gregory the elder, was "a second Adam or Moses"); idem, *Orat. 43* 35, 72 (Basil was like Moses); and idem, *Orat. 18* 14-15, 24, 29 (on Gregory the elder and Moses). In each of these texts the likening of a man to Moses (really Philo's Moses), serves to applaud a man's virtues, character, and rôle as leader.

BASIL THE GREAT

Gregory of Nyssa's *In lauden Basilii fratris* is a panegyric delivered on an early anniversary of his great brother's death. It is dominated by an artificial *sygkrisis*, by comparisons (too frequent for modern tastes) of Basil with many biblical figures. Thus we read of how Basil was not inferior to Paul (11-12), to John the Baptist (13-14), to Elijah (15-18), to Samuel (19).[84] But the chief analogy is with Moses (20-23). Very near the beginning there is this: "Him, I mean, the vessel of election, Basil, sublime in life and eloquence, who was fair unto God from birth (*ton asteion tō theō*—cf. Acts 7:20), who was venerable in character from his youth, who like Moses was instructed in all knowledge of profane learning" (*paideuthenta... pasē sophia tōn exōthen*—cf. Acts 7:22). Near the end of the book the comparison with Moses appears once more. It accordingly forms an *inclusio*.

Not surprisingly, Gregory's primary method of comparison involved allegory. Section 20 begins as follows:

> And the great Moses is set forth as a common example for all those who look to virtue; and one could not err, should he make the virtue of the lawgiver the aim of his own life. Therefore, it surely would be without reproach to show that in what he was able, our teacher [Basil] imitated the lawgiver in his life. In what then was the imitation? A certain princess of the Egyptians having adopted Moses trained him in the education of her land; though he did not leave the breasts of his mother as long as his early age needed to be sustained by sound nurture. This

---

[84] I use the chapter divisions of J. A. Stein, *Encomium of Saint Gregory Bishop of Nyssa on his Brother Saint Basil, Archbishop of Cappadocian Caesarea* (Washington: Catholic University of America, 1928).

also truth testifies for our teacher. For though nourished by pagan learning, he always clung to the bosom of the church, strengthening and maturing his soul with teachings therefrom. Afterwards Moses denied the spurious relation of his falsely called mother. And he [Basil] did not continue for long to hold in honor that of which he was ashamed. For having shaken off the glory of profane science just as the former did the kingly office, he withdrew to the lowly life; just as Moses held even the Hebrews preferable to the treasures of Egypt.

Those who have read Gregory's *De Vita Mosis* will find all this familiar, for there too the barren Egyptian princess represents profane philosophy while Moses' natural mother is scriptural learning (2:10-13). So what is set forth in *The Life of Moses* as the proper course of virtue is, in the *Laudem Basilii*, presented as fulfilled in Basil's life.

Gregory's characteristic love of allegory also shines forth in section 21, where we read that Basil, as a priest, "led [many] through the water" and "fed [them] with heavenly nourishment."We are obviously expected to know that the crossing of the Red Sea is a type of Baptism (cf. 1 Cor. 10:1-4) and that the miracle of the manna is a type of the Eucharist (cf. John 6). Gregory left it to his readers to gather the obvious.

Besides allegorical interpretation, the *encomium* of Gregory on Basil draws analogies with Moses in three additional ways. First, analogous religious experiences are related. In section 21 it is said that Moses "was illumined by a light in the bush," and that "we are able to speak of something akin to this vision in the case of the later [Basil] also: that when it was night there came upon him while praying in the house the glow of a light; and that light was something immaterial, illuminating his room by divine power, suspended from no material thing." Similar is section 22, with its first-person plural eye-witness testimony: "Many times we perceived that he was also in the dark cloud wherein God was. For what was invisible to others, to him the initiation into the mysteries of the Spirit made visible, so that he seemed to be within the compass of the dark cloud in which knowledge about God was concealed." Note well: the text says only that Basil entered into a dark cloud; it does not mention that Moses entered such. Once more the reader's knowledge of the Bible is taken for granted.

A second method of constructing analogies involves similar external circumstances. For instance, the Scripture says that the tomb of Moses "is not found." In like manner, Basil was buried without "any material lavishness," and "out of the abundance of what he left behind no material memorial of the man was found overwhelming his reputation for the nobler part" (23). Again, Moses left Egypt and "spent much time living by himself in retirement." So too Basil, who "left the turmoils of the city and this worldly circumstance, and was wont in the most secluded region to philosophize with God" (21).

The third way in which Gregory created Basil in the image of Moses was by bestowing upon him Mosaic titles, including "shepherd" (*poimēn*), "lawgiver" (*nomothetēs*), and "teacher" (*didaskalos*).

What moved Gregory to liken his brother to Moses?[85] One must obviously take into consideration the aforementioned rhetorical convention: it was common in the circles near Gregory to liken Christian leaders to Moses. In Basil's case, however, more needs to be said. Gregory of Nyssa lived through a time of intense christological crisis, and both he and his brother were leading figures in the heated debate with Arianism. Now it is noteworthy that in praising the older brother, the younger chose to emphasize the theme of combat. Consider *In laud. Bas.* 22:

> Many times he arrayed himself against the Amalekites, using prayer as his shield. And when he raised up his hands, the true Moses conquered His enemy. He put an end to the witchcraft of the many sorcerers of that Balaam; they, not listening to the true word but obeying the ass-like doctrines of demons, kept their mouths ineffectual towards wickedness, since the prayer of our teacher placed a curse upon their fine words.

This same motif, of Basil as Mosaic holy warrior, appears also in sections 9 and 10, where the career of "the noble soldier of Christ" (2) is introduced by reference to Arius, Aetius, Eunomius, and Eudoxius, heretics all. These last stealthily carried idolatry back into the world after the victory of Christ had cast it out. But "when almost all had come under its sway, then the great Basil was exhibited by God" (10). The battle with heresy, especially Arianism, goes far to explain the Moses typology and the comparisons with other heroes of the faith. Gregory upheld his own orthodoxy by setting his brother's anti-Arian ministry within the general course of salvation-history: it was yet one more instance of God raising up a teacher to crush the opponents of true religion. In this way Basil became the Moses of his generation, the charismatic who led God's people to triumph over

---

[85]For what follows I am much indebted to M. Harl, "Moïse figure de l'évêque dans l'Eloge de Basile de Grégoire de Nysse (381)," in *The Biographical Works of Gregory of Nyssa*, ed. Andreas Spira (Philadelphia: Philadelphia Patristic Society, 1984), 71-119. — For a later comparison of Basil to Moses see Joannes Monachus, *Hymn Bas.* 3.

their enemies. "Moses saved his people, delivering them from tyranny. This people bears witness to the like in our lawgiver by whose priesthood they were restored to the promise of God" (21). By thus interpreting Basil, Gregory simultaneously interpreted the struggle against Arianism. To understand Basil aright was to understand aright the struggle, yet ongoing when Gregory wrote, for an orthodox Christology. In sum, the effusive praise of his brother as a new Moses was a rhetorical means of condemning heresy and upholding the true faith.

THEODORET'S MONKS OF SYRIA

In Theodoret of Cyrrhus' life of the fourth century Syrian monk, James (or Jacob) of Nisibis, there is, in chapter 4 (= *Rel. Hist.* 1:4), a memorable tale of how "the man of God" was offended by certain girls who were washing clothes in a stream. These girls, "far from feeling awe at his novel appearance," not only stared at James but failed to cover their heads; indeed, they did not "even let down their clothes, which they had taken up." Indignant—in Theodoret's eyes justifiably indignant—the itinerant monk, desirous "to display God's power opportunely," uttered a curse that instantly worked to stop the stream in which the young ladies stood. The curse also turned the maidens' hair prematurely gray: "their black hair was changed, and they looked like young trees decked in spring with the leaves of autumn." But in response to the cessation of the life-giving water, the populace of that place, as may readily be imagined, protested, begging James to remit the punishment and restore the stream. He acquiesced; and, upon the utterance of a prayer, the water flowed once more. James also kindly determined to restore the youthful appearance of the offending girls; they, however, refused to see him, so "he let the punishment stand, as a lesson in self-control, a reason for good behavior, and a perpetual and clear reminder of the power of God."

Commenting upon this strange sequence of events, Theodoret spoke of "the miracle of this new Moses." What provoked such a characterization?[86] Despite the manifest dissimilarities, the story of Moses bringing forth water in the desert was certainly in Theodoret's

---

[86]Whether Theodoret was the first so to label James I have not been able to discover. Later on eastern church tradition gave James the nickname, "the Moses of Mesopotamia."

mind, for he added that James' wonder resulted not *"from the blow of a rod* but received its efficacy from the sign of the cross" (*Hist. Rel.* 1:5). Perhaps a few lines after this we should find an additional allusion to Moses, one far more subtle. James, we are told, "did not, like the great Elijah, hand over those shameless girls to carnivorous bears" but instead applied only "a harmless correction," which circumstance much excited Theodoret's "admiration for his [James'] gentleness" (ibid.; on Moses' proverbial gentleness see p. 180).

Theodoret's account of James mentions Moses one other time. The story of the siege of Nisibis (in 338) at the hands of Sapor II, king of the Persians, is told in chapters 11-12. Here we are informed that the citizens "begged the man of God" to ascend the wall and "rain down curses" on the enemy camp. James did so; and as he spoke, so God did, "persuaded as by Moses." "A plague" was sent, that is, "a cloud of gnats and mosquitoes," which had the desired effect of scattering the impious emperor and his hostile forces.

Aside from chapters 4 and 11-12, Theodoret's brief biography of James of Nisibis does not otherwise name Moses. Also, I have found no inexplicit or subtle references to the lawgiver. This means that no developed typology emerges. We simply have two miracle stories which reminded Theodoert of events in the Pentateuch.

The situation is similar in Theodoret's life of Julian, known as "Saba" (*Hist. Rel.* 2). In this we learn that Julian, "like some Moses," spent extended time on a mountain in "ineffable contemplation" (2:4); that, finding himself in the desert with a thirsty young man, he brought forth "a spring of water:" "just as Moses once of old by striking with his rod that infertile rock caused a flood of fertile river-water, in order to satisfy the thirst of those many thousands, so this man of God by watering with his tears that most arid sand drew forth streams of spring-water, to cure the thirst not of many myriads but of a single adolescent" (2:7, 8); and that Julian, to escape being honored, set out to visit the isolated Mount Sinai and so came to the "rock where Moses, the leader of the prophets, hid when he was counted worthy to see God, in so far as it is possible to see Him" (2:13).

The stories of James of Nisibis and of Julian Saba are not the only ones in Theodoret's *History of the Monks of Syria* to tell of holy men who imitated the great Moses. *Hist. Rel.* 26:7 claims that the famous Symeon Stylites fasted for forty days, "like the men of God Moses and Elijah," while 26:2 informs us that the first pillar sitter was, as a youth, a shepherd "and so comparable to those great men the patriarch Jacob, the chaste Joseph, the lawgiver Moses, the king and prophet David,

[and] the prophet Micah."[87] Also noteworthy is *Hist. Rel.* 10:7, although it may be an interpolation from someone other than Theodoret:[88]

> A precipitous rock overhangs the retreat which he had built; it had hitherto been completely dry and moistureless. Here he made a conduit, leading from the summit to the monastery, as if the production of water was in his power. Full of trust in God, clearly confident that he had won God's goodwill, and with unwavering faith, he rose in the night and went up to the top of the conduit before rousing his disciples for the customary prayers. After entreating God in prayer, with confidence in the One who does the will of those who fear him, he struck the rock with the staff with which he happened to be supporting himself. Water burst forth and poured out like a river; entering the monastery by the conduit and abundantly serving every need, it is evacuated into the sea nearby, and to this day is manifested the operation of the grace, like that of Moses, of the great Theodosius. This story on its own suffices to manifest the man's familiar access to God.

I note that the last sentence may well be a tacit allusion to Moses' familiarity with God (Num. 12:8, etc.).

What, we may now ask, was Theodoret's purpose in presenting so many monks as in certain respects duplicates of Moses? The answer lies in the general purpose of his *History*, which was to make a record of and commend a group of people whose behavior was startling, even to the ancients. The harsh asceticism, oft times well nigh incredible, of the Syrian monks, was interpreted as an outward sign of an invisible grace and commended by exhibition of its continuity with the past. This is why Moses is only one of many monkish models: Elijah is also frequently mentioned, and the more unusual practices of some of the biblical prophets also receive notice, as in *Rel. Hist.* 26:12:

> I ask fault-finders [critics of Symeon Stylites] to curb their tongue and not to let it be carried away at random, but to consider how often the Master has contrived such things for the benefit of the more easy-going. He ordered Isaiah to walk naked and barefoot, Jeremiah to put a loincloth on his waist and by this means address prophecy to the unbelieving, and on another occasion to put a wooden collar on his neck and later an iron one, Hosea to take a harlot to wife and again to love a woman immoral and adulterous, Ezekiel to lie on his right side for forty days and one his left for one hundred and fifty, and again to dig through

---

[87]Simeon's Mosaic features are enlarged upon in the early Syriac *Vita*; see S. Ashbrook Harvey, "The Sense of a Stylite. Perspectives on Simeon the Elder," *VC* 66 (1986):376-94. English text now in R. Doran, *The Lives of Simeon Stylites* (Kalmazo: Cistercian, 1992), 103-98.

[88]See the comments of R. M. Price in his edition of *A History of the Monks of Syria* (Kalamazoo: Cistercian, 1985), 93, n. 5.

a wall and slip out in flight, making himself a representation of captivity, and on another occasion to sharpen a sword to a point, shave his head with it, divide the hair into four and assign some for this purpose and some for that... . The Ruler of the universe ordered each of these things to be done in order to attract, by the singularity of the spectacle, those who would not heed words and could not bear hearing prophecy, and make them listen to the oracles... . Just as the God of the universe ordered each of these actions out of consideration for the benefit of those inured to ease, so too he has ordained this new and singular sign [Simon on his pillar] in order by its strangeness to draw all men to look... .

Whether this passage does justice to the symbolic gestures of Israel's prophets we need not argue. One thing is clear: for Theodoret, the new gathered esteem from its resemblance to the old. Moreover, such gathering of esteem for his heroes was precisely one of Theodoret's purposes in constructing his Moses typologies. For the life of the lawgiver, as comprehended by post-Philonic readers, was biblical proof that "while surfeit follows on the pleasure of bodies, divine desire does not admit the laws of satiety" (*Rel. Hist.* epilogue 4-5). In other words, the Syrian ascetics, in living the angelic life, that is, a life victorious over bodily needs, were only following in the footsteps of the great Moses and others of olden times like him.

BENEDICT OF NURSIA

The writings of Pope Gregory I, or the Great (ca. 540-604), are filled with citations of and allusions to the Scriptures; and, as one might expect of him, the many and fantastic miracle stories in his *Dialogues* as often as not recall biblical narratives.[89] As illustration consider *Dial.* 1:10, wherein is told the tale of a certain dead Marcellus, brought to life again by the wonderworking Fortunatus, bishop of Todi. Marcellus, according to Benedict, had two devoted sisters, and he died just before Easter. Furthermore, we are informed that Fortunatus, upon learning of Marcellus' demise, "could not restrain his tears." Anyone familiar with John's Gospel cannot miss the loud echoes of chapter 11. There Jesus, immediately before Passover, weeps and then raises Lazarus, a man with two devoted sisters, Mary and Martha. Gregory's account, however, conveys none of this information: the parallels with the

---

[89]See M. Mähler, "Évocations bibliques et hagiographiques dans la vie de saint Benoît par saint Grégorie," *RBén* 83 (1973):145-84; O. Rousseau, "Saint Benoît et le prophète Élisee," *Revue du moyen-âge latin* 144 (1956):103-14.

biblical story go unmentioned. It is up to the informed reader to draw the connections. But not all of Benedict's analogies in the *Dialogues* are unexpressed. On the contrary, explicit parallels between Christian saints and biblical persons are fairly frequent; see, for an example, 1:2 (on Libertinus and Elijah).

When one reviews the many fabulous yarns Gregory wove about Saint Benedict (ca. 480-547), author of the famous monastic Rule, the latter's status as a new Elijah and a new Elisha is inescapable. In 2:6 Benedict raises an iron blade from the bottom of a lake (cf. 2 Kings 6:1-7). In 2:8 ravens obey him (cf. 1 Kings 17:4, 6). And in 2:13 Benedict bilocates (cf. 2 Kings 5:25-27). As miracle worker, then, Benedict's types were, as Gregory plainly indicates (2:8), Elijah and Elisha. There is one story, however, in which Moses serves as the model. *Dial.* 2:5 reads:

> Three of the monasteries the saint had built… stood on the bare rocky heights. It was a real hardship for these monks always to go down to the lake to get water for their daily needs. Besides, the slope was steep and they found the descent very dangerous. The members of the three communities therefore came in a body to see the servant of God. After explaining how difficult it was for them to climb down the mountainside every day for their water supply, they assured him that the only solution was to have the monasteries moved somewhere else.

> Benedict answered them with fatherly words of encouragement and sent them back. That same night, in company with the little boy Placidus, he climbed to the rocky heights and prayed there for a long time. On finishing his prayers, he placed three stones together to indicate the spot where he had knelt and then went back to his monastery, unnoticed by anyone. The following day, when the monks came again with their request, he told them to go to the summit of the mountain. "You will find three stones there," he said, "one on top of the other. If you dig down a little, you will see that almighty God has the power to bring forth water even from that rocky summit, and in His goodness relieve you of the hardship of such a long climb."

> Going back to the place he had described, they noticed that the surface was already moist. As soon as they had dug the ground away, water filled the hollow and welled up… .

Given Benedict's habitual method of alluding to biblical miracles through key phrases, the use of "water from… that rock" is suggestive: it directs us to Exodus 17 and Numbers 20. That a reference to those texts was in fact intended is confirmed by the summary in *Dial.* 2:8, which looks back to 2:5: "The water streaming from the rock reminds one of Moses."

J. M. Petersen, after observing that the circumstances of the monks of the three mountain monasteries could be likened to those of the

Israelites in the desert, affirms that Gregory wanted to present Benedict "as a new Moses, leading the chosen into a wilderness."[90] Of this I am doubtful. The difficulty is that, to my knowledge, nowhere else in the *Dialogues* does Benedict emulate Moses. There is therefore no extended comparison. So can prudence claim anything more than that Gregory sought to convey that one marvel of Benedict was like one marvel of Moses? I think not. In truth, Gregory was not so much interested in likening Benedict to Moses as in comparing two wonders. To what end? Benedict knew Christians who, in an uninspiring age without martyrs, thought the days of miracles past; and he was determined, despite his belief in the superiority of internal virtues over external marvels,[91] to demonstrate that, to the contrary, contemporary Italy was not bereft of signs and wonders: there were miracles aplenty, and of the same quality as those in the Bible.[92] The feats of Elisha and Elijah and even Moses were being done again, thereby demonstrating the continuing truth of the maxim, With God all things are possible.

CONCLUDING OBSERVATIONS

Of the five concluding observations made after review of the Jewish sources, four hold equally for the Christian documents. First, for Christians as for Jews, Moses was a well-used type because he was many things, an occupier of many offices. Gregory Thaumaturgis, James of Nisibs, and Benedict of Nursia were likened to Moses because they were miracle workers. Constantine and Basil the Great were given the same distinction for different reasons: they were perceived as significant figures in salvation-history, men who turned the wheel of history. Ephrem the Syrian was compared to Moses in order to laud his virtuous character. And the Jesus tradition adopted Moses for all three reasons—and for others as well. When we come to Matthew, then, it will be wise to remember that its Moses typology might have been stimulated by multiple factors.

The Christian sources are, secondly, at one with the Jewish in this, that comparison with Moses generally serves to exalt a man, not

---

[90]Petersen, *Dialogues of Gregory*, 48.

[91]Cf. *Dial.* 1:12; the commendable sentiment is often expressed in the *Magna Moralia*, a document more easily appreciated than the *Dialogues*.

[92]Cf. *Dial.* l, preface 7; 1:2; 3:25; 4:43; and see the comments of Carole Straw, *Gregory the Great: Perfection in Imperfection* (Berkeley: University of California, 1988), 67-69.

denigrate the lawgiver. There are indeed occasions when the stress upon the superiority of the new dispensation does engender a detrimental comparison. Hence there are texts which make Jesus or Peter or Paul Moses' superior. But by and large that is, as I have amply shown, a subsidiary motif: it does not consistently run throughout the various comparisons with Moses. Far more often than not the lawgiver is a positive figure, and likeness to him is invariably complimentary. The point is really inevitable, because to seek for a likeness to one's hero is to seek for another hero. What Christian would have wished to compare Jesus with Pharaoh?

Thirdly, the parallels between Christian figures and Moses, as between Moses and Jewish figures, always exist amid sundry differences, and there is always much matter extraneous to a typology. The truth of this is sufficiently patent from the preceding pages and requires no more illustration. But I underline the point yet once again, because it proves much criticism of proposed typologies to be spurious (cf. pp. 94-95).

Fourthly, many men were, in Jewish sources known to Matthew, likened to Moses; and a cloud of Christian witnesses suggests that, in the ecclesiastical tradition of the evangelist, Jesus had already been set beside the lawgiver. Hence, by the end of the first century C.E., there was both Jewish and Christian precedent for portraying important people in general and Jesus in particular as being like Moses. It follows that the extended Moses typology in the First Gospel, to be established forthwith, was no aberration but an instance of a well-established literary custom.

We come finally to the point of dissimilarity between the Jewish and Christian texts: the Jewish typologies tend to be more subtle, less explicit than those in the Christian tradition. Leaving aside the first-century sources which implicitly liken Jesus to Moses, there is only one example in my review of a typology which consistently demands an intimate knowledge of Scripture. I refer to Athanasius' *Life of Anthony*. Otherwise the parallels between a particular saint and Moses are most often in the open and plainly announced: there is little room for constructing speculative typologies. What accounts for this fact?

As the church entered the second century its Jewish population shrank; and all the post-first-century texts I have examined were written by and for Gentiles. So the difference indicated is largely one between Jewish and Gentile texts. Of its cause I am unsure. One hesitates to offer the generalization that ancient Jews were more steeped in the Scriptures than ancient Christians. Learned Gentiles, such as Origen, knew the Bible inside out; and if one wants an example of such in an unlearned man, Anthony of Egypt will suffice (witness his letters). Moreover, the Old and New Testaments played much the same role in Christian worship and devotion as the Tanak in Jewish worship and devotion, so one wonders how there could have been significant disparity between the Scripture knowledge of Jews and Gentile Christians. We should remember in this connection that, so often in the first few centuries, the latter were converts, with all the enthusiasm for religion and religious books that implies. Nevertheless, perhaps the very success of Christianity as a missionary religion, which meant the constant swelling of ranks with the theretofore scripturally illiterate, made implicit literary allusions in works for general consumption less appropriate: considerate authors had to keep in mind the constant influx of neophytes. But then we are faced by the many inexplicit and often subtle allusions throughout Gregory's *Dialogues*, a popular work if ever there was one.[93]

Whatever the truth of the matter, here I need only observe that the author of the First Gospel belonged to the Jewish world, not to the later world of Gentile Christians. Matthew was a Jew, steeped in the Bible and Jewish custom, and his church, although it participated in the Gentile mission, remained fundamentally Jewish.[94] His literary habits must be judged accordingly. While the alleged discovery of an inexplicit but significant typology in a book composed by a third or fourth century Gentile Christian would be attended by doubt, Matthew belonged to an earlier and very different world. And in that world literary subtlety directed at keen and informed imaginations was, or so I shall now seek to show, nothing out of the ordinary.[95]

[93]Jeffrey Richards, *The Popes and the Papacy in the Early Middle Ages, 476-752* (London: Routledge and Kegan Paul, 1979), 259, uses the phrase, "accessible to ordinary people."

[94]Davies and Allison, *Matthew*, l:7-58; J. A. Overman, *Matthew's Gospel and Formative Judaism* (Minneapolis: Fortress, 1990).

[95]It would be fascinating to explore further the second Moses theme in Christianity, from antiquity to the present. The aforementioned figures only introduce a complex and extensive subject. Additional examples: (i) PG 115.565ff. reports that St. Mamas, the third cent. Cappadocian, was a new Moses who spent forty days in prison without food or drink. (ii) Ulphias, apostle to the Goths (311-83), is like Moses in Philostorgius' *Historia ecclesiastica* (PG 65:470). (iii) Bishop Nicholaus of Myra, about whom we may know nothing at all, except that he later became "Santa Claus," is a new Moses in Pseudo-Romanos, *Apud Myros, O sancte 9* (in J. B. Pitra, *Analecta Sacra Spicilegio Solesmensi I*, Paris, 1876). (iv) In John of Ephesus, *Lives* 2 (on Zʿura), Zʿura plays the part of Moses, Justinian that of Pharaoh; see Susan Ashbrook Harvey, *Asceticism and Society in Crisis: John of Ephesus and the Lives of the Eastern Saints* (Berkeley: University of California, 1990), 85. (v) Saint Patrick of Ireland was said to have abounded in meekness, to have fasted on a mountain for forty days and forty nights, to have heard God speak to him out of a fire, to have been the leader of God's people, to have died in his one

hundred and twentieth year, and to have been buried in an unknown place; see *The Tripartite Life of Patrick* (ed. W. Stokes; London: Eyre and Spottiswoode, 1887) and the *Leabhar Breac Homily on St. Patrick* (Dublin, Royal Irish Academy, MS 23), two sources which are conveniently excerpted and adapted in *Celtic Christianity*, ed. C. Bamford and W. P. Marsh (Hudson, New York: Lindisfarne, 1987), 54-55, 60. (vi) Felix's *Life of St. Guthlac*, the English hermit (? 673-714), as translated in C. W. Jones, *Saints Lives and Chronicles in Early England* (Ithaca: Cornell, 1948), 123-60, gives its hero a Mosaic aura. (vii) For the comparing of various popes with Moses see Krieller, "Moses und Petros," 256-57. (viii) In later times many Puritan leaders were likened to Moses, as were Charles II and William and Mary.

PART II
THE NEW MOSES IN MATTHEW

Four _____

REVIEW OF TEXTS

Before surveying the evidence for Matthew's new Moses theme, two prefatory remarks are in order, the first being this: the explicit comparison of, and especially the implicit drawing of parallels between, Jesus and others, must be reckoned a compositional habit of Matthew. Illustrations of explicit comparison include 12:38-41 ("something greater than Jonah is here"), 42 ("something greater than Solomon is here"); and 16:13-14 ("'Who do men say that the Son of man is?' And they said, 'Some say John the Baptist, others say Elijah, and others Jeremiah or one of the prophets'"). A signal instance of implicit parallelism, a parallelism that runs throughout the whole Gospel, appears when we set certain verses pertaining to John the Baptist along side certain verses pertaining to Jesus:[1]

John the Baptist	Jesus
John said: "Repent, for the kingdom of heaven is at hand" (3:2)	Jesus said: "Repent, for the kingdom of heaven is at hand" (4:17)
John said to Pharisees and Sadducees: "You brood of vipers" (3:7)	Jesus said to the Pharisees: "You brood of vipers" (12:34)
John said: "Every tree therefore that does not bear good fruit is cut down and thrown into the fire" (3:10)	Jesus said: "Every tree that does not bear good fruit is cut down and thrown into the fire" (7:10)

[1]In addition to what follows see John P. Meier, "John the Baptist in Matthew's Gospel," *JBL* 99 (1980):383-405.

The people regarded John as a prophet (11:9; 14:5)	The people regarded Jesus as a prophet (21:ll, 26, 46)
John was rejected by "this generation" (11:16-19)	Jesus was rejected by "this generation" (11:16-19)
Herod the tetrarch was responsible for John's death	Pilate the governor was responsible for Jesus' death
John was seized (*krateō*, 14:3)	Jesus was seized (*krateō*, 21:46)
John was bound (*deō*, 14:3)	Jesus was bound (*deō*, 27:2)
Herod feared the crowds because they held John to be a prophet (14:5)	The chief priests and Pharisees feared the crowds because they held Jesus to be a prophet (21:46)
Herod was asked by another to execute John and grieved so to do (14:6-11)	Pilate was asked by others to execute Jesus and was reluctant so to do (27:11-26)
John was buried by his disciples (14:12)	Jesus was buried by a disciple (27:57-61)

Also noteworthy are the many parallels between Jesus and his disciples: these must strike even the casual reader. A sampling:

The disciples	Jesus
They are to heal every disease and every infirmity (10:l)	He heals every disease and every infirmity (4:23)
They are to preach that "the kingdom of heaven is at hand" (10:7)	He preaches that "the kingdom of heaven is at hand" (4:17)
They are to cast out demons (10:8)	He casts out demons (9:32-33, etc.)
They are to heal lepers (10:8)	He heals lepers (11:5)

They are to raise the dead (10:8)	Jesus raises the dead (11:5)
They are not to go to the Samaritans (10:6)	He does not go to the Samaritans (15:24)
They will be handed over to sanhedrins (10:17)	Jesus is handed over to the Sanhedrin (26:57-68)
They will be dragged before governors (10:18)	Jesus is taken before the governor (27:1-2, 11-26)
They will be called Beelzebul (10:25)	Jesus is called Beelzebul (9:34; 10:25)

From such obvious and extended assimilation of Jesus and John the Baptist and of Jesus and his disciples we may extract that Matthew was wont to comprehend his Lord and illustrate his significance through comparison with others. This important fact is more than consistent with the thesis I shall be urging.

My second opening remark is that the Gospel of Matthew is not an expansive work, and it is nearly devoid of decoration. Where is the superfluous sentence? Almost every word is required and pregnant with meaning. We have here the antithesis of a flowery, Victorian novel, from which numerous details could be stricken with little but aesthetic loss (or, as the case might be, gain). This should be constantly kept before the mind while following my subsequent argument, for I shall often be reckoning as full of import a thing which might seem to some a light matter—such as the addition of "and forty nights" to Matt. 4:2. For our evangelist, however, paper was presumably a limited commodity; further, his book was, we may imagine, written with catechetical and liturgical ends in view. It was therefore of first advantage that he fill every word with meaning; and this he did by, among other things, embedding allusion after allusion. The upshot was augmentation of his Gospel by means of its linkage to other texts: the First Gospel adds to itself by implicitly interacting with earlier works.[2]

---

[2]See further below, pp. 284-87.

THE BIRTH AND INFANCY NARRATIVE
(1:18-2:23)

The existence of a Moses typology in Matt. 1-2 has been affirmed by many modern commentators, and rightly so.[3] Certain events in the Gospel strikingly resemble certain traditions about Moses, language from Exodus is plainly borrowed (as in 2:19; cf. Exod. 4:19-20), and a biblical text having to do with the deliverance from Egypt (Hos. 11:1) is expressly quoted (2:15). The inference appears inevitable. Thus it is that even Saito, who otherwise disputes the existence of a Moses typology, cannot enlarge his doubt sufficiently to purge the Mosaic features altogether from the infancy narrative: he can only wash Matthew's hands of them, that is, assign them to pre-Matthean tradition.

Previously, on pp. 19-20, I listed six devices commonly used in constructing typologies: explicit statement, inexplicit borrowing, reminiscent circumstances, key words or phrases, structural imitation, and resonant syllabic and/or word patterns. I should now like to show that, in Matthew 1-2, all but the last of these devices has been employed in the construction of an extensive typology. The effect is an infancy narrative permeated by Mosaic motifs.

Explicit statement. 2:15 quotes MT Hos. 11:1: "Out of Egypt have I called my son." Did the evangelist take these words, against their original sense, to be a genuine prophecy of Jesus?[4] There is nothing at all messianic about Hos. 11:1 or its context, nor can the object of the sentence be in doubt when one reads the prophet: the son is Israel of old. One is accordingly tempted to credit Matthew with bad faith, or, no less condescendingly, with an inept hermeneutical method. But I believe we should instead entertain the possibility that our author, with his keen knowledge of Scripture, was neither naively oblivious of, nor intentionally refused to perceive, the obvious meaning of Hos. 11:1. This last, after all, begins with, "When Israel was a child, I loved him." It is one thing to assert that Matthew's hermeneutical methods

---

[3]See below, p. 293, n. 1; also Raymond E. Brown, *The Birth of the Messiah* (Garden City: Doubleday, 1977), 110-19; Michael Goldberg, *Jews and Christians: Getting Our Stories Straight* (Nashville: Abingdon, 1985), 144-49; Perrot, "Recits d'enfance," 512; T. Saito, *Mosevorstellungen,* 51-72 (see p. 18, n. 27); H. M. Teeple, *The Mosaic Eschatological Prophet,* 74-75 (regarding the Mosaic motifs as "Matthew's invention");Anton Vögtle, "Die matthäische Kindheitsgeschichte," in *L'Évangile selon Matthieu: Rédaction et Théologie,* ed. M. Didier (BETL 29: Gembloux: Leuven University, 1972), 153-83; and Paul Winter, "Jewish Folklore in the Matthean Birth Story," *HeyJ* 53 (1954):34-42.

[4]So Luz, *Matthew,* 1:146, n. 24.

were far from ours, quite another to imply that he could not comprehend the plain sense of a Hebrew sentence.[5] Surely it is reasonable, at least initially, to assume that he knew what Hosea intended to say. But what then did Matthew think himself to be doing when he introduced Hos. 11:1 with, "This was to fulfil what the Lord had spoken by the prophet"?

In ancient Jewish sources concerned with eschatological matters the redemption from Egypt often serves as a type for the messianic redemption, and the prospect of a new exodus is held forth: before the consummation, there will be another exodus followed by another return (cf. pp. 194-99). In view of this well-attested fact, it would, I think, have been no extraordinary thing for Matthew to have found such expectation played out in the life of the Messiah, and all the more when we take into account the circumstance that Q had already portrayed Jesus as repeating or recapitulating certain experiences of Israel (see pp. 165-66). All this suggests that 2:15 is a typological interpretation of Jesus' story: "in Jesus the exodus from Egypt is repeated and completed."[6] As one recent commentator has expressed himself:

> Hosea's words are not a prediction, but an account of Israel's origin. Matthew's quotation thus depends for its validity on the recognition of Jesus as the true Israel, a typological theme found elsewhere in the New Testament, and most obviously paralleled in Matthew by Jesus' use of Israel-texts in the wilderness [in chapter 4]... ; there too it is as God's *son* that Jesus is equated with Israel.[7]

This interpretation means that the reader of Matthew 1-2 is to behold in Jesus' story the replay of another, that of the exodus from Egypt, a story whose hero is Moses. In other words, 2:15, by quoting Hos. 11:1, tells us that there is parallelism between what unfolds in Matthew 2 and what unfolded long ago in Egypt. The quotation does not, I hasten to add, make plain the extent of that parallelism. Yet it cannot but encourage the thoughtful reader to set the story of Jesus and the story of the exodus—which is the story of Moses—side by side and ask: how exactly are they similar?

---

[5]I believe, and have elsewhere argued, both that Matthew knew Hebrew and that he mined most of the formula quotations himself; the evidence that he used a book of testimonies does not amount to proof; see Davies and Allison, *Matthew*, 1:32-58; 2:323-24; also George M. Soares Prabhu, *The Formula Quotations in the Infancy Narrative of Matthew* (AnBib 63; Rome: Biblical Institute Press, 1976).

[6]Luz, *Matthew 1-7*, 146.

[7]R. T. France, *Matthew*, Tyndale New Testament Commentaries (Leicester: Inter-Varsity, 1985), 86. Cf. my article, "The Son of God as Israel: A Note on Matthean Christology," *IBS* 9 (1987):74-81.

At this point some might raise an objection: 2:15 makes Jesus the new Israel, not the new Moses. That is, Jesus the Son corresponds to Israel the son, not to the lawgiver; hence, on the redactional level, there can have been no interest in a Moses typology. Just such an argument has been forwarded by Saito. But against this, where is the tittle of evidence that Matthew did not construe Jesus' status as the new Israel and his identity as another Moses as correlative conceptions? Was his thought really so constricted and wooden as to prohibit such? In Deutero-Isaiah the servant is, at least sometimes, Israel; but he is also one like Moses (see pp. 68-71). Moreover, the Messiah was, at least in rabbinic sources, to be both like Moses and a king; but in ancient thought a king represented, could indeed be said to be, his people: so why imagine that Matthew was unable to equate the Messianic king like Moses with true Israel? Even more to the point: if one claims that in chapter 2 Matthew turned the Moses typology of the pre-Matthean tradition into an Israel typology (so Saito), what does one make of chapter 4, where similar reasoning would lead one to urge—as has Teeple—that the evangelist did just the opposite, namely, turned the Israel typology of Q into a Moses typology (see p. 167)? The truth is, such an alleged inconsistency as this exists only in the eye of the beholder, and Matthew beheld something else. I contend that for him, Jesus' experience of another exodus made him both like Israel and like Moses.[8] Jesus is many things in the First Gospel, and there is no more tension or contradiction between maintaining that Jesus is simultaneously like Moses and the embodiment of true Israel than in saying that Jesus is the son of Abraham and the Son of David.

Implicit citation. Matt. 2:19-21 recounts Jesus' return from Egypt to Israel. As the commentaries generally recognize, the verses depend upon Exod. 4:19-20:

Matthew	Exodus (LXX)
But when Herod died,	After these many days the king of Egypt died.
behold, the angel of the Lord appeared in a dream	The Lord said
to Joseph in Egypt, saying, "Rise, take the child	to Moses in Midian:

---

[8]See further Vögtle, "Kindheitsgeschichte," 175-77. He convincingly demonstrates the harmony between the quotation of Hos. 11:1 and Matthew's Moses typology.

and his mother	
and go	"Go back
to the land of Israel,	to Egypt,
for those seeking	for all those seeking
the life of the child	your life
have died."	have died."
And he rose and took	Moses, taking
	his wife
the child	and his children,
and his mother,	
	mounted them on asses,
and went unto	and returned to
the land of Israel.	Egypt (MT: the land of Egypt).

Particularly striking is the plural in Matt. 2:20: "those seeking... have died." Herod is the only immediate antecedent. This might be explained as a "rhetorical" or "allusive" plural, with reference to Herod's coactors in 2:3-4 (BDF § 141). But it is easier to believe that the language of Exod. 4:19 was retained without perfect grammatical adjustment, in order to make the parallel with the sentence from Exodus unmistakable.

According to Ulrich Luz,

> The differences between Matt. 2:13-23 and the Moses haggadah are quite great.... Not only the cleverness of the mother or the father but God's intervention saves the child Jesus; Jesus flees to Egypt, (the adult) Moses flees from Egypt. In the passage deliberately adduced by Matthew, Exod. 4:19f., Moses has his correspondence in the father of Jesus, not in Jesus. Thus it is not so that in Matt. 2:13-23, as the late passage *Pesiq.* 49b = Midr Ruth on 2:14 = 5:6 (Str-B I 86f.) says, the last deliverer is like the first one. If a correspondence is maintained, it is that between Herod and the Pharaoh, not that between Jesus and Moses.[9]

These remarks are problematic and afford yet one more illustration of the fallacy of discrediting a typology by adding up differences between type and antitype. It is true that in Exod. 4:19-20 Moses takes his family back to Egypt whereas in Matt. 2:19-21 it is Joseph, not Jesus, who performs that task; and the destination in the Gospel is, further, now Israel, not Egypt. But the observation does not establish Luz's prohibitory inference, for it misses the clear point of comparison. Jesus is the object of "those seeking the life of the child" (Matt. 2:20), a clause

---

[9]*Matthew*, 1:144, n. 13.

with its parallel in Exod. 4:19, "all those seeking your life." In this last Moses is the object, and it is precisely here that the parallelism lies, as the rest of the Gospel makes manifest. In 1:18ff. Joseph, as we shall see soon enough, is like Amram, Moses' father, while Jesus is like Moses, the savior of Israel. Surely that circumstance should dictate how one reads chapter 2. Nothing has prepared us to think of Joseph as Mosaic. Much, however, has prepared us to think of Jesus as such. Hence the parallelism of 2:19-21 should be unfolded as follows:

—Moses went into exile, as did Jesus

—Moses was in exile until the king seeking his life expired,

   an event supernaturally communicated; so too with Jesus

—Moses, like Jesus later, returned from exile with his family

Pace Luz, we do have here resemblance between the first redeemer and the last. Indeed, such resemblance was, one presumes, precisely the reason for the borrowing from Exod. 4:19.

   Similar circumstances. The following parallels between Matthew 1-2 and traditions about Moses are those most obvious, and the majority of them have been noted and discussed by others before me:

The story of Moses According to Josephus, *Ant.* 2:210-16, Amram, the noble and pious father of Moses, was fearful, ill at ease, and at a loss as to what to do about his wife's pregnancy, for Pharaoh had decreed death for male infants; being in such a state, God appeared to the man in a dream, exhorted him not to despair, and prophesied his son's future greatness	The story of Jesus While Joseph, the just father of Jesus, is contemplating his course of action with regard to his wife's pregnancy, the angel of the Lord appears to him in a dream and bids him not to fear, then prophesies his son's future greatness (1:18-21)
Moses was remembered as Israel's "savior,"[10] and Joseph, *Ant.*	"You will call his name Jesus, for he shall save his people

---

[10]See Artapanus *apud* Eusebius, *Praep. ev.* 9:27.21-22 (*diasōsanta, apolysai*); Josephus, *Ant.* 2:216; *LAB* 9:10; Acts 7:25 (*didōsin sōterian autois*); *b. Sota* 12b ("the savior of Israel"—

2:228, associated his very
name with an Egyptian verb for

from their sins" (1:21)

"save": "It was indeed from this very incident [the rescue of the infant
Moses from the water] that the princess gave him the name recalling
his immersion in the river, for the Egyptians call water *mou* and those
who are saved *esēs*; so they conferred on him this name compounded
of both words" (cf. C. Ap. 1:286: "Moses" signifies "one saved out of the
water")

At the time of Moses' birth, the king, Pharaoh, gave the order to do away with every male Hebrew child (Exodus 1)	Near the time of Jesus' birth, the king, Herod, gives the order to do away with the male infants of Bethlehem (2:16-18)
In extra-biblical tradition, Herod slaughtered the Hebrew infants because he learned of the birth of the future liberator of Israel (Josephus, *Ant.* 2:205-209; *Tg. Ps.-J.* on Exod. 1:15; etc.)	Herod orders the slaughter of Hebrew infants because he has learned of the birth of Israel's liberator (2:2-18)
According to Josephus, *Ant.* 2:205, 234, Pharaoh learned of Israel's liberator from scribes, and in the *Jerusalem targum* on Exod. 1:15 it is said that Jannes and Jambres, chief magicians, were the source of information[11]	Herod learns of the coming liberator from chief priests, scribes, and magi (2:1-12)
Unnamed astrologers foretold Israel's deliverer (so *b. Sanh.* 101a; *b. Sota* 12b; and *Exod. Rab.* on 1:22)	The magi see a star and interpret it as signifying the birth of Israel's deliverer (2:1-2)

on the lips of Pharaoh's magi); *Exod. Rab.* 1:18; Gregory of Nyssa, *Laud. Bas.* 21; and recall
the rabbinic formula, "as the first redeemer [Moses], so the last."

[11]Jannes and Jambres, designated "holy scribes" and "magicians" in Eusebius, *Praep.
ev.* 9:8 (quoting Numenius), were held in Jewish tradition to be the sons of Balaam (see
p. 109, n. 40). This is so intriguing because, as exegetical history shows, Matthew's magi
have frequently been associated with Balaam; see Davies and Allison, *Matthew,* 1:230-
231, 234-35.

According to Josephus, *Ant.* 2:206, when Pharaoh heard the scribe prophesy the deliverer, he was "seized by fear;" in the *Chronicle of Moses* all the

"When Herod the king heard this, he was troubled, and all Jerusalem with him" (2:3)

people are "seized by a great fear because of Pharaoh's dream," which dream is interpreted to signify Moses' advent (cf. below, p. 157)

Moses was forced to leave his homeland because Pharaoh sought his life (Exod 2:15); before that, as an infant, he was under the shadow of death and kept safe by divinely ordered circumstances (Exodus 2:1-l0; Philo, *Mos.* 1:12; Josephus, *Ant.* 2:217-27)

Jesus is providentially taken from the land of his birth because Herod seeks to kill him (2:13-14)

After the death of Pharaoh, Moses was commanded by God to return to Egypt, his homeland; *tethnēkasin gar pantes hoi zētountes sou tēn psychēn* (Exod. 4:l9)

After the death of Herod, Joseph is commanded by an angel to return to Israel, his homeland; *tethnēkasain gar hoi zētountes tēn psychēn tou paidiou* (2:19-20)

Moses took his wife and his children and returned to Egypt (Exod. 4:20)

Joseph takes his son and his wife and goes back to Israel (2:21)

There are, I should like to submit, a few additional parallels which, although less obvious, will remunerate review. (l) David Daube, in his book on *Rabbinic Judaism and the New Testament*, conjectured that the *Passover Haggadah* interprets Exod. 2:25 ("God saw the people of Israel and God *knew*") in a sexual sense (*yada* ʿ= both "to know" and "to have sexual intercourse with"), thereby attributing the conception of Moses to God's direct intervention.[12]

Most, including myself at one time, have quickly dismissed the conjecture. Thus Raymond Brown, in *The Birth of the Messiah*, relegates the possibility to a footnote under the unflattering adjective, "dubi-

---

[12]David Daube, *The New Testament and Rabbinic Judaism* (London: University of London, l965), 5-9.

ous."[13] There are, if we overlook the flight in the face of certain cherished theological convictions, three problems: (i) the proposed interpretation is not explicit in any extant Jewish literature; (ii) Josephus and the *Liber Biblicarum Antiquitatum*, both from the first century, make it plain that Amram fathered Moses; and (iii) Moses could not have been virginally conceived in any event because he was not the first-born: Aaron and Miriam came before him, by natural means. These problems, it is held, take us to a dead-end.

There are nonetheless reasons for further investigation, for Daube's proposal is not unattested by evidence—not all of it noticed by him. For one thing, Josephus had this to say about Moses' birth: the piety of Amram and Jochebed, their faith "in the promises of God was confirmed by the manner of the woman's delivery, since she escaped the vigilance of the watch, thanks to the gentleness of her travail, which spared her any violent throes" (*Ant.* 2:218). According to this, Moses' mother was not subject to the curse of Eve, as recorded in Gen. 3:16: "I will greatly increase your pangs in childbearing; in pain you shall bring forth children." This same tradition reappears in *b. Sota* 12a and *Exod. Rab.* 1:20. Clearly some Jews believed, by Matthew's time, that at least Moses' *delivery* was extraordinary. Is there any evidence that his conception was also considered extraordinary?[14]

The haggadah has it that Jochebed, Moses' mother, was old when she conceived the deliverer. According to *b. B. Bat.* 120a, "As it is written, 'And there went a man of the house of Levi [Amram], and took to wife a daughter of Levi;' how could she be called 'daughter' when she was a hundred and twenty years old?"[15] The text explains: "This teaches that the signs of maidenhood [*sîmānê- naʾărût*] were restored in her. The flesh was again smooth, the wrinkles were

---

[13]Brown, *Birth*, 524, n. 21.

[14]We should keep in mind that Judaism did know of the possibility of extradordinary conceptions. *1 En.* 6-7; *1QapGen.* 2; *T. Sol.* 5.3; and *Prot. Jas.* 14.1 reflect the belief that angels could impregnate human beings. There is also the bizarre story of the miraculous conception and birth of Melchizedek at the end of some mss. of 2 Enoch (chapter 71)—although this is of uncertain date and origin. That a divine begetting of the Messiah should be found in *1QSa* 2.11-2 is doubtful; but perhaps attention needs to be directed to the obscure text in *b. Yeb.* 64a-b: R. Ammi stated: 'Abraham and Sarah had hidden [or: undeveloped] genitals (*ṭumṭumîn*); for it is said: "Look to the rock whence you were hewn and to the hole of the pit whence you were digged;" and this is followed by the text: "Look unto Abraham your father, and unto Sarah that bore you." R. Nahman stated... Our mother Sarah was incapable of procreation; for it is said, "And Sarah was barren; she had no child." She had not even a womb.'

[15]Other sources say she was one hundred and twenty-six years, still others one hundred and thirty; but to my knowledge Jochebed is always old when her age at the time of Moses' conception or birth is mentioned.

straightened out and beauty returned." This notion, overlooked by Daube, that Jochebed's youth was restored before the conception of Moses, is attested also in *Tg. Exod.* 2:1; *Exod. Rab.* l:19; and *b. Sota* 12a.[16] Now there seems little doubt as to the meaning, in *b. B. Bat.* 120a, of "the symptoms of maidenhood were restored," especially because, in context, the case of Jochebed is illustrative of how the daughters of Zelophehad, who did not marry until forty, past which the text says conception is impossible, could still conceive: not only were Jochebed's wrinkles removed, but her reproductive mechanism was renewed; that is, her fertility and presumably hymen were restored.[17] If this interpretation be correct, Jochebed was a virgin immediately before Moses was conceived. Now this does not, I freely confess, entail that Moses was conceived virginally. Yet it is certain that, in the rabbinic texts cited, Moses' birth is associated with a new and miraculous beginning.[18] Further, *b. B. Bat.* 120a and the parallel texts, interpreted as I have interpreted them, do away with one argument against Daube's proposal, namely, that Moses' conception could not have been analogous to that of Jesus because Jochebed, having already given birth to Aaron and Miriam, was not a virgin: Jewish legend restored her virginity.

A second consideration, one ignored, for understandable reasons, by Daube's critics, lends credence to his theory. Jewish tradition equated the "affliction" of Deut. 26:7 ("And he saw our affliction, and our distress, and our oppression") with sexual abstinence. As the *Passover Haggadah* puts it: "'And saw our affliction': this is enforced marital continence. As it is said: 'And God saw the children of Israel, and God knew'" (Exod. 2:25). This tradition, that the Israelites abstained from intercourse in order to prevent the slaughter of male infants is an ancient one, occurring already in *LAB* 9 (from the [late?] first century C.E.). One can therefore understand how belief in Moses' supernatural conception *might* have arisen: the tradition closely associated the time of Jochebed's impregnation with a time of sexual abstinence. The indubitable fact has given me much cause for pondering.

And it does not stand alone. According to *Exod. Rab.* 1:13, Jochebed was three months pregnant when Amram divorced her. But according

---

[16]It is interesting that while Josephus does not preserve this tradition, he does have God reassure Amram through recall of Sarah's fertility in old age: *Ant.* 2:213.

[17]In *b. Kidd.* 4a the *sîmānîm* of *na'arût* clearly denote the signs of puberty.

[18]In part this was no doubt stimulated by Exod. 2:1, which naturally implies that Moses was the first-born; but what then of Aaron and Miriam? See further below, pp. 203-204.

to *Exod. Rab.* 1:19, she was three months pregnant when Amram took her back. Visually:

1:13   conception————(3 months)————> divorce
1:19   conception————(3 months)————> remarriage

We have here, it seems, two conflicting traditions. How is their relationship to be evaluated? *Exod. Rab.* 1:13, in which Amram divorces Jochebed three months after conception, does not make much sense, for if, as the text teaches, Jochebed "was already with child, how could her husband hope to thwart Pharaoh's plan by divorcing her?" (Daube). The difficulty is not felt in *Exod. Rab.* 1:19, if it is assumed that divorce occurred before knowledge of the pregnancy came to Amram (that is, shortly after conception). Nor is there any problem in *b. Sota* 12a: here the divorce precedes both remarriage and conception, so it serves the function of saving life (cf. *Sefer ha-Zikronot*). Now the curious fact, with surprising implications, is that despite their apparent chronological contradiction, *Exod. Rab.* 1:13 and 19 agree that Jochebed conceived before she remarried; and if anyone ever believed that and simultaneously believed (as many of the sources relate) that Amram divorced Jochebed in order to circumvent Pharaoh's decree, it would follow that Jochebed became pregnant between the time that her husband divorced and then remarried her, that is, during a temporary cessation of sexual relations. As explanation, only unlawful intercourse (of which there is no trace in the tradition) or supernatural intervention offer themselves for consideration.

Let me submit one more piece of evidence. In a fascinating article on an obscure topic, P. W. van der Horst has reviewed the ancient sources which tell of individuals born in the seventh month after conception. Outside of Jewish and Christian texts he finds seven such, all men: Apollo, Dionysius, Heracles, Eurystheus, Demaratus of Sparta, Julius Caesar, and Corbulo. The first two were gods, the third a hero begotten by Zeus, the fourth a mythical king who claimed Zeus as his great-grandfather, the fifth an historical king supposedly begotten by a hero (Astrabacus), and the sixth a great dictator with a divine lineage. Only the seventh, a consul, had a simple human origin. The situation is similar in Jewish and Christian documents, for in them the following are sometimes said to have been born in the seventh month: Jesus, Mary, Isaac, Samuel, and Moses. Now Jesus was thought born of a virgin, and in *Protevangelium James* 4 Anna has clearly conceived without Joachim. As for Isaac, already in Genesis his conception is miraculous, for "it had ceased to be with Sarah after the manner of women," and only divine aid enabled her, at the infertile age of ninety, to bear a child. Further, Philo says Isaac was begotten by God (*Leg. all* 3:219; cf. *Mut. num.* 130-32, 137); and while the interpretation of his words are disputed,[19] *Tg. Ps.-J.* on Gen. 21:1 records that, "the Lord wrought a miracle for Sarah," while *Gen. Rab.* 47:2 offers that God fashioned for Sarah an ovary; and Gal. 4:21-31 may also assume a miraculous birth for Isaac, although most commentators have thought otherwise. What of Samuel? His mother, Hanna, was barren because "the Lord had closed her womb" (1 Sam. 1:5), and only in response to prayer was she opened. Moreover, "that also Jochebed and Hanna were felt to be parallel cases is proved by the fact that Hanna too, like Jochebed, is said to have been 130 years of age when she conceived Samuel... . [And] Samuel's birth has clearly been a model for the miraculous birth of Mary in the *Protevangelium Jacobi.*"[20]

The emergent pattern is undeniable: a seven months delivery in pagan or Jewish or Christian sources betokens a divine origin or a conception supernaturally assisted. So when we find, in *Tg. Ps.-J.* on Exod. 2:2; *Mek. of Rabbi Simeon ben Yohai,* p. 6 (Epstein); and *Sefer ha-Zikronot,*[21] that Moses too was born at the end of six months or in the seventh month, this is one more sign that his advent was thought of as surrounded by mysterious circumstances.

We are perfectly free to affirm, and with the evidence on our side, that Jewish tradition nowhere explicitly confirms Daube's interpretation of the line from the *Passover Haggadah.*[22] Further, the proposal under consideration suffers from the disadvantage that Josephus and Pseudo-Philo tell the story of Moses' birth in such a way as to exclude it. On the other hand, the haggadic imagination did, beyond all dispute, speculate about the supernatural circumstances of both Moses' conception and delivery.[23] So whether or not a virgin birth for the lawgiver had any currency, a proposition of greater plausibility—I do not say probability—than most have admitted, people did think of the circumstances of his advent as miraculous, as due to the direct intervention of God. Is this then not yet one more important way in which Matthew's Jesus resembles Moses?

---

[19]See P. Grelot, "La naissance d'Isaac et celle je Jésus: Sur une interprétation 'mythologique' de la conception virginale," *NRT* 94 (1972):462-87, 561-85.

[20]"Seven Months' Children in Jewish and Christian Literature from Antiquity," *ETL* 54 (1978), 358.

[21]For additional sources see Ginzberg, *Legends,* 5:397, n. 44.

[22]Although perhaps someone might want to contend that the interpretation of *Mošeh ʾîšaʾ ʾĕlōhîm* (Deut. 33:1) as "Moses, man and God" (see p. 155) might reflect such a belief.

[23]It also speculated on his infancy. Philo, for example, says he was weaned at a surprisingly early date: *Mos.* 1:18.

(2) In Matt. 1:18 it is said that Mary, after betrothal, but before marriage and before sexual intercourse, was with child of the Holy Spirit. Then, in 1:24, we read that Joseph, dispelled of suspicions regarding Mary's behavior, took her to wife. So the narrative tells of a man marrying an already-pregnant woman. The situation, to my knowledge, has its closest and perhaps only Jewish parallel in the Moses traditions. As previously indicated, *Exod. Rab.* 1:13 and 19 record that, when Amram remarried Jochebed, she was already pregnant with Moses. Whether or not the circumstance ever was (as Daube suspected) explained by a supernatural intervention, or whether it was always assumed, as *Exod. Rab.* 1:13 offers, that Amram impregnated his wife before he divorced and subsequently remarried her, there can be no denying the formal parallel: just as Joseph took to himself a pregnant wife, so too, according to certain Jewish sources, did Amram marry a woman already with child.

(3) In one of the volumes in his great study of Jewish symbols, E. R. Goodenough observed that there is an interesting scene at the Dura-Europos synagogue (west wall, north half) which may be related to Matthew 2. In the latter the new-born Jesus is adored by magi who bring three gifts: gold, frankincense, and myrrh. In the former there is a depiction of the birth of Moses, and he too seems to be presented with gifts.[24] Three Egyptian maids or princesses (depicted as nymphs) hold forth dishes, a box, and a juglet. Unfortunately, the precise significance of these objects is unknown: there is apparently no literary parallel to help us in interpretation. Goodenough, however, was fairly confident that the three women are offering gifts to the new-born savior.

Although the correctness of Goodenough's interpretation is beyond the compass of certainty—perhaps some future discovery may yet settle the matter—, it may be observed that, in later Christian art, the infant Moses does receive gifts.[25] Was the motif borrowed from the Jewish tradition? or did Christians instead assimilate the birth of Moses to that of Jesus? In the former case Goodenough's interpretation would be recommended and the parallel with Matthew 2 made firm. In the latter case we would at least have evidence that some Christians, at some point in time, thought it appropriate to liken the birth of the first redeemer to that of the last. And in either case the

---

[24]For what follows see Goodenough, *Jewish Symbols*, 9:203-17. On p. 208 he makes the comparison with Matthew 2.

[25]Goodenough, *Symbols*, 11:176, plate 174.

possibility that there might be a Mosaic background for the adventure of the magi is enhanced.

(4) According to Matt. 2:14, Joseph took "the child and his mother by night" and went into Egypt. Why the notice of time (such a rarity outside the later chapters)? Perhaps it creates a parallel with the passion narrative: at the end too it was at night that Jesus was overtaken. Or maybe *nyktos* makes plain the danger: the family had to go under cover of darkness. Or perchance the word suggests that Joseph immediately did as he was commanded, for he was commanded in a dream, and so, presumably, at night. It is more likely, however, that the cluster of motifs—flight, night, Egypt—should recall the exodus. Tradition held that Moses and the Israelites fled Egypt *at night* (Exod. 12:31-42; the fact was firmly planted in Jewish memory because the Passover was celebrated in the evening; cf. Exod. 12:8; *Jub.* 49:1, 12; etc.).

The objection to this reading is that the notice comes in 2:14, not in 2:21, where the family of Jesus leaves Egypt.[26] But this overlooks that the parallelism lies not in the identity of course taken but in the flight itself. It is true that Moses and the Israelites fled *from* Egypt, Jesus and his family *to* Egypt. But the emphasis is upon what is shared, that being the act of fleeing from hostility. Moreover, Joseph and his family were only fleeing when they exited Palestine, not when they left Egypt; so the typology is more effective with *nyktos* in 2:14, where there is urgency, instead of 2:21, where haste is unnecessary.

(5) *b. Meg.* 14a informs us that when Moses "was born, the whole house [he was born in] was filled with light." This legend, widely attested,[27] has occasionally been associated with Matthew's story of a guiding star.[28] At first sight, the parallel seems ill-considered: is a star really reminiscent of a light within a room?[29] An additional consideration, however, begets second thoughts. We inevitably regard Matthew's star as a heavenly object, that is, an energetic mass located in deep space. But in ancient Judaism stars were often thought of as living beings, and there are texts which identify them with angels.[30]

---

[26]Davies and Allison, *Matthew*, 1:261.

[27]Cf. *b. Sota* 13a; *b. Meg.* 14a; *Exod. Rab.* 1:20; *Cant. Rab.* 1:20; *Sefer ha-Zikronot*; *SB* 1:78; 2:678;

[28]E.g. Davies, *Setting*, 80.

[29]But *Sefer ha-Zikronot* refers to the bright light at Moses' birth as "like that of the sun and moon at their rising."

[30]Such as Judg. 5:20; Job 38:7; Dan. 8:10; *1 En.* 86:1,3; 90:20-27; Rev. 9:1; 12:4; *LAB* 32:15; *T. Sol.* 20:14-17; *Arabic Gospel of Infancy* 7. The whole subject of astral immortality is also

Matthew's star is in fact equated with such in the *Arabic Gospel of the Infancy* 7. Now the pertinence of this becomes evident when we admit that we are at a loss before the tale of the magi: how in the world could a star in the sky guide men, however wise, to a particular residence? I submit that our puzzlement flows from our idea of a star, which idea was not Matthew's. 2:9 ("the star they had seen in the East went before them") seems clear enough. It implies what *Prot. Jas.* 21:3 relates, that the star went "before them, until they [the magi] came to the cave," and also that the star "stood over the head of the child." Compare the words of Chrysostom: the star

> did not, remaining on high, point out the place; it not being possible for them [the magi] so to ascertain it, but it came down and performed this office. For you know that a spot of so small dimensions, being only as much as a shed would occupy, or rather as much as the body of a little infant would take up, could not possibly be marked out by a star. For by reason of its immense height, it could not sufficiently distinguish so confined a spot, and discover it to them that were desiring to see it (*Hom. on Mt.* 6:3).

While all this seems fantastic to us, it was not to Chrysostom or to the author of the *Protevangelium James*, and I see no sound reason to suppose it would have been fantastic to Matthew. On the contrary, his text, which is certainly otherwise full of miracles, and which plainly avows that the star "went before" (*proēgen autous*) the magi (2:9), requires that the guiding light came down from on high to lead the magi whither they were going. If so, we do indeed have in Matthew 2 a close parallel to the phenomenon associated with the infant Moses.

But it is another matter confidently to add this parallel to the others we have compiled in our expository pilgrimage. The reason is that the theme of a supernatural light attending the birth of a great man was not exclusively associated with Moses. It was rather a popular item of folklore, attached now to this hero, now to that hero. In *LAE* 21:3 Cain, it says, was full of light at birth, while according to *1 En.* 106:2, 10, the infant eyes of Noah sent forth visible beams which made his whole house glow; and *Liv. Proph. Elijah* 2-3 testifies that shining men greeted

pertinent, especially as human destiny was often depicted as angelic; see Dan. 12:3 (on which see the commentaries); Wisd. 5:5; *1 En.* 104:2-6 (cf. 39:5); Philo, *De gig.* 2; *1QSb* IV:25; Matt. 22:30 par.; *2 Bar.* 51:1, 5; *As. Mos.* 10:7; *T. Isaac* 4:43-48; *Apoc. Zeph.* 8:1-5; *Apoc. Adam* 5:64,14-19; 76,4-6; *CMC* 51; discussion in James H. Charlesworth, "The Portrayal of the Righteous as an Angel," in *Ideal Figures in Ancient Judaism*, ed. George W. Nickelsburg and John J. Collins (Chico: Scholars Press, 1980), 135-51. —I note that Philo, *Mos.* 1:166, speculated that the pillar of cloud that led the Israelites in the desert had "an unseen angel" enclosed within it.

the baby Elijah and wrapped him in fire. The motif of an illuminated birth-place also appears outside Jewish tradition, in legends about Hercules, Zoroaster, and Mohammed. Obviously it would be hazardous to insist that the light of Matthew 2 must have reminded ancient readers of Moses in particular.

(6) In 1:23 our evangelist inserts a quotation from LXX Isa. 7:14: "Behold, a virgin shall conceive and bear a son, and his name shall be called Emmanuel." The first nine words relate to the circumstances of Jesus' conception and birth and make them fulfillments of an ancient oracle. The last seven interpret Jesus' significance by bestowing upon him a name or title, Emmanuel. The importance of this last follows from its receiving a clarifying clause, drawn from LXX Isa. 8:8: "which, being interpreted, means, With us is God." Unfortunately, Matthew's interpretive addition obscures as much as it clarifies. Is Jesus here unequivocally designated God, as he seems to be in John's Gospel? Or should we think instead that in him God's salvific presence has been made real? While I have elsewhere tried to answer the question, one must admit that there are good arguments for both possibilities, so that a dogmatic judgment is here inappropriate.[31] One fact, however, is manifest: Jesus' appellation (Emmanuel) has God's name in it.

What might this have to do with Moses? Exod. 4:16 reads: "You [Moses] shall be to him [Aaron] as God" (MT: *lēʾ lōhîm*; LXX: *ta pros ton theon*). Similar is Exod. 7:1: "I [God] make you [Moses] God to Pharaoh" (MT: *ʾelōhîm lĕparʾ ōh*; LXX: *theon pharaō*). In these two places Moses is called *theos* or *ʾelōhîm*. Now obviously Exodus does not identify Moses with Yahweh. "God to Pharaoh" and "God to Aaron" are simply striking phrases which make Moses play the rôle of God, that is, speak for Him (see the commentaries). Nonetheless, Exod. 4:16 and 7:1 later stimulated much speculation. Philo was very intrigued by the two texts and offered commentary upon them in several books, not a little of which is difficult to understand.[32] Whatever the reader may make of Philo's sometimes obscure statements, one thing is clear: the Alexandrian did not shrink from calling Moses, in some sense, *theos*. The same may be said of Jesus ben Sira. The LXX of Ecclus. 45:2 has this: Moses was *hōmoiōsen auton doxē hagiōn*, equal in glory to the holy ones (= angels). The Hebrew is, as so often, defective. But the line was almost certainly an allusion to Exod. 4:16 and/or 7:1 and should

---

[31]Davies and Allison, *Matthew*, 1:217.

[32]*Sac.* 9-10; *Mos.* 1:158; *Mig.* 81, 84, 169; *Det.* 162; *Quod Omn. Prob.* 43-44; *Mut.* 129. See further p. 304, n. 30.

be reconstructed as: *yĕkanehô bĕ [or: ʾîš] ʾĕlōhîm*.[33] According to this, Moses was titled "God." The Samaritans also made much of Moses receiving the divine name: it well served their exaltation of the lawgiver.[34] And in the rabbinic corpus there are several texts which, under the influence of Exod. 4:16 and 7:1, (wrongly) construe the phrase, *Mōšeh ʾîš hāʾ ĕlōhîm*, found in Deut. 33:1, to mean: "Moses, man and God" (*Deut. Rab.* 11:4; *Midr. Ps.* on 90:1). For further discussion of this fascinating topic of Moses as bearer of God's name I refer the reader to Wayne Meeks' helpful study of the subject.[35]

Returning to the First Gospel, should Jesus' status as Emmanuel be in any way connected with the tradition that Moses was called "God"? In Exodus, Moses, in a certain sense, acts in the place of God, that is, functions as the deity, and so is called "God." Is this not very close to what we have in Matthew, where Jesus, although he is not (I think) simply identified with God, functions as God and so is known as "Emmanuel"? The parallel is there, but whether the text was designed to evoke it I do not know. I do note, however, that exegetical history does present us with at least one example of someone associating Moses' status as *theos* with that of Jesus. Nestorius purportedly wrote in one place: "Just as we call the Creator of all things God, and just as we call Moses 'God' (for the Scripture says, 'I have made you as a God to Pharaoh')... so also the Lord Christ we call, 'God.'"[36]

Key words and phrases. 1:18-2:23 contains a few phrases which may have been intended to sound echoes of the early chapters of Exodus. Consider these parallels:

Matthew	Exodus (LXX)
prin ē synelthein autous, 1:18	*prin ē eiselthein autas*, 1:19
zētein to paidion tou apolesai	*ezētei anelein Mōusēn* +

---

[33]See W. O. E. Oesterley, *The Wisdom of Jesus the Son of Sirach or Ecclesiasticus* (Cambridge: University Press, 1912), 204, following R. Smend, *Die Weisheit des Jesus Sirach* (Berlin: G. Reimer, 1906). Cf. the notes of Box and Oesterley in *APOT* 1:484-85.

[34]See e.g. *Memar Marqah* 1:2, 9; 2:12; 4:1; 5:3, 4.

[35]Wayne A. Meeks, "Moses as God and King," in *Religions in Antiquity: Essays in Memory of Erwin Ramsdell Goodenough*, ed. J. Neusner (Leiden: E. J. Brill, 1970), 354-71.

[36]So Justinian, *Against the Monophysites*, quoting from the *acta* of the Council of Ephesus, *Exc. Eph.* 6. See *On the Person of Christ: the Christology of the Emperor Justinian*, trans. K. P. Wesche (Crestview: Saint Vladimir's, 1991), 41-42. For a contrast between "god" as applied to Moses in Exod. 7:1 and "God" as applied to "he who was incarnate in the womb of the virgin" see Gregory the Great, *Hom. Ezek.* 3:7.

+ *anechōrēsen*, 2:13-14; *aneilen*   *anechōrēsen*, 2:15
pantas tous paidas, 2:16

tēs teleutēs Herōdou, 2:15   *eteleutēsen ho basileus*, 2:23;
                                             4:19
paralabe to paidion kai tēn   *analabōn... tēn gunaika kai*
mētera autou, 2:13   *ta paidia*, 4:20

There are also isolated words which, taken together, may have been
designed to summon the exodus period. This is above all true of the
personal names. Jesus' father shares the name of the patriarch who is
referred to at the beginning of Exodus: "Now a new king arose who
did not know Joseph" (1:18).[37] Jesus' mother bears the name of Moses'
sister, Miriam. And Jesus himself is called by the name of Moses'
successor, Joshua—a fact which should perhaps be stressed given that
Joshua was remembered as one like Moses. Furthermore, Matthew 2
moves all three people—Jesus, Joseph, Mary—to Egypt, the setting for
the first exodus story. Do these coincidences not trigger memories in
the biblically informed reader?[38]

Similar narrative structure. Matt. 1:18-2:23 is customarily divided
into three main sections:
1:18-25, the dream about and birth of the coming deliverer
2:1-12, the star, Herod's scheme, the magi's worship
2:13-23, Jesus' exile and return

One must wonder whether this tripartite structure itself is not a clue
to the narrative's background and intention. More precisely, one must
wonder whether Matthew's arrangement was not derived from the
Moses traditions. The central portion of Josephus' account of Moses'
infancy (*Ant.* 2:205-23) also contains three main acts (cf. the Whiston
and Loeb divisions):
2:205-209, Pharaoh's dream and its interpretation
2:210-16, the dream of Amram
2:217-23, Moses' birth and providential deliverance

---

[37]Both Pompeius Trogus, *Hist. Phil.* 36:2.1, and Apollonius Molon *apud* Eusebius,
Praep. ev. 9:19.3, make Joseph the father of Moses; but I hesitate to make anything of this.
[38]Cf. below, p. 161, and Frye, *Great Code*, p. 172, who also observes: "The third Sura
of the Koran appears to be identifying Miriam and Mary; Christian commentators on
the Koran naturally say that this is ridiculous, but from the purely typological point of
view from which the Koran is speaking, the identification makes good sense."

The order is not the same as in Matthew: in Josephus the parent's dream is in second position, not first. Still, the themes of the three main sections are quite similar.

This general agreement merits additional examination. Josephus' narrative, unlike that in Exodus, links Pharaoh's decree of execution to foreknowledge of the coming deliverer. That foreknowledge is gained through the prophecy of a sacred scribe. So we actually have *two prophecies* of Moses' advent—one to his nemesis, the other to his father. Thus a momentous event is about to occur, knowledge of which has been bestowed through two different means to two different parties; and with that knowledge one group will seek to kill the savior to be, the other to hide him. This, then, is more precisely the fundamental structure of *Ant.* 2:205-23.

—prophecy to deliverer's foes and decree of death
—prophecy (in a dream) to deliverer's family
—the deliverance of the deliverer from danger

This basic arrangement is not exclusive to Josephus. It recurs in the later legends about Moses's infancy and can be found in, for example, *The Chronicle of Moses* and *Sefer ha-Zikronot*. Indeed, in these last two books, as in *Tg. Ps.-J.* on Exod. 1:15 and *Sefer ha-Yašar*, the prophecy to Pharaoh comes in the form of a dream which has to be interpreted. This makes for even greater resemblance to Matthew, where the prophecy to the enemies is an ambiguous sign (a star) that has to be interpreted (by the magi and by Jewish scribes). The result is this outline:

—indirect prophecy to deliverer's foes /
                    interpretation by scribes /
                                        decree of death
—direct prophecy (in a dream) to deliverer's father
—the deliverance of the deliverer from danger

We obviously have here a conventional way of ordering the infancy traditions about Moses, one going back at least to the time of Josephus. It follows that the basic structure of Matt. 1:18ff. was not invented by the First Evangelist. It was in fact not the invention of any Christian. Rather, it was borrowed from the Jewish traditions about Moses. The three main sections of Matthew 1-2 present us with a pattern that can be found in the *Antiquities* and elsewhere.

There is a second significant structural agreement between Matthew 1-2 and the Jewish traditions about Moses. The narratives that tell of a sign granted to Pharaoh often develop in five steps:

—indirect sign to the king
—troubled feelings in response to that sign
—consultation of advisors
—interpretation of sign by scribes
—resolution to slaughter Hebrew infants
The following appears in the *Chronicle of Moses* (of unknown date):

> It happened in the one hundred and thirtieth year after the descent of the
> children of Israel into Egypt and sixty years after the death of Joseph, that
> Pharaoh had a dream: an old man stood before him and there was a
> balance in his hand; he made all the people of Egypt, men, women and
> children, climb into one scale of the balance, and in the second scale he
> placed a lamb, and the lamb outweighed all the Egyptians. The king was
> astonished and pondered in his heart this prodigy, this great vision. Then
> Pharaoh awoke, and behold it was a dream. He assembled all the wise
> men and magicians of Egypt and told them his dream. All the people were
> seized by a great fear because of the dream, until there came before the
> king one of the princes who said to him, "This dream signifies a great
> misfortune and a calamity for Egypt." The king asked him, "What is it,
> then?" He replied, "A child will be born unto the children of Israel who
> will destroy all of Egypt. But now, my Lord King, I would like to give you
> good counsel: Give the order to kill every boy who will be born to the
> children of Israel. Perhaps then the dream will not come to pass." These
> words found favor in the eyes of Pharaoh and in the eyes of his court and
> the king of Egypt spoke to the Hebrew midwives.... .

Very similar accounts appear in *Sefer ha-Yašar; Yalqut Sim ʿoni* on Exod.
1:15; and *Sefer ha-Zikronot*: in these all five elements appear. It is,
admittedly, also true that we cannot here speak of invariance: Josephus
lacks the sign and the consultation, and the *Jerusalem Targum* fails to
record Pharaoh's fear. But these exceptions notwithstanding, the
cluster of five elements and their order was, to judge from their
recurrence in several sources, well established.

What do we find in Matthew? Precisely the same pattern:
2:1-2: sign (the star) called to the king's attention
2:3: troubled feelings in response to that sign
2:4: consultation of advisors
2:5-6: interpretation of the sign by scribes
2:7-8, 16-18: resolution to slaughter Hebrew infants

To observe this is not to overlook that Matthew's episode of the good
magi has no precise parallel elsewhere,[39] nor that the sign in Mat-

---

[39] Astrologers do, however, appear in the Moses infancy traditions. In *Exod. Rab.* 1:18;
b. Sanh. 101a; and *b. Sota* 12b, for instance, they prophesy a coming savior and in effect
substitute for Pharaoh's dream and its interpretation.

thew's account is a star, not a king's dream. Still, the similarities amidst the differences are obvious and fundamental. Again I cannot but surmise that we have here more than curious coincidence. Rather, the very structure of Matthew's account reflects the Moses traditions: the new Christian stories were set in a traditional mould.

There is yet a third way in which this is true. *LAB* 9 offers a first-century account of Moses' origins, one quite different than that found in Josephus. Notably, the slaughter of infants is not attributed to knowledge of a Jewish redeemer, and, in accord with later rabbinic tradition, the prophecy to the family, given in a dream, is received not by Amram but by Miriam, Moses' sister. These variations alert us that the haggadah about Moses was anything but fixed. Different story-tellers told different versions of what happened before and after Moses' birth: motifs were developed or omitted, and others inserted, as occasion or purpose warranted (cf. the variant infancy traditions in Matthew 1-2 and Luke 1-2).

One point *LAB* 9 makes, one not made by Josephus, is this: because Pharaoh decreed the slaughter of Hebrew children, the Jewish men resolved to divorce their wives:

> And after Joseph's passing away, the sons of Israel multiplied and increased greatly. And another king who did not know Joseph arose in Egypt, and he said to his people: "Behold that people has multiplied more than we have. Come, let us make a plan against them so they will not multiply more." And the king of Egypt ordered all his people, saying, "Every son that is born to the Hebrews, throw into the river; but let their females live." And the Egyptians answered their king, saying, "Let us kill their males, and we will keep their females so that we may give them to our slaves as wives. And whoever is born from them will be a slave and will serve us." And this is what seemed wicked before the Lord. Then the elders of the people gathered the people together in mourning, and they mourned and groaned, saying, "The wombs of our wives have suffered miscarriage; our fruit is delivered to our enemies. And now we are lost, and let us set up rules for ourselves that a man should not approach his wife lest the fruit of their wombs be defiled and our offspring serve idols. For it is better to die without sons until we know what God may do" (9:1-2).

This legend, as we have had occasion to observe, reappears in the later haggadah. This is the version of *Sefer ha-Zikronot*: "When the Israelites heard the decree that Pharaoh ordained, that their male children should be thrown into the river, some of the people divorced their wives; but the others stayed married to them." A similar account also appears in *Exod. Rab.* 1:19.

The notice of divorce is usually followed by a divine intervention: Providence reassures and encourages Amram, so that he takes back his wife.[40] Divine intervention is in turn usually succeeded by the remark that Amram duly went into his wife, as in *Sefer ha-Zikronot*: "When Amram heard the words of the child [that is, the prophecy of Miriam] he went and remarried his wife whom he had divorced.... And in the third years of the divorce he slept with her and she conceived by him." The pattern here is: divorce—reassurance—remarriage.[41]

The same pattern underlies Matthew 1. Because of Mary's circumstances, which imply adultery, the just Joseph, following Jewish law, resolves to obtain a divorce.[42] Next we are informed that Joseph was deterred from his intention, for the angel of the Lord appeared to him and revealed the true cause of Mary's pregnancy. Finally, the text says that "he [Joseph] knew her [Mary] not until she had borne a son" (1:25). Despite later dogma, the meaning is that, after Jesus' birth, Joseph and Mary lived a normal life as man and wife.

Matthew's story is obviously not the same as any of those told about Amram and Jochebed. Yet its structure is recollective:

1:18-19: Joseph determines to divorce Mary
1:20-21: God reassures him
1:24-25: He takes back his wife

At some point in the tradition, it has been suggested, Joseph may have sought to divorce his wife because he learned of Herod's decree.[43] This presupposes that, in the pre-Matthean tradition, there was a stage in which act II (2:1-12) preceded act I (1:18-25): thus the parallels with Moses were once even greater than they are now. That is a possibility to which I am attracted. But it remains speculative, and all I need show is the structural resemblance between Matthew 1 and the Moses traditions. Again one cannot but feel that, while the content is not all paralleled, the structure of Matthew 1 is traditional.

Before leaving Matthew 1-2 there are four issues that should be considered, however cursorily.

---

[40]In the *Liber Antiquitatum Biblicarum*, however, Amram refuses from the first to act as have his fellows, and God rewards him accordingly—a sequence that is probably redactional; cf. Saul M. Olyan, "The Israelites Debate their Options at the Sea of Reeds," *JBL* 110 (1991):85-86.

[41]Cf. John Dominic Crossan, "From Moses to Jesus: Parallel Themes," *BibRev* 2 (1986):26.

[42]See Davies and Allison, *Matthew*, 1:202-205.

[43]See Brown, *Birth*, 115-16.

Later tradition. Happily, the parallelism between Matthew 1:18ff. and certain traditions about Moses was noticed by later readers. Indeed, they themselves sometimes enlarged the correlations. Ephrem the Syrian, for example, in *Hymn 24* on the nativity, wrote this:

> The doves in Bethlehem murmured since the serpent destroyed their
>   offspring.
> The eagle fled to Egypt to go down and receive the promises.
> Egypt rejoiced to be the capitol for repaying the debts.
> She who had slain the sons of Joseph labored to repay by the son
>   of Joseph
> the debts of the sons of Joseph. Blessed is He who called him
>   from Egypt!

Obviously Ephrem understood that Matthew's text evokes the exodus.[44] The execution of the innocents of Bethlehem was like the slaughter of babes under Pharaoh, the difference being that whereas Egypt was once the witness of execution, it later became the safe haven from it. Note also that, for Ephrem, the name of Jesus' father was associated with the patriarch whose story opens Exodus (cf. p. 156).

Ephrem's interpretation does not stand alone. On p. 104 I have already quoted some words of Aphraates which I here cite again:

> Moses also was persecuted, as Jesus was persecuted. When Moses was born, they concealed him that he might not be slain by his persecutors. When Jesus was born they carried him off in flight into Egypt that Herod, his persecutor, might not slay him. In the days when Moses was born, children were drowned in the river; and at the birth of Jesus the children of Bethlehem and in its border were slain. To Moses God said: 'The men are dead who were seeking thy life'; and to Joseph the angel said in Egypt: 'Arise, take up the child, and go into the land of Egypt, for they are dead who were seeking the life of the child to take it away.'

Commentary would be superfluous.

Ephrem and Aphraates are literary witnesses. But art history offers the same testimony: Christians recognized the parallels between Matthew 1-2 and the traditions about Moses. In the depictions of the flight of the holy family to Egypt, Joseph often has a staff, and Mary and her child are typically on an ass.[45] The donkey and the staff almost certainly come from Exod. 4:20: "So Moses took his wife and his sons

---

[44]Cf. K. E. McVey, in his translation of Ephrem the Syrian, *Hymns* (New York: Paulist, 1989), 193.

[45]See G. Schiller, *Iconography of Christian Art* (Greenwich, Conn.: New York Graphics Society, 1968), vol. 1, plates 312-333.

and set them on an ass, and went back to the land of Egypt; and in his hand Moses took the rod of God." The words, as we have learned, lie behind Matthew's account of Jesus' descent into Egypt. What evidently happened, then, was this: the assimilation of one story to the other was noticed and the assimilation then extended: just as Moses went to Egypt with staff in hand and his wife on an ass, so too later did Joseph, with staff in hand and his wife on an ass, go down to Egypt.[46]

Another example of possible assimilation in post-New Testament times concerns the belief that Mary, in giving birth to Jesus, had no labor pains. John Damascus, *De fid.* 4:14, wrote:

> It was a birth that surpassed the established order of birthgiving, as it was without pain; for, where pleasure had not preceded, pain did not follow. And just as at his conception he had kept her who conceived him virgin, so also at his birth did he maintain her virginity intact, because he alone passed through her and kept her shut.

Belief in a painless delivery is attested much earlier—in Hesychios (PG 93:1469—fifth century) and Gregory of Nyssa (PG 45:492—fourth century). It is in fact implicit in the *Protevangelium James*, which was written sometime in the second century.[47] Here Mary remains a virgin even during birth (the traditional phrase is *virginitas in partu*) and the delivery is described in this fashion: "A great light shone in the cave, so that the eyes could not bear it. And in a little that light gradually decreased, until the infant appeared" (19-20; cf. *Asc. Isa.* 11:2-16; *Od. Sol.* 19:6-10). Now we have already seen that Josephus, in narrating the circumstances of Moses' birth, purported that Jochebed had no pain; and later sources reiterate this belief: doubtless it was well known. So one may ask: did the church transfer the motif of a painless delivery from Moses to Jesus? I see no way to be sure. The notion that Mary was spared suffering could have had an independent, exegetical origin: because Christ undid the fall, his birth must have been free of the curse pronounced in Gen. 3:16 (so later Christian reflection). Or maybe meditation upon belief in Mary's perpetual virginity was the decisive catalyst. But given that Christians in other respects modelled their

---

[46]Note also that many depictions of the flight to Egypt include one of Joseph's sons from a previous marriage. This too as it happens increases the parallels with Moses: the latter was commanded to take his *children*. Cf. *Gospel of Ps.-Matthew* 18. This apocryphal gospel also explicitly states that the holy family went "by way of the desert" (17) and has Jesus miraculously supply water (20).

[47]For additional early sources see J. C. Plumpe, "Some Little-Known Early Witnesses to Mary's *Virginitas in Partu*," *TS* 9 (1948):567-77.

savior on Moses, the possibility that the story of Jochebed's easy labor stimulated belief in Mary's exemption from pain must be seriously entertained.

A possible objection. *Sefer ha-Yašar* relates that the wicked king Nimrod learned, by astrology, of Abraham's advent and of his destiny to destroy false religion; that Nimrod sent for his princes and governors to ask advice; that they told him to have the midwives kill all male Hebrew infants; that Nimrod enacted their evil counsel, so that thousands of innocents were slaughtered; that Abraham's mother, Terah, saved her infant by depositing him in a cave, which he filled with light; and that Abraham, who matured at an incredible pace, was miraculously cared for by the angels. According to P. Nepper-Christensen, these traditions about Abraham confound proponents of a Moses typology in Matthew, for they show that the resemblances between Matthew 1-2 and the Moses traditions do not establish such a typology: certain motifs were just transferred from hero to hero.[48]

Does this touch the truth? I think not. Nepper-Christensen has committed two sins of omission. First, although *Sefer ha-Yašar* may be as late at the eleventh century (its date is uncertain), the book appears to be our earliest witness to the pertinent legends about Abraham; yet it must be centuries younger than the earliest sources, such as Philo and Josephus, for the comparable tales about Moses.[49] Beyond this, one can, in the second place, document a firm tendency in Jewish tradition to assimilate the patriarch to the lawgiver (see p. 91, n. 209). So very near to hand is the thought that the story of Abraham's infancy was modelled upon the story of Moses. In other words, *Sefer ha-Yašar* offers a Moses typology: the Father of Israel anticipated the liberator. If so, what Nepper-Christensen fallaciously forwards as an objection is in truth commendation: the Abraham parallels demonstrate not the unattached nature of certain motifs but instead show us that the transference to Jesus of Mosaic infancy items was not a unique procedure. Rather, Jewish tradition undertook to honor father Abraham in the very same way.

Eschatology. Jewish tradition strongly hints that, at some point in time, the traditions about Moses' infancy were thought to foreshadow

---

[48]*Matthäusevangelium*, 167-68

[49]Geza Vermes, *Scripture and Tradition in Judaism* (Studia Post-Biblica; Leiden: E. J. Brill, 1973), 90-95, establishes, by comparative method, that the author of *Sefer ha-Yašar* used traditional materials, motifs, and literary patterns; but he does not prove the antiquity of the Abraham traditions themselves.

messianic events. In *Sefer ha-Yašar* Pharaoh's dream is interpreted to mean this: "a great evil will befall Egypt *at the end of days*." This same loaded, eschatological phrase, "the end of days," also occurs, in similar contexts, in *Sefer ha-Zikronot* and *Yalqut Sim ʿoni* on Exod. 1:15. Additionally noteworthy is the introduction of Balaam in *Sefer ha-Yašar*: he was remembered as having prophesied the Messiah (Num. 24:17; cf. *CD* 7:18-26; *T. Judah* 18:3; and the LXX and targumim for Num. 24:17). And indeed his prophesy of a victorious warrior—"a son will be born to Israel who will devastate all of Egypt and exterminate her people"—is reminiscent of Num. 24:17, where it is foretold that the star to rise in Israel will crush God's enemies.

Whether there are other messianic resonances in some of the infancy traditions—what of the use of *gōʾēl* in *Exod. Rab.* 1:18? or of "son" in Pseudo-Jonathan on Exod. 1:15 and *Sefer ha-Yašar*?—is not clear. But the evidence does suffice to support Renée Bloch: messianic elements are found in some of the materials; so for some Jews the circumstances surrounding Moses' birth were prototypical, prophetic of messianic circumstances.[50] It cannot, however, be proven that such a generalization holds for Matthew's age: for that the evidence, because much too late, falls far short. Bloch's judgement, that the messianic associations of the Moses infancy stories "explain in an obvious way" the migration of Mosaic motifs to the story of Jesus, is not established. Beyond that, the reader of chapters 2 and 3 herein knows full well that Mosaic features were often adopted without any messianic or eschatological implication. Still, the employment of the Moses traditions in later Judaism does at least supply an analogy to what transpired in early Christianity. Both Jews and Christians found it appropriate to perceive in the haggadic traditions about Moses' advent a foreshadowing of the Messiah's coming.

Tradition and redaction. One last observation. It is extremely difficult to determine which, if any, of the Mosaic elements in Matthew 1-2 should be assigned to the redactor. Elsewhere I have argued that there were three main stages in the tradition-history of 1:18-2:23, the first stage of which was Mosaic.[51] Subsequent investigation has not moved me in that judgement. The result is that I must assign to tradition most of the Mosaic elements now found in Matthew's infancy narrative. We

---

[50]"A Methodological Note for the Study of Rabbinic Literature," in *Approaches to Ancient Judaism: Theory and Practice*, ed. William Scott Green (Chico: Scholars Press, 1978), 66-67.

[51]Davies and Allison, *Matthew*, 1:190-95.

can, however, be confident that Matthew both recognized those elements he reproduced for what they were, namely, Mosaic, and that he added to their number. This follows from our analysis of the formula quotation in 2:15: "Out of Egypt have I called me son." If, with the other formula quotations, this is thought to be redactional, as probably most now think, then Matthew "helped to underline the analogy between Moses and Jesus that was crucial in the pre-Matthean story."[52] Moreover, one can also urge, as has Raymond Brown, that Matthew's appreciation of this parallelism [between Jesus and Moses] explains why he has chosen an infancy narrative which fills out the parallelism more perfectly. Just as there is an infancy narrative in the Book of Exodus showing God's hand in his career even before he began his ministry of redeeming Israel from Egypt and of mediating a covenant between God and His people, so Matthew has given us an infancy narrative of Jesus before he begins his ministry of redemption and of the new covenant.[53]

THE TEMPTATION STORY (4:1-11)

As a comparison of Matt. 4:1-11 and Luke 4:1-13 shows, Q contained a temptation narrative in which Jesus recapitulated the experience of Israel in the desert. LXX Deut. 8:3 ("And he afflicted you, and he made you famished, and he fed you with manna, which your fathers knew not, in order to teach you that man shall not live by bread alone, but that man shall live by everything that proceeds from the mouth of God") is quoted in Matt. 4:4 = Luke 4:3, Deut. 6:16 ("You shall not tempt the Lord your God, as you tempted him in the temptation [at Massah]") in 4:7 = Luke 4:12, and Deut. 6:13 ("You shall fear the Lord your God, and him only shall you serve") in Matt. 4:10 = Luke 4:7. Clearly Q told a haggadic tale much informed by Scripture: as Israel entered the desert to suffer a time of testing, so too Jesus, whose forty days was the typological equivalent of Israel's forty years of wandering. And just as Israel was tempted by hunger (Exod. 16:2-8), was

---

[52]Brown, *Birth*, 118.

[53]Ibid., 112-13. He continues in a footnote: "Although chapter divisions are a later precision, it is noteworthy that there are two chapters of 'early Moses' material in Exodus before Moses is solemnly called by the voice of God in the burning bush episode of ch. 3, just as there are two chapters of 'early Jesus' material in Matthew before Jesus is solemnly designated by the voice of God in the baptism episode of ch. 3."

tempted to put God to the test (Exod. 17:1-3; cf. Deut. 6:16), and was tempted to idolatry (Exodus 32), so too Jesus.[54]

Given his knowledge of Scripture, Matthew, we may be sure, perceived Q's typological equation of Israel's wilderness temptations with those of Jesus. The presumption is commended by the evangelist's own work in 2:15, where he introduced the typological equation: Jesus = Son = Israel (see p. 142). But if in Matthew 2 the evangelist glossed the traditional Moses typology with an Israel typology, in Matthew 4 just the opposite occurred: the evangelist overlaid the existing Israel typology with specifically Mosaic motifs.[55] The proof of this is in the phrase, "fasted forty days and forty nights." The last three words, not found in Luke 4 or Mark 1:12-13, are redactional. Why were they added? Most commentators, finding explanation in the lengthy fasts of Moses and Elijah, both of which were for "forty days and forty nights" (Exod. 24:18; 1 Kings 19:8), suggest that Matthew wished to assimilate Jesus to those two saints. Calvin, in a polemical discussion of lenten fasting, wrote:

> The nature of his [Jesus'] fast is not different from that which Moses observed when he received the law at the hand of the Lord (Exod. 24:18; 34:28). For, seeing that the miracle was performed in Moses to establish the law, it behoved not to be omitted in Christ, lest the gospel should seem inferior to the law. But from that day, it never occurred to any one, under pretence of imitating Moses, to set up a similar form of fasting among the Israelites. Nor did any of the holy prophets and fathers follow it, though they had inclination and zeal enough for all pious exercises; for though it is said of Elijah that he passed forty days without meat and drink (1 Kings 19:8), this was merely in order that the people might recognize that he was raised up to maintain the law... (*Inst.* 4:12.20).

To judge from the commentaries, few careful and biblically literate readers of Matt. 4:2 have not been moved to think of Elijah and especially Moses (cf. already Irenaeus, *Adv. haer.* 5:21:2).[56] But did the

---

[54]See further B. Gerhardsson, *The Testing of God's Son (Matt 4:1-11 & Par.)* (CB,NT 2/1; Lund: Gleerup, 1966). Note also the popular yet instructive work of Austin Farrer, *The Triple Victory: Christ's Temptation according to St. Matthew* (Cambridge, Mass.: Cowley, 1990).

[55]Cf. Teeple, *Prophet*, 76-77, arguing that the redactional *anechthe* (4:1) and *oros hypselon lian* (4:8) were drawn from the Mount Nebo tradition (cf. LXX Deut. 34:1-2: *kai anebe Mouses... epi to oros... kai edeixen auto*). According to Gerhardsson, *Testing*, 44, in Matthew 4 Jesus is "the typological equivalent to Israel, God's son, not Moses, the deliverer." The antithesis, as we shall see, is false.

[56]Note also Eusebius, *Dem. ev.* 3:2; Chrysostom, *Hom. on Matt.* 13:2; Augustine, *Serm.* 252:11; *Ep.* 55:28; Julian, frag. 2; and for modern commentators Allen, *Matthew*, 30-31; F. W. Beare, *The Gospel according to Matthew* (New York: Harper & Row, 1981), 108; Gnilka,

evangelist himself intend to provke such thought? Despite the doubts of some,[57] a long list of considerations procures our assent.

(1) Moses' fast of forty days and forty nights was not forgotten: it was, on the contrary, a much celebrated achievement, one which stuck in the memory; see Philo, *De som.* 1:36; Josephus, *Ant.* 3:99; *l Clem.* 53:2; *Barn.* 4:7; 14:2; Eusebius, *Dem. ev.* 3:2; Epiphanius, *Haer.* 77:16; *Sipre Deut.* § 131b—all of which refer to "forty days and forty nights": clearly the expression was as fixed as the fact.[58]

(2) The addition of "and forty nights" distracts from the parallelism between Jesus and Israel: unlike days, years are not divided into two parts.[59] So the insertion must serve some purpose other than promotion of the Israel typology. Observe further that Matthew, in contrast to Luke, has temptation come to Jesus *after* forty days and forty nights. This also differentiates Jesus from Israel, for Israel's temptations came *during* her forty year sojourn.

(3) Matt. 12:40 has this: "For as Jonah was three days and three nights in the belly of the whale, so will the Son of man be three days and three nights in the heart of the earth." Comparison with Mark 8:12 and Luke 11:30 (= Q) demonstrates a redactional genesis and reveals Matthew's interest in a precise chronological correspondence between certain circumstances of Jesus and certain circumstances of Jonah, his biblical model in 12:40. Neither Mark 8:12 nor Luke 11:30 offers that the sign of Jonah refers to such a correspondence: only Matt. 12:40 makes that plain. Hence 12:40 shows us that Matthew saw significance in at least one durational coincidence between Jesus and an ancient worthy, and also that he rewrote his sources in order that others might perceive the same significance. That he was similarly moved when producing 4:2 is not at all unlikely.

(4) In the Hebrew Bible forty is "a symbolic and sacred number," and, as the Church Fathers well knew, it occurs often "as a round number to designate a fairly long period of time in terms of human existence or endurance."[60] But the conventionality of the number does

---

Matthäusevangelium, 1:86; Goldberg, *Jews and Christians*, 152; Gundry, *Matthew*, 54-55; Adolf Schlatter, *Der Evangelist Matthäus* (3rd ed.; Stuttgart: Calwer, 1948), 100; also n.2 on p. 293.

[57]Such as Davies, *Setting*, 45-48. Cf. Luz, *Matthew*, 1:186.

[58]*Jub.* 1:4; *LAB* 11:15; and *Deut. Rab.* 11:10 also have "forty days and forty nights" of Moses on Sinai, but they do not mention the fasting. Contrast Josephus, *C. Ap.* 2:25 ("forty days"), although here Josephus was summarizing Apion.

[59]Thus, in Num. 14:34 and Ezek. 4:5-6, where the period of forty days stands for forty years, the word "nights" finds no place.

[60]M. H. Pope, *IDB* 3:565, s.v., "Number."

not vitiate its ability to carry a quite specific connotation in the right context, and this is so in the present case, for two reasons. (a) Matt. 4:2 refers specifically to *fasting* for forty days and nights. This is crucial. Only two figures in the Jewish Bible fast for forty days and forty nights: Moses and Elijah; and on pp. 39-45 we saw that Elijah's fast is typological: the prophet's abstention was in imitation of Moses. Surely this is suggestive. (b) While "forty days" appears with some frequency in Scripture, "forty days and forty nights" does not. In fact, in the Jewish Bible the phrase is descriptive of only these circum-stances—Noah's flood (Gen. 7:4), Moses' retirements on Sinai (Exod. 24:18; 34:28; Deut. 9:9, 11, 28, 25; 10:10), and Elijah's abstinence (1 Kgs. 19:8). Now of these circumstances, the last is imitative, and those associated with Moses are much emphasized through repetition (five times in Deut. 9:9-10:10).

(5) Outside of 1 Kings 19 we find other texts which employ "forty days (and forty nights)" as part of a strategy to recall the lawgiver. In the *Apocalypse of Abraham* 12, for instance, Abraham eats no bread and drinks no water for forty days and forty nights, and this is only one of several features which make the patriarch very much like the Moses of Jewish lore (see p. 91, n. 209). Another pertinent passage is *4 Ezra* 14, already examined (pp. 62-65). Here the Moses typology is developed and explicit, and while there is no fasting, we do read of people sitting and writing for forty days and forty nights (14:42-45). Slighty different is *2 Baruch* 76, where Baruch's universal vision is to "happen after forty days." Here, although there is neither fast nor mountain, the Moses typology is plain enough (cf. pp. 65-68). Recall that there may also be a Moses typology in *Protevangelium James* 1-4. This tells us that the father of Mary, by name Joachim, a shepherd who "betook himself to the wilderness," had a wife who miraculously conceived a child; and Joachim himself is said to have fasted forty days and forty nights.[61] The upshot, then, is that if Matthew hoped that "forty days and forty nights" would remind readers of Moses, he was in the company of other ancient authors who shared the same expectation.

(6) In the synoptics Jesus' fast belongs to a temptation narrative. There may be a parallel of sorts in Deuteronomy, for according to Deut. 9:18 and 25, Moses' fasting was occasioned by Israel's lapse into

---

[61]When Adam fasts in *LAE* 6, the phrase is, notably, "forty days": nights are not mentioned, and there is no Moses typology; cf. *3 Bar* 4:14; *T. Isaac* 4:4. It goes without saying that the same is true of Diogenes Laertius, *Vit. Pyth.* 21, according to which Pythagoras died of self-inflicted starvation "after forty days."

sin: the refusal to eat and drink was a penitential act of the one for the many. The parallel is, obviously, inexact; but the Pentateuch does link the fast on Sinai to an episode of temptation.

(7) The cryptic notice, in Matt. 4:11, that angels "ministered" (*diē-konoun*) to Jesus, probably implies that he was fed by them.[62] This of course enhances the similitude between Jesus and Israel, because in the wilderness Israel was given manna, the food of angels.[63] But there might also be a parallel with Moses. Josephus, in *Ant.* 3:99, wrote that, on the mountain, Moses ate "no foods for men." The implication seems to be that he ate some other kind of food, and just such a notion is explicit in Samaritan sources: on Sinai Moses sat at the table of angels and ate their bread (*Memar Marqah* 4:6). If such a tradition had been known to Matthew, he could well have thought that just as Moses declined bread and water but was then fed by angels, in like manner the Messiah's great fast was broken by the gift of angelic bread.

(8) We find this is *Exod. Rab.* 43:1: R. Berekah said in the name of R. Judah the Prince:

> When Israel made the golden calf, Satan stood within [before God] accusing them, while Moses remained without. What then did Moses do? He arose and thrust Satan away and placed himself in his stead, as it says, "Had not Moses His chosen stood before Him in the breach" (Ps. 106:23), that is, he put himself in the place of him who was causing the breach.

Unfortunately we do not know the date at which this tale saw the light of day. But it is remarkable, given the other parallels we have noticed, that Jewish tradition came to hold that Moses bested Satan "when Israel made the golden calf," that is, during the forty days and forty nights on Sinai.[64]

If the ramifications of the addition of "and forty nights" in Matt. 4:2 seem rather obvious, a second verse in Matthew's temptation narrative has also sometimes been thought to promote the Gospel's Moses typology: "Again the devil took him to a very high mountain, and showed him all the kingdoms of the world and the glory of them" (4:8).

---

[62]Cf. Davies and Allison, *Matthew*, 1:374.

[63]Ps. 78:25; *LAE* 2-4; 2 Esdr. 1:19; *b. Sanh.* 59b; *ARN* 1.

[64]According to Davies, *SSM*, 48, n. 1, citing David Daube, *Studies on Biblical Law* (Cambridge: University Press, 1947), 24ff., there is "no suggestion" of "a temptation of Moses... on Sinai." Is this not a bit misleading? Maybe we find no temptation story like that belonging to the New Testament; but there certainly was a tradition of encounter with the evil one. Note also *b.Sabb.* 89a, where Moses, after descending Sinai, meets Satan, who asks him where the Torah is.

Is this a reminiscence of the story that Moses went to the top of Pisgah, looked in all directions, and saw the land he would not enter (Num. 27:12-14; Deut. 3:27; 32:48-52; 34:1-4)?[65] Several considerations induce us to think that very likely it is.

(1) Matthew 4 and the Nebo traditions share a common theme: a supernatural figure (God/Satan) shows to a hero (Moses/Jesus) the entirety of a realm (all the land of Israel/all the kingdoms of the world) but the hero does not then enter or inherit it.

(2) There are verbal parallels between Matt. 4:8-9 and Deut. 34:1-4:

Matthew	Deuteronomy
kai deiknysin autō	*kai edeixen autō*
pasas tas basileias	*pasan tēn gēn*
tauta panta dōsō	*dōsō autēn*

(3) "To a very high mountain" is without parallel in Luke and may be assigned to Matthew's hand.[66] Further, I shall contend that all the other redactional insertions of *oros* are probably related to Matthew's new Moses theme.[67]

(4) If *Apocalypse of Abraham* 12 commences by moving Sinai motifs to the life of Abraham (see p. 91, n. 209), the chapter closes with an event recollective of Moses' experience on Nebo, as this was recounted by later legend: Abraham's angelic guide and interpreter promises the patriarch a universal vision: "I will ascend on the wings of the birds to show you what is in the heavens, on the earth and in the sea, in the abyss, and in the lower depths, in the garden of Eden and in its rivers, in the fullness of the universe."[68] It would appear then that *Apocalypse of Abraham* 12 combines features of the Sinai and Nebo traditions, which is precisely what many have detected in Matthew 4. Not only this, but in *Apocalypse of Abraham* 13 Azazael (= Satan), in the form of a bird, tempts Abraham: "What are you doing, Abraham, on the holy heights, where no one eats or drinks, nor is there upon them food for men. But these all [your offerings] will be consumed by fire and they will burn you up. Leave the man who is with you [Isaac] and flee." I do not wish to discount the many differences between this and

---

[65]So, among others, Donaldson, *Mountain*, 93; Gfrörer, *Heils*, 385-86; Robert H. Gundry, *Matthew: A Commentary on His Literary and Theological Art* (Grand Rapids: Eerdmans, 1982), 57; Barnabas Lindars, "The Image of Moses in the Synoptic Gospels," *Theology* 58 (1955):130; W. Wilkens, "Die Versuchung Jesu nach Matthäus," *NTS* 28 (1982):485.

[66]Davies and Allison, *Matthew*, 1:369-70; contrast Donaldson, *Mountain*, 87-88.

[67]See below, pp. 172-80, 238-42, 262-66.

[68]For the comparable Moses traditions see below, pp. 223-25.

Matthew 4. At the same time, the *Apocalypse of Abraham*, like Matthew 4, does plainly have its Mosaic hero undergo Satanic temptation in close connection with a Nebo-like experience. I should like to suggest that the resemblance may be more than coincidence. There is an old tale that, at the end of his sojourn, a melancholy Moses encountered and rebuked the angel of death[69] or Samā'ēl[70], who had come to snatch his soul. *Sipre Deut.* § 305 contains a short version of this legend, *Deut. Rab.* 11:l0a one much more protracted, in which Samā'ēl and Moses argue back and forth, and in which the latter finally rebukes the former ("Away, wicked one"—cf. Matt. 4:10) who then takes flight. That some form of this tradition was known by Matthew's day is guaranteed by the dependence upon it of the *Testament of Abraham*, a pseudepigraphon composed in the first or second century C.E.[71] In view of this, our evangelist may well have formed the notion of a thematic connection between the temptation of Jesus and the traditions about Moses on Nebo.[72]

(5) In Deuteronomy God shows Moses "all the land, Gilead as far as Dan, all Naphtali, the land of Ephraim and Manasseh, all the land of Judah as far as the Western Sea, the Negeb, and the Plain, that is, the valley of Jericho the city of palm trees, as far as Zoar." The haggada greatly expanded this vision. *Sipre Deut.* § 357 tells us that Moses was granted a vision of "all the world," and further that he saw "all unto the last day" (cf. *Mek.* on 17:14-16). We shall later have occasion to explore in detail the many texts that turn Moses' survey on Nebo into a universal vision, one embracing all the cosmos and the past as well as the future. Here it suffices to observe that in Matt. 4:8 Jesus also is granted a universal vision: "and he showed him all the kingdoms of the world and their glory."

(6) What Jesus gains from God the Father in Matt. 28:16-20, he earlier, in 4:8-10, refused to accept from the tempter. Thus the kingdoms of the world become his, but only in time, and only from God. It was, according to Philo, similar with Moses:

> His office was bestowed upon him by God, the lover of virtue and nobility, as the reward due to him. For, when he gave up the lordship of Egypt, which he held as son to the daughter of the then reigning king, because the sight of the iniquities committed in the land and his own nobility of soul and magnanimity of spirit and inborn hatred of evil led

---

[69]The angel of death = Satan in *b. B. Bat.* 16a.

[70]Samā'ēl = "the chief of Satans," Jastrow, s.v.

[71]See p. 64, n. 143.

[72]Again, Davies, *Setting*, 48, n. 15, is misleading, when, following Daube, he stipulates that there is "no suggestion" of a temptation of Moses on Nebo.

him to renounce completely his expected inheritance from the kinfolk of his adoption, He who presides over and takes charge of all things thought good to requite him with the kingship of a nation more populous and mightier… (*Mos.* 1:148-49).

As he abjured the accumulation of lucre, and the wealth whose influence is mighty among men, God rewarded him by giving him instead the greatest and most perfect wealth. That is the wealth of the whole earth and sea and rivers, and of all the other elements and the combinations which they form. For, since God judged him worthy to appear as a partner of His own possessions, He gave into his hands the whole world as a portion well fitted for His heir. Therefore each element obeyed him as its master, changed its natural properties and submitted to his command, and this perhaps is no wonder (*Mos.* 1:155-56).

That Philo's interpretation was based on tradition, or that it became known to others, is probably evidenced by Hebrews, which records something similar, albeit with a Christian twist:

By faith Moses, when he was grown up, refused to be called the son of Pharaoh's daughter, choosing rather to share ill-treatment with the people of God than to enjoy the fleeting pleasures of sin. He considered abuse suffered for the Christ greater wealth than the treasures of Egypt, for he looked for the reward (11:25-26; cf. Ephrem the Syrian, *Hymns on Paradise* 14:6).

Here too, as in Philo and Matthew 4, earthly kingship is renounced for the sake of a later and more divine reward.

Taken together, the preceding points constitute a forceful argument; and having considered them in the light of the evangelist's work in 4:2, where the redactional creation of parallelism between Jesus and Moses appears manifest, I am satisfied of the probability that the First Evangelist viewed 4:8-10 against the backdrop of Nebo and desired us, his readers, to do the same.

THE MOUNTAIN OF TEACHING (5:1-2)

"In this Sermon [on the Mount], Jesus, who is the new Moses, gives a commentary on the decalogue, the Law of the Covenant, thus giving it its definitive and fullest meanings."[73] These words, from an official publication of the Roman Catholic Church, are only a recent example of an old Christian proclivity to associate the speaker of Matthew 5-7

---

[73]*Instruction on Christian Freedom and Liberation*, Congregation for the Doctrine of the Faith, March 22, 1986 (Washington, D.C.: O.S. Catholic Conference), 36 (paragraph 62).

with Moses and Sinai. Already in the fourth century Eusebius, as proof of the proposition that "Moses and Jesus our Lord acted in closely similar ways," observed that 5:21-48 can be understood as Jesus' transformation of the Mosaic Torah (*Dem. ev.* 3:2).

The frequent association of Moses with the SM has commonly been coupled with a typological interpretation of Matthew's mountain: "And seeing the crowds he went up on the mountain; and when he sat down his disciples came to him and he opened his mouth and taught them, saying..." (5:1-2). In the nineteenth century Frederic Godet formed this judgment: "The mount where Jesus speaks is as the Sinai of the new covenant."[74] In the next century, our own, Harald Sahlin put it this way: "The Sermon on the Mount is the New Law given from the mountain by the New Moses."[75] Dozens of similar sentiments could be lifted from the literature on the the First Gospel, both popular and scholarly.[76]

But it remains to ask: is this traditional interpretation correct, that is, does it correspond to the author's intention? Robert Banks, contending that it does not, has made these observations: (i) the mountain has been moved from Mark 3:13, (ii) "explicit indications of... parallelism are absent," and (iii) *to oros* is here not Sinai but "the place of 'revelation.'"[77] Such objections, however, are ineffectual and easily countered. Even if Matthew did borrow the mountain from Mark 3:13, the source-critical question is a red herring. We must still ask: why did he insert "the mountain" precisely where he did and replace the "plain" of Q?[78] Also, why did Matthew add a reference to sitting? The lack of explicitness is no more pertinent, and Banks' complaint hollow; for most of the typologies in the Hebrew Bible are implicit; and why

---

[74]*Introduction to the New Testament: The Collection of the Four Gospels and the Gospel of St. Matthew* (Edinburgh: T. & T. Clark, 1899), 131.

[75]"The New Exodus of Salvation according to St. Paul," in *The Root of the Vine*, by A. Fridrichsen et al. (New York: Philosophical Library, 1953).

[76]I cite only Matthew Henry, *Matthew Henry's Commentary on the Whole Bible* (Peabody: Hendrickson, 1991), 1628 ("Christ preached this sermon, which is an exposition of the law, upon a mountain, because upon a mountain the law was given"); Teeple, *Prohpet*, 78-82; J. Wilkens, *Der König Israels*, vol. 1 (Berlin: Furche, 1934), 82-83; and Frederick J. Murphy, *The Religious World of Jesus* (Nashville: Abingdon, 1991), 373-74. See also n. 3 on p. 293.

[77]*Jesus and the Law in the Synoptic Tradition*, SNTSMS 28 (Cambridge: University Press, 1975), 231.

[78]See Luke 6:17. Similarly, the objection of Nepper-Christensen, *Matthäusevangelium*, 177, that the historical Jesus must have done much near mountains, is beside the point. Even if Jesus delivered all of Matthew 5-7 on a mountain, the question would remain: why did the evangelist bother to record the fact?

our evangelist could not have utilized the simple and common device of the implicit allusion, a device ubiquitous in ancient Jewish and Christian writings, not to mention all of world literature, is utterly baffling. As for the third remark, which draws an inexplicable dichotomy, it just begs the question.

No more persuasive are the comments of Donaldson. In addition to observing, what is wholly true but wholly irrelevant, that the parallelism could be greater—against what typology could this objection not be launched?—and that it is not explicit—who could ever have said that it was?—he affirms, first, that "wherever Moses typology is present in Matthew, it is not dominant, but is transcended and absorbed by a higher Son-christology," secondly, that Jesus also sits on a mountain in 15:29-31, which has no Sinai background, and, thirdly, that 5:1-2 goes with 4:23-25, which is bereft of Mosaic motifs.[79] The first affirmation is problematic not only because one may doubt that Matthew's Son of God Christology is as absorbent as often assumed (cf. pp. 311-19), but also because the SM, so far as I can see, has no *direct* connection with a Son of God Christology, so how could such absorption take place here? The second claim fails in view of the comments to be made below, on pp. 238-42: there *is* a Mosaic background to 15:29-31. As for the third point, it presupposes, without explanation, that if 5:1-2 contains Sinai motifs, 4:23-25 should also, to which two rebuttals may be returned: (i) why? and (ii) the assertion that 4:23-25 has no Mosaic associations can be queried, for Jewish tradition took Exod. 19:8 ("And all the people answered and said") and 19:ll ("The Lord will come down upon Mount Sinai in the sight of all the people") to entail that, at the foot of Sinai, none were dumb or blind, and that therefore all the people had been healed; so already *Mek.* on Exod. 19:ll and 20:18.[80] Consequently it is not impossible that our evangelist prefaced the SM with a healing summary because he wished the circumstances of Jesus' inaugural address to mimic those of Sinai.

If the usual protests against perceiving a Sinai typology in Matt. 5:1-2 are empty of force, what may be said on the other side?[81]

(1) Jesus "goes up" on the mountain. The Greek is, *anebē eis to oros.* Now in the LXX, *anabainō + eis to oros* occurs twenty-four times. Of

[79]Donaldson, *Mountain*, 113.
[80]For later references see Ginzberg, *Legends*, 2:374; 3:78, 213; 6:176.
[81]The following carries forward arguments I first made in "Jesus and Moses (Mt 5:1-2)," *ExpT* 98 (1987):203-205.

these, a full eighteen belong to the Pentateuch, and most refer to Moses.[82] Surely this statistic strengthens whatever association there might be between Matt. 5:1-2 and Moses' reception of the Torah.

(2) Jesus "sits" on the mountain. Most commentators remark that the reference to posture emphasizes the speaker's rôle as teacher, for rabbis and others sat when they taught.[83] But there is more, much more. In Deut. 9:9 (a text which might be alluded to in Matt. 4:2), Moses speaks these words: "When I went up the mountain to receive the tables of stone, the tables of the covenant which the Lord made with you, I remained on the mountain forty days and forty nights; I neither ate bread nor drank water." The word translated "remained" is *wāʾēšeb*. BDB lists, as the second and third meanings of *yāšab*, "remain" and "dwell" respectively. But the first meaning given for the verb is "sit," and in *b. Meg.* 21a we find this:

> One verse says, "And I sat in the mountain" [Deut. 9:9], and another verse says, "And I stood in the mountain" [Deut. 10:10]. Rab says: He [Moses] stood when he learned and sat while he went over [what he had learned]. R. Hanina said: He was neither sitting nor standing, but stooping. R. Johanan said: "Sitting" here means only "staying," as it says, "And you stayed in Kadesh many days" [Deut. 1:46]. Rabba said: The easy things [he learned] standing and the hard ones sitting.

Can the tradition that Moses sat on Sinai be traced back to Matthew's time or before? It is possible that the First Gospel itself holds the proof, in 23:2: "The scribes and the Pharisees sit on Moses' seat." Unfortunately, the precise meaning of "Moses' seat" (cf. *Pesiq. R. Kah.* 1:7) is uncertain, and it would be unwise to infer anything more than a connection between Moses and sitting.[84] No more enlightening is *T. Mos.* 12:1-2: "And when he [Moses] had finished speaking these words, Joshua again fell at the feet of Moses. And Moses grasped his hand and raised him into the seat before him." This, although certainly intriguing, is too cryptic to serve us. But matters are otherwise with

---

[82]Exod. 19:3, 12, 13; 24:12, 13, 18; 34:1, 2, 4; Num. 27:12; Deut. 1:24, 41, 43; 5:5; 9:9; 10:1, 3; 32:49.

[83]Ezek. 8:1; Matt. 23:2; Luke 4:20-27; Acts 16:13; *m. Abot* 1:4; 3:2, 6; *ARN* 6; Eusebius, *H.E.* 5:20. The Hebrew word for "school" (*yěšîbâ*) means "sitting" (cf. Ecclus. 51:23).

[84]I think it too tenuous to equate "Moses' seat" with "the throne of Torah," the place where the synagogue elders sat (cf. W. G. Braude and I. J. Kapstein, *Pesikta de Rab Kahana* [Philadelphia: Jewish Publication Society of America, 1975], 17, n. 59), and then to connect that with the tradition that God's throne was on Sinai (see n. 86). For one thing, in the first century "Moses' seat" was probably only a way of speaking; only later did synagogues have seats for teachers built into them; see I. Renov, "The Seat of Moses," in *The Synagogue*, ed. J. Gutman (New York: KTAV, 1975), 233-38.

Philo. In *Sacr.* 8 we are informed: "There are still others, whom God has advanced even higher, and has caused them to sit beside himself (*hidruse de plēsion heautou*). Such is Moses to whom He says, 'stand here with Me.'" The text quoted is LXX Deut. 5:31, according to which the lawgiver stood beside God on Sinai. But Philo himself interpreted the verse to mean that Moses *sat* beside God.[85] Is this not evidence that the tradition found in *b. Meg.* 21a was in currency by the turn of the era?

Another clue turns up in *4 Ezra* 14. We have already observed how, from beginning to end, this chapter, which recounts a second giving of the Torah, borrows elements from Exodus: there is an extensive typology here (pp. 62-65). It is therefore striking that the posture of those who, like Moses of old, write the divine commandments, is remarked upon: for forty days and forty nights they *sit* (v. 42). The time span certainly belongs to the Moses typology. The sitting, I strongly suspect, does also.

There is still additional evidence to be considered, evidence proving that the picture of Moses sitting on Sinai was familiar in Matthew's Jewish world. The Pentateuch does not disclose much about what Moses did when he was alone on Sinai, a prudent silence which pious imagination could not abide. Thus at some juncture there arose the supposition that, on the mountain, Moses underwent a heavenly ascent, complete with angelic encounters.[86] The antiquity of this idea, that to go to Sinai was to go to heaven, is, as we shall see, guaranteed by several things. It indisputably predates Matthew's time.[87]

---

[85]Cf. Goodenough, *Symbols*, 9:119, n. 215. —Should we compare Revelation's expression, "the throne of God and of the lamb"?

[86]See e.g. *Sipre Deut.* § 306; *ARN* A 2; *b. Sanh.* 38b; *b. Šabb.* 88b-89a; *3 En.* 15B; *Midr. Ps.* 8:2; *Cant. Rab.* 8:11; *Pesiq. R.* 20:4; 25:3; *Pirqe R. El.* 46. For later ascension texts in which Moses travels through the heavens to behold all see Moses Gaster, *Studies and Texts*, vol. 1 (London: Maggs Brothers, 1925), 125-43 ("The Revelation of Moses A," "The Revelation of Moses B"). In both Targum Onkelos and Targum Pseudo-Jonathan on Exod. 24:10, the throne of God appears on Sinai (cf. the so-called *Prayer of Jacob* 8: "You who s[i]t upon (the) mountain of h[oly] [S]inaios"; for God's throne on a mountain see *l En.* 13:8; 24:3; 25:3; *T. Levi* 2:5ff.; 5:1; etc.). For a collection of texts which refer to or tell about Moses' ascension see the notes to Ginzberg, *Legends*, 3:109-19. For critical discussion see K.-E. Grözinger, *Ich bin der Herr, dein Gott!* (Bern: Herber Lang,, 1976), 130-214; J. P. Schulz, "Angelic Opposition to the Ascension of Moses and the Revelation of the Law," *JQR* 61 (1971):282-307. Sometimes Moses himself ascends (on a cloud), sometimes Sinai itself goes to heaven.

[87]Morton Smith, it is important to observe, has demonstrated that 4QMa, frag. 11, col. 1, a pre-Christian, Palestinian text, which tells of an individual enthroned in heaven, is not likely to be about the archangel Michael (so M. Baillet); rather, the fragment relates the ascension and deification of a human figure. Unfortunately the individual's identity is unknown. Do we have here fragments of a lost Moses or Enoch pseudepigraphon? See Morton Smith, "Ascent to the Heavens and Deification in 4QMa," in *Archaeology and the Dead Sea Scrolls*, ed. L. H. Schiffmann (JSPSS 8; Sheffield: JSOT, 1990), 181-88.

Moses' ascent into heaven was sometimes portrayed as a coronation or enthronement. According to Samaritan legend, Moses "sat on a great throne and wrote what his Lord had taught him" (*Memar Marqah* 4:6).[88] Rabbinic tradition also presumably knew of this enthronement, as *Tanhuma, wāʾērāʾ* § 7 intimates (cf. *Exod. Rab.* 8:1; see SB 1:175). According to this, God has shared his glory with others, and in the case of Moses, the man was made "God" (Exod. 7:1), crowned with light (Exod. 34:29), given the royal sceptre (Exod. 4:17), and made "king in Jeshurun" (Deut. 33:5). Moses' enthronment on Sinai seems to be presupposed.[89]

The same may be claimed for Philo, *Mos.* 1:155-58, part of which I quoted earlier. This purports that God shared his possessions with his friend Moses, who was "named God and king of the whole nation" when he entered "into the darkness where God was, that is into the unseen, invisible, incorporeal and archetypical essence of existent things." Here the climb to Sinai's peak is construed as an ascent into heaven, albeit a very Platonic heaven. Compare *Quaest. Exod.* 2:29, where Exod. 24:2 ("Moses alone shall come near to God") is interpreted to mean that Moses ascended to God and "became kin to God and truly divine." We are reminded of the rabbinic teaching that Moses was "a man when he ascended on high, a God when he descended below" (*Pesiq. R. Kah.*, supplement 1:9).

In Philo and Exodus Rabbah one has to read a bit between the lines. But it is otherwise with Eusebius, *Praep. ev.* 9:29.4-6, which preserves material from the lost work of Alexander Polyhistor, quoting the *Exagoge* of Ezekiel:

> I [Moses] dreamt there was on the summit of mount Sinai a certain great throne extending up to heaven's cleft, on which there sat a certain noble man wearing a crown and holding a great sceptre in his left hand. With his right hand he beckoned to me, and I stood before the throne. He gave me the sceptre [cf. *Exod. Rab.* 15:15] and told me to sit on the great throne[90] [cf. Philo, *Sacr.* 8]. He gave me the royal crown [cf. *Exod. Rab.* 15:15] and he himself left the throne. I beheld the entire circled earth both beneath the earth and above the heaven, and a host of stars fell on its knees before me; I numbered them all. They passed before me like a squadron of soldiers. Then, seized with fear, I rose from my sleep.

---

[88]For additional texts see Meeks, *Prophet-King*, 232-36.

[89]See further Meeks, "Moses as God and King."

[90]*eis thronon megan eipen kathēsthai.* "Although it is never said that the figure seated upon the throne is God, the fact that the throne reaches to the vaults of heaven... makes this probable." So C. R. Holladay, "The Portrait of Moses in Ezekiel the Tragedian," in *Society of Biblical Literature 1976 Seminar Papers*, ed. George MacRae (Missoula: Scholars Press, 1976), 449. In view of the parallel texts about Moses' ascension, "probable" is too weak a word.

Eusebius also transmitted the following interpretation of this fantastic dream, as delivered by Moses' father-in-law:

> O friend, that which God has signified to you is good; might I live until the time when these things happen to you. Then you will raise up a great throne and it is you who will judge and lead humankind; as you beheld the whole inhabited earth, the things beneath and the things above God's heaven, so will you see things present, past, and future.

The enthronement of Moses in the *Exagoge* of Ezekiel is a fascinating episode whose importance is, for many reasons, exceptional, and its interpretation has naturally been the subject of some debate.[91] For our immediate purposes, however, enough is plain: the tradition that, on Sinai, Moses sat on the divine throne, must go back to at least the time of Ezekiel the Tragedian, that is, probably to the second century B.C.E.[92]

---

[91]See the brief overview in Larry W. Hurtado, *One God, One Lord: Early Christian Devotion and Ancient Jewish Monotheism* (Philadelphia: Fortress, 1988), 57-59.

[92]Moses' enthronement on Sinai should just perchance be considered very old tradition independent of the Pentateuch. The myth of a heavenly ascent followed by the reception of heavenly tablets and enthronement was part and parcel of Mesopotamian royal ideology, and the pattern seems to be reflected in both biblical and extra-biblical traditions about Moses. See G. Widengren, *The Ascension of the Apostle and the Heavenly Book* (Uppsala: A. B. Lundeqvistska, 1950), esp. 7-58. I would further add, although this is even more speculative, that the tradition of Enoch's enthronement (*l En.* 45:3; 51:3; 55:4; 61:8; 69:27-29) may have been modelled upon that of Moses, and in any case there were probably in pre-Christian times rival traditions about Enoch and Moses as enthroned with or beside God; cf. P. W. van der Horst, "Moses' Throne Vision in Ezekiel the Dramatist," *JJS* 34 (1983):21-29. —I must here mention the so-called Jewish Orpheus, whose longer recension (in Eusbeius, *Praep. ev.* 13:12.5) apparently includes an account of someone's heavenly ascent (see M. Lafargue, "The Jewish Orpheus," in *Society of Biblical Literature 1978 Seminar Papers*, ed. P. J. Achtemeier [Missoula: Scholars Press, 1978], vol. 2:137-43): "And no one has seen the ruler of mortal men, except a certain unique man, an offshoot from far back of the race of the Chaldeans. For he was knowledgeable about the path of the star, and how the movement of the sphere goes around the earth, both in circular fashion, but each on its own axis. He rides in spirit through the air and through the water of the stream. A comet makes manifest these events—he had a mighty birth. Yes he after this is established in the great heaven on a golden throne" (lines 25-33). Unfortunately the interpretation of these lamentably turgid lines is controversial. The phrase, "of the race of the Chaldeans," as well as the tradition that "the unique man" was learned in matters astronomical, which is said of Abraham in Ps.-Eupolemus in Eusebius, *Praep. ev.* 9:17; Artapanus in ibid., 9:18; Josephus, *Ant.* 1:158, 167-68; *LAB* 18:5; *b. B. Bat.* 16b; etc., seem to point us to the patriarch. But Philo, *Mos.* 1:5, called Moses "a Chaldean," as did Justin Martyr, *1 Apol.* 53, and the lawgiver is explicitly mentioned in lines 40-41. Moreover, Philo purported that Moses was exceptionally learned in "the Chaldean science of the heavenly bodies" (*Mos.* 1:23), and the assertion that "the unique man" is the only one to have seen God suggests Moses. Thus the possibility that Pseudo-Orpheus recounts or reflects the apotheosis of Moses and his sitting on a throne cannot be excluded. I note that M. Lafargue, in *OTP* 2, 796-77, thinks of Moses rather than Abraham (evidently a reversal of his earlier opinion).

I am not, let me make plain, proposing that Matt. 5:1-2 be directly related to the traditions of Moses' *enthronement* on Sinai—although it may be worth recalling that some commentators have dimly sensed a royal motif in Matt. 5:1-2. The point is simply this: the image of Moses sitting on Sinai, whether on a throne or some other seat, was firmly established in the imagination of pre-Christian Jews.[93] It was therefore a resource Matthew could have utilized had he wished.

(3) Others did so wish. More than one ancient author advanced a Moses typology by making his main character sit. I refer the reader to what has already been said concerning both *4 Ezra* 14, where the scribes receiving the Torah sit for forty days and forty nights (see p. 63), and Athanasius' *Vita Antonii*, in which the Mosaic hero is often said to have sat on his mountain and communed with God (see p. 115). Additionally noteworthy is John 6:3, whose language is so close to Matt. 5:1-2: *anēlthen de eis to oros Iēsous kai ekei ekathēto meta ton mathētōn autou*: Jesus went up into the mountain and sat there with his disciples. This is part of the preface to a long and dramatic chapter which draws several clear and explicit parallels between Jesus and Moses; hence the interpretatation of John's mountain as a "Christian Sinai," to use Raymond Brown's term,[94] commends itself.[95]

Notice may also be taken of the Merkabah text in *b. Hag.* 14b.[96] In this an angel speaks from the midst of a fire (cf. Exodus 3) to R. Johanan b. Zakkai and R. Eleazar b. Arak as the latter is expounding the "work of the Chariot." Subsequently Johanan relates that once, when he and R. Jose the priest were on Mount Sinai, sitting as at a banquet (cf. Exod. 24:11), a voice invited them to ascend to the heavenly banqueting chambers. Now the use of Sinai imagery in Merkabah visions is elsewhere attested, and in the present instance the two rabbis *sit* on Sinai, which circumstance may accordingly be regarded with some plausibility as a Mosaic motif.

(4) If the vocabulary of 5:1-2, which introduces the SM, draws on biblical texts about Moses and Sinai, the same is true of 8:1, which

---

[93]For additional references to Moses sitting see Exod. 2:15; 18:13-14; *Mek.* on Exod. 18:13-14 (Moses' father-in-law "saw him behaving like a king who sits on his throne while all the people around him stand"); *ARN* A 12 (Moses on Nebo); *Deut. Rab.* 11:10. Did the notion that Moses was a scribe (cf. Josephus, *C. Ap.* 1:2; *Tg. Onk.* to Deut. 33:21)—scribes sat for their work—contribute to this picture?

[94]Raymond Brown, *John*, 1:232.

[95]See further Theo Preiss, "Étude sur le chapitre 6 de l'Évangile de Jean," *ETR* 46 (1971):144-56.

[96]For what follows see D. J. Halperin, *The Merkabah in Rabbinic Literature* (American Oriental Series 62; New Haven: American Oriental Society, 1980), 128-33.

concludes the SM: *katabantos de autou apo tou orous*. This is almost identical with LXX A Exod. 34:29, which recounts Moses' descent from the holy mountain: *katabainontos de autou apo tou orous* (cf. also 19:14; 32:1, 15). Moreover, a participial form of *katabainō + de + autou + apo + tou orous* appears in the Septuagint only once, in the passage cited (LXX B has *ek* for *apo*).

Having made my four points, I am prepared to affirm that Matt. 5:1-2 was designed by the First Evangelist to summon distinct recall. For those properly informed of and alive to Jewish tradition, the two verses constitute a Mosaic preface: the mountain is typologically analogous to Sinai, and when Jesus sits thereon, his posture evokes the image of the lawgiver. To what end the construction of such a preface was directed will be considered in short order. But first 5:3 and 8 require attention.

TWO BEATITUDES (5:5, 8)

"Blessed are the meek, for they shall inherit the earth." So Matt. 5:5, a logion absent from Luke but not for that reason to be reckoned to Matthean redaction.[97] Exegetical history has now and again associated this, the third beatitude, in both its parts, with Moses. In Judaism Moses was meekness' own self:

Num. 12:3: "Now the man Moses was very meek, more than all men that were of the face of the earth."

Ecclus. 45:4: God "sanctified him [Moses] through faithfulness and meekness."

Philo, *Mos.* 1:26: "Each of the other passions, which rage so furiously if left to themselves, he [Moses] tamed and assuaged and reduced to meekness."

ibid. 2:279: "Moses... [was] the meekest and mildest of men."

b. Ned. 38a: "The Holy One, blessed be He, causes his divine presence to rest only upon him who is strong, wealthy, wise, and meek; and all these are deduced from Moses."

---

[97]Davies and Allison, *Matthew*, 1:434-36.

Tanhuma Bereshit l: "As for the Torah, humility is her imprint and Godfearingness her crown, as it says, 'The end of humility is the fear of the Lord' (Prov. 22:4) and 'The beginning of wisdom is the fear of the Lord' (Ps. 110:10). These two gifts were combined in Moses, who was 'exceedingy humble' (Num. 12:3) and who 'feared to behold God' (Exod. 3:6)."

Given passages such as these[98] it is no surprise to learn that some have illustrated the *praus* of Matt. 5:5a by remembering Moses. One example: when Theodoret of Cyrrhus sought to characterize the "simplicity of character, gentleness of behavior, and modesty of spirit" displayed by the monk Romanus, on account of which "he emitted the radiance of divine grace," the bishop joined Matt. 5:5 and Num. 12:3: "'Blessed are the meek, for they shall inherit the earth.' And this was the distinguishing feature of the achievements of Moses the lawgiver: 'Moses', he says, 'was very meek, more than all men that were on earth'" (*Rel. Hist.* 11:2).

Like 5:5a, Matt. 5:5b has also on occasion cultivated memories about Moses. Eusebius, in *Dem. ev.* 3:2, commented: "Moses… promised a holy land and a holy life therein under a blessing to those who kept his laws; while Jesus Christ says likewise: 'Blessed are the meek, for they shall inherit the earth.'" For Eusebius the third beatitude did not bring to mind Moses' meekness but rather Moses' rôle as the one who promised Israel inheritance of the land,[99] and thus he instanced the text as belonging to the parallels between Messiah and lawgiver: both gave the same promise to their followers (cf. Deut. 4:1).

Perhaps we should follow the interpretive lead of Theodoret and Eusebius and set Matt. 5:5 against the Moses traditions. Moses was, in meekness, the exemplar. He promised the Israelites inheritance of the land. *And he himself did not enter the land.* From this last fact, sufficiently unexpected to have engendered much rabbinic reflection, one might extract that the third beatitude pledges something Moses never gained. On such an interpretation, the members of the new covenant would be more blessed than the chief figure of the old: if, in the past, the meek one did not enter the land, now, that the kingdom of God has come, "the meek… shall inherit the earth." Compare 11:11: the least in the kingdom is greater than all those who came before.

---

[98]See also Origen, *Exod. hom.* ll:6; Jerome, *Ep.* 82:3; *Apophthegmata Patrum*, PG 65, Syncletica ll; John the Persian 4; Antiochus Monachus, *Hom.* 115.

[99]The parallel is stronger if Matthew's *tēn gēn* be translated "the land (of Israel)" instead of "(all) the earth." But against this see Davies and Allison, *Matthew*, 1:450-51.

One hesitates to pronounce whether or not the Mosaic interpretation of Matt. 5:5 should be endorsed. It is encouraging that, on the two other occasions Matthew used *praus*, he was, we shall find, thinking of Moses (see pp. 218-33, 248-53). But against the proposed reading is the apparent dependence of 5:5 upon Ps. 37:11 ("But the meek shall possess the land"): that verse and its context make no reference, explicit or otherwise, to Moses. Also in the way is the circumstance that no other beatitude can have anything to do with Moses—unless it be 5:8, which refers to the beatific vision: "Blessed are the pure in heart, for they shall see God." This might be taken to promise Christians the felicity of beholding what Moses beheld, or what he did not behold, depending upon one's interpretation of Exodus 33.[100] But this can be no more than a conjecture, one without, to my knowledge, patristic or modern support. So the verdict on 5:5 must be: not proven.

JESUS AND THE TORAH (5:17-48)

5:17-20, the preamble to 5:21-48, has as its first function the prevention of misunderstanding—although its plain message has all too often been ignored. Many readers, ancient and contemporary, have construed 5:21-48 as a series of "antitheses"—that is the word so commonly used—which overturn the Torah. But, to judge from 5:17-20, there are in the first place no antitheses because in the second place there is no overturning of the Torah. Jesus, according to Matthew, neither dismissed the Torah nor released his followers from its imperatives. The commandments given to Moses, so far from having been drained of their ancient life, are still the living, active word of God. "Think not that I have come to abolish the law and the prophets. I have come not to abolish them but to fulfil them. For truly, I say to you, not an iota, not a dot, will pass from the law until all is accomplished. Whoever then relaxes one of the least of these commandments and teaches men so shall be called least in the kingdom of heaven...".

Not only does 5:17-20 rebut in advance a wrong interpretation of 5:21-48, it also supplies the reader with a clue as to the right interpretation. 5:20, in announcing that the righteousness of Jesus' followers must exceed that of the scribes and Pharisees, anticipates that Jesus' words in the subsequent paragraphs will, in their moral stringency,

---

[100]See further below, pp. 218-21. Some spoke of Moses seeing God, others of him not seeing God, still others of his seeing God in a partial or imperfect fashion.

exceed those of the Torah. Thus the tension between Jesus' teaching and the Mosaic law is not that those who accept the former will transgress the latter; rather is it that they will achieve far more than they would if the Torah were their sole guide.[101] As the *pleion* of 5:20 and the *perisson* of 5:47 imply, Christian righteousness means doing more. So although there is continuity with the past, there is also newness in the present, and it does not surprise when 5:21-48 goes beyond the letter of the law to demand even more.

Structurally, 5:21-48 consists of six paragraphs, each illustrating the truth of 5:17-48:

Moses forbade murder.
  Jesus forbids anger.

Moses condemned adultery.
  Jesus condemns the adulterous thought.

Moses permitted divorce.
  Jesus restricts that permission.

Moses gave rules for taking oaths.
  Jesus rules that oaths should not be taken at all.

Moses recommended the precept, "eye for eye, tooth for tooth."
  Jesus denies the precept's application to personal disputes.

Moses required love of neighbor.
  Jesus requires love of the enemy, in effect, love of all.

The paragraphs whose basic content has just been indicated are all introduced by variations on a formula:

a You have heard that it was said to those of old
  b. But I say to you

a You have heard that it was said
  b. But I say to you

---

[101]For this and what follows see Davies and Allison, *Matthew*, 1:481-566. Herein I must, for reasons of constricted space, neglect a score of controversial issues and just lay down my own judgments. I beg the reader's indulgence for the seemingly apodictic sentences.

a It was said
  b. But I say to you

a Again, you have heard that it was said to those of old
  b. But I say to you

a You have heard that it was said
  b. But I say to you

a. You have heard that it was said
  b. But I say to you

The first portion of the recurring formula (marked a) in each instance introduces instruction which can be found in the Pentateuch:

5:21 = Exod. 20:13; Deut. 5:17
5:27 = Exod. 20:14; Deut. 5:18
5:31 = Deut. 24:1-4
5:33 = Lev. 19:12
5:38 = Exod. 21:24; Lev. 24:20; Deut. 19:21
5:43 = Lev. 19:18

The second half of the formula (marked b) in every case prefaces Jesus' teaching, which transcends[102] a traditional commandment by making additional, difficult demands. (5:18, note well, rejects only subtraction from the law, not addition to it.) The meaning of the formula therefore is this: You (my listeners) have heard (in Scripture) that it was said (by God through Moses) to those of old (the wilderness generation)...; but I (Jesus) say to you.... It follows that, in 5:21-48, Jesus is directly dealing with the words of Moses—but not so much interpreting them as qualifying and adding to them.

This fact, that Jesus' words stand beside and supplement those of Moses, is not explicitly stated. But for ancient Jewish readers explicitness would have been otiose. It was only too obvious that Jesus was quoting Moses and then adding to him. But how would this remarkable circumstance—remarkable because we possess no precise parallel—have been understood?

The first clue is the macrotext, or larger context. We have already reviewed quite a number of texts in Matthew 1-5 which together make

---

[102]Cf. the formulation in Eusebius, *Dem. ev.* 3:2.

Jesus another Moses. Particularly significant is 5:1-2, where the Sinai typology leads one to anticipate new revelation delivered by a new Moses. This expectation is met, especially in 5:21-48, where Jesus twice enlarges upon the decalogue itself (5:21-30). Hence 5:21-48 continues the Moses typology: Jesus is another lawgiver. In this connection one should recall that, in Judaism, Mosaic characteristics transmigrated to later legislators and teachers (for example, Ezekiel and Hillel); and that in *4 Ezra*, where the scribe receives the old revelation of Sinai *plus additional, new revelation*, the Moses typology is extensive. Insofar then as Matthew made his teacher and revealer into another Moses, he was only being conventional.

But that is not the end of the matter. We must not forget the identity of the SM's speaker: he is the Messiah. In other words, he is the fulfillment of eschatological expectation, the culmination of Israel's history. This inevitably raises a question: should we, as have some, speak of "messianic Torah"?[103] My answer is that we should: Jesus is the Moses-like Messiah who proclaims the eschatological will of God on a mountain typologically equated with Sinai.

In contending this I do not assume that "messianic Torah" was to hand as a well-defined conception in Matthew's world, nor that our use of the expression is free of ambiguity. Our evangelist did not have access to a ready-made notion which we can easily document and which he could simply lay upon his hero. At the same time, an examination of certain texts will clarify my claim and help us to understand why the First Evangelist interpreted the Messiah's teaching as an eschatological law against which the first law is to be measured.

(i) Matthew probably associated Jesus' office as teacher with his status as Messiah. This follows from the expectation, attested in many texts from divers times and places, according to which the Messiah and/or some other eschatological figure will bring eschatological instruction. A sampling:

—Isa. 42:1-4: the servant (= Jesus the Messiah for Matthew; cf. Matt. 12:18-21) will bring *mišpāt* and *tôrâ*.

---

[103]So Birger Gerhardsson, *Memory and Manuscript: Oral Tradition and Written Transmission in Rabbinic Judaism and Early Christianity* (2nd ed.; Uppsala and Lund: Gleerup, 1964), 327. Cf. Ferdinand Hahn, *The Titles of Jesus in Christology* (London: Lutterworth, 1969), 44, opposing Gerhard Barth, "Matthew's Understanding of the Law," in G. Bornkamm, G. Barth, and H. J. Held, *Tradition and Interpretation in Matthew* (London: SCM, 1963), 153-59, and rightly observing that there was hardly one firm conception of what a "messianic Torah" might be: one cannot establish what was or was not possible in Matthew's time on the basis of later rabbinic sources.

—*CD* 7:18: the messianic oracle in Num. 24:17 ("A star shall come forth out of Jacob and a scepter shall rise out of Israel") is referred to "the Interpreter of the law."

—*4Q175*: this quotes Deut. 18:18-19 in an anthology of messianic texts, implying that the Qumran community expected an eschatological prophet like Moses, of whom God said: "I will put my words into his mouth and he shall tell them all that I command them."

—*ll Q Melch.* 2:15-21: "an anointed one, a prince" (cf. Dan. 9:25) will proclaim peace and salvation (cf. Isa. 52:7) and instruct those who mourn in Zion (cf. Isa. 61:2-3) "in all the ages of the world."

—*l En.* 51:3: the Elect One, the Son of man, will sit on God's throne, and "from the conscience of his mouth shall come out all the secrets of wisdom" (cf. 46:3; 49:3-4).

—*Ps. Sol.* 17:43: the Messiah's "words will be purer than the finest gold, the best. He will judge the peoples in the assemblies, the tribes of the sanctified. His words will be as the words of the holy ones, among sanctified peoples."

—*Tg. Onq.* to Gen. 49:11: the Messiah and those with him will study the Torah.

—*Tg. Isa.* to 53:5: peace will come through the Messiah's teaching, and those who "gather around his words... will be forgiven."

—*Gen. Rab.* 98:9: "When he, about whom it is written, 'Lowly and riding upon an ass' (Zech. 9:9) will come... he will elucidate for them the words of the Torah... and elucidate for them their errors. R. Hanina said: 'Israel will not need the teachings of King Messiah in the world to come, for it is said, "Unto him the nations shall seek" (Isa. 11:10)—not Israel.' If so, why will King Messiah come, and what will he come to do? To gather the exiles of Israel and to give them thirty commandments."[104]

One should also not overlook John 4:25, which purports that a Samaritan woman, in conversation with Jesus, expressed her faith that, when

---

[104]Additional rabbinic texts in SB 4/1:1-3.

the Christ comes, "he will show us all things" (cf. *Memar Marqah* 4:12).[105]

(ii) Rabbinic sources witness to a variety of beliefs about the fate of the Torah in the messianic age and/or the age to come[106]—that it will stay the same, inviolate forever,[107] that obscure parts will become clarified,[108] that certain sacrifices and festivals will cease,[109] that the laws covering things clean and unclean will be revised,[110] or even that there will be a new Torah.[111] One is sorely tempted to call upon this last belief to elucidate Matthew and the SM. But the texts attesting it are all very much later than the first century.[112] I therefore cannot in good conscience propose that we simply read the First Gosepl in their light. Nonetheless, the rabbinic texts referred to remain indirectly instructive, for they incontestably show us that some rabbis, at some points in time, did entertain speculative thoughts about possible changes in the Torah; and if they did so we must ask why in this particular Matthew could not have anticipated them. This is all the more true when notice is taken of Gal. 6:3: "Bear one another's burdens and so fulfil the law of Christ" (*ton nomon tou Christou*). Now the Hebrew equivalent of the expression in parenthesis, *tôrātô šel Mā šiah*, appears in *Mid. Qoh.* 11:8: "the Torah which a man learns in this world is vanity compared with the Torah of the Messiah." The coincidence of phrase with Paul may not be coincidence. Gal. 6:3 could be the proof that pre-Christian Judaism already spoke of the Messiah's Torah. Of this, however, we must remain unsure: independent invention of the same phrase cannot be reckoned impossible. Yet of one thing we may be confident. Paul, whatever he meant by it, could refer to Jesus Christ as having his own *nomos*.[113] I believe that Matthew's Gospel also presents us with the *nomos* of the Messiah—if not in terminology then in substance.

---

[105]As further background one should recall the common promise of eschatological wisdom and knowledge; see Hab. 2:14; LXX Hos. 6:2-3; *1QpHab*. VII:1-5; XI:1-2; Matt. 11:25 par.; 13:35. There is also much material in Raymond E. Brown, *The Semitic Background of the Term "Mystery" in the New Testament* (FBBS; Philadelphia: Fortress, 1968).

[106]For detailed discussion see Davies, *Setting*, 156-90.

[107]See *y. Meg.* 1:70d; *Exod. Rab.* 6:1; 33:7; *Lev. Rab.* 19:2; SB l:244-47.

[108]E.g. *m. ʿEd.* 8:7; *m. Sek.* 2:5; *b. Ber.* 35b; *b. Hag.* 25a; *b. Menah.* 45a.

[109]*Yal.* on Prov. 9:2; *Lev. Rab.* 9:7.

[110]*Midr. Ps.* on 146:7; *Lev. Rab.* 13:3.

[111]*Lev. Rab.* 13:3; *Tg.* on Isa. 12:3; *Tg.* on Cant. 5:l0; *Midr. Qoh.* 2:1; *Yal.* on Isa. 26:2.

[112]Although the use of *kainē entolē* in John 13:34 and of *kainos nomos* in *Barn.* 2:6 may suggest an earlier currency for the concept.

[113]See further Heinz Schürmann, "'Das Gesetz des Christus' (Gal 6,2)," in *Neues Testament und Kirche*, ed. Joachim Gnilka (Freiburg: Herder, l974), 282-300.

(iii) The Dead Sea Scrolls are further cause for pursuing the issue. *1QS* IX.9-ll[114] and *CD* VI.14[115] seem to imply the expectation that the sect's laws, based on its interpretation of the Torah, will be improved upon in the future. But much more significant is the *Temple Scroll*. This document not only reproduces much Pentateuchal legislation but also adds to and alters some of that legislation—and does so in the first person singular, with reference to God himself. Moreover, M. O. Wise has urged that the redactor's omissions of portions of Deuteronomy 12-26, when not due to avoidance of redundancy or rejection of legislation presupposing polygamy or remarriage after divorce, can be plausibly explained in terms of eschatological expectation.[116] Thus most of Deuteronomy's rules concerning aliens, slaves, lending, and boundary markers were omitted because thought inappropriate for the coming era. Further, the scroll assumes that all twelve tribes are in the land, as eschatological expectation dictated (*llQTemple* 57:11-12).[117] Now if Wise is correct in all this, he has finally given us the demonstration that pre-Christian Judaism not only contemplated a messianic Torah but actually produced one. Unfortunately, the reach of this study on Matthew prohibits examination of the merits and demerits of Wise's work as well as review of the competing theories. But if new Qumran discoveries and future scholarship confirm the direction of Wise's arguments,[118] the ramifications for New Testament studies will be considerable.

(iv) Gregory of Nyssa wrote:

> One can divide wickedness under two headings, one concerned with works, the other with thoughts. The former, the iniquity which shows itself in works, he [God] has punished through the old law. Now, however, he has given the law regarding the other form of sin, which punishes not so much the evil deed itself, as guards against even the beginning of it (*Beat.* 6).

---

[114]"They shall not depart from any counsel of the law, walking in all the stubborness of their hearts; but they shall judge by the first judgements by which the men of the community began to be disciplined, until there shall come a prophet and the Messiahs of Aaron and Israel."

[115]"They [those of the covenant] shall take care to act according to the exact interpretation of the law during the age of wickedness."

[116]*Temple Scroll*, passim; idem, "The Eschatological Vision of the Temple Scroll," *JENS* 49 (1990):155-72.

[117]For the eschatological ingathering of the tribes see the texts cited in my article, "Who will come from East and West? Observations on Matt. 8.11-12 = Luke 13.28-29," *IBS* 11 (1989):158-70; also T. A. Bergen, "The 'People coming from the East' in 5 Ezra 1.38," *JBL* 108 (1989):675-83.

[118]Also pertinent and tending in the same direction as Wise's works are the contributions of Wacholder, *Dawn,* passim, and Morton Smith, "Helios in Palestine," *Eretz Israel* 16 (1982):199-214.

This interpretation of the SM is not the whole truth; but it is very far from being wholly false. Matthew, we should not doubt, believed that Jesus, to great degree, focused on the interiority of the command- ments.

There is already an emphasis upon such interiority in the Tanak, as in Ps. 40:8 ("I delight to do thy will, O my God; thy law is within my heart") and Deut. 30:11-14 ("The word is very near to you; it is in your mouth and in your heart, that you can do it"). There is also Psalm 37, v. 31 of which reads: "The law of God is in his heart; his steps do not slip." There is some reason, beyond the later rabbinic evidence (see SB 1:199-200), to think that this last verse might have been understood by early Christians to pertain to eschatology. Matt. 5:5 quotes LXX Ps. 37:11 ("and the meek shall inherit the earth") and transforms it into an eschatological promise; and the Qumran community applied portions of Psalm 37 to the Teacher of Righteousness, the prince of wickedness, and the final destruction of evildoers (see *4QpPs^a*). But much more telling for the point I wish to make, which is that the interiority of the Torah would have been for Matthew an eschatological conception, is Jer. 31:31-34:

> Behold, the days are coming, says the Lord, when I will make a new covenant with the house of Israel and the house of Judah, not like the covenant which I made with their fathers when I took them by the hand to bring them out of the land of Egypt, my covenant which they broke, though I was their husband, says the Lord. But this is the covenant which I will make with the house of Israel after those days, says the Lord: I will put my law within them, and I will write it upon their hearts; and I will be their God and they shall be my people. And no longer shall each man teach his neighbor and each his brother, saying, "Know the Lord," for they shall all know me, from the least of them to the greatest, says the Lord; for I will forgive their iniquity and I will remember no more.

We need not here enter into the minefield that is this text, except to observe what is certain: according to Jeremiah 31, a new covenant will be established, the Torah will be interiorized, and the sins of God's people will be forgiven. Now it is more than suggestive that the three forecasts of Jeremiah all find their match in Matthew: Jesus the Messiah instituted a new covenant (26:28), stressed the internal di- mensions of the commandments (5:21ff., etc.), and gave his life as a ransom for many (20:28; 26:28). Moreover, most commentators have supposed that Matt. 26:28 ("this is my blood of the covenant... for the forgiveness of sins") alludes to Jer. 31:31 and so implicitly proclaims in Jesus' deeds the realization of Jeremiah's words (cf. Luke 22:17; 1

Cor. 11:25). It is consistent with this that Jer. 31:31-34 has regularly been understood by Christians from a very early time to have been realized in Jesus Christ.[119] What follows? I am lured to believe that Matthew 1-5 presents Jesus as the new lawgiver, the eschatological revealer and interpreter of Torah, the Messiah who brought the definitive, end-time revelation, a revelation for the heart, as foretold by Jeremiah's ancient oracle (cf. Justin, *Dial.* 11).

THE SM'S CLOSING TRIAD (7:13-27)

The SM winds down with a series of warnings which may be grouped into three subsections:
1. The two ways (7:13-14)
   a. Exhortation (13a)
   b. The wide gate and easy way (13b-c)
   c. The constricted gate and hard way (14)

2. False prophets (7:15-23)
   a. Exhortation (15a)
   b. The deeds of the false prophets (15b-20)
   c. Their judgement (21-23)

3. The two builders (7:24-27)
   a. The wise builder (7:24-25)
   b. The foolish builder (7:26-27)

This closing portion might, for five reasons, remind a reader of the Pentateuch's closing book. To begin with, Deuteronomy contains a prominent collection of warnings near its end, in chapters 28-30, warnings directed, like those of Matt. 7:13-27, against people who will not obey the divine imperatives. Next, Matt. 7:15-23 addresses the problem of false prophets, and the Pentateuchal legislation on that subject belongs to Deuteronomy 13 and 18. Thirdly, the two-way theme appears in Matt. 7:13-14; and that theme, so prominent in ancient Judaism and early Christianity, has its roots in Deuteronomy. Note especially Deut. 11:26 ("Behold, I set before you this day a blessing and a curse"); 30:1 ("And when all these things come upon

---

[119]See 2 Corinthians 3; 6:17-18; Heb. 8:8-12; and C. H. Dodd, *According to the Scriptures* (London: Fontana, 1965), 44-46.

you, the blessing and the curse, which I have set before you…"); and 30:15 ("I have set before you this day life and good, death and evil"). 30:1 and 15 particularly interest because they belong to the same neighborhood as Deut. 31:1; 31:24; and 32:45, verses which, I shall argue, are imitated by Matt. 7:28. Moreover, Matthew's particular antithesis, *zōē— apōleia*, appears in Deut. 30:15-20: "I have set before you life (LXX: *zōē*)…. But if your heart turns away… you shall perish utterly" (LXX: *apōleia apoleisthe*). In the fourth place, the wording of Matt. 7:24-27, which enjoins hearing (*akouei, akouōn*) Jesus' words (*logous*) to do (*poiei, poiōn*) them, echoes LXX Deut. 31:12: *akousontai poiein pantas tous logous tou nomou toutou*. Lastly, Deut. 28:15-30 is reminiscent of the parable of the two builders: "But if you will not obey the voice of the Lord your God or be careful to do all his commandments and his statutes which I command you this day, then all these curses shall come upon you and overtake you…. You shall build a house and you shall not dwell in it."

Should we infer that Matt. 7:13-27 was constructed with an eye on the concluding chapters of Deuteronomy, that the end of the SM simulates the end of the Pentateuch? Those of us who postulate the existence of Q will not be able to attribute to Matthew either the combination of *akouein + logous + poiein* in vv. 24 and 26 or the location of the parable of the two builders at the close of the SM, this because Luke 6:46-49 exhibits the same features, which features, it follows, already belonged to Q's sermon on the plain. That circumstance, however, is offset by another. A comparison of both 7:13-14 (on the two ways) and 7:15-23 (on false prophets) with Luke 6:43-44 and 13:23-24 suggests that the two subsections owe as much to Matthean redaction as to tradition. To judge by Luke, neither the alternative of the two ways nor the directions for discerning false prophets belonged to Q's sermon on the plain.[120] Instead it was evidently Matthew's creativity which gave to the SM's conclusion the form and content it now has, a form and content which, we have seen, might remind one of Deuteronomy. When to this is added the knowledge that in other particulars the First Evangelist designed the SM to recall the law of Moses, one begins to wonder whether 7:13-27 was not likewise so designed. To do more than wonder, however, would perhaps be unwise; and I am content simply to call attention to a possibility.

---

[120]Cf. Davies and Allison, *Matthew*, 1:694-95,

THE TRANSITIONAL FORMULA (7:28-29)

Five times Matthew placed the following refrain at the end of a major discourse:

7:28   *kai egeneto ote etelesen ho Iēsous*
          tous logous toutous

11:1   *kai egeneto ote etelesen ho Iēsous*
          diastassōn tous dōdeka mathētais autou

13:53   *kai egeneto ote etelesen ho Iēsous*
          tas parabolas tautas

19:1   *kai egeneto ote etelesen ho Iēsous*
          tous logous toutous

26:1   *kai egeneto ote etelesen ho Iēsous*
          pantas tous logous toutous

The first six words are in each case the same. Thereafter the words vary, although a demonstrative pronoun occurs in four instances, and each second half of the formula refers to Jesus' teaching—to his words (7:28; 19:l; 26:1), to his instruction of the twelve (11:1), to his parables (13:53).

Matthew's transitional formula[121] has usually been discussed in connection with the Gospel's structure. Bacon, as is well known, made it the key to his Pentateuchal outline (pp. 293-98). But there is a second issue which 7:28-29 and its parallels provoke. The repetition of a transitional formula throughout a Jewish book is a well-attested phenomenon. "The Israelites (again) did what was evil in the sight of the Lord" punctuates Judges: 2:11; 3:7, 12; 4:l; 6:l; l0:6; 13:1. And the Pentateuch offers several variations on the basic form, "These are" + type of teaching[122] + agent of teaching:[123] Lev. 26:46; 27:34; Num. 30:16; 36:13; Deut. 1:1; 6:l. There is also a formula that appears three times in Deuteronomy, in 31:1, 24; and 32:45:

    kai sunetelesen Mōusēs
      lalōn pantas tous logous toutous

---

[121]"Transitional formula" is more accurate than "concluding formula."

[122]"Statutes," "judgments," "laws," "words," "commandments."

[123]"That the Lord established through Moses," "that the Lord gave to Moses," "that the Lord commanded (through) Moses."

henika de sunetelesen Mōusēs
grapōn pantas tous logous tou nomou toutou

kai sunetelesen Mōusēs
lalōn panti Israēl

A few commentators have believed that Matthew's five-fold formula was forged under the memory of these three texts.[124] In Deuteronomy, as in Matthew, we have a recurring transitional formula, the first half of which is more stable than the second half. Further, *tous logous toutous* recurs in three of the Matthean texts and in two from Deuteronomy. The additional similarities can be seen from this analysis:

introductory element, with opening *kai* in all but one case
+ *(sun)teleō*
+ subject (Jesus or Moses)
+ type of authoritative speech delivered
(usually with demonstrative pronoun)

The texts from Matthew and Deuteronomy all fit this common form.

Is the parallel fortuitous, or was Matthew's formula intended to function as an allusion? Luz objects that, if an allusion were intended, more words would be shared; thus the passages from Deuteronomy lack *egeneto*, and Matthew has the simplex, *teleō*, instead of the compound, *sunteleō*.[125] But these observations hardly free the mind of doubt, for not only does the Huck-Greeven *Synopse* print *sunetelesen* for Matt. 7:28, but is it prudent to insist that an allusion be, in effect, a quotation? Certainly there are other Matthean texts whose allusive nature is obvious and yet the correspondence with Scripture is far from perfect. The evangelist, had he wished, could readily have assimilated Matt. 2:19-21 even more completely to Exod. 4:19-20. That he did not so wish is a simple fact. Moreover, there are scriptural quotations, such as those in 2:23 and 27:9-10, which are, to understate the matter, inexact—so inexact that their very source is disputed. Should this not halt us from issuing a pontifical *a priori* regarding what

---

[124]E.g. P. Dabeck, "'Siehe, es erscheinen Moses und Elias' (Mt 17,3)," *Bib.* 23 (1947):176; H. Frankemölle, *Jahwebund und Kirche Christi* (NTAbh, n.F. 10, 2nd ed.; Münster: Aschendorf, 1984), 334, 370; Gnilka, *Matthäus*, 1:283-84; A. Ogawa, *L'histoire de Jesus chez Matthieu* (Europäische Hochschulschriften 23/116; Frankfurt am Main: Lang, 1979), 115-16; Teeple, *Prophet*, 82. For other parallels see LXX Num. 16:31; Ps. 72:20; *4 Ezra* 7:1; *2 Bar.* 87:1.

[125]*Matthew*, 1:455.

Matthew might have written but did not—particularly when we remember that allusions, as opposed to quotations, are by definition informal and only partially reproduce earlier texts? I am inclined to accept what Luz rejects, namely, that the redactional refrain in Matt. 7:28-29; 11:l; 13:53; 19:l; and 26:l recalls another refrain, one belonging to the end of Deuteronomy and the story of Moses.

In favor of this conviction is a textual decision with which the critic is faced: for Matt. 7:28 one can either read *etelesen*, as does NA[26], or one can read *sunetelesen*, as does HG. If we adopt the latter reading, the parallel with Deut. 31:1, 24 and 32:45 is all the closer. But if we accept the former, it seems a very good guess that the resemblance to Deut. 31:1, 24 and 32:45, verses which employ *sunetelesen*, was recognized; and just as scribes sometimes assimilated NT citations to the LXX, so here too: the parallel, so far from being overlooked, was enhanced. I note that the textual apparatus in Legg shows that *sunetelesen* is also reproduced by witnesses in ll:l and 26:l.

One last point. Although others have rendered a different verdict,[126] it is my best judgment that there is probably no significance in the fact that Matthew's formula appears five times. One could, I suppose, observe that some have divided Deuteronomy into five sections (Deut. 1-3; 4-ll; 12-26; 27-30; 31-34),[127] or that the law code in Deut. 12-26 falls into five parts (12:2-28; 12:29-17:13; 17:14-18:22; 19:1-25:19; 26:1-l5).[128] But the formula which our evangelist apparently imitated appears only three times. More worthy of reflection perhaps is that Matthew's basic structure, marked by his five-fold formula, is that of narrative followed by discourse followed by narrative followed by discourse, etcetera. This is also more or less true of most of Exodus -Deuteronomy: sections of law and narrative alternate.

OVERVIEW OF MATTHEW 1-8

(i) The new exodus. Having reviewed the pertinent portions of Matthew 1:1-8:1 it remains to inquire whether the parallels we have discerned between Moses and Jesus are parts of some greater whole. Did Matthew hand us an unordered heap of semblances, or did he

---

[126]See Appendix I, pp. 296-97.

[127]See Duane L. Christensen, in *Mercer Dictionary of the Bible*, ed. Watson E. Mills (Macon: Mercer, 1990), 211, s.v. "Deuteronomy."

[128]S. D. McBride, "Polity of the Covenant People: The Book of Deuteronomy," *Int.* 41 (1987):229-44.

intend something more? It is my view that the many allusions to Moses cohere into a pattern, a structure of meaning. All along we have been examining the pieces of a jigsaw puzzle; and, when they are all put together, a distinct image stares back at us. I refer not to the face of Moses but rather to a picture of which he is only a part, albeit a very important part.

Matthew commenced by replaying the plot of Exodus 1-2 and of the haggadah that grew up around those chapters; thus the circumstances of Mary's pregnancy, the prophecy of Israel's savior, the issuance of Herod's decree, and the saving of Jesus' life are all recollective.[129] What comes next? The text jumps forward many years,[130] quotes a new exodus text from Isaiah (3:3), and then tells of Jesus' experience of baptism—which ritual, be it noted, Paul likened to the passing of Israel through the Red Sea (1 Cor. 10:1-5).[131] After that we read that Jesus, like Moses, fasted for forty days and forty nights (4:2), after which (5:1-2) he climbed a mountain and, having sat down, critically engaged the Mosaic Torah and delivered fresh imperatives (cf. 7:28-29). Does not the whole sequence inexorably push us to the conclusion that in Matthew's opening chapters we have to do not just with parallel personages (Jesus and Moses) but with parallel plots, that an extensive typology underlies all of Matthew 1-7, that the story of Jesus is the story of a new exodus, that Matt. 1:1-5:2 contains a predictive

---

[129]I also note that if Matthew opens with a genealogy, Exodus 1:1-7 supplies a list of Israelite ancestors.

[130]Is it just coincidence—I ask the question; I give no answer—that the jump from Matt. 2:23, where the infant Jesus goes to Nazareth, to 3:1ff., where the adult Jesus comes to John, has a parallel in Exodus 2, where the narrative passes from the naming of Moses (2:10) to his adulthood (2:11)? "I drew him out of the water" is followed immediately by "One day, when Moses had grown up, he went out to his people and looked upon their burdens." The LXX has: *egeneto de en tais hēmerais tais pollais ekeinais megas genomenos Mōusēs*... . Comparable are Matthew's debated *de*, the use of *en tais hēmerais*, and the abutment of events from infancy and adulthood.

[131]We do not know if the comparison was conventional (as Goodenough, *Symbols*, 10:135, claimed: "Paul certainly did not invent the idea that the passage of the Red Sea was baptism *into Moses*") or whether it was invented by the apostle; but the link in rabbinic sources between baptism and the phrase, "enter under the wings of the Shekinah" (*b. Yeb.* 46b, etc.), favors the former possibility. —In later Christian literature and art of course Moses' passing through the Red Sea, as well as the imitative crossings of the Jordan by Joshua, Elijah, and Elisha, came to be prefigurations of the baptism of Jesus and Christians; see Jean Daniélou, *The Bible and the Liturgy* (Notre Dame: University Press, 1956), 86-98. The same prefiguration is implicit in Matthew. But this, apart from the quotation of Isaiah in v. 3, only appears from Matthew's schematization in chapters 1-7. Little emphasis upon the new exodus or new Moses theme emerges when chapter 3 is examined in isolation. At most there are hints of such. I refer the reader to the exhaustive treatment of Davies, *Setting*, 26-45, upon which I cannot improve.

structure which leads the alert reader to anticipate, in the event justly, the revelation of another law?[132] Following Austin Farrer and Michael Goulder,[133] I have no misgivings in returning whole-hearted assent.[134]

More than consistent with this conviction is the existence of other ostensible historical narratives which not only contain Moses typologies but also borrow the plot of the exodus. Here it suffices to advert to the discussion in chapters two and three, especially to what was said regarding Joshua, 1 Samuel, the *Jeremiah Apocryphon*, and Eusebius' *Ecclesiastical History*. In constructing an extended exodus typology Matthew was scarcely playing the rôle of an innovator. The archaic plot of the exodus was constantly updated by both Jews and Christians; it was ever old, ever new.

Having established this fact, a crucial observation falls to be considered: Matthew's text has a profound eschatological dimension— something missing from Joshua, 1 Samuel, the *Jeremiah Apocryphon*, and Eusebius' *Ecclesiastical History*. The Gospel concerns the Messiah, a figure of the latter days. Thus its new exodus is to be understood against those Jewish texts which, according to the principle that the end is declared from the beginning (Isa. 46:10), announce an eschatological exodus. Representative are the following:

Hos. 2:14-15: "Therefore, behold, I will allure her, and bring her into the wilderness... And there she shall answer as in the days of her youth, as at the time when she came out of the land of Egypt."

Isa. 10:24-26: "Therefore thus says the Lord, the Lord of hosts: 'O my people, who dwell in Zion, be not afraid of the Assyrians when they smite with the rod and lift up their staff against you as the Egyptians did. For in a very little while my indignation will come to an end, and my anger will be directed to their destruction. And the Lord of hosts will wield against them a scourge, as when he smote Midian at the rock

---

[132]I have elsewhere, following Davies, tried to relate the SM to the triadic declaration of Simeon the Just as recorded in *m. 'Abot* 1:2: "Upon three things the world stands: upon Torah, upon temple service, and upon *gĕmîlût hăsadîm*." This is worth noting because it underlines the comprehensive character of the SM: it is Matthew's version of the three rabbinic pillars by which the world is sustained. See my article, "The Structure of the Sermon on the Mount," *JBL* 106 (1987):423-45; also W. D. Davies and Dale C. Allison, Jr., "Reflections on the Sermon on the Mount," *SJT* 44 (1991), pp. 283-310.

[133]See Appendix IV, pp. 307-11.

[134]Note also the remarks of S. H. Hooke, *Middle Eastern Mythology* (Baltimore: Penguin, 1963), 169-70.

of Oreb; and his rod will be over the sea, and he will lift it as he did in Egypt.'"

Isa. 11:15-16: "And the Lord will utterly destroy the tongue of the sea of Egypt; and will wave his hand over the River and smite it into seven channels that men may cross dryshod. And there will be a highway from Assyria for the remnant which is left of his people, as there was for Israel when they came up from the land of Egypt."

Ezek. 20:33-38: "As I live, says the Lord God, surely with a mighty hand and an outstretched arm, and with wrath poured out, I will be king over you. I will bring you out from the peoples and gather you out of the countries where you are scattered, with a mighty hand and an outstretched arm, and with wrath poured out; and I will bring you into the wilderness of the peoples; and there I will enter into judgment with you face to face. As I entered into judgment with your fathers in the wilderness of the land of Egypt, so I will enter into judgment with you, says the Lord God. I will make you pass under the rod, and I will let you go in by number. I will purge out the rebels from among you, and those who transgress against me; I will bring them out of the land where they sojourn, but they shall not enter the land of Israel. Then you will know that I am the Lord."

Additional, related texts include Isa. 4:5; 40:3-5; 48:20-21; 51:9-11; Jer. 31:31-34; Mic. 7:15; *1QM* XI:10; Rev. 11:6; *2 Bar.* 29:8; *Sib. Orac.* 7:149; *Deut. Rab.* 2:2.[135] When Jews looked to the future they saw the past. For them, the distant time of Moses and the longed-for latter days mirrored one another.

Particularly interesting for comparison with Matthew are Jer. 16:14-15 ("Therefore, behold the days are coming, says the Lord, when it shall no longer be said, 'As the Lord lives who brought up the people of Israel out of the land of Egypt,' but 'As the Lord lives who brought up the people of Israel out of the north country and out of all the countries where he had driven them.' For I will bring them back to their own land which I gave to their fathers") and Isa. 52:11-12 ("Depart, depart, go out thence, touch no unclean thing; go out from

---

[135]Discussion in B. Anderson, "The Exodus Typology in Second Isaiah," in *Israel's Prophetic Heritage*, ed. B. Anderson and W. Harrelson (New York: Harper & Row, 1962), 177-95; J. Fischer, "Das Problem des neuen Exodus in Isaias c. 40-55," *TQ* 110 (1979):111-20; H. Sahlin, "The New Exodus of Salvation," in *Root of the Vine*, 81-95.

the midst of her, purify yourselves, you who bear the vessels of the Lord. For you shall not go out in haste, and you shall not go in flight, for the Lord will go before you, and the God of Israel will be your rear guard"). According to the former, future oaths will refer not to the exodus from Egypt but to the new saving event, which is therefore greater than its historical analogue: the first exodus will in some sense be superseded. According to the latter, "in the new exodus disquietude will be replaced by calm. The new exodus will therefore not simply be a remanifestation of an older prototype, but will have qualitative distinctions of its own"[136] (cf. Isa. 43:18-19).

That the hope for a new exodus, which might surpass the old, was very much alive in Matthew's time, is a familiar fact, one demonstrated especially by the Dead Sea Scrolls. These feature a community that entered the desert in order to prepare the way for a new exodus (cf. 1QS VIII:12-14, quoting Isaiah 40:3). That community structured itself on analogy with the structure of Mosaic Israel and also anticipated that its eschatological battle would be a memory come to life (see 1QM III-IV, X); as 1QM XI:8 has it: "Thou will do to them as Thou did to Pharaoh, and to the captains of his chariots in the Red Sea."[137]

In addition to the Dead Sea Scrolls there is Rev. 15:2-4, a text presumably composed very near Matthew's time. Here those who have conquered the beast and its image and the number of its name stand beside a sea of glass and "sing the song of Moses" (cf. Exodus 15; Deuteronomy 32). Clearly the deliverance from the Red Sea is here the typological equivalent of the eschatological deliverance, and the song in Revelation "celebrates a new and greater exodus."[138] Also quite pertinent for our understanding of Matthew in its historical context are the several new exodus motifs in the Pauline epistles[139] and especially the popular prophets whose sad and partial stories Josephus recorded. We had occasion to examine these on pp. 78-83 and deemed it most likely that more than one must have fruitlessly sought, by reliving certain exodus experiences, to prove himself the eschatological prophet like Moses (cf. Matt. 24:26). Now if I may so put it, what we have in Matthew is the obverse of Josephus' capsule summaries of

[136]Fishbane, Interpretation, 364.

[137]See further Frank More Cross, Jr., The Ancient Library of Qumran and Modern Biblical Studies (Garden City: Doubleday, 1961), 78, n. 36a.

[138]J. P. M. Sweet, Revelation (Philadelphia: Westminster, 1979), 239.

[139]See esp. 1 Cor. 10:1-4; 11:25; 2 Corinthians 3-4; and the remarks of Davies, Paul and Rabbinic Judaism (rev. ed.; Philadelphia: Fortress, 1980), 100-110, 141-46, 250-53, 313-14; also Sahlin, as in n. 135.

failed leaders. That is to say, the Gospel is the literary record not of an unsuccessful eschatological prophet like Moses but a successful one, who for Christians had accomplished a new exodus. This is in part the implication of Matt. 3:3: "For this [John the Baptist] is he who was spoken of by the prophet Isaiah when he said, 'The voice of one crying in the wilderness: Prepare the way of the Lord, make his paths straight.'" The line from Isa. 40:3 is, in its original context, a proclamation of the eschatological exodus (cf. the application in the Dead Sea Scrolls). In Matthew (as in Mark 1:3) it helps cast the shadow of the exodus over the story of Jesus.

At this juncture let me revert to an issue earlier considered (p. 142). Some commentators have played the new Moses and new exodus themes against each other, as though emphasis upon one must lead to de-emphasis upon the other. I disagree, and not just because there are other texts which integrate the two themes. There are two additional and important facts, the first being that Matthew wished to open his story by telling of a new exodus, the second that it was impossible for there to be another exodus without the participation of the people of God, those to be redeemed—but when Jesus came into the world the new covenant community, the *ecclesia*,[140] did not yet exist: disciples had not been called, and the church had not yet been built upon Peter the rock (4:18-22; 16:13-20). Or, to be more precise, the *ecclesia* did exist, but it then consisted solely of its leader, Jesus himself—as I think Hos. 11:1, quoted in Matt. 2:15, implies: Jesus = Son = Israel. Thus narrative circumstances dictated that, at the book's beginning, the new Moses also be the new Israel; and so when we discover that Jesus is, in Matthew 2 and 4, not only very much like Moses but also very much like Israel, what prohibits giving both facts their full force? There is an analogy to all this in Exodus, where it is related that, when the golden calf was made, every Israelite save one forsook Yahweh. That individual was of course Israel's leader, Moses, who for a time became the remnant: he himself was true Israel (cf. 1 Kings 19:14). And as with the first redeemer, so with the last: if Moses once constituted the people of God, the Mosaic Messiah did no less.[141]

---

[140]For this term see 16:18; 18:17. The word is used of the exodus community in LXX Deuteronomy.

[141]It is also pertinent that "almost every key element in Moshe's early life—e.g., rescue from death by royal decree, rescue from death by water, flight into the desert, meeting with God on the sacred mountain—foreshadows Israel's experience in the book of Exodus. The key theme of the distinction between Israel and Egypt, so central

(ii) The new creation. There is a minor yet important theme that shows itself more than once in Matthew's opening chapters. I refer to the theme of the new creation.[142] The Gospel opens with two loaded words, *biblos geneseōs*. These words, which I take to be the book's title, appear together only twice in the Septuagint, in Gen. 2:4 and 5:1 (cf. 6:9). Further, "*Genesis*" was already, among Greek-speaking Jews of Matthew's time, the name for the first book of Moses, as is conclusively established by Philo, *Poster C.* 127; *Abr.* 1; and *Aet. mund.* 19. Obviously Matthew selected his opening words with the intention of sending thoughts back to the primeval history. The evangelist also accomplished this end by designating Jesus "son of Abraham" (1:1) and by heading his genealogy with the three patriarchs, Abraham, Isaac, and Jacob. And then there is 3:16, where the Spirit of God descends as a dove upon Jesus. Although many interpretations of this have been offered, it is altogether likely that 3:16 implies a parallel between the baptism of Jesus and the creation of the cosmos. Just as the Spirit of God "brooded"—the Hebrew verb is used of a bird in Deut. 32:11 (cf. *b. Hag.* 15a)—over the face of the waters at the inception of things, so did the Spirit of God, in the form of a dove, move over the waters when Jesus was baptized.[143]

What does the new creation motif have to do with the new Moses theme? The two things are complimentary when we take into account the principle, *ta eschata hōs ta prōta*: the last things (will be) as the first (*Barn.* 6:13). This sentiment, a fundament of eschatological expectation,[144] incorporated both the creation of the world and the exodus from Egypt; that is, Jews who imagined the end foresaw both a new creation and a new exodus. It is therefore no surprise that both things were sometimes envisaged at once. Two examples:

---

to the Plague Narrative and to Israelite religion as a whole, is brought out beautifully in the depiction of Moshe's development from Egyptian prince to would-be liberator to shepherd in the wilderness.... What is important in these early chapters of Exodus, then, is not the customary focus on the young hero's deeds... but on what he shares with his people, or, more precisely, how he prefigures them." So Everett Fox, *Genesis and Exodus: A New English Rendition* (New York: Schocken, 1991), 235.

[142]In addition to the following see Davies, *Setting*, 67-72.

[143]See further Davies and Allison, *Matthew*, 1:331-34; also my article, "The Baptism of Jesus and a New Dead Sea Scroll," *BAR* 18 (1992), pp. 58-60. The patristic texts which associate baptism with the primitive waters of Genesis (see Jean Daniélou, *The Bible and the Liturgy*, 70-75) are here in continuity with the canonical Gospels.

[144]Cf. *4 Ezra* 7:30 and the *paliggenesia* of Matt. 19:28. Discussion in Nils A. Dahl, "Christ, Creation, and the Church," in *Jesus in the Memory of the Early Church* (Minneapolis: Augsburg, 1976), 120-40.

Isa. 51:9-11: "Awake, awake, put on strength, o arm of the Lord; awake, as in days of old, the generations of long ago. Was it not thou that didst cut Rahab in pieces, that didst pierce the dragon? Was it not thou that didst dry up the sea, the waters of the great deep; that didst make the depths of the sea a way for the redeemed to pass over?. And the ransomed of the Lord shall return, and come to Zion with singing; everlasting joy shall be upon their heads; they shall obtain joy and gladness, and sorrow and sighing shall flee away."

2 Bar. 29:3-8: "And it will happen that when all that which should come to pass in these parts has been accomplished, the Anointed One will begin to be revealed. And Behemoth will reveal itself from its place, and Leviathan will come from the sea, the two great monsters which I created on the fifth day of creation and which I shall have kept until that time. And they will be nourishment for all who are left. The earth will also yield fruits ten thousandfold. And on one vine will be a thousand branches, and one branch will produce a thousand clusters, and one cluster will produce a thousand grapes, and one grape will produce a cor of wine. And those who are hungry will enjoy themselves and they will, moreover, see marvels every day. For winds will go out in front of me every morning to bring the fragrance of aromatic fruits and clouds at the end of the day to distill the dew of health. And it will happen at that time that the treasury of manna will come down again from on high, and they will eat of it in those years because these are they who will have arrived at the consummation of time."

Also noteworthy is Isa. 43:15-21, where "the Creator of Israel," who once made a way in the sea and extinguished chariot and horse, army and warrior, promises to do "a new thing," which is explicated as another exodus: "I will make a way in the wilderness and rivers in the desert... for I give water in the wilderness, rivers in the desert, to give drink to my chosen people." Not unrelated are certain promises made by the Apocalypse of John: those who overcome will, at the consummation, not only eat of the tree of life, as did Adam and Eve: they will also be given manna, as was Israel of old (Rev. 2:17; 22:2).[145]

It is my suggestion that, in Matthew, the new exodus that is the historical renewal of Israel in the person of the Mosaic Messiah is simultaneously a new creation, that is, a renewal of the world. To what degree, however, we should regard as predominately eschatological the mingling of exodus themes with creation motifs is problematic. For the creation and the exodus were associated even outside the

---

[145]Further texts and discussion in R. Le Déaut, *La Nuit Pascale* (AB 22; Rome: Pontifical Biblical Institute, 1963).

sphere of eschatological speculation.[146] Wisd. 19:6 affirms that "the whole creation in its nature was fashioned anew" when God preserved the Israelites as they fled from Egypt; and *LAB* 15:5-6 compares the parting of the Red Sea to the creative act of Gen. 1:9: "Let the waters under the heavens be gathered together into one place." Already the Hebrew Bible, as is well known, moves Rahab, the female monster of chaos, from creation contexts (Job 9:13; 38:8-11) to Exodus contexts (Ps. 89:11; Isa. 51:9-10). The Bible further offers two competing rationales for observing the Sabbath, one involving commemoration of the creation (Exod. 20:9-11), the other involving commemoration of the exodus (Deut. 5:15). Even more significant for our purposes, however, is the lesser known fact that the book of Exodus itself implicitly likens the advent of Moses to a new creation. In Exod. 1:5-7 we read that in Egypt the Israelites "were fruitful and increased greatly; they multiplied and grew exceedingly strong; so that the land was filled with them." The striking redundancy is not just overdone rhetoric. The repetition is rather the repetition of Gen. 1:28 ("Be fruitful and multiply, and fill the earth and subdue it; and have dominion...") and 9:1-2 ("Be fruitful and multiply, and fill the earth. The fear of you and the dread of you shall be upon every beast..."). "The Exodus passage has," to quote James S. Ackerman, "preserved the five-fold verb structure of [the Genesis texts]... and three of the verbs are the same in all three passages,[147] so we can assume that it [Exod. 1:5-7] is inviting us to perceive" connections between Exodus 1 and both Genesis 1 and 9; specifically, "the destiny of man, as announced at the Creation and after the Flood, is in the process of being fulfilled by the descendants of Israel." [148]

Closely following upon the allusions to Adam and Eve and Noah there are promptings to recall Genesis 11 and the tower of Babel. If I may cite Ackerman again: in both Exod. 1:8-14 and Gen. 11:1-9

---

[146]There is much useful material in R. Chernus, *Redemption and Chaos: A Study in the Symbolism of the Rabbinic Aggada* (Ann Arbor: University Microfilms, 1978).

[147]*pārâ, rābâ, malē'*.

[148]J. S. Ackerman, "The Literary Context of the Moses Birth Story (Exodus 1-2)," in *Literary Interpretations of Biblical Narratives*, ed. K. R. R. Gros Louis et al. (Nashville: Abingdon, 1974), 77. Cf. Terence E. Fretheim, "The Plagues as Ecological Signs of Historical Disaster," *JBL* 110 (1991), 385, n. 3: "That the phrase 'the land was filled with them' in Exod 1:7 is intended as an explicit reference to Gen 1:28 and 9:1 is no doubt evident in the absence of any reference to Egypt or Goshen, the mention of which would have blurred this link. In some sense Israel is represented as having fulfilled the creational command, and hence Israel is a microcosmic fulfillment of God's intentions for the creation."

there is an emphasis on human ingenuity. Both [passages] are introduced by the interjection *haba* 'come now,' with the main verb in the Hebrew cohortative 'let us,' followed by *pen* 'lest,' describing the situation which the protagonists are seeking to avoid. Both stories refer to building activity and describe similar building materials [Gen. 11:3: *nilbĕnâ lĕbēnîm… hōmer*; Exod. 1:14: *bĕhōmer ûbilbēnîm*; 5:7: *lĕbōn hallĕbēnîm*]. Both stories stress that man's proud wisdom and purposive activity were in vain, and can lend to his own destruction, when they run counter to the order of things perceived by Israel. In each story man's purposive activity precipitates a divine counteraction which results in redemptive dispersion, first in Abraham, then in Israel….[149]

The silent gesturing towards Genesis continues in Exodus 2. Moses' mother, it is said, put her infant son in a *tēbâ*, an ark (2:3). Is there significance in this? Many have so thought.[150] Gen. 6:14 reads: "Make for yourself an ark of gopher wood… and cover it inside and out with pitch." Exod. 2:3 reads: "She took for him an ark of bulrushes, and daubed it with bitumen and pitch." The correspondences are striking: *tēbâ* appears in the Hebrew Bible only in these two places, and in both instances the person whom the ark is to serve is similarly indicated (*lĕkâ; lô*). Moreover, "the building materials for the *tēbah*" are specified "in a construct chain; puns involving words for 'pitch' are found in both (*kpr* in Genesis and *hmr* in Exodus); the vessel is twice sealed, 'inside and out' in Genesis and 'with pitch and with mortar' in Exodus."[151] One can hardly avoid the thought that Moses was a second Noah. If Noah, the savior of all living things, was preserved upon the waters in an ark, it was not otherwise with Moses, the savior of Israel.

The primeval history is also evoked by Exod. 2:2. According to this, Moses' mother "saw that he [Moses] was good." *ra ᶜâ + kî-tôb*, otherwise unattested outside Genesis, echoes the refrain of Genesis 1: "And God saw that it was good." The parallel is recognized in *Exod. Rab.* 1:20: "The sages say: When Moses was born the whole house became flooded with light; for here it says: and she saw him that he was a goodly child, and elsewhere it says: And God saw the light that it was good."[152] One also remembers that the traditions of Jochebed's recovered virginity, her second legal marriage, and her immunity from birth pangs, all previously discussed, convey that Moses marked a

[149]Ibid., 81. Cf. Isaac M. Kikawada and Arthur Quinn, *Before Abraham was* (Nashville: Abingdon, 1985), 117.

[150]Note e.g. U. Cassuto, *A Commentary on the Book of Exodus* (Jerusalem: Magnes, 1967), 18-19, and Sarna, *Exodus*, 28.

[151]So Kikawada and Quinn, *Before Abraham was*, 85.

[152]Cf. Kikawada and Quinn, ibid., 114-15.

brand new beginning: his birth was a new event, different from the earlier births of his brother and sister, and it escaped the curse of Gen. 3:16. The sort of thing here implied appears in and was extended by Samaritan tradition, according to which Moses renewed the creation, opened Eden, and held in his hands the rod of Adam.[153] In short, Moses was another Adam.

Beyond the back references to Genesis already observed, Ackerman has wondered whether Moses' attempt to halt the combat of two Hebrew men (Exod. 2:11-15) should be related to the tale of Cain and Abel, and also—here he gropes for too much—whether, in Exod. 2:17, the driving of the women away from the well, their source of life, might not have something to do with the driving of Adam and Eve from paradise. However those matters may stand, Ackerman asks: "Is the narrative [in Exodus], moving back with its allusions through the primeval story sequence, portraying a God who, through Moses and the people of Israel, is in the process of reversing the alienation and broken community which had been man's condition since earliest times?"[154] He answers with this:

> Pharaoh's Babel-like building activity is doomed to fail because bondage crushes the human spirit. Moses in the ark is, like Noah, the presence of life for mankind because he will point the way to freedom. His intention to prevent one Hebrew brother from smiting another is an attempt to overcome the hostility between brothers which had existed since Cain killed Abel. Paradoxically, the seven daughters are driven away by the shepherds because God, confirming the new situation of pride and hostility embodied in man's disobedience, had driven Adam and Eve out of Eden, away from the tree of life.[155]

I am inclined to suppose Ackerman is close to the truth, partly because later in Exodus there are additional ties to the creation narrative.[156] The destructive ten plagues, which leave a wrecked empire, are seemingly the antitheses of the ten wonderful words of creation,[157] as certain contrasting parallels suggest:

Exod. 7:14: Aaron lifted his   Gen. 1:10: God created the

---

[153]Evidence in Meeks, *Prophet-King*, 222-23.

[154]"Literary Context," 114-15.

[155]Ibid.

[156]For what follows see Ziony Zevit, "The Priestly Redaction and Interpretation of the Plague Narrative in Exodus," *JQR* 66 (1976):193-211.

[157]Gen. 1:3, 6, 9, 11, 14, 20, 24, 26, 28, 29; cf. *m. 'Abot* 5:1, 4.

staff over the "gatherings of their waters" (miqwēh mêmêhem)

"gatherings of the waters" (miqwēh hammayim)

Exod. 8:3: "the Nile will swarm (šeras) with frogs"

Gen. 1:20: "Let the waters swarm with swarms" (yišrĕsû ...šeres)

Exod. 8:16-19: Aaron struck the "dust" ('ăpar) of the earth and from it came lice (or: gnats)

Gen. 2:7: God created human beings from the "dust" ('āpār) of the ground

Exod. 9:1-7: the hand of the Lord killed "the cattle in the field, the horses, the asses, the camels, the herds, the flocks of the Egyptians"

Gen. 1:25: "And God made the beasts of the earth according to their kinds and cattle according to their kinds, and everything that creeps upon the ground according to its kind"

Exod. 10:15: the locusts "ate all the plants ('eśeb) in the land and all the fruit (pĕrî) of the trees ('ēs) which the hail had left; not a green thing remained, neither tree ('ēs) nor plant of the field through all the land of Egypt"

Gen. 1:11: "The earth brought forth vegetation, plants ('eśeb) yielding seeds according to their own kinds, and trees ('ēs) bearing fruit (pĕrî) in which is their seed, according to its kind"

Exod. 10:22-23: "there was thick darkness (hōšek) in all the land of Egypt... but all the people of Israel had light ('ôr) where they dwelt"

Gen. 1:2: "darkness (hōšek) was upon the face of the deep;" 1:4: "God separated the light (ha'ôr) from the darkness"

Exod. 12:29: God smote the first-born in the land of Egypt, and all the first-born of the cattle

Gen. 1:24, 26: God created human beings, God created cattle

Having observed these correlations, Ziony Zevit commented:

> At the end of the narrative in Exodus, Israel looks back over the stilled water of the sea at a land with no people, no animals and no vegetation,

a land in which creation had been undone. Israel is convinced that her redeemer is the Lord of all creation.... He who had just reduced order to chaos was the same as he who had previously ordered the chaos.[158]

Long ago Philo offered a very similar interpretation: "God's judgment was that the materials which had served to produce the world should serve also to destroy the land of the impious; and to show the mightiness of the sovereignty which he holds, what he shaped in his saving goodness to create the universe he turned into instruments for the perdition of the impious whenever he would" (*Mos.* 1:96).[159]

There is at least one additional way in which the Pentateuch joins Moses and the creation. "The completion and consecration of the tabernacle in which the Lord is to dwell [Exodus 39-40] are narrated in terms that repeat, or recover, the original creation."[160] Seven times in Exodus 39 there appears the formula, "They/he made/prepared... as the Lord had commanded Moses" (39:1, 5, 7, 21, 26, 29, 31). Both the seven-fold repetition and the content resemble Genesis 1-2 and its formula: "And God said... and it was so." Further, that "Moses saw all the work... [and] blessed them" (Exod. 39.43) calls to mind the recurrent "God saw" of Genesis 1, which culminates in the blessing uttered upon creation's completion (Gen. 2:1-3); and when we read that, after "Moses finished the work" (*wayĕkal Mōšeh ʾet-hamméláʾkâ*), the divine cloud covered the tent of meeting, which circumstance communicates that the people of God have finally rested from their journeys (Exod. 40:33-38), one thinks of Gen.2:1-3: "God finished his work" (*wayĕkal ʾĕlōhîm... mĕlaʾkĕtô*) and rested from "all the work which he had done." Lastly, that the construction of the tabernacle inaugurated a new time is suggested by the date assigned to its completion: "in the *first* month in the second year, in the *first* day of the month..." (Exod. 40:17). It does seem that "Genesis and Exodus

---

[158]"Three Ways to look at the Ten Plagues," *BR* 6 (1990):23.

[159]There are also structural parallels between Genesis 1 and Exodus 7-12. Cf. Sarna, *Exodus*, 77. The pattern in Genesis is 3 acts of creation + 3 acts of creation + final act pertaining to God alone. The pattern of the plagues is 3 plagues + 3 plagues + 3 plagues + final plague whose agent is God alone (cf. p. 211). It is also just possibly relevant to note that both Psalm 78 and 105 preserve the tradition of seven plagues (cf. the seven days of Genesis).

[160]Richard H. Moye, "In the Beginning: Myth and History in Genesis and Exodus," *JBL* 109 (1990):596-97. See in the addition to what follows M. Weinfeld, "Sabbath, Temple, and the Enthronement of the Lord: The Problem of the Sitz im Leben of Genesis 1:1-2:3," in *Mélanges bibliques et orientaux en l'honneur de M. Henri Cazelles*, ed. A. Caquot and M. Delcor (AOAT 212; Neukirchen-Vluyn: Neukirchen; Kevelaer: Butzon and Bercker, 1981), 501-12.

[comprise] a narrative unit that closes with a repetition of the creation and blessing with which it opened,"[161] so that the building of the Israelite sanctuary is interpreted as imitation of the world's creation and a participation in its perfection.

The significance of the preceding paragraphs for Matthew should be evident. Jewish sources sometimes construe the exodus as a second creation; sometimes they interpret the eschatological denouement as a new creation and a new exodus; and sometimes they join creation motifs to the story of Moses. We accordingly find in Judaism literary precedent for the cluster of themes I have traced in Matthew's initial chapters. Thus when Jesus, the Mosaic Messiah, undergoes another exodus and inaugurates a new creation, he not only brings to realization certain eschatological expectations: he also leaves a record that recapitulates a rich literary tradition.

THE MIRACLES OF CHAPTERS 8-9

Christians have frequently compared the miracles of Moses with the wonders of Jesus. The *Acts of Pilate* makes Nicodemus speak as follows to Pilate:

> What do you intend to do with this man? This man does many signs and wonders, which no one has done nor will do. Let him alone and contrive no evil against him. If the signs which he does are from God, they will stand; if they are from men, they will come to nothing. For Moses also, when he was sent by God into Egypt, did many signs which God commanded him to do before Pharaoh (5:1).

Compare with this *Ps.-Clem. Rec.* 1:57: "As Moses did signs and miracles, so also did Jesus. And there is no doubt but that the likeness of the signs proves him [Jesus] to be that prophet of whom he [Moses] said that he should come 'like myself.'" Eusebius, who also saw the evangelical miracles as proof that Jesus was the prophet of Deut. 18:15, 18, wrote in similar fashion: "Moses by wonderful works and miracles authenticated the religion that he proclaimed; Christ likewise, using his recorded miracles to inspire faith in those who saw them, established the new discipline of the gospel teaching" (*Dem ev.* 3:2).

The common abutment, in early Christian literature, of the wonders of Jesus and Moses can be no surprise, for the lawgiver was

---

[161]Moye, "In the Beginning," 597; cf. M. Fishbane, *Text and Texture* (New York: Schocken, 1979), 11-13.

remembered as an especially great miracle worker. Indeed, his stature as such grew over the centuries. The dramatic combat with Pharaoh's magicians, the spectacular parting of the Red Sea, and the several wilderness miracles, led to much reflection on Moses' extraordinary abilities. In time a whole corpus of magical charms and writings— including *The Key of Moses*, *The Eighth Book of Moses*, and *The Secret Book of Moses*—was assigned to the lawgiver.[162]

But what are the causes for surmising, as did B. W. Bacon and several others,[163] that the reader of Matthew 8-9 in particular should be put in mind of Moses? Consider these possible correlations:

—In Exodus 7-12 there are ten plagues. In Matthew 8-9 there are ten miracles.[164]

—In Matt. 8:1-4 Jesus heals a leper. Moses also healed a leper (Num. 12:10-16; cf. Exod. 4:6-7)—a fact of some note as stories of the remission of leprosy are rare in Judaism. Eusebius, *Dem. ev.* 3:2, observed the parallel.

—Moses is named in Matt. 8:4: "Show yourself to the priest, and offer the gift that Moses commanded." This order makes Jesus abide by the law, that is, makes him act in accord with Moses. Is 8:4 then programmatic for what follows?

—It was characteristic of Moses that he worked his wonders *en logois*, by his words (Ecclus. 45:3). Similarly does Jesus cast out demons and perform miracles *logō*, by his word (8:16).

---

[162]See John G. Gager, *Moses is Greco-Roman Paganism* (SBLMS 16; Nashville: Abingdon, 1972), 134-61.

[163]B. W. Bacon, *Studies in Matthew* (New York: Henry Holt, 1930), 187-89; Kastner, *Moses*, 165-69; Schoeps, *Theologie*, 93-97 (citing Mic. 7:15: "As in the days when you came out of the land of Egypt I will show them marvelous things"); Teeple, *Prophet*, 82-83 (citing Schoeps).

[164]On the significance of the number ten see H. A. Brongers, "Die Zehnzahl in der Bibel und in ihrer Umwelt," in *Studia Biblica et Semitica Theodoro Christiano Vriezen*, ed. W. C. van Unnik and A. S. van der Woude (Wageningen: H. Veenman en Zonen, 1966), 30-45. He demonstrates that ten can function as seven often does, to indicate fullness, completeness, perfection. Recall the ten commandments and the tithe; see also Gen. 24:10, 22; 31:7; Lev. 26:26; Num. 14:22; 1 Sam. 1:8; Ruth 4:2; Job 19:3; Eccles 7:19; Zech. 8:23; *Jub.* 19:8; Philo, *Mos.* 1:96 (ten is "a perfect number"); Matt. 25:1-13; Rev. 2:10; Josephus, *Bell.* 6:423; 4 *Ezra* 5:46; *m. 'Abot* 5:1-6. On p. 37 Brongers suggests that the accomplishment of ten miracles in Matthew 8-9 is a sign of messianic "Vollmacht."

—According to extra-biblical tradition, Moses raised the dead (see Artapanus in Clement of Alexandria, *Strom.* 1:23; and Eusebius, *Praep. ev.* 9:27). In Matt. 9:18-26 Jesus raises the dead.

—In Matt. 8:23-27 Jesus calms and then crosses the sea of Galilee. Some have thought his power reminiscent of Moses' ability to part the Red Sea. Eusebius wrote: Moses "made the sea dry with a strong south wind. For Scripture says: 'Moses stretched forth his hand over the sea, and the Lord drove back the sea with a strong south wind,' and he adds: 'The waves congealed in the midst of the sea.' In like manner, only much more grandly, our Savior 'rebuked the winds and the sea, and there was a great calm'" (*Dem. ev.* 3:2). One may add (i) that "even the land and sea obey him" (Matt. 8:27) is similar to what Philo observed of Moses: "each element obeyed him as its master" (*Mos.* 1:156); (ii) that whereas Matt. 8:23-27 may be interpreted in terms of the old creation motif of the struggle against chaos,[165] that same motif was traditionally associated with the miracle of the Red Sea,[166] and (iii) that according to LXX Ps. 105:9-10 God "rebuked" the Red Sea (*epetimēse ... thalassē*) and so saved (*esōsen*) Israel, while according to Matthew Jesus "rebuked" (*epetimēsen*) the winds and the sea (*thalassē*) in response to his disciples' request that he "save" them (*sōson*).

Elsewhere I have complained that Bacon's proposal is problematic because although there may be ten miracles in Matthew 8-9, there are only nine miracle *stories*,[167] and further that the miracle stories of 8-9 are parcelled out into three different groups—8:2-15; 8:23-9:8; and 9:18-34.[168] Visually:

8:1-22	8:1-4 a healing	
	8:5-13 a healing	+ summary report and words of Jesus, 8:16-22
	8:14-15 a healing	

[165]Davies and Allison, *Matthew*, 2:75.

[166]See Ps. 77:16 and Cross, *Canaanite Myth*, 37-44; also Bernard F. Batto, "The Reed Sea: *Requiescat in Pace*," *JBL* 102 (1983):27-35.

[167]9:18-26, the healing of a ruler's daughter and of the woman with an issue of blood, is a unit. Cf. Meier, *Matthew*, 79-80.

[168]Davies and Allison, *Matthew*, 2:1-2.

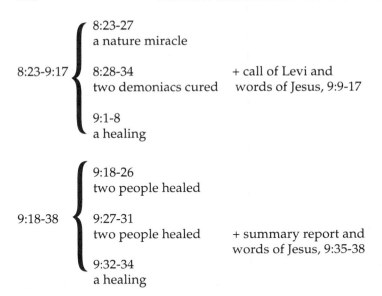

8:23-9:17
- 8:23-27 a nature miracle
- 8:28-34 two demoniacs cured   + call of Levi and words of Jesus, 9:9-17
- 9:1-8 a healing

9:18-38
- 9:18-26 two people healed
- 9:27-31 two people healed   + summary report and words of Jesus, 9:35-38
- 9:32-34 a healing

My presumption was that Exodus offers nothing similar. But live and learn: I was mistaken. A strikingly similar pattern does appear to order the ten plagues of Exodus. As Rashbam (Samuel ben Meir, the French Tosaphist) remarked, in his twelfth-century commentary on Exodus, the first and second, fourth and fifth, and seventh and eight plagues are preceded by warnings. The third, sixth, and ninth—whose narratives are uniformly brief—are not. Should we then group the first nine plagues into three sets of three, with the tenth, which, in contradistinction to the other plagues, has no natural grounding, standing apart as climactic? This is suggested by other patterns. Thus the first, fourth, and seventh plagues occur "in the morning" (*babōqer*). Again, the first three plagues involve Aaron holding Moses' staff while the seventh, eight, and ninth group themselves together by the circumstance that in each instance Moses stretches forth his hand. There is also an apparent pattern with regard to the introductory command in each pericope:

Command	Plague			Verse
"You stand" (a form of *ysb*)	1	4	7	7:15; 8:16; 9:13
"Go in to Pharaoh" (*bō' 'el Phar'ōh*)	2	5	8	7:26; 9:1; 10:1
no common feature	3	6	9	————

Furthermore, one recent commentator has offered that if plagues 1, 2, and 3 demonstrate the superiority of God and his agents over against the Egyptians and their magicians (7:17; 8:10, 18-19), 4, 5, and 6 show God's presence in the land and his ability to distinguish Israel from Egypt and shelter the former from calamity (8:22; 9:4, 6), while 7, 8, and 9, the most powerful plagues, substantiate God's incomparability (9:14, 18, 24; 10:6, 14).[169]

Whatever the correct source-critical solution to Exodus 7-12 may be (many proposals have been forwarded), the plagues as they stand readily allow themselves to be grouped into three sets of three, as the chart on the opposite page illustrates.[170] Moreover, we need not wonder whether the triadic arrangement of the plagues was known to the ancients. Although his analysis differs from the one I have given, Philo did in fact find three triads in Exodus 7-12; see *Mos.* 1:97ff.[171]

The structural parallel between Exodus 7-12 and Matthew 8-9 has moved me to reconsider my earlier judgment. There is not only a common number of miracles to be reckoned with but also a shared pattern: in both Exodus and Matthew there are ten miracles, and in both narratives there is a 3 x 3 pattern. Is this just coincidence? Or did Matthew arrange Jesus' miracles so that they would mirror the wonders of Moses? I am no longer quite so sure that Bacon has been executed at the scaffold of criticism. Nonetheless, my uncertainty has not been sufficient to foster full-fledged repentance. There remains the incongruity, perhaps (I admit) more jarring to us than to the ancients, between plagues of judgment and miracles of mercy: do they naturally invite comparison? Worse still, there is an obvious structural disparity: in Matthew, unlike Exodus, the final miracle is neither separated from the others nor climactic—it is in fact a model of pruned simplicity, a surprising anticlimax:

> As they were going away, behold, a dumb demoniac was brought to him. And when the demon had been cast out, the dumb man spoke; and the crowds marveled, saying, "Never was anything like this seen in Israel." But the Pharisees said, "He casts out demons by the prince of demons."

[169]So Richard J. Clifford, in *NJBC*, 48.

[170]This reproduces page 76 of Sarna, *Exodus*, and is reprinted with permission. (The verses are cited according to the Hebrew text.)

[171]God "distributed the punishments in this wise: three belonging to the denser elements, earth and water, which have gone to make our bodily qualities what they are, He committed to the brother of Moses; another set of three, belonging to air and fire, the two most productive of life, He gave to Moses alone; one, the seventh, He committed to both in common; and the other three which go to complete the ten He reserved to Himself."

The Literary Structure of the Plagues Narrative

Plague	Exodus source	Forewarning	Time indication of warning	Instruction formula	Agent
First 1. Blood	7:14-24	yes	"in the morning"	"Station yourself"	Aaron
2. Frogs	7:25-8:11	yes	none	"Go to Pharaoh"	Aaron
3. Lice	8:12-15	none	none	none	Aaron
Second series 4. Insects	8:16-28	yes	"in the morning"	"Station yourself"	God
5. Pestilence	9:1-7	yes	none	"Go to Pharaoh"	God
6. Boils	9:8-12	none	none	none	Moses
Third series 7. Hail	9:13-35	yes	"in the morning"	"Station yourself"	Moses
8. Locusts	10:1-20	yes	none	"Go to Pharaoh"	Moses
9. Darkness	10:21-23	none	none	none	Moses
Climax 10. Death of Egyptian firstborn	11:4-7 12:29-30	yes	none	none	God

The most compelling criticism, however, is another: the grouping of material into triads occurs elsewhere in Matthew, as does the 3 x 3 pattern,[172] and the use of triads for structuring narrative material is well attested in old Jewish texts: it does not specifically characterize the miracle tradition of Exodus.[173] In fact, in this particular we merely have to do with a common way of organizing oral traditions, one which appears in literature from all over the world. The tale of Goldilocks and the three bears, for instance, is, just like the SM, a series of triads within triads. So my conclusion, although accompanied now by a little less conviction, remains that Bacon was probably wrong about Matthew 8-9: I here doubt the presence of a Moses typology.

THE MISSIONARY DISCOURSE (MATTHEW 10)

Jesus, according to 9:35-38, the preface to the missionary discourse, had mercy on the Jewish crowds, for they were "as sheep without a shepherd" (*hōsei probata me echonta poimēna*). The phrase in quotation marks was, according to the theory of Markan priority, borrowed from Mark 6:34; but ultimately its source was the Tanak:

---

[172]See my article, "The Structure of the Sermon on the Mount," *JBL* 106 (1987):423-45; also Davies and Allison, *Matthew*, 1:58-72.

[173]See Allison, "Structure." Note also the apparent 3 + 3 + 1 pattern in Genesis 1:1-2:3 (P):

Day	Created thing	Association	"And God said"	"Let there be"
1	light	heaven	v. 3	v. 3
2	firmament to separate waters	water and sky	v. 6	v. 6
3	dry land vegetation	land	vv. 9,11	vv. 9,11
4	lights in sky	heaven	v. 14	v. 14
5	creatures of sea and air	water and sky	v. 20	v. 20
6	animals that live on land and human beings	land	vv. 24,26	vv. 24,26

7   God rests

Cf. S. R. Driver, *The Book of Genesis* (3rd ed.; London: Methuen, 1904), 2; U. Cassuto, *A Commentary on the Book of Genesis*, Part I (Jerusalem: Magnes, 1978), 17; Gordon J. Wenham, *Genesis 1-15* (WBC; Waco: Word, 1987), 6-7.

Num. 27:15-17: Moses said, "Let the Lord, the God of the spirits of all flesh, appoint a man over the congregation, who shall go out before them and come in before them, who shall lead them out and bring them in; that the congregation of the Lord may not be as sheep which have no shepherd" (LXX: *hōsei probata hois ouk esti poimēn*).

1 Kings 22:17: the prophet Micaiah proclaimed: "'I saw all Israel scattered upon the mountains, as sheep that have no shepherd (LXX: *hōs poimnion ho ouk esti poimēn*)'; and the Lord said: 'These have no master; let each return to his home in peace.'"

2 Chron. 18:16: this is a doublet of 1 Kings 22:17; at the relevant point the LXX reads: *hōs probata hois ouk estin poimēn*.

Judith 11:19: Judith to Holofernes: "Then I will lead you through the middle of Judea, till you come to Jerusalem; and I will set your throne in the midst of it; and you will lead them like sheep that have no shepherd (*hōs probata hois ouk estin poimōn*), and not a dog will so much as open its mouth to growl at you."

Our question is this: did Matthew intend "as sheep without a shepherd" to allude to one or more of these texts, or did the evangelist instead adopt a conventional expression which had come to possess a life of its own?

There are perhaps reasons to discern in the phrase a connection with Num. 27:17 in particular. Not only does this last supply the closest verbal parallel, but in both the Gospel and the Pentateuch the shepherd of Israel[174] appoints a successor or successors—Joshua in one case, the twelve in the other. Hence one might maintain that just as Moses gives "authority" (MT: *hôd*) to Joshua, "a man in whom is the Spirit" (Num. 27:18), so that Joshua will further Moses' ministry, similarly Jesus gives his *exousia* to the twelve, through whom the Spirit will speak (10:20), so that they will continue his work. Supportive of such a comparison are, first, that elsewhere in the First Gospel the twelve may be typologically related to Joshua (see pp. 262-66) and, secondly, that Matthew acquired "as sheep without a shepherd" from Mark 6:34, which verse belongs to a story that many have found

---

[174]For Jesus as shepherd see Matt. 2:6; 25:32; 26:31. Moses, despite all his achievements, was always remembered as a shepherd: Exod. 3:1; Num. 27:12-23; Ps. 77:20; Philo, *Mos.* 1:60-66; Josephus, *Ant.* 2:263-64; *LAB* 19:3, 9; *Mek.* on Exod. 14:31; *Est. Rab.* 7:13; etc.; additional references in Bloch, "Moïse," 138-39. Cf. Clement of Alexandria, *Strom.* 1:23; Jerome, *Life of Malchus* 5 (where Malchus, a shepherd in the desert, likens himself to Moses). For the possibility that Heb. 13:20 ("God... led up from the dead the great shepherd of he sheep") is an allusion to Isa. 63:11 (where God "raises up from the earth the shepherd of the sheep") and so makes Christ as shepherd surpass Moses see B. F. Westcott, *The Epistle to the Hebrews* (2nd ed.; London: Macmillan, 1892), 448.

reminiscent of Exodus 16, where Moses promises the manna (cf. pp. 238-42). So a case can be made.

But how strong is that case? Matt. 9:35-38 reminds one as much of 1 Kings 22:17 as Num. 27:17; for in l Kings 22 "as sheep which have no shepherd" serves to characterize the condition of Israel and implicate the reign of Ahab. Matters are similar in Matthew, where the Pharisees allege: "By the prince of demons he casts out demons" (9:34). Jesus' words are a "charge against the leaders of the Jews, that being shepherds they acted the part of wolves. For so far from amending the multitude, they even marred their progress" (Chrysostom, *Hom. on Mt.* 32:4).

Another reason for hesitating to detect in Matt. 9:35 an allusion to Num. 27:17 and Moses is this: the several other occurrences of "as sheep without a shepherd" do not seem to hark back to Num. 27:17. That is, l Kings 22:17; 2 Chron. 18:16; and Judith ll:l9 do not allude to Num. 27:17. Neither do the related expressions in Isa. 13:14; Ezek. 34:5-6; Zech. 10:2; 13:7; Josephus, *Ant.* 8:404; and 2 *Bar.* 77:13. Consequently it cannot be shown from other texts that "as sheep without a shepherd" carried specifically Mosaic connotations.

There is a second way to link Matthew's missionary discourse with Moses. In the Pentateuch the lawgiver is associated with a group known as the phylarchs (MT: *nĕśî'îm*; LXX: *archontes* [*tēs synagōgēs*]),[175] which group was chosen to help in the first census. According to Num. 1:1-16:

> The Lord spoke to Moses in the wilderness of Sinai, in the tent of meeting, on the first day of the second month, in the second year after they had come out of the land of Egypt, saying, "Take a census of all the congregation of the people of Israel, by families, by fathers' houses, according to the number of names, every male, head by head; from twenty years old and upward, all in Israel who are able to go forth to war, you and Aaron shall number them, company by company. And there shall be with you a man from each tribe, each man being the head of the house of his fathers. And these are the names of them men who shall attend you. From Reuben, Elizur the son of Shedeur; from Simeon,

[175]See esp. W. Horbury, "The Twelve and the Phylarchs," *NTS* 32 (l986):503-27. For what follows I am much indebted to this article. References to the princes include Exod. 16:22; 22:27; 34:31; 35:27; Lev. 4:22-26; Num. 7:1-88; l0:4, 14-28; 17:16-28; 21:18; 27:2; 31:13; 32:2; 34:16-29; 36:1; Josh. 9:15-21; 14:l; 21:1; 22:9-34; 1 Kings 8:l; Ezek. 45:8; Alexander Polyhistor, in Eusebius, *Praep. ev.* 9:30. Josephus, *Ant.* 3:219-22, seems to presuppose a tradition according to which the phylarchs came together "two by two"—which of course reminds one of Mark 6:7: "And he [Jesus] called to him the twelve and began to send them out two by two."

Shelumiel the son of Zurishaddai.... These were the ones chosen from the congregation, the leaders of their ancestral tribes, the heads of the clans of Israel.

Although I have elided all but two of them, twelve men (LXX Num. 7:2: *dōdeka archontes*) are here named, one for each tribe. The circumstance is reminiscsent of Matt. 19:28, where the twelve apostles represent the twelve tribes of Israel. Further, the list of names in Num. 1:5-16 (introduced with *kai tauta ta onomata*) is the closest formal parallel to Matt. 10:1-4 of which I am aware (and Matthew's text opens with *ta onomata estin tauta*).

That Matthew wanted Jesus' selection of the twelve apostles to recall Moses' appointment of the twelve phylarchs is a possibility not to be blithely dismissed. Certainly some have thought the two groups related.[176] Bengel, in his commentary on Matt. 19:28, remarked that twelve was the number of the princes; and long before Bengel, Origen, when explicating Exod. 18:21-22, where Moses is told to appoint princes (cf. Num. 1:16), cited Matt. 19:28 (*Hom. on Exod.* 11:6). One may also in this connection quote Thomas Hobbes, who offered the following as one illustration of Jesus' fulfillment of Deut. 18:18: "For as Moses chose twelve Princes of the tribes, to govern under him; so did our Saviour choose twelve Apostles, who shall sit on twelve thrones, and judge the twelve tribes of Israel."[177]

Beyond the testimony of past readers, one may observe (i) that if the twelve distributed the multiplied loaves to the five thousand and four thousand (Matt. 14:19; 15:37), Exodus 12 indicates that the phylarchs communicated to Moses the facts about the gathering of manna and (ii) that if Matt. 19:28 records the appointment of the twelve to be eschatological governors, the phylarchs were sometimes thought of as a ruling "body taking precedence immediately after high priest and monarch, and before the *gerousia*."[178] I do not, however, believe it is useful to travel any further over the evidence; for the theme of governing is peripheral to Matthew 10, the phylarchs were not missionaries, and the titles of the apostles and princes were different. Even more importantly, Horbury has demonstrated that, before Matthew's time, the glorification of the high priest and sanhedrin fostered a tendency, apparent in Josephus, Pseudo-Philo, and the *Pseudo-*

---

[176]Cf. Gfrörer, *Heils*, 369-74; also Schoeps, *Theologie*, 95-96.
[177]*Leviathan* 41; quoted by Horbury, "Phylarchs," 504.
[178]Horbury, ibid., 521.

Jonathan Targum, to underplay the importance and authority of the phylarchs. When to this it is added that there were, besides the phylarchs, other well-known Jewish bodies whose number was twelve,[179] one cannot confidently claim that Origen and Bengel and Hobbes are a good guide to Matthew 10.[180]

A third means of connecting Matthew 10 with Moses comes from R. E. Morosco.[181] In his opinion, Matt. 9:35-ll:l is structured according to a Hebrew Bible *Gattung*, that of the comissioning story. In particular, it resembles Exod. 3:1-4:17, the calling of Moses. The typical commissioning narrative is supposed to exhibit these elements: introduction, confrontation, commissioning, objection, reassurance, conclusion; and, according to Morosco, Matt. 9:35-ll:l may be analyzed accordingly:

9:35-38—introduction
10:1-4—confrontation
10:5-23—commissioning
10:24-42—reassurance
11:1—conclusion

I introduce this thesis only to dismiss it: it is invalidated by a lack of evidence. There is, as Morosco himself acknowledged, no objection in Matthew 10. Additionally, the verbal and thematic parallels between Matthew 10 and Exodus 3-4—including *idou*, *ophis*, and the mention of leprosy—are imperfect and slight, signifying nothing.

What conclusion, in retrospect, may be reached about Moses in Matt. 9:35-11:l? That the missionary discourse was consciously modelled upon Exod. 3-4 is a proposition to be rejected. That Jesus' appointment of the twelve should recall Moses' appointment of the twelve phylarchs is not so dubious, but it too fails to persuade: proof is lacking. Lastly, that the editor used the traditional phrase, "as sheep without a shepherd," to stir memories of Moses, is a tantalizing possibility that does not arouse incredulity; but, again, the evidence does not abound. In sum, therefore, the presence of a Moses typology in Matthew 10 is not forcibly felt, and it may not be there at all.

---

[179]Genesis 49—the twelve patriarchs; Num. 13:2-3—the twelve spies (although Philo, *Mos.* 1:221, identified these as princes); *lQS* viii:1—the council of the community; *1QM* ii.1-3—twelve priests and twelve levites (cf. *11QTemple* 57:11-13); *4QOrdinances* ii.4; iii.4—a court of twelve; *4QpIsa* —twelve chief priests; Josephus, *Bell.* 2:292—the twelve leading men of Caesarea. Discussion in J. M. Baumgarten, "The Duodecimal Courts of Qumran, Revelation, and the Sanhedrin," *JBL* 95 (1976):59-78.

[180]Eusebius, *Dem. ev.* 3:2, associates the twelve disciples not with the phylarchs but with another group, the twelve spies.

[181]"Matthew's Formation of a Commissioning Type-Scene," *JBL* 103 (1984):539-56.

THE GREAT THANKSGIVING (11:25-30)

At that time Jesus declared, "I thank thee, Father, Lord of heaven and earth, that thou hast hidden these things from the wise and understanding and revealed them to babes; yea, Father, for such was thy gracious will. All things have been delivered to me by my Father; and no one knows that Son except the Father, and no one knows the Father except the Son and any one to whom the Son chooses to reveal him. Come to me, all who labor and are heavy laden, and I will give you rest. Take my yoke upon you, and learn from me; for I am gentle and lowly in heart, and you will find rest for your souls. For my yoke is easy, and my burden is light."

P. Levertoff, when reviewing these famous lines, was reminded of the lawgiver: "What is said of Moses (Dt 34.10-12) is true in a much higher degree of Him [the Son of God]."[182] A. E. J. Rawlinson was similarly put in mind of Moses: the "fundamental idea" of Matt. 11:27-30 is "the idea of 'knowing and being known' in relation to God," and of this the best illustration is the lawgiver: "the greatness of Moses as a prophet is explained by the consideration that he was one 'whom the Lord knew face to face' [Deut. 34:10]."[183] A connection between Deut. 34:10 and Matt. 11:27 was also suggested by Dabeck,[184] and more recently Martin Hengel expressed himself this way:

The statement at the end of the Torah (Deut. 34.10): "And there has not arisen a prophet since in Israel like Moses, whom the Lord knew face to face, none like him for all the signs and wonders which the Lord sent him to do" is corrected by Jesus in terms of John the Baptist in Luke 16.16 and in terms of himself in Matt. 11.27 = Luke 10.22.[185]

Compare the words of P. Pokorny: "In terms of content it [Matt. 11:27 par.] is a reinterpretation of the saying about the unsurpassingly close relationship between Moses and God attested in Deut. 34.10."[186]

In my estimation Levertoff and the others just cited have correctly, if dimly, or at least without elaboration, perceived a crucial connection: Matt. 11:25-30 was indeed, as has been intermittently hinted, composed with Moses in mind.[187] But much more needs to be said.

---

[182]P. Levertoff, "Matthew," in C. Gore, H. C. Goudge, and Al Guillame, ed., *A New Catholic Commentary on Holy Scripture* (London: Macmillan, 1928), 156.

[183]*The New Testament Doctrine of the Christ* (London: Longmans, Green, and Co., Ltd., 1926), 263.

[184]"Moses und Elias," 177.

[185]*The Son of God* (Philadelphia: Fortress, 1976), 68-69.

[186]*The Genesis of Christology* (Edinburgh: T. & T. Clark, 1987), 55, n. 138.

[187]In the following pages I develop suggestions first made in "Two Notes on a Key Text: Matthew 11:25-30," *JTS* 39 (1988):472-80; cf. Davies and Allison, *Matthew* 2:271-97.

Matt. 11:25-30 is, in all its parts, a christological monument beneath which are buried three famous and crucial texts about Moses. I refer to:

Exod. 33:11-23: Thus the Lord used to speak to Moses face to face, as a man speaks to his friend. When Moses turned again into the camp, his servant Joshua the son of Nun, a young man, did not depart from the tent. Moses said to the Lord, "See, thou sayest to me, 'Bring up this people;' but thou hast not let me know whom thou wilt send with me. Yet thou hast said, 'I know you by name, and you have also found favor in my sight.' Now therefore, I pray thee, if I have found favor in thy sight, show me now thy ways, that I may know thee and find favor in thy sight. Consider too that this nation is thy people." And he said, "My presence will go with you, and I will give you rest." And he said to him, "If thy presence will not go with me, do not carry us up from here. For how shall it be known that I have found favor in thy sight, I and thy people? Is it not in thy going with us, so that we are distinct, I and thy people, from all other people that are upon the face of the earth?" And the Lord said to Moses, "This very thing that you have spoke I will do; for you have found favor in my sight, and I know you by name." Moses said, "I pray thee, show me thy glory." And he said, "I will make all my goodness pass before you, and will proclaim before you my name 'The Lord;' and I will be gracious to whom I will be gracious, and will show mercy on whom I will show mercy. "But," he said, "you cannot see my face; for man shall not see me and live." And the Lord said, "Behold, there is a place by me where you shall stand upon the rock; and while my glory passes by I will put you in a cleft of the rock, and I will cover you with my hand until I have passed by; then I will take away my hand, and you shall see my back; but my face shall not be seen."[188]

Num. 12:1-8: Miriam and Aaron spoke against Moses because of the Cushite woman whom he had married, for he had married a Cushite woman; and they said, "Has the Lord indeed spoken only through Moses? Has he not spoken through us also?" And the Lord heard it. Now the man Moses was very meek, more than all men that were on the face of the earth. And suddenly the Lord said to Moses and to Aaron and Miriam, "Come out, you three, to the tent of meeting." And the three of them came out. And the Lord came down in a pillar of cloud, and stood at the door of the tent, and called Aaron and Miriam; and they both came forward. And he said, "Hear my words: If there is a prophet among you, I the Lord make myself known to him in a vision, I speak with him in a dream. Not so with my servant Moses; he is entrusted with all my house. With him I speak mouth to mouth, clearly, and not in dark speech; and he beholds the form of the Lord.

---

[188]This texts shares several elements with the prayer of David in 2 Samuel 7, and a literary connection one way or the other is apparent; cf. Aurelius, *Fürbitter Israels*, 109-11. But I cannot see that 2 Samuel 7 is to be brought into our discussion here.

Deut. 34:9-12: And Joshua the son of Nun was full of the spirit of wisdom, for Moses had laid his hands upon him; so the people of Israel obeyed him, and did as the Lord had commanded Moses. And there has not arisen a prophet since in Israel like Moses, whom the Lord knew face to face, none like him for all the signs and the wonders which the Lord sent him to do in the land of Egypt, to Pharaoh and to all his servants and to all his land, and for all the mighty power and all the great and terrible deeds which Moses wrought in the sight of all Israel.

These three scriptures are thematically related,[189] for each concerns the reciprocal knowledge between Moses and God.[190] They are in addition verbally linked.[191] It is thus only natural that Exod. 33:11-23; Num. 12:1-8; and Deut. 34:9-12, which together fostered much speculation regarding the delicate issue of how anyone could see God, were often associated and considered in the light of one another. Let me illustrate:

Ecclus. 45:3-5: God "gave him [Moses] commands for the people, and showed him part of his glory [cf. Exod. 33:18-23]. He sanctified him through faithfulness and meekness [cf. Num. 12:3]; he chose him out of all mankind. He made him hear his voice, and led him into the thick darkness, and gave him the commandments face to face [cf. Deut. 34:10], the law of life and knowledge, to teach Jacob the covenant and Israel his judgments."

Philo, *Leg. all.* 3:100-103: "The mind of which I speak is Moses who says, 'Manifest Thyself to me, let me see Thee that I may know Thee [Exod. 33:13]; for I would not that Thou shouldst be manifested to me by means of heaven or earth or water or air or any created thing at all, nor would I find the reflection of Thy being in aught else than in Thee Who art God, for the reflections in created things are dissolved, but those in the Uncreate will continue abiding and sure and eternal.' This is why God hath expressly called Moses and why He spake to Him.... Moses has God for his Instructor... but Bezalel is instructed by Moses. And all this is just as we should expect. For on the occasion likewise of the rebellion of Aaron, Speech, and Miriam, Perception, they are expressly told 'If a prophet be raised up unto the Lord, God shall be known unto him in a vision' and in a shadow, not manifestly; but with Moses, the man who is 'faithful in all His house, He will speak mouth to mouth in manifest form and not through dark speeches'" (Num. 12:6-8).

Philo, *Quis rerum* 262: "What of Moses? Is he not everywhere celebrated as a prophet? For it says, 'if a prophet of the Lord arise among you, I will be known to him in vision, but to Moses in actual appearance and not through riddles" (Num. 12:6, 8); and again, 'there no more rose up a prophet like Moses, whom the Lord knew face to face'" (Deut. 34:10).

---

[189]Deut. 34:9-12 was probably composed with Exodus 33 in mind.
[190]Cf. the paraphrase in Philo, *Poster C.* 13: *tou horan kai pros autou horasthai.*
[191]"Face to face:" Exod. 33:11; Deut. 34:9-12 (cf. Num. 12:8: "mouth to mouth"); "know:" Exod. 33:12-13; Num. 12:6; "prophet:" Num. 12:6; Deut. 34:10.

Ps.-Clem. Hom. 17:18: "It is written in the law, that God, being angry, said to Aaron and Miriam, 'If a prophet arise from amongst you, I shall make myself known to him through visions and dreams, but not so as to my servant Moses; because I shall speak to him in an outward appearance, and through dreams [cf. Num. 12:6, 7], just as one will speak to his own friend' [cf. Exod. 33:11]. You see how the statements of wrath are made through visions and dreams, but the statements to a friend are made face to face [cf. Exod. 33:ll; Deut. 34:10], in outward appearance, and not through riddles and visions and dreams, as to any enemy" (cf. Num. 12:6-8).

Sipre Num. § 103: "'[Clearly, and not in dark speech, and he beholds] the form [of the Lord]' (Num. 12:8): This refers to a vision of the Lord's speech. But perhaps it refers to his seeing the vision of the [actual] Presence of God? Scripture states, 'He said, "You shall not be able to see my face, for no man can see me and live"' (Exod. 33:20).... . '...and he beholds the form of the Lord': This refers to the view of the back [of the Lord]. You maintain that 'form' refers to the back. But perhaps it is [not to the back at all] but to the very face of God? Scripture states, 'And I shall remove my hand and you may see my back' (Exod. 33:23). This refers, then, to the view of the back. 'You shall not be able to see my face' (Exod. 33:20) refers to the view of the front."

Sipre Deut. § 357: "'Whom the Lord knew face to face' (Deut. 34:10). Why is this stated? Because it is said, 'He said, "Show me your glory"'" (Exod. 33:18).

Chrysostom, *Hom. on Matt.* 78:4: "But the lips of Moses, because he was exceedingly gentle and meek ('for Moses,' it is said, 'was a meek man above all the men which were upon the face of the earth' [Num. 12:8]), He [God] so accepted and loved, as to say, 'Face to face, mouth to mouth, did He speak, as a man speaketh unto his friend'" (Exod. 33:11).

There is also, in addition to these and similar passages,[192] the evidence from Paul, to be considered below. Moreover, according to LXX Num. 12:8, Moses "saw [*eiden*] the glory [*doxa*] of the Lord." But in the Hebrew Moses "sees [*yabbît*] the form [*těmunat*] of the Lord." The substitution of "glory" for "form" and the use of an aorist (adverting to some past occasion) mean that the LXX translator construed the verse in Numbers as a reference to Moses' vision of God's glory as told in Exodus 33-34.[193] The same interpretation was made by the author of the *Pseudo-Jonathan Targum* on Num. 12:8, which mentions "the back of the Shekinah," an unmistakable allusion to Exodus 33. I further note that the LXX ties Num. 12:6-8 not only to

---

[192]Cf. Tertullian, *Adv. Prax.* 14; *Adv. Marc.* 4:23; *Memar Marqah* 5:3; and (for a much later example) Moses Maimonides, *Guide for the Perplexed* 2:45.
[193]Cf. D'Angelo, *Hebrews*, 7.

Exodus 33 but also to the end of Deuteronomy. LXX Deut. 34:5 renders the MT's ʿebed YHWH not with *ho pais tou theou*, as one might have expected, but with *oiketēs Kyriou*, which depends upon Num. 12:7: "my servant in all my house."

Returning to Matt. 11:25-30, careful investigation reveals that it gives to Jesus several attributes that Jewish tradition, on the basis of Exodus 33-34; Numbers 12; and Deuteronomy 34, had already bestowed upon Moses. Verse 27 ("All has been handed to me by my Father; and no one knows the Son except the Father, and no one knows the Father except the Son") is a claim to exclusive and reciprocal divine knowledge—which is also what Exodus 33 and 34 claim for Moses when read (as they so often were) in the light of Numbers 12 and Deuteronomy 34: God knew Moses, Moses prayed that he might know God, whereupon God dramatically revealed himself in a unique and unprecedented fashion, so that reciprocal knowledge—"face to face"—was obtained.[194] That the parallel between Matt. 11:25-30 and Exodus should not be reckoned undesigned but rather a key for interpretation follows from several facts which now fall to be considered.

(1) In Matt. 11:25-30 the declaration of reciprocal knowledge is made in a prayer, while in Exod. 33:12-13 it is in a prayer that Moses confesses God's knowledge of him and then asks to know God.

(2) Both Matt. 11:25-30 and Exod. 33:12-13 introduce a promise of rest. Indeed, the end of Exod. 33:14 ("And he said, 'My presence will go with you, and I will give you rest'" [LXX: *kai katapausō hymas*]) supplies the closest LXX parallel to the final clause of Matt. 11:28: "Come to me, all who labor and are heavy laden, and I will give you rest" (*kagō anapausō hymas*).[195]

(3) Moses was Judaism's great exemplar in meekness, and this role of his was not forgotten by Christians. For the evidence I refer the

---

[194]According to Exodus, God revealed only his back, so while Moses' petition was answered, it was not answered as anticipated. Hence some interpreters have urged that God really denied Moses what he sought; so Philo, *Poster C.* 13; *Spec. leg.* 1:42-43; *Fug.* 164-65; *Mut. nom.* 7-10; cf. John 1:18. But Ps. 103:7 declares that God showed his ways (cf. Exod. 33:13) to Moses, and that is the dominant interpretation in the history of exegesis; cf. Exod. 34:5-9; Heb. 11:27; Gregory of Nyssa, *Vit. Mos.* 2:19-20; Theodoret of Cyrrhus, *Hist. Rel.* 2:13.

[195]It is perhaps significant that, according to Exod. 5:4-5, Moses pleaded with Pharaoh to let the Israelites "rest from their burdens" (MT: *wôhišbatem ʾōtam missiblōhām*; LXX: *katapausomen autous apo ton ergon*); and more than once Deuteronomy records Moses promising Israel that, upon possessing the land, she will have rest and abatement from troubles: 3:20; 12:9-10; 25:19 (cf. Josh. 1:13, 15).

reader to pp. 180-81. The classic proof text was Num. 12:3, which was sometimes associated with the vision in Exodus 33-34: "Now the man Moses very meek, more than all men that were on the face of the earth" (see above). The joining of meekness with the intimate knowledge of God which we find in Matt. 11:25-30 was therefore prepared for by, and would have been recognized as characteristic of, the traditions about Moses (cf. Ecclus. 45:3-5; Chrysostom, *Hom. on Matt.* 78:4).

(4) The words of 11:27, "nor does anyone know the Father," should probably be related to Exod. 33:20 and the tradition there encapsulated: God said to Moses: "No man shall see me and live." Tertullian at least drew the connection: "With regard to the Father, the very gospel... will testify that He was never visible, according to the word of Christ: 'No one knoweth the Father, save the Son.' For even in the Old Testament He had declared, 'No man shall see me and live'" (*Adv. Marc.* 2:27; cf. *Adv. Prax.* 24). On Tertullian's reading Matt. 11:27 stands very near John 1:18: "No one has seen God at anytime. God the only Son, who is in the bosom of the Father, he has made him known." The meaning of this last has been expressed by Raymond Brown as follows:

> Naturally it is the failure of Moses to have seen God that the author wishes to contrast with the intimate contact between Son and Father. In Exod xxxiii 18 Moses asks to see God's glory, but the Lord says, "You cannot see my face and live".... Against this OT background that not even the greatest representatives of Israel have seen God, John holds up the example of the only Son who has not only seen the Father but is ever at His side.[196]

This interpretation of John 1:18, which is confirmed by the express contrast with Moses in John 1:17, parallels precisely Tertullian's interpretation of Matt. 11:27. For this coincidence is no good explanation. I strongly suspect that John 1:17-18 was in fact composed under the influence of the tradition behind Matt. 11:25-27(30) par. If so, the express mention of Moses in John 1:17-18 is strong support for my Mosaic interpretation of Matt. 11:25-30.

(5) In 11:27 Jesus avows: "All has been handed over to me by my Father." This unexplained utterance is, in its Matthean context, not about power but revelation: Jesus has been given—when? where? how?—the whole revelation of God, that is, eschatological revelation: his gnosis is full.[197] This is yet one more trait that should be considered

---

[196]*John* 1:36.
[197]See A. M. Hunter, "Crux Criticorum—Matt. 11.25-30," *NTS* 8 (1962):436.

Mosaic, this because the Moses of haggadah, for reasons readily understood, came to enjoy what the Moses of history surely never knew, namely, near omniscience. The wedding to Sinai of Torah—all Torah, both oral and written—entailed the unsurpassed learning of its human channel. What could not have been known by the man who, among other things, wrote a book which was understood to recount the creation of the world, prophesy messianic events,[198] and describe much in between, including the author's own death? Already the *Exagogue* of Ezekiel has Moses recount this: "I beheld the entire circled earth, both beneath the earth and above the heaven; and a host of stars fell at my feet, and I numbered them all;" and the text goes on to announce that Moses saw all "things present, past, and future." Most startling here is the assertion, to my knowledge unparalleled, that Moses numbered stars. In Jewish tradition it was precisely this that human beings, with their comparatively feeble mental powers, cannot do; see Gen. 15:5; 22:17; Deut. 1:10; Ps. 147:4; Isa. 40:26; *1 En.* 93:14; *LAB* 21:2 *b. Sanh.* 39a; *Gk. Apoc. Ezra* 2:32. The rule is: only God can count stars. But in Ezekiel's *Exagogue* Moses is the exception.

In representing Moses as a repository of encyclopedic learning, the *Exagogue* does not stand alone: many are the texts which proclaim the lawgiver's far-reaching, supernatural knowledge. Consider the following catena of quotations from various times and places:

Jub. 1:4: "And the Lord revealed to him what (was) in the beginning and what will occur (in the future), the account of the division of all of the days of the Covenant and the testimony" (cf. 1:26).

Ep. Aristeas 139: "Our lawgiver being a wise man and specially endowed by God to understand all things…".

LAB 19:10: "And he [God] showed him [Moses] the place from which the clouds draw up water to water the whole earth, and the place from which the river takes its water, and the land of Egypt, and the place in the firmament from which only the holy land drinks. And he showed him the place from which the manna rained upon the people, even unto the paths of paradise. And he showed him the measurements of the sanctuary and the number of sacrifices and the signs by which they are to interpret the heavens."

LAB 19:14-16: after God showed Moses how much "time has passed and how much remains," Moses "was filled with understanding."

2 Bar. 59:4-11: "He [God] showed him [Moses] many warnings together with the ways of the Law and the end of time… and then further, also

---

[198]Moses was considered a prophet and his book prophetic; see p. 61, n. 135.

the likeness of Zion with its measurements which was to be made after the likeness of the present sanctuary. But he also showed him, at that time, the measures of fire, the depths of the abyss, the weight of the winds, the number of the raindrops, the suppression of wrath, the abundance of long-suffering, the truth of judgment, the root of wisdom, the richness of understanding, the fountain of knowledge, the height of the air, the greatness of Paradise, the end of the periods, the beginning of the day of judgment, the number of offerings, the worlds which have not yet come, the mouth of hell, the standing place of vengeance, the place of faith, the region of hope, the picture of the coming punishment, the multitude of the angels which cannot be counted, the powers of the flame, the splendor of lightnings, the voice of the thunders, the orders of the archangels, the treasuries of the light, the changes of the times, and the inquiries into the Law."

Sipre Deut § 357: "He [God] showed him [Moses] all the world from the day it was created until the day when the dead will come to life."

b. Meg. 19b: "The Holy One, blessed be He, showed Moses the minutiae of the Torah, the minutiae of the scribes, and the innovations which would be introduced by the scribes."

Memar Marqah 5:1: "His [Moses'] span includes the knowledge of the beginning and its goes on to the day of vengeance."

I shall at this point cease quoting, although not for lack of material. Let me just add three observations: (i) Moses' proverbial knowledge and wisdom were the presupposition for the use of his name in the magical papyri and on amulets (see n. 162); (ii) the tradition that the great Greek thinkers were not autodidacts but borrowed heavily, if without acknowledgement, from "the all-wise Moses" (Clement of Alexandria, *Paed.* 2:10.83), is well-attested, as is the idea that Moses was a top-notch scientist and first-rate inventor; Artapanus went so far as to contend that Moses invented philosophy;[199] (iii) Moses' near omniscience was occasionally connected specifically with one of the three key texts beneath Matt. 11:25-30, namely, Num. 12:1-8. *Sipre* offers as its first interpretation of 12:8 (Moses is "faithful in all my house") this: "All that is above and all that is below have I revealed to him [Moses], all that is in the sea and all that is in the dry land." The same understanding of Num. 12:8 appears in *Midr. Ps.* 24:5:

Another comment on "The earth is the Lord's and the fullness thereof:" R. Azariah, R. Nehemiah and R. Berechiah told the parable of a king who

---

[199]See Eusebius, *Praep. ev.* 9:27.4; cf. Eupolemus, in Clement of Alexandria, *Strom.* 1:23.153 and Eusebius, *Praep. ev.* 9:26.1; Aristobulus, in Eusebius, *Praep. ev.* 13:13.3-8; Philo, *Sacr.* 8-10; Josephus, *C. Ap.* 1:1-5; Justin, *l Apol.* 44, 46, 59; Theophilus, *ad Autol.* 39; Eusebius, *H.E.* 6:13.7.

had two stewards, one in charge of the house and the other in charge of the fields. The one in charge of the house [cf. Num. 12:8] knew all that happened in the house and all that happened in the fields. . . . Even so, Moses, who had gone up to heaven, knew the upper as well as the nether worlds.

In view of the considerable foregoing evidence, I submit that when Matt. 11:27a affirms that Jesus received "all (revelation)" from the Father, it is maintaining for him what much Jewish tradition maintained for Moses. In other words, 11:27a bestows upon Jesus yet one more Mosaic characteristic.

(6) In 11:29 Jesus invites his hearers to take up *ton zygon mou*, "my yoke." In Matthew's day "yoke" was a metaphor for obedience, subordination, and servitude; and we find such expressions as "yoke of wisdom" (Ecclus. 6:30; 51:26), "yoke of the Messiah" (*Ps. Sol.* 7:9; 17:30), and "yoke of the kingdom" (*3 En.* 35:6). But, to judge from the literary remains, "yoke" was associated above all with the Torah, as in Jer. 5:5; Acts 15:10; Gal. 5:1; and *2 Bar.* 41:3 (cf. *2 En.* 48:9). Rabbinic literature also attests to this: "yoke of the Torah" (*'ôl tôrâ*) and "yoke of the commandments" (*'ôl miswôt*) are frequent.[200] One understands why J. C. Fenton found in Matt. 11:29a "the idea of Jesus as the second Moses, the teacher of the new law."[201] The disciple of Jesus is encouraged to take up not the yoke of the Torah given through Moses but rather, as of first importance, the yoke of the Son of God.

(7) The order of the two major clauses in Matt. 11:27 has always been thought a bit peculiar: only the Father knows the Son, only the Son knows the Father. Our natural tendency—shared by certain Christian scribes, as the ms. tradition attests—is to put the subject of God's unknowability first: it is the greater mystery. But in Exod. 33:12-13 the statement of God's knowledge of Moses prefaces Moses' request to know God: "Thou hast said, 'I know you [Moses] by name'" introduces "Show me thy ways, that I may know thee." This supplies a sensible cause for Matthew's unexpected order. The clause about knowledge of the Son comes before that about knowledge of the Father because the Gospel text replicates the order of Exod. 33:12-13, where God's knowledge of Moses is indicated before Moses makes his request for knowledge of God.[202]

(8) Paul wrote in 1 Cor. 13:12: "For now we see in a mirror dimly, but then face to face. Now I know in part; then I shall understand fully

---

[200]Cf. *m. 'Abot* 3:5; *m. Ber.* 2:2; additional texts in SB 1:608-10.
[201]J. C. Fenton, *Saint Matthew* (Baltimore: Penguin, 1963), 187; cf. Davies, *Paul,* 150.
[202]Cf. also John 10:15: "As the Father knows me and I know the Father."

even as I have been fully understood." This differs from Matt. 11:27 in that (a) eschatology is no longer realized (full understanding belongs to the future) and (b) knowledge is no longer exclusive (all the elect will someday understand). Nonetheless, Matt. 11:27 and 1 Cor. 13:12 are conceptually very close, which matters so much because the latter contains an allusion to Moses.[203] Paul introduced his remarks about knowing and being known with a contrast between seeing in a mirror dimly and seeing face to face. In doing so he was, as is generally recognized, drawing upon Num. 12:8, where God speaks "mouth to mouth"[204] to Moses, not in dark speech (*wĕlôʾ bĕhîdōt*; LXX: *ou di ainigmatōn*)[205] but rather, according to the unpointed Hebrew, *mrʾh*. This last is usually read as *marʾeh*, as in BDB, s.v. This is the vocalization behind the RSV: "clearly." Similarly, the NEB has "openly." There are, however, several rabbinic passages which take *mrʾh* to mean *marʾâ*, "mirror" (SB 3:452-54). This explains 1 Cor. 13:12: the passage presupposes the exegetical tradition according to which Num. 12:8 means that God spoke to Moses "(as) in a mirror." Thus *di esoptrou en enigmati* is the antithesis of *bĕmarʾ ā wĕlô bĕhîdōt*: Paul borrowed the phrase about Moses and simply removed the negation. This seems to imply admittedly that the special, direct mode of communication which Moses alone once had should be understood as a pointer to the knowledge Christians will receive only at the end, and one may doubt that Paul could really have thought that Moses, notwithstanding his undeniable greatness, enjoyed a revelatory experience Christians can only anticipate. Perhaps the proper conclusion is that the scriptural allusions do not amount to strict interpretation but are rather free, *ad hoc* adaptations of certain key phrases. But however one resolves that issue, the crucial fact for our purposes is established: when ruminating upon the subject of knowing God and being known by him, Paul turned his thoughts to the lawgiver.

(9) In John 15:14-15 (which just might reflect knowledge of Matt. 11:28 par.) there is this: "You are my friends if you do what I command you. No longer do I call you servants, for the servant does not know what his master is doing; but I have called you friends, for all that I have heard from my Father I have made know to you." The margin of

---

[203]Cf. Bede, *Commentary on 1 John*, on 3:2.

[204]Paul changed "mouth to mouth" to "face to face" (cf. Exod. 33:11; Num. 14:14; Deut. 5:4; 34:10; Ecclus. 45:5; *Barn.* 15:l; *Memar Marqah* 5:3; etc.) because his subject was sight, not speech, and because Jewish tradition had long associated Num. 12:8 (which has "mouth to mouth") with Exod. 33:11 and Deut. 34:10 (which have "face to face").

[205]BDB, s.v., defines *hîdâ* as "riddle, enigmatic, perplexing saying or question."

Nestle-Aland cites for comparison Exod. 33:11: "Thus the Lord used to speak to Moses face to face, as a man speaks with his friend." Raymond Brown also, in his commentary on John 15:15, refers to Exod. 33:11: "In the OT the supreme revelation of Yahweh to Moses on Sinai was as intimate as a man speaking to his *philos* (Exod. 33:11)."[206] What the verse in John and that in Exodus share is the link between friendship and personal revelation. This does not entail, I concede, that John 15:15 depends upon Exod. 33:11. It does, however, at least raise again the good possibility that when early Christians reflected upon Jesus as revealer they sometimes thought about Moses and what is said of him in Exodus 33 and 34. Consequently John 15:15 offers itself as additional warrant for discerning a link between Exodus 33 and Matthew's *Jubelruf*.[207]

(10) In 11:29b Matthew's Jesus declares: "And learn of me because I am meek and lowly in heart." Attention has already been called to the Mosaic background of meekness. Here notice needs to be directed to "learn of me."[208]

In Judaism one "learned" Torah.[209] In the First Gospel one "learns" of and from Jesus—with the implication that Jesus is or takes the place of Torah—an idea certainly found elsewhere in early Christianity, including Paul,[210] John,[211] and Hermes (*Sim.* 8:3.2: the law is the Son of God). One takes up the yoke of Jesus and one studies him. Thus he is "all that God has made known of his nature, character, and purpose, and of what he would have man be and do."[212]

Earlier I indicated that Jesus' words are eschatological Torah. But there is in Matthew no departmentalization of word and deed, no disjunction of person and speech. The two rather form an inseparable unity: Jesus embodies his utterance.[213] He therefore is, as Lactantus put it, a "law alive" (*Div. inst.* 4:17; cf. already Justin, *Dial.* 11: the eternal law is Christ).

---

[206]*John* 2:683.

[207]For Moses as God's friend see *Jub.* 21:15, 20; Philo, *Ebr.* 94; *Mos.* 1:156-57; *Somn.* 1:193-94, 231-32; etc.; *LAB* 24:3; 25:3, 5; 32:8; 33:4; Origen, *De prin.* 3:2.5; *Sib. Orac.* 2:245. "Friend of God" was also often used of Abraham (so already 2 Chron. 20:7).

[208]The Greek, *mathēte ap emou*, could be translated either "learn of me" or "learn from me." But in the present instance both amount to the same thing.

[209]Cf. Ps. 118:71, 73; *LAB* 11:2; Josephus, *Ant.* 16:43; *m.' Abot* 2:8, 14; *b. Ketub.* 50a; etc.

[210]Davies, *Paul*, 147-76.

[211]See C. H. Dodd, *The Interpretation of the Fourth Gospel* (Cambridge: University Press, 1953), 82-86; Glasson, *Moses*, 45-64, 86-94.

[212]Moore, *Judaism* 1:263, defining "Torah."

[213]For this aspect of Matthew see W. D. Davies and Dale C. Allison, Jr., "Reflections on the Sermon on the Mount," *SJT* 44 (1991): 283-310.

The same thought lies latent in 11:19: "Yet Wisdom is justified from her deeds."[214] It is generally agreed that "deeds" is here redactional (Luke 7:35 has "all her children"), and further that "her deeds" forms an *inclusio* with the *ta erga tou Christou* (= "the deeds of Christ") of 11:2. If so, we are left with the equation, "the deeds of Christ" = "the deeds of Wisdom," which equation implies another: "Christ" = "Wisdom." Whether that equation was already implicit in Q, as some have thought, or whether, as seems more likely to me, Matthew himself first planted the idea in the synoptic tradition, the point for us is that, in Judaism, Wisdom and Torah were intimately joined, indeed "fundamentally interchangeable."[215] The evidence has been set out often enough, and I need not review it again here. Suffice it to refer to Ecclus. 24:23-24; Wisd. 6:18; Bar. 3:28-4:4; and 4 Macc. 1:16-17 (cf. also Deut. 4:6). These representative passages demonstrate that the identification of Wisdom with Torah was a first-century commonplace. What follows? Because Wisdom and Torah were one, Matthew's equation of Jesus with Wisdom[216] bolsters my argument that the evangelist also identified Jesus with Torah.

Now what does all this have to do with Moses? Under Persian influence, the Graeco-Roman world was quite familiar with the idea of the king as a living law:[217]

> Now laws are of two kinds, the animate [*empsychos*] law, which is the king, and the inanimate, the written law (Pseudo-Archytas of Tarentum, in Stobaeus 4:1.132).

> The king is animate law [*nomos empsychos*], or is a legal ruler. So for this reason he is most just and most lawful (Diotogenes in Stobaeus 4:7.61).

> In general the good king must be sinless and perfect in word and deed; since he must be what the ancients call animate law, creating a law-abiding spirit and unanimity, and thrusting out lawlessness and strife (Musonius, in Stobaeus 4:7.67).[218]

[214]In addition to what follows see Jack M. Suggs, *Wisdom, Christology, and Law in Matthew's Gospel* (Cambridge: Harvard, 1970).

[215]Hengel, *Son of God*, 50.

[216]Some have also found the equation in 23:37-39; see Suggs, *Wisdom*, 70-71; but for another opinion see Marshall D. Johnson, "Reflections on a Wisdom Approach to Matthew's Christology," *CBQ* 36 (1974):44-64.

[217]See E. R. Goodenough, "The Political Philosophy of Hellenistic Kingship," in *Yale Classical Studies*, vol. 1, ed. A. H. Harman (New Haven: Yale, 1928), 55-102; also Dvornik, *Political Philosophy*, 2:453-557.

[218]Cf. Aristotle, *Polit.* 1284A; Ps.-Aristotle, *Ep. ad Alexander*; Xenophon, *Cyrop.* 8:1.22; Philolaus in Stobaeus 4:7.62; Plutarch, *Mor.* 780C; idem, *Artoxerxes* 23:3.

Moreover, Hellenistic Jews, persuaded that Moses was a king who lived his own words (cf. p. 303), and stimulated by the use of "Moses" as a designation for the Pentateuch,[219] made Moses the living Torah: "Moses and the law were more or less identified and the concept and the name were *de facto* frequently inter- changeable."[220] As Philo wrote: Moses was "the reasonable and living impersonation of law" (*nomos empsychos*; *Mos.* 1:162; cf. 2:3-5; Clement of Alexandria, *Strom.* 1:29). But, as we have seen, that is precisely what Matthew's Jesus is—the "living impersonation of law." Once more, therefore, Matt. 11:25-30 leads us back to the first lawgiver.

(11) W. D. Davies, in private correspondence, has wondered whether *hoi kopiōntes kai pephortismenoi*, "who labor and are heavy laden" (11:28), might not be exodus language. Pharaoh put slave masters over the Israelites. He ruthlessly forced them into hard labor. And, to recall Exod. 1:11-14, he made their lives bitter with hard labor in brick and mortar and with all kinds of work in the fields (cf. 2:11). Did not the Hebrews labor, and were they not heavy laden until Moses delivered them? One could urge that the Jesus of Matt. 11:25-30 promises to do what Moses did, namely, deliver his people from their burdens and labors. The problem with this proposal, however, is that neither *phortizō* nor *kopiaō* appears in LXX Exodus 1-2, nor have I found them or *zygon* elsewhere used of the slavery in Egypt. So it would probably not be wise to endorse Davies' suggestion. On the other hand, I have, for what it is worth, discovered that at least one other reader seems to have associated the language of Matt. 11:28 with Israel's plight in Egypt. In "A Soliloquy of One of the Spies left in the Wilderness," Gerard Manley Hopkins—a man who lived in the Bible—wrote this:

Give us the tale of bricks as heretofore;
To plash with cool feet the clay juicy soil.
Who tread the grapes are splay'd with stripes of gore,
    And they who crush the oil
Are splatter'd. We desire the *yoke* we bore,
    The *easy burden* of yore.

[219]Luke 16:29; 24:27; Acts. 15:21; 26:22; 2 Cor. 3:15; Ignatius, *Smyrn.* 5:l; Origen, *Comm. on Matt.* 12:43. Cf. the expression, "the Torah [or: law] of Moses:" 1 Kings 2:3; 2 Chron. 23:18; Neh. 8:l; Dan. 9:ll; Ecclus. 24:22; Tob 7:10; Bar. 2:2; 2 Macc. 7:30; *1QS* v.8; *CD* xv.2,12; Luke 2.22; John 7:23; Heb. 10:28; *b. Šabb.* 89a; etc.

[220]Georgi, *Opponents*, 135. I would add that, for Matthew, Moses must have been living prophecy.

(12) The verb used for the transmission of revelation from the Father to the Son in 11:27 is *paradidōmi*—"all has been handed over (*paredothē*) to me by my Father." This verb and the related simplex, *didōmi*, along with the Hebrew, *māsar*, were, in certain contexts, technical terms for the transmission of Torah; and they were used both for the handing over of the law to Moses and for Moses' bequeathment of that law to others. As *m.*⁾ *Abot* l:l puts it: *Mōšeh qibbēl tôrâ missînai ûmsārâ lîhôšû ʿa*: Moses received the Torah from Sinai and handed it on to Joshua. Compare LXX Deut. 10:4 (*kai edōken autas* [commandments] *Kyrios* to me [Moses]"); Ecclus. 45:5 ("God gave [*edōken*] him [Moses] commandments before his face"); Justus of Tiberias in Eusebius, *Chronicon apud* Georgius Syncellus, *Chron.* 2, preface (Moses "handed down [*paradedōkota*] oracles and utterances in sacred scripture"); also *LAB* 11:2; *Apost. Const.* 8:12.25; *Apoc. Paul* 8; and *PGM* 12:92-94. In early Christian art the transmission of the law to Moses was, presumably in imitation of Jewish models, regularly depicted by a hand, with scroll, extending itself from heaven.[221]

It is crucial to observe that Jesus, according to Matt. 11:27, not only received revelation directly from God: he also passed on revelation. So what we have in the Gospels is precisely what we have in Judaism, namely, a chain of tradition through which the divine revelation is canalized through human intermediaries. If Moses received the law and handed it on to Joshua, Jesus likewise received revelation and in turn made it known to others (cf. "and to whomever the Son wishes to reveal[222] him"). Pictorially:

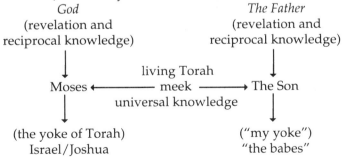

$$\begin{array}{ccc}
God & & The\ Father \\
(\text{revelation and} & & (\text{revelation and} \\
\text{reciprocal knowledge}) & & \text{reciprocal knowledge}) \\
\downarrow & \text{living Torah} & \downarrow \\
\text{Moses} \longleftarrow & \text{meek} \longrightarrow & \text{The Son} \\
\downarrow & \text{universal knowledge} & \downarrow \\
(\text{the yoke of Torah}) & & (\text{"my yoke"}) \\
\text{Israel/Joshua} & & \text{"the babes"}
\end{array}$$

---

[221]See Goodenough, *Jewish Symbols*, 9:112. Cf. *Deut. Rab.* 11:l0.

[222]For "reveal" (*apokalyptō*) with Moses as subject see *LAE* title; *b. Menah.* 29b; *Deut. Rab.* 11:l0; etc.

As this illustrates, both Moses and Jesus were thought of as being, on the human level, the prime movers in a chain of transmitted revelation.[223]

Before leaving 11:25-30, two cautionary words are in order. First, it would be wrong, in view of 5:17-20, to make the quick induction that one should take up the yoke of Jesus *instead of* the yoke of Torah, or that one should learn from Jesus *instead of* from Moses. As the living, eschatological Torah, Jesus embraces the first Torah: "Think not that I have come to abolish the law and the prophets" (see pp. 182-90). The new incorporates the old. There is no antithesis. One must also beware of reading into 11:25-30 polemic against Moses, and of finding unwarranted contrasts between the two lawgivers. This is not to say that the superiority of Jesus here has no place. Matthew makes it plain that Jesus Christ is the one Son of the Father[224] and so the chief mediator, which entails that Moses can no longer be the supreme *arbiter* (*T. Mos.* 1:14; cf. 3:12). In addition, one might observe that whereas Jewish tradition sometimes made Moses receive the Torah from angels,[225] Jesus received his revelation directly. Still, I detect no attack upon Moses or his Torah in 11:25-30. Jesus does not avow that Moses had no reciprocal knowledge of God, that he was not meek, or that he did not embody Torah; and it is nowhere implied that to take up the yoke of Jesus requires laying down the yoke of Moses. There is, to be sure, an inevitable diminution of Moses in Matt. 11:25-30, for the Son has become the focus of revelation, moving aside what was for Judaism its inadjustable center; but that is not at all the same thing as polemic. In

---

[223]It is wholly appropriate that both Moses and Jesus were known as "the lawgiver;" for Moses see Aristobulus *apud* Eusebius, *Praep. ev.* 8:l0.3, 9; Nicolas of Damascus *apud* Josephus, *Ant.* 1:95; Cleodemus Malchus *apud* Josephus, *Ant.* 1:240 (cf. Eusebius, *Praep. ev.* 9:20.3); *Ep. Arist.* 131, 139, 148, 153; Philo, *Mos.* 1:1; 2:2-3, 8; etc.; Josephus, *C. Ap.* 2:145; Nicarchus *apud.* a Byzantine lexicon (see *Anecdota Graeca* 1 [1814], 1:381); Ptolemy Chennos *apud* Photius, *Bibl.* 190; Aristides, *Apol.* 14; *Apoc. Paul* 48; Clement of Alexandria, *Strom.* 2:15; Origen, *De prin.* 4:1.1; *Pseudo-Clem. Hom.* 2:16; Eusebius, *Dem. ev.* 3:2; Julian, *C. Gal.* 238C; for Jesus see Justin, *Dial.* 12:2; 14:3; Clement of Alexandria, *Strom.* 1:26; 2:5; *Apost. Const.* 3:9.4; 6:22.5; etc.

[224]Occasionally in the literature Moses is designated God's "son," but so rarely that it would be unwise to make anything of it for the interpretation of Matt. 11:25-30. Moses is addressed as *ho pais* in Ezekiel's *Exagogue* and, according to Philo, *Q.E.* 2:29. Moses came near to God *kata suggenē tina oikeiotēta*, "in a kind of family relation." "My son Moses" appears in the *Midrash of Moses' Death* (in Jellinik, *Bet ha-Midrash* l:121) and "son of the house of God" in *Memar Marqah* 4:1. Note also that *T. Levi* 17.2 (he 'shall speak to God as a father') *may* refer to Moses.

[225]Cf. Acts 7:38, 53; Gal. 3:19; Heb. 2:2; Josephus, *Ant.* 15:136; *ARN* B 2.

11:25-30, as throughout Matthew, Moses is not Jesus' rival or adversary but his prophetic forerunner and typological predecessor.[226]

My second cautionary word is this: while the tradition-history of Matt. 11:25-30 is perhaps impossible to untangle, so that opinions differ considerably, one inference, for which I have elsewhere marshalled the evidence, commands assent: "learn from me, for I am meek and lowly of heart" (v. 29b) is redactional.[227] The point is vital, for 11:29a extends the Moses typology present elsewhere in the passage. It follows that, because he added to them, our evangelist must have recognized, and wanted his readers to recognize, the allusions to Moses.

THE SERVANT OF DEUTERO-ISAIAH

Matt. 12:15-21 contains this:

> Jesus... withdrew from there. And many followed him, and he healed them all, and ordered them not to make him known. This was to fulfil what was spoken by the prophet Isaiah [in 42:1-4]: "Behold, my servant whom I have chosen, my beloved with whom my soul is well pleased. I will put my Spirit upon him, and he shall proclaim justice to the Gentiles. He will not wrangle or cry aloud, nor will any one hear his voice in the streets; he will not break a bruised reed or quench a smoldering wick, till he brings justice to victory; and in his name will the Gentiles hope."

According to this, the longest citation of Scripture in Matthew, Jesus is *ho pais mou*, "my servant." The title is comprehensive: Jesus' lifework fulfills the prophecies made by Deutero-Isaiah concerning the mysterious, humble, suffering servant.

Because there are additional places in the First Gospel where Jesus' identity as Isaiah's servant is manifest or implied, that identity cannot be pushed to the periphery of Matthew's Christology.[228] The redactional

---

[226]We must keep clearly in mind that Matthew could have polemicized against a certain interpretation of Moses without thinking he was criticizing Moses himself. For instance, to criticize the Pharisees' Moses was not necessarily to criticize Moses himself. —A typical example of the sort of claim I am opposing appears in Goldberg, *Jews and Christians*, 156: "all analogies between Jesus and Moses are radically undermined" because Jesus, not Moses is Emmanuel—to which one must respond: if such were the view of the evangelist, why did he (as Goldberg fully recognizes) draw so many analogies in the first place? Did he set out to deconstruct his own work?

[227]See Davies and Allison, *Matthew* 2:237-38, 290.

[228]See further David Hill, "Son and Servant: An Essay on Matthean Christology," *JSNT* 6 (1980):2-16.

8:17 cites MT Isa. 53:4: "He took our infirmities and bore our diseases." This, in straightforward fashion, identifies Jesus' ministry with the ministry of the servant. More cryptically, at both the baptism and the transfiguration a heavenly voice conflates words from Ps. 2:7 and Isa. 42:1, the latter a text about the servant (3:17; 17:3).[229] Then there is 20:28, in which Jesus declares himself willing to give his life as "a ransom for many." The phrase in quotation marks probably, despite the doubts of some, depends upon Isaiah 53.[230] Finally, there are the solemn words of the last supper concerning "the blood of the covenant which is poured out for many for the forgiveness of sins" (26:28): these have often been thought to draw upon, among other sources, Isa. 53:12.[231]

There are perhaps reasons to associate Jesus' status as servant with the new Moses theme. Moses bore the title, ʿebed / pais. That title was of course also borne by others, especially kings and prophets; but, in Jewish sources, "servant" is more closely connected with the lawgiver than any other individual. The MT itself (mostly in Deuteronomy and the Deuteronomic history) labels Moses ʿebed forty times; and in Exod. 14:31 (the people "believed in the Lord and in his servant Moses") and Num. 12:7-8 (see p. 219) the appellation is specially emphasized. Matters are much the same outside of Scripture: "servant" is most characteristic of the lawgiver—so much so that assembly of all the data would nearly be an interminable task.[232]

Given the facts just adduced, one wonders not that the title "servant" was employed in the construction of several Moses typologies. Thus Joshua, Jeremiah, the suffering servant, Anthony, and Constantine were all Mosaic, and all were, in that connection, called "servant."[233] Should this be a clue to interpreting Matthew?

The question perhaps wields more force from the circumstance that the Isaianic servant, identified by Matthew with Jesus, is in certain respects Mosaic (pp. 68-71). Did our evangelist know this, and so understand that by being the servant Jesus was being Mosaic? Intriguingly enough, Matt. 26:28 mixes allusions to Exod. 24:8 and Isa. 53:12. Here exodus and servant themes meet.

---

[229]See Davies and Allison, *Matthew* 1:336-41.

[230]W. J. Moulder, "The Old Testament Background and the Interpretation of Mark x. 45," *NTS* 24 (1977), 120-27.

[231]Rudolf Pesch, *Das Abendmahl und Jesu Todesverständnis* (QD 80; Freiburg: Herder, 1978), 93-101.

[232]See further p. 56, n. 121.

[233]E.g. Josh. 24:29 (cf. Judg. 2:8); Jer. 1:4; 6:24; Isa. 42:1; Athanasius, *Vit. Ant.* 85; Eusebius, *Vit. Const.* 1:6.

The issue can be approached from still another angle. As the servant, Jesus gives his life as a ransom for many and pours out his blood (20:28; 26:28). In other words, he makes atonement with his life. The possible background for this idea of self-sacrificial atonement has been diligently sought, to no universally agreed upon conclusion. A few, however, have looked to the Moses traditions.[234] According to Exod. 32:32, Moses prayed: "But now, if thou wilt forgive their sin—and if not, blot me, I pray thee, out of thy book which thou hast written." As early as the *Mekilta* Moses is thought to have offered himself as an atoning redeemer: Exod. 32:32 is cited as proof that "the patriarchs and the prophets offered themselves on behalf of Israel" (*nātěnû napšām 'al Yiśrā'ēl*).[235] Did Matthew already know such an interpretation? Unfortunately it does not sufficiently appear from the extant evidence when Jews began to interpret Exod. 32:32 as does the *Mekilta*.

The foregoing considerations suffice to provoke reflection; and that Matthew associated the servant motif with his Moses typology is an appealing inference. But that inference is spoiled by a paucity of evidence and a double difficulty: in the allusions to and quotations of servant passages I detect no redactional activity conforming Jesus to Moses; and had Matthew wished to cast a Mosaic shadow over the servant, how could he have resisted citing, in 12:21, the MT for Isa. 42:4: "and the coastlands wait for his law?"[236] In conclusion, then, there are conflicting indicators, and we are left only with a possibility, not a probability: Matthew's servant Christology is certainly congruent with his Moses typology, but any claim for more than that would be unfounded.

THE DEMAND FOR A SIGN (12:38; 16:1)

In Matt. 12:38 "some scribes of the Pharisees" challenge Jesus to make a supernatural display: "Teacher, we wish to see a sign (*sēmeion*) from you." Similarly, in 16:1 the Pharisees and Sadducees make a "test," asking Jesus "to show them a sign (*sēmeion*) from heaven." In both instances Jesus has, on previous occasions, preformed stupendous signs and wonders, and he will do so again. But all his marvelous

---

[234]So e.g. Schoeps, *Theologie*, 94-95.

[235]Cf. *Sipre Deut.* § 355; *b. Ber.* 32a; *b. Sota* 14a; discussion in Bloch, "Moïse," 129.

[236]The question assumes that Matthew knew the Hebrew we know; but the LXX could witness to a lost Hebrew text form; see R. H. Gundry, *The Use of the Old Testament in St. Matthew's Gospel* (NovTSup 18; Leiden: E. J. Brill, 1967), 115-16.

works have availed and will avail not, for the unbelief of his opponents cannot be undone: and in the end judgement will fall upon them (cf. 12:41-42, 45, etc.).

There is a like sequence in the traditions about Moses. According to Exod. 7:8, God told Moses and Aaron: "When Pharaoh says to you, 'Prove yourselves by working a miracle' (LXX: *sēmeion ē teras*[237]), then you shall...". So Pharaoh confronted Moses and requested a miracle. As the story goes, of course, Moses worked wonders aplenty, but Pharaoh's heart was hardened: he disbelieved his own eyes and indeed opposed Moses to the bitter end, to the extinction of his own army at the Red Sea.

One could, if so inclined, press the parallelism between Matthew's two pericopae and Exodus 7 a bit further. A few verses before Matt. 12:38, 12:27 records that Jesus challenged the Pharisees by referring to the exorcisms of others: "And if I cast out demons by Beelzebul, by whom do your sons cast them out?" This might remind one of Exodus, where several of Moses' miracles are imitated by Pharaoh's magicians: not everything the lawgiver did was matchless. The parallel is all the more interesting because the ten plagues were interpreted as attacks upon the gods (cf. *Jub.* 47:5), and gods were often equated with demons; hence Moses was remembered as having battled demons. In the plague narrative of *Jubilees* we find this:

> And Prince Mastema stood up before you and desired to make you fall into the hand of Pharaoh. And he aided the magicians of the Egyptians, and they stood up and acted before you. Thus we let them do evil, but we did not empower them with healing so that it might be done by their hands. And the Lord smote them with evil wounds and they were unable to stand because we destroyed (their ability) to do any single sign. And despite all the signs and wonders, Prince Mastema was not shamed until he had become strong and called to the Egyptians so that they might pursue after you... (48:9-12).

That such an interpretation was well known is suggested by *CD* v.17-19: "For in ancient times Moses and Aaron arose by the hand of the Prince of Lights and Satan in his cunning raised up Jannes and his brother [see p. 109, n. 40] when Israel was first delivered."[238] Like Jesus, Moses was remembered as a miracle-worker who fought the devil.[239]

---

[237]Cf. Artapanus in Eusebius, *Praep. ev.* 9:27: "the king then told Moses to perform some sign (*sēmeion*) for him."

[238]Cf. *T. Jos.* 20:2: "the Lord will be with you [the sons of Israel] in the light, while Beliar will be with the Egyptians in the dark."

[239]*Jub.* 48:15 goes on to relate that Mastema was "bound" (cf. Matt. 12:29) at the Red Sea.

Also perhaps suggestive is a clause that appears in both 12:39 and 16:4: *genea ponēra kai moichalis sēmeion epizētai*: an evil and adulterous generation seeks a sign. The *dôr hammidbār*, the generation of Moses (which was often associated with the wicked generation of the flood) drew to itself the adjectives "evil" (*hārâ/ponēra*—Num. 32:13; Deut. 1:35) and "faithless" (cf. Deut. 32:20: *ouk estin pistis en autois*—this is the sense of "adulterous" in the synoptics). Some authorities even affirmed that "the generation of the wilderness will have no share in the world to come" (*m. Sanh.* 10:3). Did Matthew then think that the contemporaries of Jesus, in their stubborn refusal to believe, were akin to the generation of Moses? There can be no doubt that at least the formulation in Matt. 17:17 (*genea apistos kai diestrammenē*) depends upon Deut. 32:5 (*genea... diestrammenē*; cf. Phil. 2:15).

Do we have indication enough that Matthew was thinking of Moses and his circumstances when he wrote 12:38 and 16:l? Had we only Matthew to hand, I might imagine that we do. But we instead have to hand also Mark and Luke; and Luke 11:20, the parallel to Matt. 12:28, has Jesus respond to the Pharisees' criticism with this: "But if it is by the finger of God that I cast out demons, then the kingdom of God has come upon you." This last is, as Eusebius understood (*Dem. ev.* 3:2), a transparent back-reference to Exod. 8:18-19: "The magicians tried to produce gnats by their secret arts, but they could not. There were gnats on both humans and animals. And the magicians said to Pharaoh, 'This is the finger of God.'" The implication is that Jesus and Moses both did what demons cannot do (cf. *Exod. Rab.* 10:7); that is, they accomplished what only God can accomplish.[240] The point is critical. For I am persuaded, along with others who have examined the issue, that Luke's allusive "finger of God" probably stood in Q,[241] and would our evangelist, had he been constructing a Moses typology, have dropped a phrase so suggestive of a parallel between the first redeemer and the last? It has been urged that a dislike for anthropomorphisms here overrode Matthew's wish to make Jesus like Moses. The evangelist, however, did not shrink from writing of "the right hand of the Power" (26:62). More likely is it that he omitted "finger" because it had magical connotations.[242] But if that considera-

---

[240]Cf. Manson, *Teaching*, 82-83. "Finger of God" also appears in Exod. 31:18 and Deut. 9:10 (cf. Ps. 8:30); but in these places the context offers no real point of contact with the synoptic subject matter.

[241]See Davies and Allison, *Matthew* 2:340-41.

[242]See John Hull, *Hellenistic Magic and the Synoptic Tradition* (SBT 28; London: SCM, 1974), 129. (The substitution of *pneuma* nicely links 12:18, 28, and 31-32.)

tion sufficed to override the retention of a good parallel with Moses, we must doubt how concerned our author was to establish in chapter 12 the likeness of Jesus to Moses.

THE MULTIPLICATION MIRACLES (14:13-21; 15:29-39)

Eusebius, contending that Deut. 18:15-18 prophesied Jesus, linked the gospel feeding miracles with the story of the manna:

> Moses again fed the people in the wilderness: for Scripture says: Behold, I give you bread from heaven. And after a little: "It came to pass as the dew ceased round about the camp, and behold on the face of the wilderness a small thing, like white coriander seed, as frost upon the ground." And our Lord and Savior likewise says to his disciples: "O ye of little faith, why reason among yourselves, because you have brought no bread? Do you not yet understand, neither remember the five loaves of the five thousand, and how many baskets you took up? Neither the seven loaves of the four thousand, and how many baskets you took up?" (*Dem. ev.* 3:2, quoting Exod. 16:4, 14; and Matt. 16:8; cf. Cyril of Alexandria, *Comm. on Lk.* 48).

Do these words reflect a faithful appreciation of Matthew's intention?[243] The Fourth Gospel, drawn up very near Matthew's time, encourages investigation of the issue, for in it the feeding of the five thousand belongs to a chapter full of Mosaic motifs. Further, John records that the crowd, when it learned what had happened, took Jesus to be the prophet like Moses (see p. 82). But is John a good guide to Matthew?

The First Evangelist almost certainly understood the twin gift miracles of chapters 14 and 15 to anticipate the eucharist (cf. 26:20-29) and to foreshadow the messianic banquet;[244] and surely he was not oblivious of the striking similarities with 2 Kings 4:42-44, where Elisha feeds one hundred men with two barley loaves, and some is left over. Can we then suppose that he additionally understood 14:13ff. and 15:32ff. to suggest a parallel with Moses? In my view that is not impossible. Matthew's narrative, just like John's, is, in general, sufficiently dense to bear a multiplicity of meanings, so that the existence of one allusion need not exclude another; and I note that at least most of the commentaries on John 6 find in the feeding of the five thousand references to the exodus, to the eucharist, and to eschatology.

---

[243]Gfrörer, *Heils*, 364-65, thought so.
[244]Davies and Allison, *Matthew* 2:480-82.

Let us begin, then, with Mark, Matthew's source for 14:13ff. and 15:29ff. There does seem to be a relation between the two Markan feedings (6:34-44; 8:1-10) and the Moses traditions.[245] Apart from the words shared with Exodus, perhaps not all of them random trifles,[246] these observations may be registered:

(i) manna was identified as a sort of "bread" (Deut. 8:3; Neh. 9:15; John 6:31-34; etc.); and what Jesus multiplied was bread;

(ii) according to 6:40, the people sat in groups of hundreds and fifties (6:40), which arrangement is reminiscent of Exod. 18:21 and of the camps of the Qumran sectaries, who sought to reproduce the organization of Israel's wilderness period (see *1QS* 2:21-22; *CD* 13:1-2);

(iii) if Jesus multiplied loaves *and fishes, Sipre Num.* § 95 records that the Israelites ate fish in their desert wanderings (cf. Wisd. 19:12);

(iv) "Jesus and the disciples cross the sea to the wilderness place, and then the hungry are fed; in Exodus the Israelites cross the sea, wander in the wilderness, become hungry, and are fed with manna;"[247]

(v) Mark 6:34 remarks that the Jewish crowds were like sheep without a shepherd, and this, in its present context, could make Jesus Mosaic (cf. Num. 27:17 and see pp. 213-15);

(vi) if the manna fell in the evening (Num. 11:9), Jesus fed the crowd when the hour grew late (Mark 6:35);

(vii) whereas Mark has two similar feeding stories, the Pentateuch contains, in two separate books, two different accounts of the miracle of the manna, accounts which would not have been recognized by our spiritual forebears as doublets (see Exodus 16; Numbers 11).

---

[245]This is widely acknowledged, although its importance variously assessed; in addition to the commentaries see William Richard Stegner, *Narrative Theology in Early Jewish Christianity* (Louisville: Westminster/John Knox, 1989), 53-81.

[246]*anapausis/anapausō*: Exod. 16:23; Mark 6:31; *artos*: Exod. 16:3, 4, 8, 12, 15, 29, 32; Mark 6:37, 38, 41, 44; *ginōskō*: Exod. 16:6, 12; Mark 6:33, 38; *didōmi*: Exod. 16:8, 15, 29; Mark 6:37, 41; *erēmos*: Exod. 16:1, 3, 10, 14, 32; Mark 6:35; *kyklō*: Exod. 16:13; Mark 6:36; *ouranos*: Exod. 16:4; Mark 6:41; *synagō*: Exod. 16:5, 16; Mark 6:30; *syn/epitassō*: Exod. 16:16, 24, 32, 34; Mark 6:39; *topos*: Exod. 16:29; Mark 6:31, 32, 35; discussion in Stegner, ibid., 61-72.

[247]Stegner, ibid., 58.

One understands why Cranfield, in his commentary on Mark 6:34-44, cited *Eccles. Rab.* 1:28: "As the former redeemer caused manna to descend, as it is stated, Behold, I will cause to rain bread from heaven for you (Exod. 16:4), so will the latter redeemer cause manna to descend...".[248]

When we turn to Matthew, however, one possible reminder of Moses—"they were like sheep without a shepherd"—has been uprooted and moved elsewhere (see p. 213). Furthermore, Davies, in his exploration of the issue under review, failed to detect any redactional activity fortifying the presence of the new Moses theme in Matt. 14:13-21.[249] He concluded his misgivings with this: while there may be "undertones of the New Exodus motif," Matthew "reveals no accentuation of any such motif;" indeed, "by omitting Mark vi.34 at this point... it might be argued that Matthew has rejected an element which might be taken to point to a New Moses...".

Should this be the last word? The first sign that maybe it should not be appears from 14:21 and 15:38: "And those eating were about five/four thousand men, besides women and children" (*chōris gunaikōn kai paidion*). The words in parenthesis—passed over quickly by the commentators—are editorial and underline the crowd's vastness. But is that their only service? According to Exod. 12:37, the number of souls in the wilderness was "six hundred thousand men on foot, *lĕbad mittāp.*" While the LXX translates the last two words with *plōn tēs aposkeuēs*, the meaning of the Hebrew is "besides women and children" (cf. Philo, *Vit. Mos.* 1:147; Josephus, *Ant.* 2:317). Further, Num. 11:21 informs us that an exasperated Moses, when wondering how to feed the multitude that had exited Egypt, observed that "the people among whom I am number six hundred thousand (men) on foot... ". As in Matthew, and as in Exod. 12:37, only the number of men, not the number of individuals to be fed, is given. Should we then entertain the notion that the concluding words of Matthew's pericope were designed to allude to the way the people in the wilderness were numbered?

Another question perhaps worth raising concerns the possible allusion to LXX Ps. 107:4-9 in Matt. 15:29-39:[250]

---

[248]C. E. B. Cranfield, *The Gospel according to Mark* (rev. ed.; Cambridge: University Press, 1977), 222.

[249]*Setting*, 48-49. He did not, however, investigate the parallel in 15:29-39.

[250]Cf. J. Gnilka, *Das Matthäusevangelium*, 2 vols. (HTKNT; Freiburg: Herder, 1986, 1989), 2:37.

They wandered in the waterless wilderness (LXX: *en tē erēmō*—cf. Matt. 15:33). They found no way to an inhabited city. Hungry and thirsty, their soul fainted in them. Then they cried to the Lord in their affliction, and he delivered them from their distress. And he led them by a straight way (LXX: *eis odon*—cf. Matt. 15:32), that they might reach an inhabited city. Let them thank the Lord for his mercies, and his wonders to the sons of men. For he satisfies (*echortase*—cf. Matt. 15:37) the empty soul, and the hungry he fills with good things.

These lines can and have been given an historical sense, so that they refer not to just any band of desert pilgrims but to the wilderness wanderings of the exodus period in particular.[251] Did Matthew perhaps lend such a sense to Ps. 107:4-9, and did he have it in mind when composing 15:29-39?

That question probably cannot be answered. There is, however, another point to be made, this one indubitable: the prologue to Matthew's second feeding was designed to recall the setting of the sermon on the mount.[252] After the introductory *para tēn thalassan tēs Galilaias*, which exactly repeats 4:18, these parallels present themselves:

4:23ff.	15:29ff.
anebē eis to oros, 5:1	*anabas eis to oros*, 29
kathisantos autou, 5:1	*ekathēto ekei*, 29
ochloi polloi, 4:25, gathered for the following episode	*ochloi polloi*, 30, gathered for the following episode
kai etherapeusen autous, 4:24	*kai etherapeusen autous*, 30
the distinction between the disciples (*mathētai autou*) and the crowd, 5:1	the distinction between the disciples (*mathētas autou*) and the crowd, 32

Especially and irresistibly reminiscent of the SM is the notice that Jesus sat on the mountain, and to this there is no Markan parallel; so we must

---

[251]See N. H. Snaith, *Five Psalms (1; 27; 51; 107; 134)* (London: Epworth, 1938), 17-21. Cf. Dahood, *Psalms*, 3:80-83.

[252]Cf. Donaldson, *Mountain*, 131. He even speaks of 15:29-31 and 4:23-5:1 as forming "the opening and closing brackets of an inclusion."

all the more inquire into Matthew's intention. Why the correlations between 4:23ff. and 15:29ff.?

We have previously learned that the lawgiver, according to Jewish sources, sat on Sinai, and also that Matt. 5:1-2, where Jesus sits on a second mount of lawgiving, plays a key rôle in a developed Moses typology. It follows that Matthew designed the introduction to his second multiplication story to recall a scene with strong Mosaic associations. The reason? My guess is that the evangelist did indeed interpret Jesus' bread miracle as did John and Eusebius, namely, as analogous to the manna episode. Certainly those who rightly understand 5:1-2 will have their perception of 15:29ff. colored accordingly.

At this juncture an earlier remark invites reconsideration. I stated, on p. 238, that Matthew's text is often polysemous and that 14:13ff. and 15:29ff. could accordingly send vectors in several directions at once. I do not now wish to retract that statement, but here it may be a tad misleading. In Matthew's Jewish-Christian world the exodus from Egypt, the last supper, and the messianic banquet were not three isolated events. An intricacy of association rather obtained among them. The exodus had been typologically recapitulated at the last supper (pp. 256-61) and would again be typologically recapitulated at the consummation, which would see the return of the heavenly manna. Matthew therefore did not envisage the exodus, the eucharist, and the messianic banquet as three discreet events on the world's time line; instead they were for him superimposed images, and all three reproduced a fundamental pattern of Jewish religious experience, one involving redemption, bread, and covenant. Perhaps the difficult line in the *Pater Noster*, *ton arton hēmōn ton epiousion dos hēmin sēmeron* (6:11), is indicative of this, for interpreters have often construed it as an intersection of allusions—to Exod. 16:4 (the daily gathering of the manna), to the eucharist (*didōmi + artos* is common to 6:11 and 26:26; this is the dominant patristic interpretation), and to the eschatological manna (cf. Jerome, *Comm. in Matt.* 6:11, citing the *Gospel of the Hebrews*).[253] Thus if Matt. 14:13ff. and 15:29ff., which anticipate the Lord's supper and the messianic banquet, also exhibit points of contact with the manna episode, that is nothing but expected. How indeed could it be otherwise? The exodus, the eucharist, and the end were, through an induction of association, inseparably linked in the chains of memory. So anything prospective of the eucharist and the eschatological feast was, by an inner logic, additionally retrospective of the exodus.

[253]See Davies and Allison, *Matthew* 2:607-10.

THE TRANSFIGURATION (MATT. 17:1-8)

In *The Glory of God and the Transfiguration of Christ*, A. M. Ramsey wrote that whereas Moses' glory on Sinai was reflected, Christ's glory was unborrowed.[254] This setting of Tabor's light beside that of Sinai is a commonplace in the Christian tradition. Ephrem the Syrian, anticipating Ramsey, declared that "the brightness which Moses put on was wrapped on him from without," and in that differed from the light of Christ, which shone from within in the womb, at the baptism, and "on the mountain top."[255] Earlier than Ephrem, Eusebius drew a parallel between Moses on Sinai and Jesus transfigured:

> When Moses descended from the mountain, his face was seen to be full of glory; for it is written: "And Moses descending from the mountain did not know that the appearance of the skin of his face was glorified while he spoke to him. And Aaron and all the elders of Israel saw Moses, and the appearance of the skin of his face was glorified" (Exod. 34:29). In the same way, only more grandly, our savior led his disciples "to a very high mountain, and he was transfigured before them, and his face shone as the sun, and his garments were white like the light" (*Dem. ev.* 3:2, quoting Matt. 17:2).

Although their emphasis upon a contrast between Jesus and Moses may be excessive, the words of Ramsey, Ephrem, and Eusebius plainly unfold what is already implicit in Mark's account of the transfiguration. Whatever the history beneath Mark 9:2-10, the tradition aimed to remind readers of what took place at a much earlier time, when Moses descended Sinai with the law. This follows from the parallels with Exodus 24 and 34:[256] both Mark and the Torah refer to (i) a high mountain (Exod. 24:12, 15-18; 34:3; Mark 9:2);[257] (ii) a cloud that descends and overshadows that mountain (Exod. 24:15-18; 34:5; Mark 9:7); (iii) a voice from the cloud (Exod. 24:16; Mark 9:7); (iv) the radiance of the central figure (Exod. 34:29-30, 35; Mark 9:2-3);[258] (v) the

---

[254]Philadelphia: Westminster, 1946, 120.

[255]*Hymns on the Church* 36:5-6; see S. Brock, *The Luminous Eye: The Spiritual World of St. Ephrem* (Rome: C.I.I.S. Rome, 1985), 71.

[256]See David Friedrich Strauss, *The Life of Jesus Critically Examined* (Philadelphia: Fortress, 1972), 540-46; cf. Donaldson, *Mountain*, 142-43. Contrast Rudolf Bultmann, *History of the Synoptic Tradition* (rev. ed.; Oxford: Basil Blackwell, 1963), 260.

[257]Sinai is a low mountain in some Jewish texts, but these seem to be uniformly late; see Ginzberg, *Legends* 6:31, n. 183, to the text on 3:83. Note esp. Philo, *Mos.* 2:70: Sinai is "the highest in the region."

[258]The issue of the original meaning of the story in Exodus is irrelevant for the interpretation of the synoptics; for even if one contends that *qāran* means "becomes horned" or "disfigured," the LXX, the Peshitta, the targumim, and Pseudo-Philo all attest that Exodus was most commonly understood to say that Moses was glorified or became radiant.

fear of those who saw the radiance (Exod. 34:29-30; Mark 9:6; cf. *l En.* 89:34); (vi) the presence of a special group of three (Exod. 24:1; Mark 9:2); and (vi) occurrence after six days (Exod. 24:16; Mark 9:2). In addition to all this, Moses and Elijah, who both converse with the transfigured Jesus, are the only figures in the Jewish Bible of whom it is related that they spoke with God on Mount Sinai: so their presence together makes us think of that mountain.

It beggars belief to entertain coincidence for all these parallels. It also beggars belief to suppose that the scripturally learned Matthew missed them.[259] In fact, everything argues that he added to their number.[260] Among the Matthean manipulations of Mark's text are the following: Moses has been given the honor of being named before Elijah; "and his face shone like the sun" has been added; the cloud has been made "bright" (*phōteinē*); "in whom I am well pleased" has been inserted; and the order of *akouete autou* has been reversed. Various suggestions for these alterations can and have been made; but simplicity recommends one proposition to account for them all: Matthew rescripted Mark in order to push thoughts towards Moses. Thus the lawgiver now comes first, and no priority of significance is given to Elijah. "Face" and "sun" recall the extra-biblical tradition that Moses' face (cf. Exod. 34:29) shone like the sun (Philo, *Vit. Mos.* 2:70; 2 Cor. 3:7-18; *LAB* 12:1; *Sipre Num.* § 140; *b. B. Bat.* 75a; *Deut. Rab.* ll (207c); this is to be related to the idea that Moses on Sinai went to the place of the sun—*LAB* 12; cf. 2 *Bar.* 59:11). *Phōteinē* alludes to the Shekinah, which accompanied Israel and Moses in the wilderness—and tradition associated Moses' radiance with the glory of the Shekinah.[261] The citation of Isa. 42:1 ("in whom I am well pleased") makes Jesus the 'ebed YHWH, a figure with Mosaic associations (see pp. 68-71, 233-35). Finally, the change to *autou akouete*[262] strengthens the allusion to LXX Deut. 18:15 (*autou akousesthe*), which speaks of a prophet like Moses (cf. Tertullian, *Adv. Marc.* 4:22).

It might be objected to all this that Matthew, had he been desirous of recollecting Moses, would have mentioned Jesus' "skin," for according to Exod. 34:29, "the skin of his face shone." But to insist upon

---

[259]Certainly Luke did not; see Bruce Chilton, "The Transfiguration: Dominical Assurance and Apostolic Vision," *NTS* 27 (1980):121-22.

[260]Cf. Davies, *Setting*, 50-56; also O. Lamar Cope, *Matthew: A Scribe Trained for the Kingdom of Heaven* (CBQMS 5; Washington: Catholic Biblical Association of America, 1976), 99-102.

[261]*Sipre Num.* § 1; *Tg. Ps.-Jon.* on Exod. 34:29-30.

[262]So HG, against NA[26]; the mss. are divided.

this would be pedantic. The skin of Moses often goes unmentioned in retellings of or allusions to Exodus 34 (cf. 2 Cor. 3:7-18; *LAB* 12:1); and the targumim—Ps-Jonathan, Onkelos, Fragment, and Neofiti—have nothing corresponding to the MT's *'ôr*.[263] Likewise unpersuasive is the counter that the chief background for Matt. 17:2-8 is to be found in eschatological expectation.[264] It is true that, according to Jewish expectation, the righteous will, in the end, undergo a transformation and become glorious and luminous, while their garments will glisten.[265] Nothing, however, moves us to set the Mosaic and eschatological interpretations against one another.[266] Matthew might readily have imagined that the radiance, exhibited by Moses and Jesus, was an anticipation of eschatological glory.[267] Compare the thought in *Tanna de Be Eliyyahu*:

> To him who gives thanks for his afflictions and rejoices over them, God grants life in this world and in the world to come eternal life; "for a lamp are the commandments and the Torah is light" (Prov. 6:23). Why then did Moses merit that his countenance should shine, even in this world, with a light destined for the righteous in the next world...? Because he was always striving, yearning, and watching to make peace between Israel and the Father in heaven (Friedmann, p. 17).

Tanna de Be Eliyyahu is, to be sure, far too late to establish anything about Matthew's day. But the natural inference made in it is presupposed by certain Amoraic materials[268] and appears independently in Ephrem the Syrian, in *Hymns on Paradise* 7:10: "In Moses he (God)

---

[263]The LXX has nothing for *'ôr pěnê Mošeh* in 34:35, and LXX B Exod. 34:29 has the variant *chrōmatos*; see further William H. Propp, "The Skin of Moses' Face—Transfigured or Disfigured?," *CBQ* 49 (1987):376-77.

[264]So Schweizer, *Matthew*, 349; Gnilka, *Matthäusevangelium* 2:93.

[265]Cf. Dan. 12:3; *l En.* 38:4; 104:2; *2 Bar.* 51:1-3, 10, 12; *4 Ezra* 7:97; additional references in SB 1:752-53; 4/2:941-42.

[266]Cf. Luz, *Matthäus* 2:509: 17:1-9 is a "'polyvalente' Geschichte."

[267]That Matt. 17:2-8 has more than one layer of meaning is nearly the consensus of the commentaries, which typically inform us that the Son of God's metamorphosis is proleptic of both the resurrection of Jesus and the general resurrection.

[268]Several texts teach that Moses shone for the same reason that angels do—he fed upon the splendor of the Shekinah. For Moses see *Exod. Rab.* 3:1; 47:5, 7; *Lev. Rab.* 20:10; *Num. Rab.* 2:25; *Pesiq. R. Kah.* 26:9. For the angels see *3 En.* 22:7, 13; *Num. Rab.* 21:16; *Pesiq. R. Kah.* 6:1. This matters because angelic existence was often held to be prophetic of the saints' heavenly future, and *b. Ber.* 17a expressly says that those who live in the world to come will feed upon the Shekinah; so the idea of feeding upon the Shekinah is common to the Sinai traditions and eschatology. Additional discussion in R. Chernus, *Mysticism in Rabbinic Judaism* (SJ 11; Berlin: de Gruyter, 1982), 74-87. Chernus rightly infers that the Merkabah mystics, who sometimes claimed that their ecstatic experiences involved feeding upon the Shekinah (*Ma 'aseh Merkabah* 3 for example), must have thought of themselves as reliving Sinai and anticipating paradise.

depicted for you a parable: his cheeks, ashen with age, became shining and fair, a symbol of old age that in Eden becomes young." I am satisfied that Jesus' transfiguration moves thoughts both backward and forward in time: it is a replay of Sinai and a foretaste of things to come.[269]

Seemingly the most cogent objection to the Mosaic interpretation of the transfiguration is this: many stories from antiquity attribute radiance to others besides Moses, so why should the motif be especially associated with him? *b. B. Bat.* 58a and *Gen. Rab.* on 2:4 tell us that Adam, before the fall, emanated light like the sun (cf. SB 4/2:887, 940-41). *Sefer ha-Yašar* recounts that the infant Abraham was transfigured. *b. B. Bat.* 75a speaks of Joshua's radiance. *Joseph and Aseneth* 18-20 purports that Aseneth, on her wedding day, was transformed into beauteous light. *LAB* 12:7 relates the fiction that those who were compelled against their wills to worship the golden calf were revealed by their shining faces. *Hist. Rech.* 11-12 says that the Rechabites "dwell in light" and are covered with a covering of glory "similar to that which clothed Adam and Eve before they sinned." *ARN* B 13 records that R. Eliezer once had a visible aura. For the same phenomenon in Christian documents see Acts 6:15 (cf. Add Est. 15:13-14); *Acts of Paul and Thecla* 3; *Mart. of Montanus and Lucius* ll; PG 65, Arsenius 27; Joseph of Penephysis 7; Pambo 1, 12; Silvanus 12; and Sisoes 14. Lastly, there are pagan parallels. One example: Marinus, *Proclus* 3 (Proclus' "appearance was most agreeable, for not only did he possess the beauty of just proportions, but from his soul exuded a certain living light, or miraculous efflorescence, which shone over his whole body, which is quite indescribable"); *ibid.* 23 (when Proclus taught "it seemed that his eyes filled with a shining splendor, and all over his face spread rays of divine illumination").

In view of all the evidence, it must be conceded that the motif of radiance was far from being exclusively associated with Moses. But knowledge of this fact does not disturb my contention, for it must also be admitted that, on the other hand, the emission of light *was* sometimes understood to harken back to Moses. The luminosity of Abraham

---

[269]Cf. the recent interpretation of Stegner, *Narrative Theology*, 83-103. —For texts which give Sinai eschatological associations or which transfer its imagery to the end see Isa. 2:1-4; 4:2-6; *l En.* l; 25:3, 5; Rev. 4:5; *Liv. Proph. Jer.* 11-19; *b. Ber.* 17a; *Pesiq. R. Kah.* 37a, 144b. The giving of the law at Sinai came more and more to resemble an apocalyptic event; cf. *LAB* 11:3; *4 Ezra* 3:18-19; *b. Zeb.* 116a. It has sometimes been offered that the *parousia* scene in l Thess. 4:15-17 was modelled upon Exod. 19:10-18; see J. Dupont,ΣYN XPIΣTΩI (Bruges: Editiones de l'Abbaye de Saint-Andre, l952), 64-73.

in *Sefer ha Yašar* belongs to an extensive Moses typology (see p. 91, n. 209); and the legend that Joshua shone like the moon was based upon the belief that Moses gave to him some of his glory:[270] "'And you shall put some of your honor upon him' (Num. 17:20), but not all your honor. The elders of that generation said: The countenance of Moses was like that of the sun, the countenance of Joshua like that of the moon" (*b. B. Bat.* 75a). Note also the following, from *PG* 65, Pambo 12: "They said of Abba Pambo that he was like Moses, who received the glory of Adam when his face shone. His face shone like lightening and he was like a king sitting on his throne." This associates not only Pambo and Moses but Moses and Adam, an association also attested in Ephrem, *Comm. on Gen.* 2:15: "Just as Israel was unable to look upon the face of Moses, so were the animals unable to look at the radiance of Adam and Eve. When they (the animals) received their names they passed in front of Adam with their eyes cast down." Lastly, a seventeenth century example: however the circumstance be understood, Sabbatai Sevi was thought by many who saw him to have a face of fire—and the sources explicitly connect this with Moses. Baruch of Arezzo reported: envoys from Poland "saw his face shining with a great light, like the face of our teacher Moses."[271] Sabbatai Sevi's brothers likewise testified: "After being anointed messiah by the patriarchs, his face was exceedingly bright and shining, like the face of Moses after the giving of the law."[272] It is my contention that just as Sabbateans associated their savior's sun-like face with the lawgiver, so was it with the early believers of Jesus. Although radiance was not, in the environment of ancient Christianity, invariably a Mosaic motif, the confluence of circumstantial details between Matt. 17:1-9 par. and Exodus 24 and 34 means that the mount of transfiguration was, for the evangelists, including Matthew, a second Sinai, where a miracle of old was repeated.

One final point. It is natural to see in 17:1-9 the greater than Moses theme; for, at the last, Moses and Elijah disappear, and the reader is left with the command to "hear him," that is, the one Son of God, Jesus. Care must nonetheless be taken not to press this or that detail in an attempt to exalt Jesus over Moses. Jesus' superiority to Moses is only a very minor theme of the transfiguration narrative. Maybe it is worth remarking that there is one particular which could be used, if one were

---

[270]Cf. LXX Num. 27:20 and the targumim on that verse; also *Sipre Num.* § 140.
[271]Scholem, *Sabbatai Sevi*, 132.
[272]Ibid., 142.

so inclined, to exalt Moses over Jesus. Matthew's text says nothing about a veil, and it is plain that Jesus' luminosity was temporary. But the targumim on Deut. 34:7 affirm that Moses did not lose his glory: it stayed with him until death (cf. *Tg. Onk.* and *Tg. Neofiti* on Num. 27:20). Similarly, *LAB* 19:16 has Moses transfigured on Pisgah as well as Sinai.[273] The Bible itself teaches that Moses' glory did not forsake him:

> But whenever Moses had went in before the Lord to speak with him, he took the veil off, until he came out; and when he came out, and told the people of Israel what he was commanded, the people of Israel saw the face of Moses, that the skin of Moses' face shone; and Moses would put the veil upon his face again, until he went in to speak with him (Exod. 34:34-35).

Thus whereas the visual glory of Jesus was fleeting, that of Moses endured.[274] Now I do not at all imply that this fact matters for the interpretation of Matt. 17:1-9. The point is rather that had matters been reversed, so that it was Moses, not Jesus, who lost his radiance, the commentators would have made much of it. There are, however, always differences between a type and its antitype, either of which can be, depending upon predilection, promoted or demoted by inventive interpretation. This fact should warn. The superiority of Jesus to Moses is an assumption of our Gospel more than it is an assertion, and it is not to be discovered in every exegetical nook and cranny.

THE ARRIVAL IN JERUSALEM (21:1-17)

According to Matt. 21:1-17, Jesus entered Jerusalem to public acclaim. To illuminate the event, the evangelist quoted from Zech. 9:9, which contains this: "Behold, your king comes to you." The word "king" signals a major theme of the passage, a theme reinforced by the crowds' chant of "Hosanna to the Son of David" (v. 9, quoting Ps. 118:25; cf. v. 15).

In addition to playing a royal rôle, Jesus is also "the prophet:" "And the crowds said, 'This is the prophet Jesus from Nazareth of Galilee" (v. 11). This confession, redactionally inserted, is neither false nor

---

[273]Cf. *Deut. Rab.* 11:3; *Memar Marqah* 5:4. Additional references in Ginzberg, *Legends* 3:93, 119, 143, 438; 6:37, 204, 50, n. 260, 60, n. 309, 6l, n. 311.

[274]There are, however, also texts according to which Moses' radiance gradually diminished or was given to Joshua; see Belleville, *Reflections of Glory*, 67, 75.

superficial. Although it does not convey the whole truth (what one title does that?), it is true as far as it goes: Jesus is indeed "the prophet" (cf. p. 313).

Two initial observations raise the possibility of a Mosaic background for Matt. 21:1ff. The first is this: v. 11 uses a definite article. Jesus is not *prophētēs* but *ho prophētēs*, not "a prophet" but "the prophet." This could well advert to the expectation of the prophet like Moses (as in John 6:14).[275] Secondly, the prophetic and kingly offices are here present at once, which matters because Wayne Meeks has documented the rich tradition—found in Philonic, rabbinic, and Samaritan sources—that depicts Moses as the prophet-king, and that tradition is of some importance for Johannine Christology. Are matters perhaps similar in the First Gospel?

21:4-5 preserves one of the so-called formula quotations:

> This took place to fulfil what was spoken by the prophet, saying, "Tell the daughter of Zion, Behold, your king is coming to you, humble, and mounted on an ass, and on a colt, the foal of an ass" (Zech. 9:9).

Schoeps and Teeple, in their reviews of the new Moses theme in Matthew, both heard in the quotation from Zechariah definite Mosaic echoes. Why? Because rabbinic tradition drew a parallel between Exod. 4:20 ("So Moses took his wife and his sons and set them on an ass, and went back to the land of Egypt; and in his hand Moses took the rod of God") and Zech. 9:9 ("Rejoice greatly, O daughter of Zion! Shout aloud, O daughter of Jerusalem! Lo, your king come to you; triumphant and victorious is he, humble and riding on an ass, on a colt the foal of an ass"):

> Rabbi Berekiah said in the name of Rabbi Isaac: "As the first redeemer was, so shall the latter Redeemer be. What is stated of the former redeemer? And Moses took his wife and his sons, and set them upon an ass (Exod. 4:20). Similarly will it be with the latter Redeemer, as it is stated, Lowly and riding upon an ass (Zech. 9:9; *Eccles. Rab.* 1:28; cf. *Sam. Rab.* 14:9 (45b); *Pirke R. El.* 31).

One could, then, interpret the fulfillment of Zechariah's oracle as establishing Jesus' status as Mosaic Messiah.

Discordant with this congenial conjecture, however, is the relatively late date of the requisite rabbinic traditions: proof of their early circulation is lacking. In addition, the LXX does not draw any obvious lines of connection between Exod. 4:20 and Zech. 9:9, so most com-

[275]Cf. Teeple, *Prophet*, 83.

mentators have either ignored or rejected the suggestion that the
messianic ass of Matt. 21:9 possesses Mosaic associations.[276] But there
is much more to our issue than these mitigating facts.

(i) Exod. 4:20 stands behind a portion of Matthew's infancy narrative and there it promotes a typological correlation between the
Messiah and Moses.[277]

(ii) 21:5 depicts Jesus as "meek" (*praus*). The same adjective occurs
in 5:5, where it may or may not recall Moses, and in 11:29, where the
Mosaic aura is manifest. So there has already been preparation for
understanding Jesus' meekness to mark him as one like Moses.

(iii) The following appears in Matt. 21:15-16:

> But when the chief priests and the scribes saw the wonderful things that
> he did, and the children crying out in the temple, "Hosanna to the Son
> of David!" they were indignant; and they said to him, "Do you hear
> what these are saying?" And Jesus said to them, "Yes; have you never
> read, 'Out of the mouth of babes and sucklings thou hast brought
> perfect praise'?"

Why the insertion of this episode, with its quotation of Ps. 8:3?[278] Safely
ignoring the poltry proposal that it adds "local color,"[279] I submit that
the answer lies in the Moses traditions. The *Mekilta* on Exod. 15:1 cites
Ps. 8:3 in connection with the exodus and interprets "you have
ordained ('ôz"[280] to refer to song (cf. LXX: *ainon*). It thus links Psalm 8
with the song of Exodus 15. The exegetical conflation is not peculiar to
the *Mekilta*. Because 'oz is common to Exod. 15:2 and Ps. 8:3, the two
texts were often brought together, and from this developed[281] the well-
attested belief that, at the Red Sea, children praised God. *t. Sota* 6:4 has
this:

> R. Jose the Galilean says: When the Israelites came up out of the sea…
> they recited a song of praise. When the babe lying on its mother's lap
> and the suckling at his mother's breast saw the divine presence, the
> former raised his neck and the latter let go of his mother's breast, and
> they all responded with a song of praise, saying, "This is my God, and

---

[276]Cf. Davies, *Setting*, 59-60.

[277]See pp. 142-44. The omission of the donkey from Matt. 2:19-21 *could* be explained
by a desire to save it for the entry.

[278]There is a remote parallel in Luke 19:39-40: "And some of the Pharisees in the
multitude said to him, 'Teacher, rebuke your disciples.' He answered, 'I tell you, if these
were silent, the very stones would cry out.'" Two differences are, for our purposes, very
important: Luke refers neither to children nor to Psalm 8:3.

[279]So Lindars, *Apologetic*, 204.

[280]The first meaning of ôz is "strength," but it can also mean "stronghold" (BDB, s.v.).

[281]Or did the story exist before its exegetical foundation?

I will glorify him." R. Meier said, even foetuses in their mother's wombs sang a song of praises (cf. *b. Ber.* 56b; *b. Sota* 30b; *Targ. Yer.* on Exod. 15:2; *Midr. Ps.* 8:5).

The pre-Matthean genesis of this tradition is vouched for by Wisd. 10:21, according to which, when Israel crossed the Red Sea, Wisdom "rendered the tongues of infants articulate" (*glōssas nēpiōn ethēken tranas*). Matthew, it follows, inserted into his story of Jesus a motif— the supernatural singing of children as recorded in Psalm 8—that recognizably belonged to another story. In this circumstance I see yet one more attempt to conform Jesus to Moses: their lives were marked by parallel events.

(iv) 21:15 informs us that the high priests and the scribes saw *ta thaumasia ha epoiēsen*, the wonders which Jesus did. The words ring remembrance of the very last verse in the Pentateuch, where we read of *ta thaumasi... ha epoiēse Mōusēs*. Is the parallel inadvertent, or one of those seemingly minute singularities imbued with typological meaning?

(v) Matt. 21:5 purports that Jesus rode on "an ass and on a colt, the foal of an ass." This is strange indeed. How does a man, unless he is performing a stunt, ride two animals at once? The Christian artistic tradition, in its main types of the entry, has usually depicted just one ass. When a second is shown, it is an unridden youngster behind the adult.[282] But how then did Matthew come to write what he did? Two heads are better than one, for obvious reasons. Not so obvious is why Matthew thought the same of donkeys. Did he multiply one ass (so Mark) by two for the same unfathomable reason that he turned the one demoniac of Mark 5:1-17 into two demoniacs, or can we perchance recover his intention?

I should like to offer a solution which, if memory serves, I have not read elsewhere. Both MT Exod. 4:20 and MT Zech. 9:9 plainly refer to one animal. LXX Zech. 9:9, on the other hand, is ambiguous: while one animal is probably in view, one could, if so inclined, take it to refer to two. What of LXX Exod. 4:20? In disagreement with the Hebrew, it plainly has Moses return to Egypt with *hypozygmia*, beasts. Now because LXX Exod. 4:20 has been absorbed into the infancy narrative, we may suspect the evangelist paid it some attention, and perhaps the verse holds the key to the locked door of Matt. 21:5. My suggestion is this: according to the principle that the last things are as the first, and

---

[282]G. Schiller, *Iconography of Christian Art*, vol. 2 (Greenwich, Conn.: New York Graphic Society, 1968), 18-23 and plates 31-50.

according to the interpretive methods of his day, which encouraged the association of two texts sharing a common word, our evangelist, like later rabbinic exegetes, connected Zech. 9:9 with Exod. 4:20; and by interpreting one text in the light of the other and bringing to bear a harmonizing hermeneutic, the ambiguous LXX Zech. 9:9 was made to refer to two animals because of the plural *hypozygmia* of LXX Exod. 4:20. I freely confess that my proposal cannot be proven. But it is far more likely than that Matthew could not make out the meaning of a biblical text (whether in Hebrew or Greek), or that he mentioned two donkeys because Mark's *neon* implied a colt and its mother, or that he just happened to know the true historical circumstances and deemed them worthy of accurate record. Certainly elsewhere Matthew read one Scripture in the light of another and conflated biblical texts (see the commentaries on 2:6; 3:17; and 27:9-10).[283]

(vi) The extent to which Moses was popularly associated with an ass can perhaps be gauged from this, that the association appears even in pagan literature. Tacitus, *Hist.* 5:3, wrote that Moses found water in the wilderness by following a herd of wild asses. The following comes from Diodorus Siculus:

> When Antiochus... made war against the Jews he entered the sacred shrine of the god, where only the priest is allowed to go. In it he found a stone image of a thick bearded man seated on an ass and holding a book in his hand. He assumed that it was a statue of Moses who founded Jerusalem (34.1).

Whether or not this last should be traced to Poseidonius, and whether or not it is a perverted version of some Jewish tradition, there was a pagan belief that Jews worshiped an ass.[284] That belief, needless to say, was uninformed slander. But we should not doubt that Moses was indeed remembered within Judaism, as without, as a man who rode upon an ass (cf. Exod. 4:20; *Gen. Rab.* on 32:6; *Pirqe R. El.* 31).

Although I do not wish to dogmatize, I am persuaded, in view of the evidence recapitulated above, that the new Moses theme is part and parcel of Matt. 21:1ff. The narrative is, in important respects, akin to John 6, where the comparison and contrast with Moses is explicit. In John the crowd acclaims Jesus "the prophet" (v. 14) and seeks to make

---

[283]According to John P. Meier, *Law and History in Matthew's Gospel* (AnBib 71; Rome: Biblical Institute, 1976), 17, Matthew must have misunderstood the Hebrew parallelism of Zechariah because no "theological purpose or symbolic meaning" can be found in the doubling of the animals. If I am correct, Meier is incorrect.

[284]See Victor Tcherikover, *Hellenistic Civilization and the Jews* (New York: Atheneum, 1970), 365-66.

him king (v. 15) while Jesus, for his part, acts in ways which remind one of Moses. What of Matthew? Here too Jesus shows himself to be like the lawgiver, with the result that the crowd concludes that he must be "the prophet" (v. 11) and should be made king (v. 9; cf. v. 15). Both Matthew and John, I believe, interpreted Jesus to be, among other things, the prophet-king like Moses.

CHAPTER 23

Two propositions may be dismissed at once. The first, offered by Hahn and Garland, that Jesus is, according to 23:2 + 8-10, the only rigthful occupant of the chair of Moses, reads too much into the text;[285] and the second, forwarded by Dabeck and Le Déaut,[286] that the beatitudes of 5:1-12, taken in conjunction with the woes of chapters 23, correspond to the blessings and curses of Deuteronomy 27 and 28, falls before Davies' words:

> Neither in order, number, content nor audience is there here any real parallel. Curses and Blessings in Deuteronomy are invoked upon all Israel: in Matthew on the Pharisees and the "New Israel" respectively; in Deuteronomy Curses and Blessings occur in close propinquity: in Matthew they are divided. Matt. vii. 24-27 does indeed offer a miniature parallel, of a loose kind, to Deut. xxvii, xxviii, but recourse to this parallelism is not necessary because Blessings and Curses were a common feature of first-century Judaism, rabbinic and sectarian.[287]

But there might, one could argue, still be a sideglance at Moses in vv. 8-10, where "rabbi" (*rabbî* = *didaskalos*, v. 8) and "teacher" (*kathēgētēs*, v. 10) are reserved for Jesus.[288] In rabbinic sources Moses is, sufficiently often to render documentation superfluous, *rabbenû*, "our teacher." Should we then entertain the notion that Jesus—"you have one teacher, Christ," v. 10—has stripped Moses of his traditional title and usurped his office? Perhaps so; but I harbor reservations. The emphasis of 23:8-10 is manifestly upon contemporary, not ancient authorities: "*You* are not to be called rabbi," "nor are *you* to be called teacher." The

---

[285]Hahn, *Titles*, 386, 405-406, and David E. Garland, *The Intention of Matthew 23* (NovTSup 52; Leiden: E. J. Brill, 1979), 60-61. Cf. Dabeck, "Moses und Elias," 176.

[286]See Dabeck, *ibid.*, and Le Déaut, *Pascale*, 314-15. Dabeck obtained seven beatitudes by following M.-J. Lagrange, *Evangile selon saint Matthieu*, 7th ed. (Paris: J. Gabalda, 1948), 80-81, where it is argued that 5:11-12 only develop v. 10 and that the Greek translator added a beatitude.

[287]*Setting*, 60.

[288]The "one teacher" of 23:8 is not God but Jesus.

text just does not address the subject of what to call biblical worthies. 23:9, for instance, makes "father" the exclusive property of God. Does this really require displeasure with Luke's Lazarus, who addresses the patriarch in whose bosom he dwells as "Father Abraham" (Luke 16:24)? Elsewhere Jesus, who is the disciple's constant example, and the evangelist himself, display no reluctance to use "father" with traditional biological sense; see 4:21; 10:35-37; 15:4-5; 19:29. How then can the compass of Matt. 23:8-10 be unbounded? A literal and unrestricted application would entail censorship of all in the Jewish Bible who call anyone save God "father"—unthinkable for Matthew. The inevitable conclusion is that one hesitates to include within the circumference of the hyperbolic 23:8-10 any but contemporary religious leaders; and therefore it is problematic to discover in those verses, with their characteristic overstatement, the detachment of a traditional title from Moses and its exclusive transfer to Jesus. The concern of the passage lies elsewhere.

THE ESCHATOLOGICAL DISCOURSE
(MATT. 24:3)

The tradition that, on Mount Sinai, Moses gathered eschatological secrets and beheld the future, is known from several sources. *Jub.* 1:1-4 is one such source:

> In the first year of the exodus of the children of Israel from Egypt, in the third month on the sixteenth day of that month, the Lord spoke to Moses, saying, "Come up to me on the mountain, and I shall give you two stone tablets of the Law and the commandment, which I have written, so that you may teach them." And Moses went up to the mountain of the Lord. And the glory of the Lord dwelt upon Mount Sinai.... And the Lord revealed to him both what was in the beginning and what will occur in the future, the account of the division of all of the days of the law and the testimony.

Related accounts appear in the *Exagogue of Ezekiel* (see p. 177), *LAB* 19; *4 Ezra* 4:5; *2 Baruch* 4; *Sipre Deut.* § 357; *Tg. Ps.-Jn.* on Deut. 34:1; and *Memar Marqah* 5:3. The *Temple Scroll* may also be cited, for it is the record of a revelation ostensibly given to Moses on Sinai (cf. 51:6-7), a revelation which included what is to come (e.g. column 29).

Moses is not the sole individual in old Jewish sources to receive, while on a mountain, revelation of future events. Mention may also be made of Abraham (*Apoc. Abraham* 21-23), Naphtali (*T. Naph.* 5:1-8), Baruch (*2 Bar.* 13:1), and Ezekiel, whose vision of the heavenly temple was reviewed in chapter 2. It is conspicuous that of the four persons just named, three were, in the sources just cited, likened to Moses. For the evidence I refer to what has been said on pp. 50-53 (Ezekiel), 65-68 (Baruch), and 91 (Abraham). Clearly Sinai was, before and after the first century, the prototypical mountain of future revelation.[289]

This raises a question for the student of Matthew. Is Sinai typologically present in Matthew 24? Here too knowledge of the future is granted on a mountain: "As he sat on the Mount of Olives, the disciples came to him privately, saying, 'Tell us, when will this be, and what will be the sign of your coming and of the close of the age?'" Prediction after prediction follows.

Two observations. First, Jesus is not only on a mountain but sitting on a mountain, which gives the reader a feeling of familiarity, for this has happened before: in both 5:1-2 and 15:29, where the new Moses theme is present, Jesus also sits on a mountain. Secondly, "the close of the age" (*synteleias tou aiōnos*—redactional) "appears also in 28:20 in a strikingly similar context: Jesus on a mountain giving instructions to his disciples for the period leading up to the close of the age. So it is apparent that in Matthean thought these two mountain scenes were linked together."[290] We shall have occasion soon enough to observe that the mountain scene of 28:16-20, like those in 5:1-2 and 15:29, contains Mosaic features, which means that those who read and reread Matthew will link 24:3 with at least three other passages, in all of which Jesus is like Moses. So what then of 24:3? Does it too add to Matthew's Moses typology?

I am unsure. Redaction criticism is unable in this instance to offer confirmation, for it cannot report any significant importations into Matthew's source which might betray an interest in Moses. The mountain, the sitting, and the revelation were all to hand in Mark. Further, whereas Mark 13:3 has Jesus sit *eis to oros*, Matt. 24:3 has him sit *epi tou orous ton elaiōn*. The changes, from *oros* to *orous* and from *eis* to *epi*, while fully understandable grammatically, distance the text from both 5:1-2 and 15:29. In these last we have (i) a form of *anabainō* + (ii) *eis to oros* (unspecified) + (iii) *kathēmai/kathizō*; and while our evangelist could readily have composed Matt. 24:3 to conform to this pattern, he did not: *anabainō* is missing, *epi tous orous* replaces Mark's *eis to oros*, the mountain is specified (it is "the mount of Olives"), and *kathēmai* is in initial position. Hence if Matthew did indeed want his

---

[289]Cf. Donaldson, *Mountain*, 72.
[290]Donaldson, *Mountain*, 158.

readers to tie threads from 24:3 back to 15:29 and 5:1-2 and so associate the eschatological discourse with Mosaic passages, he did nothing to assist them in their endeavor. For this cause, then, I cannot pass beyond the interrogatory mode: should Matt. 24:3, where Jesus sits on a mountain and reveals the future, summon the specter of Moses?

THE LAST SUPPER (26:17-30)

According to Northrop Frye, "the Gospels could hardly be more careful than they are to synchronize the Crucifixion with the feast of the Passover, to make it utterly clear that the Passion, as they saw it, was the antitype of the Passover sacrifice."[291] The words are true enough if one is referring to John. But in the synoptics it is the last supper, not the crucifixion itself, that is, strictly speaking, synchronized with the Passover proper. Thomas Hobbes wrote:

> And for the other Sacrifice, of eating the Paschall Lambe, it is manifestly imitated in the Sacrifice of the Lords Supper, in which the Breaking of the Bread, and the pouring out of the Wine, do keep in memory our deliverance from the Misery of Sin, by Christs Passion, as the eating of the Paschall Lambe, kept in memory the deliverance of the Jews out of Bondage of Egypt. Seeing therefore the authority of Moses was but subordinate, and hee but a Lieutenant to God; it followeth, that Christ, whose authority, as man, was to bee like that of Moses, was no more but subordinate to the authority of his Father (*Leviathan* 41).

It is natural enough to associate the man who instituted the Lord's supper with the man who instituted the passover—and Hobbes was certainly not the first to do so. According to Ferdinand Hahn, the paschal expectations of the early church, which so influenced the tradition of the Lord's supper, belonged "to the total complex of the idea of Jesus as the eschatological prophet and the new Moses."[292] This association posits the paschal character of the Lord's supper as a corollary of Jesus' status as the eschatological prophet like Moses. Is there any evidence that Matthew himself posited such, or that he in any way viewed the Jesus of Matt. 26:17-30 as Mosaic?

Let us begin with 26:17-19:

> Now on the first day of Unleavened Bread the disciples came to Jesus, saying, "Where will you have us prepare for you to eat the passover?" He said, "Go into the city to such a one, and say to him, 'The Teacher

[291]*Code*, 173.
[292]*Christology*, 383-84. Cf. Salhin, "New Exodus," 93-94.

says, My time is at hand; I will keep the passover at your house with my disciples.'" And the disciples did as Jesus had directed them, and they prepared the passover.

The puzzle of whether the last supper was in fact, as this pericope seemingly requires, a passover meal, has furrowed many brows. John 13:1-4 and 18:28 appear to assume it was not; and certain features in the synoptics themselves have been thought incongruent with Matt. 26:17-19 par. and rather in harmony with John. We need not, however, wait for a judgement on that issue here. The crucial point is that, however it really was, Matthew's own conviction is patent: the last supper was a passover meal.

This is crucial because passover was a remembrance of the exodus, a retelling of the drama of Israel's redemption during the days of Moses—and those who remembered the exodus relived it. "In every generation let each one of us look to himself as though he came forth from Egypt" (*m. Pesah.10:5*). *To participate in the passover ritual was to internalize and enter into the past:* "*We* were Pharaoh's slaves in Egypt, and the Lord our God brought *us* forth from there with a mighty hand and an outstretched arm" (the *Passover Haggadah*). So Matthew's narrative, by informing us that Jesus observed the passover, implies that he too suffered exile, endured slavery, and celebrated freedom. In other words, he ritually made present events from the life of Moses. Now given this, and given Matthew's penchant for embedding in his narrative parallels between the first redeemer and the last, did he here indulge that penchant once more? Did he, as we might anticipate, take advantage of the opportunity afforded him by a story in which Jesus commemorates the release from Egyptian bondage?

Most modern commentators detect three scriptural allusions in Matt. 26:26-29—to Exod. 24:8, to Isa. 53:11-12,[293] to Jer. 31:31-34.[294] While in this they are probably correct, it must be conceded that only a parallel of thought, not language, exists between the synoptic passage and Jer. 31:31-34,[295] and the correlation with Isa. 53:11-12 is

---

[293]According to Schoeps, *Theologie*, 94-95, the suffering of Jesus, interpreted against Isaiah 53, corresponds to the traditions, based upon Exod. 32:32 ("But now, if thou will forgive their sin—and if not, blot me, I pray thee, out of thy book which thou has written"), that Moses offered himself as an atoning redeemer (see p. 69 above): "The primitive community must have understood Deut. 18:15 precisely as an announcement through Moses of the suffering of Jesus (so Luke 24:27, 44; Acts 26:22)" (p. 95). This is not an opinion that has commended itself to others.

[294]See Robert H. Gundry, *The Use of the Old Testament in St. Matthew's Gospel* (NovTSup 18; Leiden: E. J. Brill, 1967), 57-59.

[295]See Wolff, *Jeremia*, 131-34.

imperfect, especially if the LXX is consulted.[296] The only absolutely certain and unambiguous echo of Scripture is to be heard in the phrase, *to haima mou tēs diatēkēs*. These words are unmistakably from Exod. 24:8: "Moses took the blood and dashed it on the people, and said, 'See the blood of the covenant (LXX: *to haima tēs diatēkēs*) that the Lord has made with you in accordance with all these words." Does this fact not invite us to imagine a typological correspondence? Through blood Moses was the mediator of the old covenant. Through blood Jesus is the mediator of the new covenant.

But all this was already given by Matthew's tradition, and the redaction critic wants to find some sign that our author himself thought of Jesus as Moses' antitype in 26:17-30. According to Davies, no such sign exists. Matthew made "certain liturgical improvements," added "with you" in v. 29, and introduced "the forgiveness of sins," a phrase "probably intended to connect 'the blood of the covenant' with the New Covenant of Jer. xxxi.31f." (which ends with "I will forgive their iniquity, and remember their sin no more"). Therefore nothing in Matthew's account "necessarily point[s] to an emphasis on the Exodus motif as such."[297] The issue, however, is not so easily settled.

The LXX for Jer. 31:34 (36:33) reads: *hileōs esomai tais adikiais autōn kai tōn hamartiōn autōn ou me mnēsthō eti*. Only one word—*hamartia*—is shared with Matt. 26:28. Perhaps that suffices to constitute an allusion as the thought is the same: God will forgive sins. But there may well be a better explanation for Matthew's addition of "for the forgiveness of sins." I have already noted that the allusion to Exod. 24:8 is much firmer than that to Jer. 31:31-33. I should now like to raise the possibility that *eis aphesin hamartiōn* is to be connected with the former, not the latter.

Exod. 24:8 says nothing at all about the forgiveness of sins. It is, however, otherwise with targums *Onkelos* and *Pseudo-Jonathan* (but not *Neofiti*). The former reads: "And Moses took blood... and sprinkled it upon the altar *to make atonement* for the people and he said: Behold the blood of the covenant which the Lord has made with you in all these words." The currency in the first century of this interpretation of the Sinai offering as expiatory is guaranteed by Heb. 9:19-22, where it is taken for granted that the blood Moses sprinkled was for

---

[296]Pesch, *Abendmahl*, 96.
[297]*Setting*, 59.

the forgiveness of sins. Perhaps, then, Matthew's addition of "for the forgiveness of sins" does indeed reflect the influence of Exod. 24:8.

A second possible pointer in the direction of Moses is 26:19: "And the disciples did as Jesus had directed them, and they prepared the passover." The Greek is: *kai epoiēsan hoi mathētai hōs synetaxen autois ho Iēsous kai hētoimasan to pascha.* Except for the final four words, this differs considerably from its ostensible source, Mark 14:16: "And the disciples set out and went to the city, and found it as he had told them; and they prepared the passover." Matthew's sentence is much closer to Matt. 1:24 and 21:6. But it also has a good parallel in Exod. 12:28: "Then the people of Israel went and did so; as the Lord had commanded Moses and Aaron, so they did." Both the structure and vocabulary of this resemble Matt. 26:19:

Matthew	MT/LXX
kai epoiēsan	*wayya(ăśû / kai… epoiēsan*
hoi mathētai	*běnē-Yiśrā)ēl / hoi huiou Israēl*
hōs	*ka)ăšer / katha*
synetaxen	*siwwâ / eneteilato*
autois	*YHWH / Kurios*
ho Iēsous	*et-Mōšeh wě)ăhărōn / tō Mōusē kai Aarōn*

I would be content to dismiss the linguistic resemblances as coincidence were it not for a conjunction of content: just as Matt. 26:19 concludes Jesus' directions for passover preparation, so too does Exod. 12:28 follow Moses' instructions for *pesah.* Is this just happenstance?

A third consideration stimulates even more reflection. Matthew's version of the last supper is foreshadowed by two stories, the feeding of the five thousand and the feeding of the four thousand.[298] Observe the following parallels between 14:13-21 and 26:20-29:

The feeding of the five thousand	The last supper
opsias de genomenēs	*opsias de genomenēs*
anaklithenai	*anekeito*
labōn	*labōn*
artous	*arton*
eulogesen	*eulogēsas*

[298]See esp. Gundry, *Matthew*, 289-95.

klasas   eklasen
edoken tois mathetais   dous tois mathētais/edōken autois
ephagon   phagete
pantes   pantes

These parallels, which appear in precisely the same order in the two passages and which extend beyond those in Mark,[299] demonstrate that the feeding of the five thousand was for Matthew an allegory of the eucharist.

Whenever one text anticipates another, the result is mutual enrichment: both are colored by each other. How does this work in the present instance? Two stories in which, it seems, Jesus is Mosaic, foreshadow a narrative in which Jesus, like Moses, issues instructions for the preparation of passover and then mediates a covenant in blood for the forgiveness of sins. This must provoke thought. Can the last supper really be insulated from the evangelist's new Moses Christology?

The Mosaic interpretation of Matt. 26:17-30 which I tentatively propose has a striking parallel in Heb. 9:15-22:

> Therefore he is the mediator of a new covenant, so that those who are called may receive the promised eternal inheritance, since a death has occurred which redeems them from the transgressions under the first covenant. For where a will is involved, the death of the one who made it must be established. For a will takes effect only at death, since it is not in force as long as the one who made it is alive. Hence even the first covenant was not ratified without blood. For when every commandment of the law had been declared by Moses to all the people, he took the blood of calves and goats, with water and scarlet wool and hyssop, and sprinkled both the book itself and all the people, saying, "This is the blood of the covenant which God commanded you." And in the same way he sprinkled with the blood both the tent and all the vessels used in worship. Indeed, under the law almost everything is purified with blood, and without the shedding of blood there is no forgiveness of sins.

Here the surpassing self-sacrifice of Jesus is compared with the sprinkling of blood told of in Exod. 24:6-8. This is reminiscent of the comparison I suggest we should perhaps find in Matthew. Further, upon closer inspection the parallel is even more exact. Heb. 9:20 reads: "This is the blood of the covenant which (touto to haima tēs diathēkēs hēs)...". There is no "this is" (touto) in Exod. 24:8. The MT prefaces "the blood" with hinneh, the LXX with idou. Why the modification? The

---

[299]Matthew added opsias de genomenēs in 14:15 diff. Mark 6:35, and changed edidou (Mark 6:41) to edoken.

commentators who address the question usually return the obvious answer: we are to detect assimilation to the tradition of the Lord's supper (cf. Mark 14:22, 24; 1 Cor. 11:24-25).[300] But if this is correct, then the writer of Hebrews was put in mind of the Lord's supper when he likened Jesus' mediation of a new covenant in blood to the inauguration of the old covenant through Moses' sprinkling of blood. This is precisely what we may have in the First Gospel.

THE DEATH OF JESUS (MATT. 27:45-54)

Several strange things happened, so Matthew tells us, when Jesus died. The sun went dark (27:45). Then the temple veil was rent (27:51). Then the earth quaked (27:51). And then the dead rose up (27:52-53). What happened when Moses died? There are no prodigies at the end of Deuteronomy. Fancy, however, did not fail to make up the lack: it surrounded Moses' passing with a cascade of wonders. Tradition tells that the angels mourned, the heavens were shaken, lightnings flashed, and a heavenly voice spoke. The early circulation of such legends is guaranteed by *Pseudo-Philo* 19:16 ("the angels mourned at his (Moses') death, and the lightnings and the torches and the arrows went all together before him. And in that day the hymn of the heavenly hosts was not sung") and 2 *Bar.* 59:3 ("the heavens which are under the throne of the Mighty One were severely shaken when he [God] took Moses with him"). So one just might apprehend in the circumstances surrounding the crucifixion the visage of the lawgiver.

But I am of a different mind. Extraordinary phenomena were, in antiquity, eagerly added to the narratives of great men and the tales of their deaths. In this Moses was no one special. According to *T. Adam* 3:6 there was, when Adam expired, a thick darkness for seven days (cf. *LAE* 46). In 2 *En.* 67 a murk is said to have covered the earth when Enoch walked with God and was not, for God took him. Virgil wrote that when Julius Caesar was murdered on the ides of March, the sun was, from the sixth hour until night, in eclipse, and there was an earthquake (*Georgics* 1:463ff.). Ambrose reported that darkness coincided with the death of Theodosius I (*De Obitu Theodosii Oration* 1), and Marinus related the same of Proclus (*Proclus* 37). Various miracles also

---

[300]O. Michel, *Der Brief an die Hebräer* (6th ed.; Göttingen: Vandenhocek and Ruprecht, 1966), 319-20; C. Spicq, *L Épître aux Hébreux*, vol. 2 (EB; Paris: J. Gabalda, 1953), 264.

attended the deaths of certain rabbis.[301] One could go on and on: the theme belongs to world mythology and literature. Thus trees bloomed out of season and powder fell from the sky when Buddha slipped away, and as Francis of Assisi left the body, larks, otherwise only heralds of dawn, sang at night.

It is additionally problematic for the proposal under scrutiny that, of the four supernatural phenomena in Matt. 27:45-54—darkness, destruction of veil, earthquake, resurrection—only one (earthquake) has, to my knowledge, a parallel in the traditions of Moses' death.[302] No less unsettling is this: if the darkness at noon appears to fulfill the Day of the Lord oracle in Amos 8:9-10 ("I will make the sun go down at noon," "I will make it like mourning for an only son"), the rending of the veil seems to symbolize the end of the temple, while the earthquake in Jerusalem and the resurrection of the holy ones make real the prophetic texts in Ezek. 37:12 and Zech. 14:4-5[303]—all of which is to say: the signs in Matthew 27 are suffused with eschatological meaning. They are not Mosaic.

MATTHEW'S CONCLUSION (28:16-20)

Perhaps most modern commentators have detected in 28:16-20 an allusion to LXX Dan. 7:13-14, where the Son of man is given *exousia*. They are persuasive. Others, not so persuasive, have proposed that 2 Chron. 36:23 informs Matthew's closing sentences. But what about the persistent feeling, usually expressed in tentative fashion, that Matt. 28:16-20 should evoke the image of Moses?[304]

We may begin with the reference to "the mountain." This, even by itself, is suggestive; for we have previously seen that on at least four

---

[301]Paul Fiebig, *Jüdische Wundergeschichten des neutestamesntlichen Zeitalters* (Tübingen: J. C. B. Mohr, 1911), 38-49, 57-61.

[302]That the darkness of the crucifixion should not be connected with the plague of darkness in Egypt has been demonstrated by Davies, *Setting*, 84-85. Contrast Goldberg, *Christians and Jews*, 195.

[303]See on all this Dale C. Allison, Jr., *The End of the Ages has Come* (Philadelphia: Fortress, 1986), 26-33, 40-46.

[304]Cf. R. E. Brown, *A Risen Christ in Eastertime* (Collegeville: The Liturgical Press, 1991), 34 (cf. p. 37); Dabeck, "Moses," 176; R. T. France, *Matthew* (Tyndale New Testament Commentaries; Grand Rapids: Eerdmans,1985), 412; Gundry, *Matthew*, 593-94; B. J. Hubbard, *The Matthean Redaction of a Primitive Apostolic Commissioning* (SBLDS 19; Missoula: Society of Biblical Literature, 1974), 151-75; Ben F. Meyer, *The Church in Three Tenses* (Garden City: Doubleday, 1971), pp. 160-67; K. Smyth, "Matthew 28: Resurrection as Theophany," *ITQ* 42 (1975), 259-71.

occasions (4:8; 5:1-2; 15:29; 17:1-2) and perhaps five (24:3) Jesus' appearance on a mountain is joined to the new Moses theme. Given this recurrent connection, presumption inclines us to look for Moses also in 28:16-20—especially when it is added that Moses ended his earthly course on a mountain[305] and that of all the figures in the Christian Bible, Moses and Jesus are the two whose narratives, from beginning to end, are most punctuated by significant mountain scenes.

There is another reason for suspecting the new Moses motif to be present in 28:16-20. Following B. J. Hubbard, the pericope contains elements frequently attested in commissioning narratives found in the Hebrew Bible.[306] Hubbard's precise delineation of a well-defined *Gattung* is not, I admit, without problems; but his collection of commissioning stories which share common features is quite useful; and when one examines his data with our topic in mind, intriguing results emerge. Of the twenty-seven Hebrew Bible commissioning narratives studied, in five "the observance of all that God has commanded is mentioned. In four of these instances, the wording in the LXX is similar to that in Mt. 28:20.... ."[307] These are the four instances: Exod. 7:2 ("But you [Moses] will say to him [Pharaoh] all that I command you" [*panta hosa soi entellomai*]); Josh. 1:7 ("to observe and to do as Moses my servant commanded you" [*eneteilato soi*]); 1 Chron. 22:13 ("you will prosper if you are careful to do the ordinances and decisions which the Lord commanded [*eneteilato*] Moses for Israel"); and Jer. 1:7 ("and whatever I command you [*kai kata panta hosa ean enteilōmai soi*] you will speak").[308] Three of the four texts, as Hubbard observes, mention Moses. What he fails to remark is that the fourth, Jer. 1:1-l0, belongs to a Moses typology.[309] What follows? The imperative to do all that has been commanded, when it is part of an Old Testament commissioning story, and when the LXX uses *entellomai*, invariably mentions Moses or depends upon tradition about him. What then of Matthew?

It is crucial to notice that among the members of Hubbard's *Gattung*, three are about God, or God through Moses, commissioning the lawgiver's successor: Deut. 31:14-15, 23; Josh. 1:l-9.[310] Is there any particular relationship between Matt. 28:16-20 and these three pas-

---

[305]Deuteronomy 34; Josephus, *Ant.* 4:324; *LAB* 19:8, 16; *Liv. Proph. Jer.* 17; *Slavonic Life of Moses* 16.

[306]*The Matthean Redaction*, passim.

[307]Ibid., 91.

[308]Additional parallels, not found in commissioning narratives, include Exod. 29:35; 34:32; Deut. 1:3; and 2 Chron. 33:8—all of which are directly associated with Moses.

[309]See above, pp. 56-62.

[310]*Pace* Hubbard, Josh. 1:1-9 is the unit to be considered, not 1:1-11.

sages? There indeed is. If one subtracts from 28:16-20 the elements evidently drawn from Daniel 7[311] and those features which, because paralleled in other resurrection narratives, presumably derive from the appearance tradition,[312] these remain: the mountain, the command to go and disciple the nations, the imperative to observe all Jesus has commanded, and the promise of perpetual divine presence. We have already seen that the mountain recalls Moses. What of the other three items? All have parallels in Josh. 1:1-9. Josh. 1:2 tells Joshua to "go" (cf. LXX v. 9: *hou ean poreuē*) and cross the Jordan. Josh. 1:7 enjoins Joshua to "observe and to do as Moses my servant commanded you" (see above). And Josh. 1:9, the pericope's conclusion, promises God's presence: "for the Lord your God is with you where you go" (LXX: *meta sou Kurios ho theos sou eis panta hou ean poreuē*). Moreover, with the exception of 1 Chron. 22:1-16, where David is like Moses and Solomon like Joshua, and where Joshua 1 is being imitated,[313] only two commissioning narratives in the entire Hebrew Bible end with the promise of divine presence: Deut. 31:23 (God's commissioning of Joshua in the MT, Moses' commissioning of Joshua in the LXX) and Josh. 1:1-9 (God's commissioning of Joshua). As if that were not striking enough, there is, besides Josh. 1:1-9, only one other commissioning narrative in the LXX with the following four elements—*poreuomai*, repetitive *pas*, the instruction to do what has been commanded (with *entellomai*), and the promise of divine presence (with *meta*). That text is Jer. 1:1-l0, which, as already noted, is modelled upon the Moses traditions. Should we not then infer that Matt. 28:16-20 is, like 1 Chron. 22:1-16 and Jer. 1:1-l0, a commissioning narrative with Mosaic associations?

The case is bolstered by examination of *The Testament of Moses*. In this Moses, before he speaks of things to come, commissions Joshua (1:6-18). The text, which clearly combines the commissioning accounts of Deut. 31:14-15 and Josh. 1:1-9,[314] has Moses commence with this:

---

[311]"All authority in heaven and earth has been given to me" and "in the name of the Father, Son, and Holy Spirit" (see below).

[312]Appearance to the eleven (cf. Mark 16:14-18; Luke 24:36-49; John 20:19-23); recognition and doubt (cf. Mark 16:14-18; Luke 24:37, 41; John 20:24-29; the motif is traditional, but its expression in Matt. 28:17 [*prosekynēsan, edistasan*] is redactional; cf. 14:31-33); speech of the risen Lord. Also, the form, (a) setting, (b) appearance of Jesus, (c) disciples' response, (d) commission, and (e) promise, is traditional (cf. Mark 16:14-18; Luke 24:36-49; John 20:19-23).

[313]See above, pp. 37-39.

[314]Such a conflation was altogether natural: Josh. 1:1-9 incorporates almost all of Deut. 31:14-15, and literary dependence one way or the other, or composition by the same hand, is obvious.

"Go forward with all your strength, that you may do everything which has been commanded..." (*omnia quae mandata sunt ut facias*). These words strongly resemble Matt. 28:18-20, and they are embedded in a commissioning narrative, one delivered at the end of the speaker's earthly tenure. Moreover, the narrative emphasizes God's lordship (vv. 11-12), mentions "the nations" (v. 13—*gentes*), focuses on Joshua's study and preservation of the Mosaic Torah (vv. 16-17), and ends with a reference to "the consummation of the end of days" (*in consummatione exitus dierum*). So my contention, that Matthew used traditions about the commissioning of Joshua to formulate 28:16-20, where Jesus' followers are commissioned to go forth and teach the observance of all the commandments, can cite precedent: the author of *The Testament of Moses*, when working with Deuteronomy 31 and Joshua 1, constructed a commissioning narrative in many ways reminiscent of Matt. 28:16-20.

Having discovered the Mosaic background of 28:16-20, it remains to inquire to what degree that background should be attributed to Matthew himself as opposed to the tradition. Thus we come to the problem of tradition-history.

The attempts to assign 28:16-20 in its entirety to redaction, or to divine in it isolated sayings which Matthew brought together do not carry conviction.[315] Rather, beneath Matthew's conclusion there lies a pre-Matthean appearance story whose primitive form was, as Hubbard has argued, on the basis of his examination of the canonical appearances of Jesus to the eleven, probably not far from the following: "Jesus appeared to the eleven. When they saw him they were glad, though some disbelieved. Then he said: preach (the gospel) to all nations. (Baptize) in my name for the forgiveness of sins. (And behold,) I will send the Holy Spirit to you."[316] I would only add that "to all the nations" may be late, even Matthean. But that aside, how did the primitive narrative develop into what we know today? The scriptural background in Daniel 7 and Joshua 1 gives us important clues, although of course any solution must remain hypothetical.

J. Schaberg has plausibly urged that the liturgical formula, "in the name of the Father, the Son, and the Holy Spirit," developed out of a pre-Matthean midrash upon Daniel 7, a text which features a heavenly triad—the Ancient of Days, the one like a son of man, and the angels.[317]

[315]See J. P. Meier, "Two Disputed Questions in Matt 28:16-20," *JBL* 96 (1977):407-24.
[316]*The Matthean Redaction*, 122-23.
[317]*The Father, the Son, and the Holy Spirit* (SBLDS 61; Chico: Scholars Press, 1982), 111-41.

If her thesis be accepted and if, as seems most reasonable, the phrase in 28:18, *edothē moi pasa exousia en ouranō kai epi (tēs) gēs*, be assigned to tradition, not redaction,[318] then, we may infer, someone before Matthew interpreted the appearance story by relating it to Daniel's vision: Jesus is the vindicated Son of man. The revised account may have looked something like this: "Jesus appeared to the eleven. When they saw him they were glad, although some disbelieved. Then he said: 'All authority in heaven and earth has been given to me. Preach the gospel. Baptize in the name of the Father, the Son, and the Holy Spirit. (And behold,) I will send the Holy Spirit to you.'"

What is the difference between this and Matt. 28:16-20? There are, apart from the specification of Galilee (dictated by the adoption of Mark 14:28 and 16:7), four main elements missing from our hypothetical second stage: the setting on a mountain, the command to go and make disciples, the order to do all that Jesus commanded, and the assurance of Christ's presence. Now we have already considered these four elements—and they are precisely what gives the pericope its Mosaic aura. So a third stage of the tradidition, we may justly surmise, reinterpreted the appearance of Jesus to his own in terms of Moses' commissioning of Joshua.

There is every reason to identify the third stage with the redactional stage,[319] so that the Mosaic features and the editorial additions coincide. It follows that Matthew designed his conclusion so as to generate an implicit parallel between Jesus and Moses. Just as the lawgiver, at the close of his life, commissioned Joshua both to go into the land peopled by foreign nations and to observe all the commandments in the law, and then further promised his successor God's abiding presence, so similarly Jesus: at the end of his earthly ministry he told his disciples to go into all the world and teach observance of all the commandments uttered by the new Moses; and then he promised his abiding presence.[320]

[318]See Meier, "Disputed Questions," 410, 413-14.

[319]See further W. D. Davies and Dale C. Allison, Jr., "Matt. 28:16-20: Texts Behind the Text," *RHPR* 72 (1992):89-98—parts of which I have here reproduced.

[320]There was, as is well known, a tradition that Moses did not die but rather, like Enoch and Elijah, ascended to heaven; see Christopher Begg, "'Josephus's Portrayal of the Disappearance of Enoch, Elijah, and Moses': Some Observations," *JBL* 109 (1990):691-93, and Loewenstamm, "Death of Moses." If Matthew and his audience knew of or accepted such, the parallel would have been all the more evident. Cf. Eusebius, *Dem. ev.* 3:2: "Even when they say that no one knew the death of Moses, or his sepulchre, so none saw our savior's change after his resurrection into the divine."

SUMMARY OF RESULTS

(i) Readers of Matthew have often found the vision of Moses' distinct shadow clouded by two obscuring prejudices, the first being the conviction that typology tends to negate historicity[321]—this is the ghost of Strauss—the second being the desire, not unfounded, to give Jesus' newness its due recognition.[322] Moses' shadow might also be obscured by those who wave the magic wand of current opinion: according to one writer, recent scholarship has, more and more, tended away from interpreting Matthew's Jesus as a new Moses.[323] But I am unsure how one measures such things, unsure that the judgement is correct, and unsure in any case that it matters. I do acknowledge that in more than one recent work the new Moses theme has in fact, for whatever reason, suffered interment.[324] But the burial is premature; and I trust that, however the reader may overcome the obstacles cited, it has become evident that Matthew embroidered brighter and thicker Mosaic threads into the fabric of his history than many have allowed. Our evangelist plainly believed that "the law of Moses... foreshadowed the mystery of Christ... by types and shadows, painting it, so to speak, as in a picture" (Cyril of Alexandria, *Hom. Luc.* 54). Discretion, to be sure, is called for. The new Moses theme remains one of many things, and not the most important. If it cannot be ignored, it is still exaggeration to say that "Matthew presents Jesus first and foremost as

---

[321]Cf. Lagrange, *Matthieu*, 82-83. —It is beyond my present purview to address this problem; but I can observe that the presence of a typology does not, despite widespread presumption to the contrary, settle, without further ado, the historical question. Typology did often contribute to fictional narratives (as in *4 Ezra*). But it also sometimes *interpreted* historical facts. Notwithstanding Eusebius' Moses typology, Constantine did win a dramatic victory at the Milvian bridge; and Gregory of Nyssa's eulogy of his brother Basil, full of *synkrisis*, is an eye-witness account.

[322]Traditional christological dogma, with its investment in Christ's uniqueness and divinity, has I think disinclined many from favoring a Christology whose principle feature is Jesus' likeness to another human being. Luther, for one, had problems with it. Thus, in his lecture on Deuteronomy 18 (translated in *Luther's Works, vol. 9: Lectures on Deuteronomy*, ed. J. Pelikan and D. Poellot [St. Louis: Concordia, 1960], 174-90), Luther sought to turn the "like me" of Deut. 18:15, 18 into "unlike me:" "It is his purpose to show that in the future there will be another priesthood, another kingdom, another worship of God, and another word, by which all of Moses will be set aside. Here Moses clearly describes his own end, and he yields his mastery to the Prophet who is to come" (p. 176). "He is not speaking here of similarity between Moses and that Prophet in regard to personal worth but of similarity in authority or office" (p. 177). "They are alike in divine authority, but with respect to the fruit of their ministry they are unlike and completely opposed to each other" (p. 179).

[323]David M. Hay, "Moses through New Testament Spectacles," *Int.* 44 (1990):243.

[324]See above, p. 18, n. 27.

a Moseslike figure."[325] The Moses typology is no more the trunk of Matthew's Christology than it is only a distal twig. It is somewhere in between: I should liken it to a main branch.

(ii) The Moses typology, especially strong in the infancy narrative and the SM, definitely shapes all of Matthew 1-7. It is also definitely present in the great thanksgiving of 11:25-30, in the narrative of the transfiguration (17:1-9), and in the concluding verses, 28:16-20. I am further inclined, but with less faith, to find the typology in the feeding stories (14:13-22; 15:29-39), the entry into Jerusalem (21:1-17), and the last supper (26:17-25). But proposals concerning the missionary discourse, the requests for a sign (12:38; 16:1), the woes of chapter 23, the eschatological discourse, and the crucifixion (27:45-53) are to be rejected or entertained as nothing more than possibilities.

An interesting observation emerges from the foregoing conclusions: the passages in which Moses' tacit presence is the strongest display an order which mirrors the Pentateuch:

Matthew	The Pentateuch	
1-2	Exod. 1:1-2:10	infancy narrative
3:13-17	Exod. 14:10-31	crossing of water
4:1-11	Exod. 16:1-17:7	wilderness temptation
5-7	Exod. 19:1-23:33	mountain of lawgiving
11:25-30	Exod. 33:1-23	reciprocal knowledge of God
17:1-9	Exod. 34:29-35	transfiguration
28:16-20	Deut. 31:7-9	commissioning of
	Josh. 1:1-9	successor

I do not want to make too much of this common sequence, for 14:13-22; 15:29-39; 21:1-17; and 26:17-25, which I at least cannot ignore, disrupt it. At the same time, there is a rough chronological agreement between certain events in the life of Jesus and their typological cousins in the Tanak, and it is not trivial. Especially significant is it that Matthew chose to commence and conclude with the Moses typology. A book's opening sets the tone, and the closing resolution usually lends meaning to all that goes before. Hence if Matthew filled the infancy narrative with Mosaic motifs and modelled his ending upon

[325]So R. H. Fuller, in R. H. Fuller and P. Perkins, *Who Is This Christ?* (Philadelphia: Fortress, 1983), 84.

Deut. 31:7-9 and Josh. 1:1-9, the new Moses theme was not at the periphery of his concerns.

(iii) Matthew's Moses typology must be regarded as conventional in scope, method, and subject. Both before and after the end of the first century other Christians composed narratives in which Jesus is much like Moses; further, heroes other than Jesus were assimilated to Moses through allusions to his story; and, as has appeared again and again, many of the motifs Matthew employed—including fasting for forty days and forty nights, sitting on a mountain, and transfiguration into light—can be found in other Moses typologies. As for the scope of Matthew's Moses typology, by which I mean its significance and relative frequency of appearance, it is also unexceptional. In Joshua, for example, the new Moses motif, which is important but not dominating, is strongest at the book's beginning, occasional through the central portion, and forcibly present at the end—all of which is equally true of Matthew.[326]

(iv) Some things, including very important things, are hidden. God, as Luther and Pascal insisted, is a good example: "Truly, thou art a God who hides thyself" (Isa. 45:15). Matthew's Moses typology is another example, if by hidden is meant inexplicit. Moses is named in the First Gospel only seven times, in 8:4; 17:3, 4; 19:7, 8; 22:24; and 23:2. I have foregone examination of most of these texts[327] for the good and simple reason that, for our purposes, they yield next to nothing: an express comparison between Jesus and Moses does not obtain even once. One is put in mind of the typology in 1 and 2 Kings, examined earlier, in which Elijah time after time imitates a Moses who goes unnamed. Here the lawgiver's presence is, so to speak, felt, not heard. It is the same in Matthew. To the implications of this surface silence I shall return in the final chapter. Here I only register the observation

---

[326]There is a modern parallel of sorts in Thomas Hardy's *The Mayor of Casterbridge*, where one of the main characters, Michael Henchard, is modelled upon Saul. The two are explicitly compared only once; but patterns of thought, structure, and phraseology suffice to establish a broad likeness; and the reader who detects these patterns is much better equipped to understand the novel than is one in ignorance; see J. Moynahan, "The Mayor of Casterbridge and the Old Testament's First Book of Samuel: A Study of Some Literary Relationships," *Publications of the Modern Language Association* 71 (1956):118-30. There is another and more recent parallel in the screen-play of Jerzy Kosinski's *Being There*. On one level this is a polemic against Christianity, or rather against its foudational figure. The bumbling main character, who, through a series of comic errors, becomes esteemed for his alleged wisdom, utters numerous agricultural parables, walks on the water, and does other Christ-like things; but his likeness to Jesus is never spelled out: interpretation is necessary.

[327]See however below, pp. 311-19.

that just as microscopes reveal the limitations of our unaided eyes, our native blindness to many worlds, so critical study informs us that Matthew holds many hidden pictures: and seeing we do not see. To read the First Gospel as one would a typical twentieth century novel is, if that is all one is doing, gravely to misread. No man is an island. Neither is Matthew. At every juncture the book presupposes that the reader is bringing to its ubiquity of allusions an intimate knowledge of Judaica, knowledge without which one is reading commentary without text.[328] In chess one can, as Saussure observed, always appraise the value of any piece merely by studying the current state of affairs: the task requires no acquaintance with previous moves. Not so with the sentences of our Gospel. Without knowledge of their historical geology, which can only come from an education into the tradition, Jewish and Christian, beneath them, significant understanding is impossible; for many of the words, phrases, pictures, and patterns of Matthew were designed to trigger "the eureka of bisociative experience,"[329] that is, they were intended to foster the discovery of analogies between the stories of Jesus and Moses—analogies which can only be formed in a mind with the proper prerequisite knowledge of Moses. To a mind bereft of such knowledge, much in Matthew will be invisible. For reading is a reciprocal process: text gives to reader, reader gives to text. And as Carlyle says somewhere, even "conclusive facts are inseparable from inconclusive except by a head that already understands and knows." We have all had the experience of hearing and understanding the words of a joke without getting the joke: we can fail to make implied connections: it is up to us. Likewise can we follow the surface of Matthew, by which I mean the plain meaning of the words, and miss all the depths. Put otherwise, the synchronic without the diachronic is, at least with regard to our Gospel, like tongues without love: it does not really get to the heart of the matter.

---

[328]Cf. the formulation of Goldberg, *Jews and Christians*, 135: "This narrative [Matthew] presupposes that one [the Jewish Bible]—and a thorough knowledge of it."

[329]I borrow this expression from Arthur Koestler, *The Act of Creation* (London: Hutchinson, 1964).

Five

CONCLUDING REFLECTIONS

It remains to consider how the new Moses theme bears on the interpretation of Matthew.

THE OLD AND THE NEW

T. S. Eliot, in a famous essay, wrote of the

> tendency to insist, when we praise a poet, upon those aspects of his work in which he least resembles any one else. In these aspects or parts of his work we pretend to find what is individual, what is the peculiar essence of the man. We dwell with satisfaction upon the poet's difference from his predecessors, especially his immediate predecessors; we endeavor to find something that can be isolated in order to be enjoyed. Whereas if we approach a poet without this prejudice we shall often find that not only the best, but the most individual parts of his work may be those in which the dead poets, his ancestors, assert their immortality most vigorously.[1]

Persuaded that uniqueness is indeed what matters most, contemporary readers of the Four Gospels, like the modern critics Eliot referred to, are ever expecting the unprecedented: Jesus should be a pioneer who, in his words and deeds, went where no one else had gone before. Witness the widespread scholarly deployment, notwithstanding sound criticism, of the so-called "criterion of dissimilarity." This is undoubtedly the most popular of all criteria for authenticating words attributed to Jesus, one I have often used myself. What is its issue? A Jesus isolated from both Judaism and Christianity, a Jesus different from

---

[1]"Tradition and Individual Talent," in *Selected Essays 1917-1932* (New York: HBJ, 1932), 4.

both his predecessors and his followers. In this connection one thinks of Joachim Jeremias, arguably the twentieth century's outstanding quester for Jesus. He sorted through the Jesus tradition largely in order to determine in what particulars Jesus had abandoned his heritage. In Jeremias' many learned books and instructive articles the unparalleled becomes the characteristic, which in turn becomes the significant. In this he represents most of us. Do we not assume, with Dr. Johnson, that "no man ever became great through imitation?" and, with Seneca, that "an imitator never comes up to the level of his model—the copy always falls short of the original?" Greatness, so we are accustomed to imagine, is not obtained by repeating the past.

But Matthew thought otherwise. For him imitation was not an act of inferior repetition but an inspired act of fresh interpretation. For him the source of Jesus' authority was not novelty but God, the author of truth. The evangelist did assuredly write that the crowds were astonished at Jesus' words, "for he taught them as one having authority, and not as their scribes" (7:29). Yet Matthew nowhere took over Mark's strong expression, "new teaching" (1:27), and surely he knew as well as we do that Jesus was not the first to utter the golden rule (7:12), and that in permitting divorce for unchastity (5:32; 19:9) Jesus was ruling like the Shammaites. Matthew did not I think suffer from what Harold Bloom, with reference to modern poets, has called "the anxiety of influence," and for him the past was not, to borrow from W. Jackson Bate, a "burden." This is not to say that the modern fetish for novelty, so intense since the eighteenth century, was foreign to the ancients. Khakheperre-sonb, a scribe of ancient Egypt, wrote the following in 2,000 B.C.E.: "Had I unknown phrases, sayings that are strange, novel, untried words, free of repetition; not transmitted sayings, spoken by the ancestors!"[2] And Philo offered that "great natures carve out much that is new in the way of knowledge" (*Mos.* 1:22). But for Matthew the strange and the new were uncertain blessings. A Jesus fundamentally discontinuous with the Jewish tradition could not have been Israel's Messiah, for the latter was a feature of the former. And yet the most obvious fact about Jesus was that he did not match expectations. His residence in Nazareth was unanticipated, his failure to persuade Israel a stumblingblock (cf. the theological labyrinth in Romans 9-11). His death as a criminal on a shameful Roman cross was a scandal, and his three-day resurrection in the

---

[2]I quote from Miriam Lichtheim, *Ancient Egyptian Literature: A Book of Readings*, vol. 1 (Berkeley: University of California, 1973), 146.

middle of history peculiar. Matthew, like the later followers of Sabbatai Sevi, who also assimilated their hero to Moses,[3] had little need to proclaim novelty. The destabilizing tradition he passed on shouted that loud enough for the deaf to hear. What our Jewish evangelist required instead was to show that the novelty was not naked, that it wore familiar dress. One wonders not at all that Matthew opened his book by naming David and Abraham, that he immediately followed 1:1 with a genealogy full of old Jewish names, that he sprinkled formula quotations throughout, that he frequently employed Septuagintal idioms, and that he constructed a Moses typology: the evangelist was determined to put the new wine in old wineskins.

I do not, let me hasten, hold forth that Matthew put no stock in the new. No: he composed a book in which Moses, while remaining normative, becomes a symbol of someone greater, a promise awaiting fulfillment, a book in which the exodus becomes history anticipating eschatology. Matthew should not be likened to those rabbis who made fidelity to the past a virtue, creativity in the present undesirable; and he would not have shared their delight in hyperbolic denials of the truly new: "Scripture, Mishnah, halachoth, oral laws not found in the Mishnah, homiletical expositions, and the decisions to be hereafter given by eminent scholars already existed and were communicated as a law to Moses from Sinai. Whence do we know this? From what is written: Is there a thing whereof it is said: See, this is new?" (*Eccles Rab.* l:9). There was in both Jewish and Christian tradition—and so in Matthew's world—a place for the new. "For behold, I create new heavens and a new earth; and the former things shall not be remembered or come into mind" (Isa. 65:17). "If anyone is in Christ, he is a new creation" (2 Cor. 5:17). "Every scribe who has been trained for the kingdom of heaven is like a householder who brings out of his treasure what is new..." (Matt. 13:52). "Behold, I make all things new" (Rev. 21:5). Still, Matthew struggled to contain the newness of the Gospel. His Jesus was not the unbegotten phantom of doceticism but the upshot of a history, Israel's *telos*. Thus the newness we do encounter in Matthew is that of completion, and it always gives us *déjà vu*: there is repetition and the past lives on.[4] Indeed, the old vindicates the new, through the resemblance of the two. In Judaism the present was regularly legitimated by the past: memories were the measure of all things (cf. the prevalence of pseudonymity.) So too, with qualification,

---

[3]See Scholem, *Sabbatai Sevi*, 584ff.
[4]Cf. the "and what is old" of Matt. 13:52.

was it for Matthew. For him discontinuity would have been falsehood, for truth required continuity. Jesus and the new creation wrought by him therefore had their significance confirmed by resonant links with the past, that is, with Israel's history. We have here the antithesis of Marcionitism, with its dichotomy between the God of Israel and the God of Jesus Christ.[5] Jesus brought to fulfillment the history of Israel; and it was axiomatic, given the past's paradigmatic character, rooted in the consistency of God, that the end be like the beginning of that history.

All this is to be emphasized because too often the parallels between Jesus and Moses have been neglected in favor of focus on the differences.[6] This may work with the Gospel of John, but it does not work with Matthew. In the First Gospel Jesus' superiority to Moses is not argued. Rather is it simply assumed. The paragraphs of 5:21-48 do, to be sure, demand more than Moses demanded, and 11:25-30 makes Jesus, not Moses, the chief mediator between God and his people. There is, however, no explicit diminishing of Moses. To grasp the point it may help to draw an analogy with Matthew's treatment of John the Baptist. There are numerous purposeful parallels between Jesus and John, as I earlier had occasion to observe (pp. 137-38). These parallels serve several functions, both literary and theological, and they should not be played down or deconstructed because of an anxiety to exalt Jesus over John. Although such anxiety may have been someone else's concern, it was not Matthew's, and so it makes a poor presupposition for exegesis. The same may be said regarding the Moses typology. Our evangelist did not suffer from any second temple inferiority complex: it was Jesus, not Moses, who was unquestionably Lord. Just as Jesus was greater than the temple and greater than Jonah and greater than Solomon (12:6, 41-42), so too was he greater than Moses. Such was Matthew's quiet confidence, within which confidence he constructed his Moses typology. So to under-

---

[5]One may compare the situation a century later with Origen. He, in the debate with Marcionites and others like them, was very much concerned with demonstrating the consistency of God's activities; see Peter J. Gorday, "Moses and Jesus in *Contra Celsum* 7:1-25," in *Origen of Alexandria*, ed. C. Kannengiesser and W. L. Petersen (Notre Dame: University Press, 1988), 313-36.

[6]Teeple, however, went astray by arguing the other extreme, that whereas Paul and John and Hebrews offer us not a Jesus like Moses but a Jesus unlike and superior to Moses, Matthew, by contrast, gives us just the opposite: a Jesus who is so like Moses that he is not his superior; see *Prophet*, 94-97. The insistence that a Moses Christology and a greater-than-Moses Christology are two different things, indeed contraries, will not endure scrutiny.

stand him aright we must follow his lead and put the emphasis where he put it: and it belongs on the parallels.

Perhaps another analogy may assist. At the time of the Reformation both the Reformers and their Roman Catholic opponents claimed to be the true heirs and interpreters of Augustine. The resultant, heated dispute generated much polemic—polemic not directed at the Church Father himself but rather against those who were perceived, rightly or wrongly, to have misappropriated him. A similar situation no doubt obtained in Matthew's world. The Matthean community was not interested in denigrating Moses but in countering his non-Christian sponsors.

CHRISTOLOGY

The First Gospel displays no independent interest in Moses. The man of God's silent yet forcible presence is in servitude to the Messiah: Moses is there to tell us about Jesus. How so? No simple answer suffices. Both Moses and Jesus were many things, and they occupied several common offices. Moses was the paradigmatic prophet-king, the Messiah's model, a worker of miracles, the giver of Torah, the mediator for Israel, and a suffering servant. And Jesus was similarly a suffering servant, the mediator for Israel, the giver of Torah, a worker of miracles, the Mosaic Messiah, and the eschatological prophet-king. It would be error to isolate any one common function or title and promote it as the *raison d'être* for Matthew's Moses typology. One should not, for instance, assert that Matthew's Jesus is Mosaic simply because he is the Messiah, or simply because he is the prophet like Moses, or simply because he gives a new law. The truth is more expansive than that.

Having said this, two observations are needful. First, the Gospel refuses to denigrate the lawgiver precisely because only the worthy are worth imitating: mimesis is flattery. This obvious fact is so often missed because the concerns of Paul and John are unconsciously read into Matthew. There is, however, as previously indicated, no polemic against Moses in Matthew. The lawgiver is not Jesus' adversary but, like the Baptist, his typological herald and foreshadow. Indeed, just as Virgil was for Dante a Christian, Moses must have been such for Matthew (as he was for the Church Fathers). And so far from it having been within the evangelist's purview to demote him, the contrary was true: given Jesus' assumed superiority, the more one exalted Moses, the more one exalted Jesus; for the one who was Lord always comfortably maintained his advance over his predecessor. Consequently those interpreters who have attenuated the lawgiver's status have focused on a presupposition and missed the main point. It was Moses' very greatness that allowed honor to pass from him to his superior look-alike.

My second point is related to Howard Clark Kee's remark that "above all, Jesus is portrayed in Matthew as a figure of authority, with respect to the interpretation of the law and to the determination of who are worthy to be members of the new community."[7] How true is this? *Exousia*, authority, is at least one of the fundamental themes of the First Gospel—as it is of Mark—and so one of the fundamental components of Matthew's Christology—as is made obvious by recollection of, among other verses, 8:27 ("What sort of man is this, that even winds and sea obey him?"); 9:6 ("The Son of man has authority on earth to forgive sins;" cf. v. 8); 10:1 ("And he called to him his twelve and gave them authority over unclean spirits"); 21:27 ("neither will I tell you by what authority I do these things"); and 28:18 ("All authority in heaven and earth has been given to me"). It is admittedly vain to inquire of Matthew's Gospel, What is Jesus' one chief attribute? That would be to reduce to simplicity the inevitably complex. But if the question were not misdirected, *exousia* might be a good answer.

How does this bear upon typology? Without prosecuting a needless demonstration of the obvious, Moses was for Judaism the personification of authority, its living definition. To him was given the Torah, and "Moses says" was interchangeable with "Scripture says" and with "God says."[8] Given this, is it coincidence that the theme of Jesus' authority frequently coincides with Matthew's Moses typology? The extensive prefigurement in 1:1-5:2 culminates in the SM, which closes with the crowd exclaiming that Jesus, unlike the scribes, teaches "as one having authority" (7:29). And in 11:25-30, which is so riddled with allusions to the Moses traditions, the thought of *exousia*, if not the word, is indisputable: the "all" that the Father has given to Jesus is revelation, which Jesus then bestows upon others as he wills. In 17:1-8 the voice from heaven, in circumstances reminiscent of Exodus 24 and 34, enjoins obedience to Jesus, the prophet like Moses: "listen to him." As for 28:16-20, modelled upon Deuteronomy 31 and Joshua 1, its dramatic use of *exousia* has already been noted. What follows? The

---

[7]Howard Clark Kee, *Knowing the Truth: A Sociological Approach to New Testament Interpretation* (Minneapolis: Fortress, 1989), 95.

[8]CD V:8; VIII:14; XIX:26-27; Matt. 22:24; Rom. 10:19; Josephus, *Ant.* 7:91; etc.

correlation between Jesus' authority and his Mosaic character was the product of design. Just as philosophers wore clothing of a certain kind in order to advertise their office, similarly did Matthew drape the Messiah in the familiar mantle of Moses, by which dress he made Jesus the full bearer of God's authority.

GROUP IDENTITY

Memory constitutes identity, wherefore amnesiacs, bereft of self-knowledge, suffer the misery of near or total loss of meaning.[9] Without the anchor of stability which is recollection, the Heraclitean river constantly sweeps all before it. And as with the individual, so with communities: identity requires memory. Thus it is that, whenever a religious group comes into being, it invariably appropriates or manu-factures for itself a sacred heritage and history, a genealogy. Only rarely if ever is there delight in, or emphasis upon, rupture with the past. The rule is proclamation of continuity with some tradition. The false prophets of Josephus inaugurated their short-lived religious movements by attempting to replay the exodus. The Reformers claimed both the Bible and Augustine (Calvin: "Augustine is completely on our side"). The Anabaptists discovered themselves in medieval her-etics, as did the Landmark Baptists later on. And Joseph Smith founded Mormonism by handing the world pre-Columbian history books. The past, adopted as tradition, is everywhere used to midwife and nurture a community's symbolic universe, if I may use the terminology of the sociologists.[10]

Which brings us to religious typology, for it has often helped to create and sustain a symbolic universe. This is because typology, which puts its perceivers in two stories at once, can provide an instant history for a community. Puritan historiography offers a fine example of this.[11] North America became, for the Puritans, the promised land,

---

[9]I am informed that the Welsh word for "madness" (*gwallgofvwydd*) means a failure in the memory.

[10]Peter L. Berger and Thomas Luckmann, *The Social Construction of Reality* (New York: Doubleday, 1966).

[11]For what follows see K. B. Murdoch, "Clio in the Wilderness: History and Biography in Puritan New England," *CH* 24 (1955):221-38; also Sacavan Bercovitch, ed., *Typology and Early American Literature* (Amherst: University of Massachusetts, 1972), esp. the essay by Mason I. Lowance, Jr., "Cotton Mather's *Magnalia* and the Metaphors of Biblical History," on pp. 139-60.

while England and the Roman Church were spoken of as the house of bondage; difficulties were fathomed through comparison with Israel's temptations in the wilderness; and leaders were likened to Abraham and Moses, men who sojourned to unknown lands. In short, the Puritans quite sincerely conceived themselves to be a new Israel in the midst of a new exodus, with a new promised land stretching before them. They relived, in their communal minds, the foundational experiences of Israel, in this way defining themselves *vis-à-vis* holy history. Such definition lent familiarity to the foreign New World and added urgency to their endeavors; it combatted the feeling of isolation from European tradition and culture; it attenuated the pains of being a people set apart; it gave the New Englanders an ancient family tree and put their activities within the grand scheme of things; and it offset the doubts of men and women conducting an uncertain experiment by dignifying them as the proprietors of the Jewish and Christian estate. "Motivated in part by a desire to define and preserve a tradition for the new colonies, so that their people might not be children vainly seeking for fathers,"[12] the Puritans used typology to confer status upon themselves and meaning upon their labors. Thus they ceased to be strangers in a strange land.

There is in all this a good parallel with the production of the First Gospel—which, be it remembered, commences with a new exodus. Its author, in writing the short story of Jesus Christ, was creating and stabilizing Christian memories—and he made sure that those memories stretched back to hoary antiquity. Matthew's audience, constituted of Jews and Gentiles, could not have shared recollections from the distant past. Not only did Christianity measure its age by decades instead of centuries, but Gentiles and Jews were not fellow heirs of any paternal acres. How then remedy the situation, that is, how construct a communal history? The Bible held the solution: Matthew and his community, like other Christians before them, read themselves into the book and so came to make it their own. Matthew's Jesus, the son of David and the son of Abraham (1:1), by fulfilling the prophecies of the Jewish Bible and by being like Moses, became the heir of Jewish history and tradition (cf. 21:43), which in turn made his followers joint heirs of the same. In other words, by uniting themselves to their Scripturally faithful Mosaic Lord, Christians were uniting themselves to the sacred past of the Jews, the one people of God: to belong to Jesus Christ was to belong to Israel's history and so to have her memories.

---

[12]Murdock, "Clio," 223.

In this way the Bible ceased to be the chronicle of a nation and became instead the charter of the church, a sort of legitimating aetiology.

The importance of validation via antiquity, although a well nigh universal phenomenon,[13] was, we can be sure, particularly pressing in Matthew's time and place. His world knew nothing of our love, sponsored by scientific advance, of innovation, nothing of the vain desire of modern philosophy and politics to wipe clean the slate of tradition and start over (recall Descartes and the French Revolution). Although we have more traditions than we care to admit, and while our political rhetoric still occasionally appeals to dead heroes and their causes,[14] we feel no necessary commitment to "practices supported by antiquity" (Tacitus, *Hist.* 5:4-5).[15] It was different with our ancestors. For them age bestowed status; innovation was suspect. Josephus composed *Contra Apionem* in order to prove the "extreme antiquity" (*palaiotaton*) of the Jewish race and to rebut those who slandered his people as comparatively "modern" (*neōteron*; see *C. Ap.* 1:1-3). The philosophical schools of Hellenism were careful to preserve lists of leaders, that is, lists of founders and their successors.[16] And the critics of early Christianity did not praise the religion's newness but condemned it as a novelty. Celsus, Porphyry, and Plotinus, who lived "in an age where religious traditions were widely held to express a people's continuity with the past and their national allegiance to constituted authority,"[17] were at one in this. When Celsus wrote that Jesus appeared "not long ago" and taught "new doctrines," he was not being complimentary. If the Jews and Egyptians were roundly admired for their faithful adherence to ancestral laws and customs, Christians were dismissed as adherents of a "*superstitio nova*" (Seutonius, *Nero* 16); they were rebuked as inventors of what Julian the Apostate disparagingly called a "new cult" (*kainēn thusian*). Apologists for the faith naturally sought to prove that, to the contrary, Christians were the legitimate descendants of true Israel. They went so far as to appropriate for the church Israel's very name.[18]

[13] I have read somewhere that Christian missionaries to the South Pacific reported that many Polynesians found the genealogy to be the most interesting and important part of Matthew.

[14] I note the attempt of the anti-abortion or pro-life movement to align itself with the abolitionists of the 1800's and the civil-rights activists of the 1960's.

[15] One recalls how fervent the debate over apostolic succession has often been. But the progress of modernity has witnessed the recession of that debate.

[16] Élie Bikerman, "La chaîne de la tradition pharisienne," *RB* 59 (1952):44-54.

[17] R. Joseph Hoffmann, ed., *Celsus: On the True Doctrine* (New York: Oxford, 1987), 34.

[18] Justin, *Dial.* 125; *Apost. Const.* 7:36.2; 35.4; Eusebius, *Frag. in Lc.* 1:32. There is much useful material in Marcel Simon, *Verus Israel* (Paris: E. de Boccard, 1964).

Eusebius is here representative. Not only did he, near the beginning of his ecclesiastical history, set out to show that the Christian principles "have not been recently invented, but were established, we may say, by the Deity in the natural dictates of pious men of old, from the very origin of our race," and that "the first and most ancient religion known, that of those pious men that were connected with Abraham, is the very religion lately announced to all in the doctrines of Christ" (*H.E.* 1:4): he also undertook to write the *Praeparatio Evangelica*, the burden of whose second half is to show that Christians are justified in calling the Hebrew past their own.

While removed from Eusebius by two centuries, Matthew's motives were in part those of the later historian. He too was much concerned to give Christians, through the adoption of Judaism, a feeling of rootedness in a glorious and renowned past. And just as his formula quotations Christianized the Torah, the heart of Jewish identity, so his presentation of the Christian Lord as another lawgiver was a second way of absorbing Judaism and contending that Jesus, not rabbinic Judaism, was the outcome of Sinai; which is to say: Matthew Christianized not only the Torah but also its author.

Matthew's method, of adoption through assimilation, was, so far from being original, then standard fare: the mingling of the histories of two men, with the aim of mingling the histories of two communities, was a rhetorical commonplace. Eusebius made Constantine into a new Moses, Israel's first and greatest king, thereby establishing the Christian empire as a legitimate continuation of Israel's ancient and holy history (see pp. 118-21). Eusebius also recreated Origen, the hero of his *Ecclesiastical History*, in the image of Socrates, thus suggesting that Christian thought, personified in the Alexandrian theologian, was the fulfillment of authentic Hellenic philosophy.[19] Outside of Christianity, diaspora Jews made David like Orpheus.[20] They further gave Moses the name Hermes[21] and put in his hand the club of Heracles.[22] In all this Hellenistic Jews were, among other things, defining their communal identity by broadening their history: the necessity for meaning was the mother of their invention. Their ontological reasoning was of the form: I was, therefore I am.

At this juncture it should be remarked that Judaism itself was no unified phenomenon and that, before and after Matthew, its different

[19]Cox, *Biography in Late Antiquity*, 87-88.
[20]Cf. the mosaic found in the Gaza strip shortly before the Six Day War.
[21]Artapanus, in Eusebius, *Prape. ev.* 9:27.6-9.
[22]Goodenough, *Symbols*, 10:119-25.

children vied for the heritage of Moses.[23] The descendants of the Pharisees, who made Hillel, their hero, Mosaic, took care to trace their beliefs back through a chain of tradition, a chain at whose head was Moses on Sinai: *m. Abot* 1:1. It was similar with the Samaritans. They, after Abraham's example, worshipped on Mount Gerizim; and clinging to what they regarded as the authentic Pentateuch as composed by Moses, they accused others of adulterating Torah and wrongly erecting a temple in Jerusalem. The Sadducees, who rejected the Pharasaic oral tradition, no doubt held a comparable attitude: they were the faithful custodians of the Mosaic past, while everyone else had been faithless. And then there is Philo. He forwarded a mystical version of Judaism for which Moses was made the chief hero and apologetical instrument. Manifestly the philosopher was concerned to show the continuity between his own interpretation of Judaism and the lawgiver. The same concern is reflected in the Dead Sea Scrolls, although they represent a very different kind of Judaism. According to the Scrolls, those outside the sect had defective faith: only the remnant in the age of wrath, the "converts of Israel" (*CD* X:2), had kept the covenant; only they did precisely all "commanded by the hand of Moses" (*1QS* I:3). Finally, let me mention the book known as *Jubilees*, which I do not regard as Essene. It has rightly been said that

> the author's strict interpretation of the Law, his appeal to a distinct set of traditions which reported the cultic life and piety of the patriarchs, his hostility to surrounding nations, his abhorrence of gentile practices, his insistent demand for obedience to God's commands in a time of apostasy, his belief that God was about to create a new spirit within his people which would make possible a proper relationship between God and Israel, and his preoccupation with adherence to a calendar of 364 days are some of the characteristics which identify him as part of a zealous, conservative, pious segment of Judaism which was bound together by its own set of traditions, expectations, and practices.[24]

And what was the justification for the traditions, expectations, and practices of that segment of Judaism? To judge by *Jubilees* itself, legitimation derived from faithfulness to what God had revealed on Sinai. In other words, from the point of view of the group itself, outsiders were guilty of not following Moses.

From the foregoing it is obvious that pre-Christian Judaism was astir with a conflict of remnants, divided by a sort of paternity dispute:

---

[23]My thoughts on this matter were prodded by T. L. Donaldson, "Moses Typology and the Sectarian Nature of Early Christian Anti-Judaism: A Study of Acts 7," *JSNT* 12 (l981):27-52. Also useful is the second chapter in Overman, *Matthew's Gospel*.

[24]O. S. Wintermute, in *OTP* 2:45.

who had and who had not been fathered by Moses? Into that dispute, already long raging, entered Matthew. And his contention, that the Christian community harbored the rightful children of Moses, had been heard often enough before: the claim itself had no uniqueness; new only was the manner of its making, with reference to Jesus. Many were the communities with a remnant mentality who sought to justify their symbolic universes by demonstrating the harmony between themselves and Moses. Their self-understanding, determined by Jewish tradition, could not have abided anything less.

APOLOGETICS

In the Byzantine *Life of St. John the Almsgiver* there is this: "Lovers of Christ, mark this miracle [John turned tin into silver]; it is not strange. For he who multiplied the five loaves and at another time converted the waters of the Nile into blood, transformed a rod into a serpent, and changed fire into dew, easily accomplished this miracle too, in order to enrich his servant and show mercy." In these lines familiarity does not breed contempt but reassurance. In a reversal of Humean logic, an unusual event in the present is made more believable because analogous with the past. A similar line of apologetical reasoning appears in Bede's *Life of Cuthbert* 2. This tells the queer tale, too long to recount here, of a child who was healed by an angel who rode upon a horse. The story ends with this: the angel was "sent by the same power who had deigned to send the Archangel Raphael to cure Tobias' eyes. If anyone thinks it strange for an angel to appear on horseback, let him read the history of the Maccabees, where angels on horseback come to defend both Judas Maccabeus and the Temple itself."

Thomas Kuhn has argued that scientists are not, as modern mythology would have it, disinterested and open-minded seekers of truth but rather paradigm-bound interpreters who discount new data when unable to fit them into established ways of thinking. Whatever one makes of Kuhn's analysis of scientific revolutions, his characterization of scientists does make them resemble the rest of us, for the new can only be contemplated through what is already believed, and in this last we always have vested interests. This is especially true in religion, which posits old stories and books as authoritative revelation. The past, or rather interpreted portions of it, become canon, the measure of truth. Earlier we examined the legislation in Ezekiel 40-48 and the endorsement of esoteric books in *4 Ezra*, which legislation and endorsement were potentially controversial—for which cause they required defence, that is, a demonstration of harmony with established norms. How was this done? In both cases Moses was, so to speak, called to the witness stand: his presence in a typology spoke on behalf of the new. For ancient Jews the resemblance of Ezekiel and Ezra to Moses must have suggested authentic continuity with the authoritative past and so supported the authenticity of the new teachings. No doubt the original Deuteronomist was also concerned to suggest such authentic continuity when he incorporated into his history the series of Moses typologies which culminates in Josiah.

A similar generalization may be made about Theodoret of Cyrrhus' *Religious History*, in which the Christian heroes are constantly and favorably compared with the biblical giants from days gone by. Here the past, present in typologies and similitudes, renders the new plausible. And so also was it with Matthew. The Moses typology was designed to inform Christology and group identity; but it additionally constituted a type of evidence. Whether we today find that evidence convincing is of course beside the point: our prejudices are irrelevant. Typology was a rhetoric of great vitality and force in ancient Judaism and early Christianity, and Matthew's early audience surely construed the parallels between Moses and Jesus as valid testimony to the Christian kerygma. In this we find a close parallel in Eusebius' *Demonstratio Evangelica*, an ostensible apology that is really a manual of dogmatic instruction. After listing numerous parallels between Jesus and Moses, Eusebius concluded with this:

> If then no one but our savior can be shown to have resembled Moses in so many ways, surely it only remains for us to apply to him and to no other the prophecy of Moses, in which he foretold that God would raise up one like himself, saying: "I will raise up a prophet to them of their brethren like you... " (Deut. 18:15). But the Old Testament clearly teaches that, of the prophets after Moses, no one before our savior was raised up like Moses, for it says: "And there has not arisen yet a prophet like Moses whom the Lord knew face to face in all his signs and wonders" (Deut. 34:10). I have then proved that the divine Spirit prophesied through Moses of our savior... (*Dem. ev.* 3:2).

Matthew I am sure would have understood these words, and he would have been happy to see his Gospel used as Eusebius used it. Indeed, I am confident that he anticipated finding readers who understood his implicit apologetic.

I need only add that by postulating an apologetical dimension to Matthew I am not implying that its author wrote for outsiders. Contemporary defences of Christianity are read primarily by doubting Thomases seeking reassurance, just as pre-Christian Jewish apologetic literature was consumed firstly by diaspora Jews struggling with Hellenism.[25] Matthew may well have hoped that his Gospel would fall into a few non-Christian hands, but he was principally concerned to edify followers of Jesus; and it was with them in mind that he constructed his Moses typology.

LITERARY METHOD

The First Gospel has this apparent defect, that its author did not trumpet all his intentions. Although he made much clear, he also left much, even of importance, unsaid. The careful reader knows this after only the first few verses, for the insertion of four women into the genealogy, a fact inescapable, must mean something. But what? We are, to our frustration, never told. Matthew was in one respect akin to Clement of Alexandria, of whom it has been said: his "preferred style of discourse is by allusion and implication."[26] Perhaps our evangelist expected too much of his readers. Or—and this is my own supposition—his first readers were better equipped than are we, which is to say they had a knowledge we lack, a knowledge, that is, of the tradition behind the Gospel, which tradition has ceased to be.

In addition to not revealing all his intentions, Matthew also failed to instruct us about his literary methods. In this regard he was like most authors, who "seldom write about the essentials of their art. A true convention in any age is accepted without comment. In the main, we cannot expect our authors to tell us what their conventions were. We shall have to hunt for ourselves."[27] What do we find when we hunt in Matthew? The first discovery is that the Gospel is like a chapter in a book. Scriptural citations and allusions—which are anything but detachable ornamentation— direct the reader to other books and so teach that Matthew is not a self-contained entity: much is missing. The Gospel, in other words, stipulates that it be interpreted in the context of other texts. This means that it is, in a fundamental sense, an incomplete utterance, a book full of holes. Readers must make present what is absent; they must become actively engaged and bring to the Gospel knowledge of what it presupposes, that being a pre-existing collection of interacting texts, the Jewish Bible. The First Gospel is a

[25]V. Tcherikover, "Jewish Apologetic Literature Reconsidered," *Eos* 48 (1956), 169-93.
[26]Mortley, "The Past in Clement of Alexandria," 194.
[27]C. W. Jones, *Saints Lives and Chronicles in Early England* (Ithaca: Cornell, 1947), 53.

mnemonic device, designed (to use the current jargon) to trigger intertextual exchanges which depend upon informed and imaginative reading.

The second discovery of our hunt is that Matthew is not only allusive but densely so. 11:25-30, for example, requires for its correct interpretation the knowledge of several texts about Moses and their traditional interplay. Acknowledgement of this fact is perhaps a special difficulty for us at the end of the twentieth century; for we live in a time of verbal inflation, of throw-away utterances. The sheer volume of verbage produced by our society, for paper and for wave transmission, has reduced the value of words, so that we now need more to say less. The result is that we are not so accustomed to the phenomenon of few words signifying much, or of paragraphs in which every sentence bears meaning to be penetrated. But Matthew was so accustomed: religious speech for him was polysemous and heavily connotative. The complex combinations of scriptural phrases found in *llQMelchezedek*, the *Mekilta*'s habit of offering multiple interpretations for single sentences and sometimes for single words, and the many subtle allusions in many of the Moses typologies discussed herein should supply us with insights into Matthew's mentality. For him it was the most natural thing in the world to construct a sentence pointing in two or more directions at once.

Maybe a parallel closer to our time will make the evangelist's habits easier to accept. Consider the following, from one of Protestantism's most famous hymns, Augustus Montague Toplady's "Rock of Ages" (1776):

> Rock of Ages, cleft for me,
> Let me hide myself in Thee!
> Let the water and the blood,
> From Thy riven side which flowed,
> Be of sin the double cure,
> Cleanse me from its guilt and power...

The first four lines allude to or draw upon at least four scriptural texts, and some of the words have more than one referent. The dominant image is of water and blood flowing from Christ's riven side to undo the guilt and power of sin. John 19:34 is clearly being alluded to: "one of the soldiers pierced his side with a spear, and at once blood and water came out." But the image of a dead Christ on the cross is not alone; it has rather been conflated with the image of water coming out of the wilderness rock which Moses struck (see Exodus 17; Numbers 20). And that is not all, for Christ is directly addressed as the rock that was cleft, and that presupposes the identification in 1 Cor. 10:4: "and the rock was Christ." Finally, in lines 1 and 2 plain use has also been made of Exodus 33, where Moses hides in the cleft of a rock while the glory of the Lord passes by. The allusions then may be set forth like this:

"Rock" (= Christ)	1 Cor. 10:4
"Rock" + "cleft" + "hide"	Exod. 33:22
"Rock" + "water" + "flowed"	Exodus 17; Numbers 20
"water" + "thy riven side" + "flowed"	John 19:34

Whether or not contemporary singers of "Rock of Ages" perceive all these allusions, many eighteenth century Protestants, having grown up hearing the Bible read every evening, probably did. And I believe that their performance in this particular may be likened to the performance of Matthew's original audience: it knew Scripture and Jewish tradition sufficiently well to hear Matthew as it was intended to be heard, as a catena of allusions.

Let me, however, subjoin a caveat. I do not believe that Matthew was too clever for his own good, that, through subtlety, he unwittingly deprived his audience of *anagnorisis*, the pleasure of recognition:[28] our evangelist should not be likened to a bad French symbolist, nor is his book like the monologues of *Finnegan's Wake*, monologues sufficiently dense with allusion to exhaust even the most learned of readers. Yet there may still have been a conscious hermeneutical gap between Matthew's author and some of his readers. B. Rajan, in a study of Milton,[29] contended that although average 17th century readers could have understood *Paradise Lost*, they would, upon reading the book, have been encouraged to increase their knowledge, this because the book leads in so many interesting directions. As Rajan put it: the reader of *Paradise Lost*

> would have been drawn into reading the literature massed behind it, the other poems written on the subject, the epic poems written in other languages, and encouraged to explore the controversies and problems on which so much of *Paradise Lost* is based. So learning is what the poem recommends rather that what it stipulates.[30]

I am in no position to pass judgement on this evaluation of Milton and his first audience. But the thing Rajan envisages, namely, a book that

---

[28]On the pleasure of detecting allusions, which fact partly explains their ubiquity in world literature, see Koestler, *Act of Creation*, 335-40.
[29]*Paradise Lost and the 17th Century Reader* (London: Chatto and Windus, 1962).
[30]Ibid., 18.

invites the reading of other books, may justly characterize Matthew. Let me explain.

Many have intuited that the First Gospel was composed with catechetical ends in view. Certainly the focus upon moral instruction, the habit of topical presentation, and the ubiquity of mnemonic devices such as repetition and the triad do, when taken together, strongly suggest this. In my estimation, the case made by Ernst von Dobschütz, in 1928, that Matthew was both rabbi and catechist, has not dissipated with time: it is as strong as ever. Hence I consider it likely that Matthew's Gospel was intended to be, among other things, a catechetical aid: "The Jewish rabbi had become a Christian teacher and now used his catechetical skills in the service of the gospel" (von Dobschütz). Now if this surmise is correct, we may imagine that, when a Jewish-Christian instructor took up Matthew as a tool of catechesis, a hundred questions would have been raised by newly-converted Gentiles. Why are there four women in the genealogy? For what reason did Jesus prohibit the Samaritan and Gentile missions? What is the meaning of not casting pearls before swine? In addition to examining, to edifying conclusions, such educating riddles, the catechist would also have had the further opportunity to unfold the Moses typology, which is filled with theological riches. Details such as "and forty nights" (4:2) and sitting on a mountain (5:1-2), when made heuristic, would have opened eyes in wonder, encouraged the faith of novices, and demonstrated that treasures old and new could always be brought forth from their Lord's story. Above all, because the understanding of such obscurities invariably involves knowledge of the Bible, the fundamental lesson of Scripture's importance would have been inculcated: to understand Jesus, one must understand Scripture. Given this sort of catechetical setting, I think it possible that Matthew, with the end of stimulating interest in the Bible, may well have planted allusions which he knew would, without assistance, escape the perception of unlearned Christians.

WORLD-VIEW

Like the numerous biblical comparisons in Cotton Mather's *Magnalia*, Matthew's Moses typology, based on allusions, is not erudite display but the fruit of a particular philosophy of history. As Northrop Frye has written,

> What typology really is as a mode of thought, what it both assumes and leads to, is a theory of history, or more accurately of historical process:

an assumption that there is some meaning and point to history, and that sooner or later some event or events will occur which will indicate what that meaning or point is, and so become an antitype of what has happened previously.[31]

Implicit in our Gospel is a vision of time, causality, and salvation, according to which history is not a random flux progressing to an unknown and undetermined end; rather, God is history's entelechy, and under the divine sovereignty, history becomes the arena of promise and fulfillment, type and antitype, prefiguration and manifestation. On this view of things, God's future never enters the present as the wholly contingent or unanticipated: there is always continuity with the sacred past. In both prototypical word and metaphorical deed, God has declared "the end from the beginning and from ancient times things not yet done" (Isa. 46:10). Salvation-history is therefore a redemptive process in which every event belongs to a nexus, and meaning belongs to the whole.

To this it must be added that the unifying sense thus given to history is Christological. For in the Gospel, history always revolves around Christ. The creation, the exodus, the monarchy, and the prophets all prefigured and presaged Jesus the Messiah; and the eschatological future will be nothing other than Jesus' *parousia*, with its attendant circumstances. So for the believing reader of Matthew, history looks like this:

Past I——————>Past II—————>Present—————>Future

| Prophecy and types of Jesus Christ | The earthly ministry of Jesus Christ | The abiding presence of Jesus Christ | The *parousia* of Jesus Christ |

If Moses, as Ezekiel the Tragedian has it, saw, on Pisgah, the past, the present, and the future, then in Matthew Jesus himself is all three: he was and is and is to come.[32] (One must be cautious, however, when drawing a line between Matthew's present and the eschatological future. The evangelist hoped the end would come sooner rather than later, and he interpreted both the past of Jesus and the experience of the church in eschatological categories.[33] Matthew's typology cannot,

---

[31]*The Great Code*, 80-81.

[32]I do not imply that Matthew must have believed in the Messiah's pre-existence: the topic is just not addressed by the Gospel.

[33]See my book, *The End of the Ages has Come* (Philadelphia: Fortress, 1985), 40-50.

accordingly, be divorced from eschatology. But this then leads to another point: given the traditional correlation between *Urzeit* and *Endzeit* in Judaism, Matthew's eschatological outlook must have nourished his typological mentality. In other words, as a student of eschatology he would have become accustomed to interpreting eschatological events as a series of antitypes. It is of interest that millennarian impulses stimulated typological construction in early 17th-century English and American Puritanism.[34])

THE PRESENCE OF THE PAST

If it is true that Jesus was, for Matthew, the hermeneutical key to unlocking the religious meaning of the Jewish Bible, it is also true that the Jewish Bible was for him the hermeneutical key to unlocking the religious meaning of Jesus. Thus our Gospel contains a defining dialectic: the past informs the present, and the present informs the past. In accord with this, the typological lines between Jesus and Moses are bidirectional: informed understanding of Jesus requires true understanding of Moses, and true understanding of Moses requires informed understanding of Jesus.

But to leave matters at that would be misleading, for Matthew required more than just knowledge of Moses. Cotton Mather wrote this in his *Magnalia*:

> this law commonly called moral, God was pleased to give to the people of Israel, as a church under age, ceremonial laws, containing several typical ordinances, partly... prefiguring Christ, his graces, actions, sufferings and benefits, and partly holding forth diverse institutions of moral duties: All which ceremonial laws being appointed only to the time of reformation, are by Jesus the True Messiah, and only law-giver, who was furnished with power from the Father for that end, abrogated and taken away (5:19.3).

Calvin penned something very similar in the *Institutes*, where he claimed that Christ's annulment of the Mosaic law, so far from derogating it, reveals its true purpose; for if the law were still in effect, we could not understand its real end, which was to prefigure Christ (2:7.16). I do not believe that Matthew the Jew—Calvin and Mather were Gentiles—would have been wholly happy with such a line of thought. 5:17-20 entails that the words of Moses, albeit perhaps

---

[34]S. Bercovitch, "Typology in Puritan New England," in *Typology and Early American Literature*, 179-81.

qualified by the Messiah's advent, have not been emasculated or taken away: they are more than instructive but insubstantial images of things to come, more than just shadows on Plato's cave wall. Jesus may in certain respects have transcended the lawgiver, and assuredly his salvific ministry ushered in new circumstances; but these facts do not amount to abolition. In the First Gospel, Moses is still an imperative.

Granted the abiding validity of the Torah, which requires not just knowing Moses but doing Moses, we can be sure that Matthew was much concerned with the preservation of his Jewish religious heritage in a church inexorably becoming Gentile. The analogy here is not with the Renaissance writers, who imitated the classical tradition in an attempt to recover the distant past, to resurrect the dead; it is instead with Irenaeus and Origen and those ancient Christians for whom full adoption of the Jewish Bible was, in the face of dualistic heresies, their way of defending the Christianity which had nurtured them, which Christianity they took to be apostolic. Matthew's stylistic imitation of the Septuagint, his formula quotations, his explicit statement on the law and the prophets, and his Moses typology—all things more than skin-deep— were deliberate strategies aimed at preserving his own patrimony: they inextricably bound the story of Jesus to Judaism.

I use the word "deliberate" because Matthew, living as he did after the fall of Jerusalem, in a period of successful Gentile missions, did not need to be a prophet to foresee whither things were tending: Christianity was fast becoming a Gentile religion. And however much our evangelist endorsed the evangelism of non-Jews (28:16-20) he cannot have been oblivious to the dangers, that is, indifferent to the possibility that the originally Hebrew gospel would be misconstrued by persons outside the orbit of Judaism, that a Gentile Christianity might define itself in opposition to its genetic inheritance and then cease watering it scriptural roots, thus becoming fertile ground for the weeds of error (as happened with Marcionitism). Prevention is better than cure, and Matthew's Gospel was written as prevention; for it was drawn up by a man with an almost Jeremian sense of foreboding, a man who solemnly undertook to write a powerful and persuasive book which would endorse the pre-Christian past and prohibit the disassociation of Christianity from Judaism, a book which would demonstrate that the Messiah himself followed in the footsteps of the lawgiver, and that therefore to abandon Moses is to abandon Jesus.

APPENDICES I–VII

APPENDICES

APPENDIX I

B. W. Bacon's Contribution

B. W. Bacon was not the first to espy Mosaic motifs in Matthew. Before him many had observed that chapters 1-2 contain a new exodus theme,[1] that the forty days fast of 4:1 recalls Exod. 34:28,[2] that the sermon on the mount (hereafter SM), in its circumstances and content, portrays Jesus as another lawgiver,[3] and that the narrative of the transfiguration records "an enhanced repetition of the glorification of Moses."[4] But to Bacon seemingly goes the

---

[1]E.g. H. J. Holtzmann, *Lehrbuch der historisch-kritischen Einleitung in das Neue Testament* (3rd ed.; Freiburg im Breslau: J. C. B. Mohr (Paul Siebeck), 1892), 379, observing parallels between Herod and Pharaoh, 2:20 and Exod. 4:19, and 2:21 and Exod. 4:20. Cf. G. H. Box, *The Virgin Birth of Jesus Christ* (London: Sir Isaac Pitman and Sons, Ltd., 1916), 20, on Matt. 2:20-21 and LXX Exod. 4:19-20: "The Evangelist intends to suggest a likeness between the divinely guided career of Moses, the instrument of Israel's redemption from Egypt, and the Messianic Redeemer who saves His people from their sins—the type, of course, being far transcended by the antitype." Pp. 21-22 affirm that Matthew saw Jesus as the fulfillment of Deut. 18:15 and explore the Jewish legends about the birth of Moses. Cf. A. Gfrörer, *Das Jahrhundert des Heils*, 354-64.
   —Incidentally, the second part of this last contains, on pp. 318-413, a much dated yet still stimulating section on Mosaic messianism and the New Testament, a section in which most of the questions Matthean students still wrestle with anent Moses in Matthew are already raised, and occasionally with insights which make the later discussion appear retrogressive.
   [2]Cf. Holtzmann, *Lehrbuch*, 379; W. C. Allen, *A Critical and Exegetical Commentary on the Gospel according to St. Matthew* (3rd ed.; ICC; Edinburgh: T. & T. Clark, 1912), 30.
   [3]Cf. Holtzmann, *Lehrbuch*, 379; P. P. Levertoff, "The Gospel according to St. Matthew," in *A New Catholic Commentary on Holy Scripture*, ed. C. Gore et al. (New York: Macmillan, 1928), 136-37.
   [4]So D. F. Strauss, *The Life of Jesus Critically Examined*, ed. P. C. Hodgson (Philadelphia: Fortress, 1972), 545.

distinction of being the first to insist that Matthew, in its entirety, is a new law whose very structure mirrors the Torah.[5]

"A half-century ago," so Bacon wrote in the late 1920's, "it was recognized that... [Matthew's] compiler has followed the plan of aggregating his teaching material from all sources into five great discourses."[6] With this fact as his guiding star, Bacon went on to contend that those five discourses correspond "to the codes of the Pentateuch, each introduced, like the Mosaic codes, by a narrative section..." (p. xiv.). The First Evangelist was "of Jewish origin and training, with unbounded reverence for the Law; consequently he... [could not] conceive of any arrangement of the 'commandments to be observed' better than the Mosaic:"

> The Torah consists of five books of the commandments of Moses, each body of law introduced by a narrative of considerable length, largely concerned with the "signs and wonders" by which Jehovah "with an outstretched and mighty arm" redeemed his people from Egyptian bondage. Matthew is a "converted rabbi,"[7] a Christian legalist. Each of the "five books" of his "syntax of the logia" of Jesus begins with an introductory narrative and closes with a stereotyped formula linking its discourse to the next succeeding narrative section (p. 8l).

All this may be pictorially represented by the following:

Preamble or Prologue:
1-2: The birth narrative

Book I: (a) 3:1-4:25: Narrative material
         (b) 5:1-7:27: The Sermon on the Mount
Formula: 7:28-29: "And when Jesus finished..."

---

[5]In 1928, however, Levertoff, "St. Matthew," 128-29, proposed the following: "The word 'logos,' whether or not applied to a source identical with Q, is, we suggest, nothing else but the Greek for the Hebrew 'Debarim,' the traditional name for Deuteronomy. If this be so, the purpose of the 'Logia,' which Matthew incorporated in his Gospel, was to present a kind of new 'Deuteronomy,' describing the life of our Lord as the 'Last Redeemer,' preparing the new Israel for the kingdom of Heaven, in a manner similar to Moses, the 'first redeemer,' as pictured in the old Deuteronomy, preparing the people for the Promised Land." Levertoff went on to maintain that the order of the Logia partly determined the structure of Matthew. Cf. F. Godet, *Introduction to the New Testament: The Collection of the Four Gospels and the Gospel of Matthew* (Edinburgh: T. & T. Clark, l889), 181-85; also E. Nestle, "Die Fünfteilung im Werk des Papias und im ersten Evangelium," *ZNW* 1 (l900):252-54.

[6]*Studies in Matthew* (New York: Henry Holt, l930), xiv. Cf. J. C. Hawkins, *Horae Synopticae* (rev. ed.; Oxford: University Press, l909), 163-65.

[7]"A converted Jewish rabbi" (*ein konvertierter jüdischer Rabbi*) was the phrase used by E. von Dobschütz, in his famous article, "Matthäus als Rabbi und Katechet," *ZNW* 27 (1928):338-48. Von Dobschütz's essay helped create an environment receptive to Bacon's portrait of Matthew as a legalist.

Book II: (a) 8:1-9:35: Narrative material
       (b) 9:36-10:42: Discourse on mission and martyrdom
Formula: 11:1: "And when Jesus had finished..."

Book III:(a) 11:2-12:50: Narrative and debate material
       (b) 13:1-52: Teaching on the kingdom of heaven
Formula: 13:53: "And when Jesus had finished..."

Book IV:(a) 13:54-17:21: Narrative and debate material
       (b) 17:22-18:35: Discourse on church administration
Formula: 19:1: "Now when Jesus had finished..."

Book V: (a) 19:2-22:46: Narrative and debate material
       (b) 23:1-25:46: Discourse on eschatology, farewell address
Formula: 26:1-2: "When Jesus finished..."

Epilogue: 26:3-28:20: From the last supper to the resurrection

Bacon was persuaded that the discovery of five books, homologous to the five books of Moses, "marks an epoch in the critical understanding and valuation" of Matthew, and "it should be made correspondingly prominent in attempts... to give the Gospel its historical position and value" (p. xvi). He did not, however, lay claim to a discovery: he flattered himself only with making a *re*discovery. J. Rendall Harris, in his *Testimonies*,[8] printed a fragment whose opening words may be rendered into English thus: "Matthew curbs the insolence of the Jews, as with bridles muzzling them in five books." Tendering an interpretation different than that of Harris,[9] Bacon took the six iambic verses to be "a prologue to Matthew after the plan of the so-called Monarchian Prologues" (p. xv), which prologue discloses that, during the time of the apologists—Bacon dated the fragment to the second century—Matthew's Gospel was imagined to contain five divisions or books.[10]

---

[8]Part I (Cambridge: University Press, 1916); Part II (Cambridge: University Press, 1920).

[9]See *Testimonies* 1:100-17; 2:90-94, 109-21. Harris, who conceded the uncertainty of the date of the lines (from a sixteenth century Mount Athos ms.), regarded them as confirmation of his theory that the apostle Matthew composed a five-part book of scriptural testimonies to Jesus Christ.

[10]See further B. W. Bacon, "The 'Five Books' of Matthew against the Jews," *Expositor* 15, series 8 (1918):56-66.

Over the past half-century or so Bacon's thesis has been much discussed. Not a few have been favorably inclined towards it.[11] It is in their favor that the structural imitation of one book by another is attested in both Jewish[12] and Graeco-Roman sources,[13] and also that there do indeed seem to be five major discourses in Matthew (5-7, 10, 13, 18, [23]24-25). And yet Bacon's far-reaching outline transgresses the facts.[14] For (i) it will not do to label Matthew 1-2 "prologue," Matthew 26-28 "epilogue;" (ii) it is untrue that each of the five books of Moses contains "commandments of Moses, each body of law introduced by a narrative of considerable length"[15] (what of Genesis?); (iii) one fails to detect any correlation between Matthew's "first book" and Genesis, his "second book" and Exodus, etc.; (iv) there is not sufficient cause to unite each discourse to a narrative and so create "books" consisting of narrative and discourse;[16] and (v) the critic must "distinguish between the use of a single, specific subtext and a topos that conventional repetition has removed from the purview of any one author or work;"[17] and with regard to the matter at hand, the division of a work into five parts may have been conventional in Matthew's first-century Jewish-Christian world—a proposition given substance by the Pentateuch, the Psalter, the Megilloth, Jason of Cyrene's Maccabean history (cf. 2 Macc. 2:23), *Jubilees*,[18] *l Enoch*, the early form of *Mishnah ᵓAbot*, Papias' *Exposition of the Oracles of the Lord* (cf. Eusebius, *H.E.* 3:39), Irenaeus' *Adversus Haereses*, and Hippolytus' memoirs (cf. Eusebius, *H.E.* 4:22); so even if Matthew does contain five sections, the implications are not obvious.[19]

---

[11]See those cited by J. D. Kingsbury, *Matthew: Structure, Christology, Kingdom* (Philadelphia: Fortress, 1975), 3, n. 13.

[12]The *Psalms of Solomon* consciously imitate the Psalter in several respects, the *Testaments of the Twelve Patriarchs* are more or less modelled on Genesis 49, and *11QTemple* in many ways follows the Pentateuch. For the Psalms and the Pentateuch see n. 19. I know of no treatment of structural imitation in Jewish books.

[13]One thinks of Virgil and of the debt of his *Eclogues* to Theocritus' *Idylls*, of his *Georgics* to Hesiod, of the *Aeneid* to Homer. For other examples and discussion see G. M. A. Grubbe, *The Greek and Latin Critics* (London: Methuen, 1965).

[14]In addition to what follows see Davies, *Setting*, 14-25.

[15]If this is indeed what Bacon mistakenly thought. But, as he expressed himself so poorly, we cannot really tell.

[16]See my article, "Matthew: Structure, Biographical Impulse, and the *Imitatio Christi*," in *The Four Gospels 1992*, ed. C. M. Tuckett et al. (BETL 100; Leuven: Leuven University Press, 1992), vol. 2, pp. 1203-1221.

[17]Greene, *Light in Troy*, 50.

[18]After the introduction there are stories about Adam, Noah, Abraham, Jacob, and Moses.

[19]Cf. Hawkins, *Horae Synopticae*, 163-64, who compares the prevalence in European literature of five-act plays and three-volume novels. At the same time, some of the books

Not one of these points is in itself, I confess, an Achilles' heel, and, because of the bare possibility that the number five connotes Moses, Bacon may always haunt Matthean studies. Nonetheless it is understandable that the company of those enamored of Bacon's structural analysis seems to wane perceptibly as the years go by, while alternative proposals proliferate. Bacon has not prevailed.

Aside from his discussion of Matthew's structure, Bacon did not much elaborate on the Mosaic elements in the First Gospel: "Moses" is not even in the index of subjects. He did, in arguing for the Jewish roots of Matthew's infancy materials, affirm that "the underlying Jewish tales... belong to the legendary story of Moses rather than Abraham; for 'the episode of the return from Egypt narrated in [chapter 2] verses 20 and 21 is clearly modelled upon the LXX of Ex. 4:19,20 (the return of Moses from Midian to Egypt).'"[20] Yet the significance of this for interpretation remained unfolded.

In only one other connection did Bacon introduce Moses. Matthew 8-9 contains "a group of ten Mighty Works, subdivided at 8:17 by a Scripture Fulfillment with transition at 9:8 to the Markan group Mk 2:13-22; 5:1-42" (p. 187); and according to Bacon, Matthew added—as "an afterthought"—two miracles, those in 9:27-31 and 9:32-34. Why? The motive was numerical: the evangelist desired to have Jesus perform "ten mighty works exhibiting the power of the 'prophet like unto Moses'..." (p. 189). In other words, Jesus' ten miracles were designed to resemble the ten plagues Moses worked in Egypt—a surmise that has appealed to others.[21]

As with Bacon's linking of Matthew's five discourses to the five books of Moses, so here too: there are difficulties.[22] The reader is referred to the discussion on pp. 207-12, where I have recorded my reasons for scepticism. Here it suffices to observe that Bacon's interpretation of Matthew 8-9 is far from manifest and that other explanations of the arrangement of the section abound (see the commentaries).

I have cited should perhaps be regarded as imitators of the Pentateuch's structure. Many have dated the canonical collection of one hundred and fifty psalms to a time after the composition of the Pentateuch, on the assumption that its division into five parts reflects "a conscious imitation of the fivefold partition of the Pentateuch;" so Mitchell Dahood, *Psalms I. 1-50* (AB 16; New York: Doubleday, 1965), xxx; cf. J. Hempel, in *IDB* 3, 943b, s.v., "Psalms, Book of." Note *Midr. Ps.* 1:2: "as Moses gave five books of laws to Israel, so David gave five books of Psalms to Israel."

[20]*Studies*, 153-54, citing G. H. Box, "The Gospel Narratives of the Nativity and the alleged influence of Heathen Ideas," *ZNW* 6 (1905):80-101.

[21]E.g. Schoeps, *Theologie*, 93.

[22]See esp. Davies, *Setting*, 86-92.

A critical examination of Bacon's work and its reception reveals that, for our purposes, his primary contribution was to stimulate the discussion. While he established neither that Matthew's structure was intended to mirror the Pentateuch, nor that Matthew 8-9 was modelled upon the plagues of Exodus, his suggestions along these lines generated much useful debate and so moved us forward—and that cannot be reckoned failure. We must moreover remind ourselves that exposition of Matthew's theology was not the heart of Bacon's enterprise. However much he in certain respects anticipated redaction criticism, he was above all passionate about the historical Jesus, a subject on which he wrote much. This explains the confession on p. xiv: "The question of sources we confess to be our deepest interest in the Studies in Mt." Bacon probed Matthew's theology, characterized as "neo-legalistic perversion," in order to forget it and then press on toward the goal for the prize of the historical Jesus. Bacon was a typical liberal quester, not a modern redaction critic.

APPENDIX II

W. D. Davies' *The Setting of the Sermon on the Mount*

When it first appeared, W. D. Davies' *The Setting of the Sermon on the Mount* eclipsed all previous discussion of the subject of Moses in Matthew, and the book has remained the fullest examination of that subject, the one treatment that compels attention. After an introductory section where, among other things, the axe is laid to the root of Austin Farrer's theory that Matthew 5-7 is modelled upon Exodus 20-24, Davies turns, on pp. 14-108, to what he calls "the setting in Matthew." Under this rubric fall three subjects: "Pentateuchal motifs," "New Exodus and New Moses," "Mosaic categories transcended."

The section on pentateuchal motifs, on pp. 14-25, is the definitive review of Bacon's analysis of Matthew's structure. Davies' conclusion, convincingly argued, is negative: "the pentateuchal approach to Matthew must remain questionable" (p. 25). The strongest of his reasons for so deciding have been given on pp. 294-97.

The next section, which spans pp. 26-93, looks at the new exodus and new Moses themes, reviewing, in order, Matthew's treatment of Mark and Q, the material peculiar to Matthew (M), and the arrangement of the ten miracles in Matthew 8-9. According to Davies, the new Moses motif is not present, explicitly or implicitly, in chapter 3, and "there is nothing to indicate that Matthew has emphasized the Exodus motif in any way…" (p. 45). In 4:1-11, the temptation narrative, "it is precarious to find even in the Matthean version… any convincing parallel between Jesus and Moses, although Jesus does re-enact the experience of the 'Son of God,' the Old Israel" (p. 48). Nor is there any accentuation of the new exodus motif in 14:13-21, the feeding of the five thousand. But in 17:1-8, the story of the transfiguration, "Matthew seems to have altered and rearranged the material in Mark, not merely for motives of simple reverence… but with the deliberate purpose of presenting Jesus after the manner of Moses, albeit a Moses whom he supersedes as 'the unique and definitive teacher of mankind'" (p. 56). Other passages, "of lesser significance,"[23] do not exhibit the new Moses theme. So Davies' review of the Markan and Q material in Matthew leads to this:

> Such New Exodus motifs as have been detected… are preserved, though hardly emphasized, in Matthew. The 'New Moses' motif as such is more rare…. Nevertheless, in two places we are probably justified in detecting the lineaments of the New Moses, in the feeding of the thousands,[24] where, however, his 'Mosaic' character is not particularly emphasized by Matthew, and in the Transfiguration scene, where this character can be regarded as deliberately developed by Matthew, Jesus being the one who replaces Moses as the one who is to be heard. The Mount of Transfiguration thus recalls the Mount from which Jesus proclaimed the Sermon in v-vii, and to this extent supports the interpretation of the Jesus of the Mount as a New Moses and a greater (p. 61).

Concerning next the material peculiar to Matthew, Davies first examines "the prologue" (Matthew 1-2), then "the epilogue" (26:1-28:20; the terminology is Bacon's). He discerns in the former not only a new creation motif and an emphasis upon the fulfillment of Davidic hopes but also the second Moses theme: Pharaoh is the model of Herod; 2:19-21 resembles Exod. 4:19-20; the magi have their parallel in the Moses traditions (Exodus 7; Josephus, *Ant.* 2:205-209, 232-37); the legend of a supernatural light flooding Moses' house at birth (se SB l:78) approximates the star which leads the magi; and, lastly, it is not unlikely that David Daube has correctly interpreted a passage in the Passover Haggadah as a reference to the conception of Moses without human father (see above, pp. 146-50). Thus "we seem to be justified in finding in the Prologue support for regarding the *SM* in the light of Sinai and the Christ of the Mount in the light of Moses, though we

---

[23]11:7; 11:5-6; the choice of the twelve; the last supper; 21:1-9; the beatitudes of chapter 5 and the woes of chapter 23.

[24]The statement is somewhat surprising given the earlier comments on pp. 48-49.

emphasize that this is never made explicit by Matthew" (p. 83). With regard to the epilogue, 26:1-28:20, there are no Mosaic undertones in 26:53[25] or 27:45-56,[26] and they are weak if present at all in 26:26-30 (the last supper); but that there is an implicit reference to Moses in 28:16-20, where Jesus, on a mountain, enjoins obedience to his commandments, is a "plausible conjecture" (p. 86).

The third part of the section on the new exodus and the new Moses themes deals with the ten miracles in 8:1-9:34, with this result: "Apart from the number ten, which itself may be a mere literary convenience, there is no indication that the shadow of Moses falls on viii.l-ix.34" (p. 90).

Before advancing to the next topic, Davies stops to summarize his results so far (pp. 92-93). The data indicate that "Matthew was well aware of that interpretation of Christ which found his prototype in Moses, and that, at certain points, he may have allowed this to colour his Gospel. But the restraint with which the New Exodus and New Moses motifs are used is noticeable." In our Gospel "there is no explicit reference to Mount Sinai; no features from the account of the giving of the Law in Exod. xix, as they are developed, for example, in Heb. xii. 18ff., appear in v. lf.; and at no point, apart from the express quotations from the Law in the antitheses, in v. 21ff., are we directly referred to the events at Sinai." Hence "we cannot but ask whether Matthew could not have been somewhat bolder in his 'Mosaism' had the idea of a New Moses played a great part in his purpose in writing the Gospel. The case would seem to be that, while the category of a New Moses and a New Sinai is present in v-vii, as elsewhere in Matthew, the strictly Mosaic traits in the figure of the Matthean Christ, both there and in other parts of the Gospel, have been taken up into a deeper and higher context."

Davies turns to the final topic of his second chapter on pp. 93-108: Mosaic categories transcended. The application of *mathētai*, the bearing of Christ's yoke (11:29: this implies a law of Christ), and the concept of being "trained" or "taught" for the kingdom (13:52) show that the relation of Christians to Jesus could "be expressed in a terminology derived from Judaism, the religion of the Law" (p. 94); and this fact well comports with the idea that Christians stand under

---

[25]"Do you think that I cannot appeal to my Father, and he will at once send me more than twelve legions of angels?" According to the *Mekilta*, Moses had access to angelic aid; see Davies, *Setting*, 40.

[26]The miracles accompanying the crucifixion.

a new Sinai and follow a new Moses. But caution is required, lest the parallel lead to imprecision. Much about Jesus does not resemble or recall Moses. (i) The commandments of the SM are Jesus' words, so that "the ethical teaching is not detached from the life of him who uttered it, and with whom it is congruous. It is personalized in him" (p. 94). (ii) Jesus himself is an object of faith (cf. 18:6; 27:42). (iii) Obedience consists of following Christ, the one who suffered, was made poor, rejected worldly honor, and served others. (iv) Jesus is not, for his disciples, "teacher" or "rabbi" but "Lord:" Jesus commands as Lord. Moses commanded as mediator (p. 97). (v) There is a kind of identity between Christians and their Lord (cf. 10:40; 18:5; 25:31-46), and the Christian life is to be understood in the light of this relationship: the imperative is based upon the indicative. Davies also urges that if by "New Sinai" is meant a revolutionary phenomenon, such cannot be the case. Matthew does not understand the six paragraphs in 5:21-48 to contain "antitheses;" and his redactional work in 12:1-14 (observance of the Sabbath), 15:1-20 (on the laws of purity), and 19:1-9 (on divorce) exhibit an "anxiety not to place Jesus in direct antithesis to Moses" (p. 105). After making some comments on Matthew 23, to the effect that what is there condemned is not obedience to the law but misinterpretation of it, Davies asserts that "the understanding of the Law of Moses both within and without the Sermon in Matthew forbids any emphasis on an antithesis to the Law of Moses and must be allowed… to temper our eagerness to see in Jesus a New Moses opposed to the first" (p. 106). At the same time, it is affirmed that "Christians, for Matthew, do stand under the 'New Sinai' of a 'New Moses' (p. 94), and that "the substance of the New Law, the New Sinai, the New Moses, are present" (p. 108).

As positions Davies has espoused on particular texts have, time and again, been examined on previous pages, I should like at this juncture to pursue a series of questions that has surfaced from reading and rereading *The Setting of the Sermon on the Mount*—questions which largely set the agenda for my own work. So, to begin: does Davies' survey, long and well-informed as it is, exhaust the pertinent evidence? Whatever Davies' intention, the answer must be negative. 11:25-30, a crucial text in my judgement, is quoted in Greek opposite page 1, but its probable Mosaic background is only intimated, never investigated. The possible parallel between 8:1 and certain verses in Exodus is not considered, nor is the resemblance between 7:28-29 and Deut. 32:45. More surprisingly, only five points of contact are observed between Matt. 1-2 and the traditions about Moses. Many others can and have been noted (pp. 140-65 herein). None of these omissions is insignificant.

Next, is Davies' failure to discuss at any length other documents, whether Jewish or Christian, which contain a Moses typology, not a debilitating handicap? In establishing the presence of the new creation motif in chapter 1 he writes: "It is also necessary to recall the whole emphasis on the coming of Christ as a new creation in the New Testament to feel the force of the argument" (p. 70, n. 2). But the same is true of the new Moses theme. It certainly appears in Luke-Acts and John as well as Hebrews, is implicit in Mark, and is a commonplace in patristic literature. Davies is not, of course, unaware of all this (cf. p. 189, n. 2). Yet the fact unaccountably receives no emphasis. Surely the appearance of a motif in other streams of the Christian tradition makes its discovery in Matthew more believable. No less importantly: there is an abundance of Jewish materials in which Moses serves as a type. Again, Davies cannot be wholly ignorant of this, for he rightly remarks that Hillel and Akiba were set over against Moses (p. 108, n. 2), and he observes the possibility that Elijah's journey to Horeb was in imitation of Moses (p. 46). These examples, seemingly so suggestive, are, however, only the proverbial tip of the proverbial iceberg. Not just Elijah and Hillel and Akiba but, as the reader of this study now knows, Joshua and Gideon and Samuel and Jeremiah and Ezekiel and still others were likened to Moses, and numerous are the narratives about them which echo the Pentateuch. How can we justly evaluate Matthew without keeping this in mind and without examining how and why other authors constructed Moses typologies? The present investigation has demonstrated that a very rich collection of relevant texts has gone unmined by Davies and others.

A third question: if one claims, as have so many, that Matthew's Jesus is greater than Moses, what Moses are we talking about? We know that there have been many Jesus Christs, for each age, each religious body, each theological school has had its own Jesus. History has handed us the Pauline Christ, the Johannine Christ, the Gnostic Christ, the Byzantine Christ, the liberal Christ: and so it goes. It has not been otherwise with Moses. There has been the Moses of P, the Deuteronomic Moses, Moses the apocalyptic seer, Moses the Hellenistic sage and philosopher-king, Moses the magician, the Talmudic Moses, and Moses the Christian saint.[27] With what Moses was Matthew acquainted? It is easy enough to discover ways in which the Jesus of Matthew outshines the Moses of the Pentateuch. But Moses lived on in Jewish imagination and tradition, a fundamental fact demanding

---

[27]Instructive here is D. J. Silver, *Images of Moses* (New York: Basic Books, 1982).

our full attention. In Matthew's time many held what might be called a "high Mosesology."[28] Davies, in his section on the transcending of Mosaic categories, observes that disciples in Matthew have faith in Christ. But in *Mek.* on Exod. 14:15 we read that the Israelites who followed Moses into the desert "believed" in him (cf. Exod. 14:31; 19:9); and Samaritanism came to make belief in Moses a tenet of its religion: "He who believes in Moses believes in his Lord" (*Memar Marqah* 4:17).[29] Again, Davies, in the same section, makes much of the *imitatio Christi* and of Jesus' embodiment of his speech. This too, however, need not take us beyond Moses, for in Hellenistic Jewish sources Moses is the perfect embodiment of virtue, his words and deeds being one (cf. Philo, *Mos.* 1:29, 48); he therefore becomes an object of imitation:

> I hope to bring the story of this greatest and most perfect (*teleiotatou*) of men to the knowledge of such as deserve not to remain in ignorance of it (Philo, *Mos.* 1:1).
> Perhaps, too, since he was destined to be a legislator, the providence of God which afterwards appointed him without his knowledge to that work, caused him long before that day to be the reasonable and living impersonation of the law (ibid. 1:162; cf. 158-59).
> The legislative faculty has for its brothers and close kinsfolk these four in particular: love of humanity, of justice, of goodness, and hatred of evil.... It is no small thing if it is given to anyone to acquire even one of these—a marvel surely that he should be able to grasp them all together. And this Moses alone appears to have attained... (ibid. 2:9-10).

[28]A "high Mosesology" might already be attested in the Pentateuch, by way of refutation; see Silver, ibid., 3-43. Among his observations are these: Moses never devised a war plan, sat on a throne, or promulgated laws (he only reported what God told him); he had no mausoleum, founded no dynasty, left no important offspring; the Torah does not say Moses freed Israel, that he did miracles, or that he led the people in the desert (God is always the subject of those activities); Moses is not depicted as a self-reliant leader but a man without freedom of judgment and action, a faithful courier who only did what he was told; he was only an agent, not a leader, ambassador, or principal; in Exod. 2:14-15 we read that Moses struck down an unsuspecting victim, hid his act, and fled in fright into the night; and Exodus reports no plan of Moses to return and help his people until God appeared to him in the bush. The force of these observations is all the stronger when one takes into account the extra-biblical traditions about Moses: these give him heroic proportions. For further discussion of the evidence that the exaltation of Moses in Judaism brought forth responses which maintained his submission to God see Cross, *Canaanite Myth*, 195-215; W. Feilchenfelt, "Die Entpersönhohung Moses in der Bible," *ZAW* 64 (1952):156-78; Friedman, *Who Wrote the Bible?*, 197-206; J. Morgenstern, "Moses with the Shining Face," *HUCA* 2 (1925):1-27; Polzin, *Moses and the Deuteronomist*. Recall that in Num. 25:6-16 Phineas upstages Moses, and that in the *Passover Haggadah* Moses all but disappears.

[29]See J. Macdonald, *The Theology of the Samaritans* (Philadelphia: Westminster, 1964), 150-52.

In these [Moses' great natural gifts], philosophy found a good soil, which she improved still further by the admirable truths which she brought before his eyes, nor did she cease until the fruits of virtue shewn in word and deed were brought to perfection (ibid. 1:66).

In speech and in addresses to a crowd he found favor in every way, but chiefly through his thorough command of his passions, which was such that he seemed to have no place for them at all in his soul, and only knew their names through seeing them in others rather than in himself (Josephus, *Ant.* 4:328-29).

We should be fully alive to the possibility that our image of Moses or the Biblical picture of Moses was not that of Matthew. In particular, we should not just assume that this or that facet of Matthew's Christology gives us a Jesus greater than Moses. Although what he meant is disputed, Philo called Moses *theos*;[30] and *Deut. Rab.* 11:4, on the basis of the *ʾîš ʾĕlōhîm* of Deut. 33:1, refers to Moses as half man, half divine being. In Ezekiel the Tragedian's *Exagoge* there is a scene in which God stands off his throne and hands his scepter to Moses, who takes the seat, as the stars bow down before him (see p. 178). Some Jews, according to *Sipre* § 357 and other sources, believed that Moses never died. It has even been argued (although the evidence is inconclusive) that, during the Persian occupation of Egypt, there was a Moses cult with shrine, perhaps at Leontopolis.[31] Be that as it may, the point is made: we must not, without further ado, identify Matthew's Moses with either the historical Moses or the biblical Moses. "Greater than Moses," with reference to Matthew, is not a category clearly defined.

My fourth question is methodological: how does one determine whether the purported discovery of an allusion is exegesis or eisegesis? This difficult question, rarely asked, demands systematic attention, and I have discussed it on previous pages. Here I raise just one issue, one posed by Davies' treatment: should possible allusions be discussed one at a time, in isolation from one another? Davies methodically looks now at this text from Mark, now at that text from Q. But a biblical typology will often consist of scattered references and allusions running over several paragraphs, even chapters, which together add up to significance. So should we not from time to time stand back and ask of proposed allusions whether they do not generate some overall pattern? This is precisely the value of Goulder's work, to which

---

[30]See Carl R. Holladay, *THEIOS ANER in Hellenistic Judaism* (SBLDS 40; Missoula: Scholars Press, 1977), 103-98. Cf. Artapanus *apud* Eusebius, *Praep. ev.* 9:27.6: Moses was reckoned worthy of "godlike honor" (*isotheou timēs*).

[31]D. J. Silver, "Moses and the Hungry Birds," *JQR* 64 (1973):124-53.

we shall next turn; and one recalls that C. F. Evans' famous study of Luke's central section gains what force it has from the cataloguing of parallels which, though in themselves weak, bear a striking similarity of sequence.[32] Even if one harbors doubt, as do I, regarding Evans' demonstration, his method has merit. The case for typology can be cumulative. Does Davies' work give due consideration to this?

Another question: on pp. 26ff. Davies examines first the baptismal material, then the temptation, then the feeding of the five thousand, then the transfiguration, then a few miscellaneous passages, then the prologue, then the epilogue, then chapters 8-9. But what would have happened had he begun with the prologue and/or the transfiguration before turning to other passages? Upon Matthew 1-2 and 17:1-8 the seal of Moses has been clearly set, and in those places Davies can perceive much evidence of a redactional tendency to insert items likening Jesus to Moses. It is generally a safe rule to start from the certain and then proceed to the uncertain; for while the latter cannot much help us with the former, the former can aid us with the latter. In the present case, why not begin with the more or less assured allusions to Moses before scrutinizing the less evident? Tracking covert allusions is hazardous business, and presumption will inevitably effect the outcome. Were one to commence with the infancy materials and/or the transfiguration, in both of which Moses is forcefully present, would there not be a greater disposition to encounter him elsewhere? This is all the more true when an observation of Davies is taken into account:

> As in the Old Testament so in the New the prologues to the various documents often illumine their contents. This is true, for example, of the book of Job, where the Prologue is designed to make the reader aware of the reason for Job's suffering, even though it is hidden from the sufferer himself, and from those around him. So in the New Testament, the prologues of the Fourth Gospel and of Mark, on examination, explain the contents of the two Gospels as a whole, while the prologue of Luke explicitly states the author's aims. We might therefore expect this to be the case with Matthew also. Indeed we might suspect this would be pre-eminently true of this Gospel, because of its so emphatic schematic character (pp. 61-62).

These words, which merit assent, move one to ask: if the prologue to Matthew is programmatic, and if, as Davies holds, it contains the new

---

[32]C. F. Evans, "The Central Section of St. Luke's Gospel," in *Studies in the Gospels,* ed. D. Nineham (Oxford: Basil Blackwell, 1955), 37-53.

Moses theme, is this not a propitious clue which should cast its light on the rest of the Gospel? What other major theme—major is the right word, as I hope I have shown—in the prologue (= Matthew 1-2) does not resurface more than once in Matthew 3-28?

One final query: does Matthew's conservative attitude towards the law stand in tension with the new Moses theme? On p. 106 Davies writes: "the understanding of the Law of Moses both within and without the Sermon in Matthew forbids any emphasis on an antithesis to the Law of Moses and must be allowed... to temper our eagerness to see in Jesus a New Moses opposed to the first." On the next page there is this: "the *SM* itself is not set forth as a 'new,' revolutionary Law, in sharp antithesis to that given on Sinai." While concurring that the SM is not Moses undone, what unstated assumptions underlie Davies' words? Most of the (Gentile) Church Fathers assuredly thought that there was more than just tension between the new covenant and the old. For them the new Moses made much the old Moses said obsolete. But it was otherwise with the Ebionites, and who is to say that Matthew was not in this respect closer to them? Could he not have believed the new Torah and the new Moses to be at one with the old Torah and the old Moses? If "the understanding of the Law of Moses both within and without the Sermon in Matthew forbids any emphasis on an antithesis to the Law of Moses," that does necessarily "temper our eagerness to see in Jesus a New Moses opposed to the first," but it does not necessarily hamper us from seeing in Jesus a new Moses *like* the first. Why has Davies tacked on "opposed to the first"? Is it because others who have detected the new Moses theme in Matthew have tended so to express themselves?[33] Perhaps so. But then it must be emphatically stated: an antitype does not inevitably subvert its type— as the numerous Jewish Moses typologies reviewed herein abundantly illustrate. Neither Paul's contrast between Adam and Christ nor the contrast of the two covenants in Hebrews 8-10 need be the model for a Moses typology in Matthew. We should not proceed from the assumption that a strong Moses typology must imply a revolutionary and unMatthean attitude towards the law. In fact, I venture that the truth—grasped by Schoeps—is just the opposite: it was Matthew's conservativism which made so congenial the new exodus and new Moses themes.[34]

[33]A famous instance: Hans Windisch, *The Meaning of the Sermon on the Mount* (Philadelphia: Westminster, 1951).

[34]I note that *The Setting of the Sermon on the Mount* is not Professor Davies' last word on the subject of Moses in Matthew. In a 1988 lecture delivered at a Princeton symposium on messianism and then again at Duke University in 1990, he has shown

APPENDIX III

Matthean Typology in the Work of M. D. Goulder

M. D. Goulder's *Type and History in Acts*[35] is, as the title indicates, a book about Acts. The opening pages, however, treat of Matthew. Goulder, writing that "typological criticism is a tool not yet accepted and valued by all scholars," and conceding that typology "improperly used… is, as its critics have objected, subjective and unscientific and dangerous" (p. 1), is anxious to demonstrate that typology can be objective and scientific and helpful. To execute the demonstration he examines the assertion of the typologist that "the sermon on the mount is the antitype of the giving of the law on Mount Sinai" (p. 2). Against the critic who replies, "Nonsense… there is no evidence of this: there are plenty of mountains in Galilee, and Jesus climbed one to instruct his disciples—that is all," Goulder answers that "almost all typology is *cumulative*," and he contends that the mountain of Matt. 5:1 is not isolated but part of a "systematic and sustained typology" (p. 2). The outcome of his discussion may be set forth in this way (cf. p. 3):

Genesis and Exodus	Matthew
Genesis: this book is the *locus classicus* for genealogies in the Hebrew Bible	l:l-17: "The book of the genesis of Jesus Christ" precedes a genealogy
Genesis 37-50: Joseph is a dreamer of dreams; in one dream he is represented by a star; he excels the wise men of Egypt	1-2: Joseph has a dream; there is a special star; wise men appear
Genesis 45-50: Joseph takes old Israel down to Egypt	2:13-15: Joseph takes new Israel down to Egypt (Hos. ll:l is quoted)

himself much more open than before to the Mosaic approach to the First Gospel. He now for example believes that a new exodus pattern does in fact run throughout the first few chapters and that 11:25-30 has as its background Exodus 33 and Moses' rôle as mediator. Our ICC commentary also reflects the development in his thinking on the matter. This does not mean that Davies' would concur with all the suggestions I make herein: that is too much for me to hope. But his change of mind, after a life-time of study, cannot but encourage others to pass beyond his earlier work and ask if there are not more hidden things to be revealed.

[35]London: S.P.C.K., 1964.

Exodus 1: Pharaoh massacres infants	2:16: Herod massacres infants
Exod. 4:19: "All the men are dead…"	2:20: "They are dead…"
Exod. 12ff.: from Egypt to Israel	2:21ff. from Egypt to Israel
Exodus 14: a desert scene; Israel passes through the water	3:1ff.: a desert scene; Jesus (= new Israel) passes through water (cf. 1 Cor. 10:1-2)
Exodus 16ff.: temptations in the wilderness for forty years; the first temptation is for bread, the second is at Massah, the third is the making of the golden calf	4:1-11: temptations in the wilderness for forty days and nights; the first temptation is for bread, the second brings a quotation of Deut. 6:16, which in its original context refers to Massah, and in response to the third temptation Jesus quotes Deut. 6:13, which concerns false gods
Exodus 18: Moses gathers seventy elders	4:17-21: Jesus gathers four disciples
Exodus 19: Moses and the commandments on Sinai	5:1-2: the SM, "where Jesus gives his 'fulfilment' of the sixth, seventh, and ninth commandments"

The number of correlations between Matthew and Genesis-Exodus is not, according to Goulder, chance's child. It is true that any one of them "might have been a coincidence and no more. But when they are placed in a definite order, accident is out of the question. A succession of this dimension has been purposefully arranged, and by St. Matthew himself and no other." He continues: "There is nowhere in the New Testament so extended, continuous, and transparent a passage modelled upon the Old Testament as Matt. 1-5, and it is to this mast that the typologist should nail his flag" (p. 6).

Having established this much, Goulder pursues the problem of method. How does one avoid subjectivity in discovering typology? How much evidence is required to establish that a biblical text was in an evangelist's mind? Goulder proposes, and discusses in some detail, three safeguards: "the need to supply catenas, and not single instances, of correspondences; the need for the coincidence of actual Greek words between type and antitype, and the rarer the better; and the need for a convincing motive for the evangelist to have composed his work in the way claimed" (p. 6).

As final justification for a typological approach to Acts, Goulder appeals to precedent. Calling upon l Maccabees, he rightly observes that it explicitly and implicitly draws parallels between Judas Maccabeus and the biblical Judah[36] as well as between Phineas and both Eleazar and Judas Maccabeus.[37] Typology was alive among ancient Jewish history writers.[38]

Type and History in Acts has unfortunately had no discernible impact upon Matthean studies. Presumably the causes are two—first, the book is about Acts, and, secondly, the author has the reputation of being something of a maverick. Nonetheless, the work is an important step forward. The concern for method, conspicuously absent from so many other discussions, is admirable. Also praiseworthy is the attempt to remove New Testament typological criticism from isolation. By citing clear examples of typology from l Maccabees, Goulder shows that the phenomenon under review was not a Christian *novum* but a Jewish commonplace. My own work has confirmed this and expands the comparative material by exploring numerous texts, both Jewish and Christian, which contain a Moses typology. Finally, Goulder's insight that typology is usually cumulative and involves a catena of allusions is most helpful. Other proponents of a Moses typology in Matthew have been content to observe that Jesus is here like Moses and there like Moses, or that the new exodus theme seemingly appears in several places. Goulder, however, has noticed that the apparent

---

[36]Cf. l Macc. 3:4 with Gen. 49.9, l Macc. 2:14 with Gen. 37:34, and, more generally, l Macc. 2:49ff. with Gen. 49.

[37]Note l Macc. 2:26 and cf. l Macc. 2:1 with l Chron. 24:7 and l Macc. 3:8 with Num. 25:11.

[38]Goulder does not note the work of Farmer, *Maccabees, Zealots, and Josephus* (New York: Columbia, 1956), which shows that the Maccabees themselves later became models and types for first-century Jewish nationalists.

allusions to Moses and the exodus in Matthew 1-5 appear in their biblical sequence:[39]

Exodus—slaughter—return—passage—temptation—mountain of
               of infants   of hero   through   lawgiving
                                               water

Matthew—slaughter—return—passage—temptation—mountain of
                 of infants   of hero   through   lawgiving
                                                 water

This is more than curious and not likely to be the upshot of chance. It would seem that the various texts with Mosaic parallels should be considered together, not in isolation from each other: our moments of recognition are to be added up. Because of their high density, and by virtue of their order, which is that of the Pentateuch, the allusions are contiguous and possess a collective integrity which establishes a typological sequence. This matters so much because it is often difficult to determine how much of the Tanak should be activated or evoked by a New Testament citation or allusion. But when a catena of New Testament texts alludes to biblical passages that are all part of the same story, then, we may surmise, that whole story should be called to mind: plot is recapitulating plot.

On the downside, Goulder's work is greatly circumscribed because (i) he has—for understandable reasons: the book's purview is Acts—looked only at Matthew 1-5 and (ii) there is, as I hope to show later, much in Matthew 1-5 that he has missed. But the one serious flaw is another. Goulder finds parallels to Matthew 1-5 not only in Exodus but also in the latter parts of Genesis. This pushes the case too far. While 1:1 does hearken back to Genesis, the existence of a Joseph typology in Matthew 1-2, although not impossible,[40] is far from

---

[39]Goulder acknowledges his debt in this particular to his teacher, A. Farrer, *St. Matthew and St. Mark* (Westminster: Dacre, 1954), 182-83, where there is this: in Matthew 2 "the male children of Israel are slaughtered by a new Pharaoh. God calls his son out of Egypt into the Land of Promise. Jesus passes the waters and undergoes one after another Israel's temptations in the wilderness. It is on such a background that the ascent of the mountain [5:1] is set, a new Sinai surely, from which Jesus delivers his interpretation of the ancient law." This fruitful proposal unfortunately swims in a sea of implausible speculation (such as: Matthew is a new Hexateuch, the beatitudes correspond to the decalogue, Matthew 13 is to be associated with Numbers) and therefore has not been sufficiently considered.

[40]Brown, *Birth of the Messiah*, 111-13.

obvious, in part because Matthew drew no key expressions from the appropriate portions of Genesis, in part because the extra-biblical traditions about Amram, the father of Moses, are more likely in the background. The demonstration of this I have already made (pp. 140-65). Here I only call attention to Goulder's remarks on the *magoi*. He wonders why, if the Joseph story lies behind Matthew 1-2, the word is not *exēgētai* or *sophoi*, as in LXX Gen. 41:8. His explanation? "In Dan. 2:2—a passage closely similar to, and in fact written in imitation of, Gen. 41—the interpretation of Nebuchadnezzar's dream is committed to enchanters and μάγοι and sorcerers and Chaldeans; and the word covers St. Matthew's need more exactly without departing from biblical precedent" (p. 8). I am unable to concur: this takes one too far afield. Certain extra-biblical traditions about Moses have his birth predicted by *magicians*.[41] Given all the other parallels in Matthew's infancy narrative to the extra-biblical traditions about Moses, is this fact not more noteworthy than the use of *magoi* in Daniel 2, a chapter otherwise without influence on Matthew 2? The lesson is plain: because Matthew and his audience "knew" a lot more about Moses than what can be gleaned from Scripture, because indeed the Scriptures were understood in the light of extra-scriptural traditions,[42] a valid typological method will not confine itself to biblical materials.[43]

APPENDIX IV

The New Moses and the Son of God: Jack Dean Kingsbury

In his influential book, *Matthew: Structure, Christology, Kingdom*, Jack Kingsbury rejected Bacon's thesis of a First Gospel divided into five parts after the fashion of the Pentateuch (pp. 2-7). Among other points made he affirmed that "as far as the 'new Moses' typology is concerned, while Matthew may in instances have permitted this to color his Gospel, it is not so dominant a trait as to render Bacon's proposal credible" (p. 5). This claim was supported solely by a footnote citing

---

[41]Davies and Allison, *Matthew*, 1:192-93.

[42]Very helpful here is Kugel, *In Potiphar's House*. Note especially his conclusions on pp. 265-68.

[43]In his later book, *Midrash and Lection in Matthew* (London: SPCK, 1974), Goulder acknowledges a Moses typology on several occasions but does not develop it; see pp. 240, 245-47, 283, 393-95.

the work of others.[44] Later on, however, Kingsbury reverted to the subject. In a section on "minor" Christological titles he sought to show that "it is not with a new Moses that the reader [of Matthew] has to do... but with the Son of God" (pp. 91-92). Three arguments were offered.

First, Kingsbury wrote that Matthew's Gospel does not raise "(the) prophet" (cf. Deut. 18:15, 18) to "the rank of what may properly be construed as a christological title"[45] (p. 88). "Prophet" is not even adequate for John the Baptist (11:9), so how much less Jesus. And in 16:13-14 and 21:11 and 46 the confession of Jesus as prophet has only "negative value" (p. 88). It is made by the crowds, whose commitment to Jesus is ambiguous. The disciples, on the other hand, confess Jesus to be the Son of God (14:33; 16:16).

Secondly, there are, Kingsbury observed, many Matthean portions which, according to others, have been influenced by the new Moses theme—Matthew 2; 3; 4:2; 5:1; 8-9; 17:1-8; 28:16-20 (cf. the previous discussion). But he asserted that in these places "Matthew is at pains to develop his Son-of-God christology" (p. 90). In Matt. 2:15, for example, Jesus is called "my Son;" and in 4:3 and 6 Jesus is tempted by the devil as "the Son of God;" and in 17:5 a voice declares the transfigured Jesus to be "my Son;" and in 28:16-20 baptism is in the name of "the Father, Son, and Holy Spirit." All this Kingsbury deemed "extraordinary" (p. 90).

Thirdly, Kingsbury wrote that "the very way in which Matthew works editorially with the term 'Moses' helps to illuminate his under-standing of the person of Jesus in these two places" (p. 91). In Mark 7:10 = Matt. 15:4 and Mark 12:26 = Matt. 22:31 a Markan mention of "Moses" has been replaced by "God." "For Moses said" is now "For God said," and "read in the book of Moses" has become "read what was said to you by God." For Kingsbury, "the point of the various editorial changes is that Matthew, in treating of the law, is intent upon following the thrust of a passage such as Exod 20:1 (the one who 'spoke' atop Mt. Sinai was 'God') at the expense of other pentateuchal passages which stress the mediating role of Moses" (p. 91). Why? "Because the Jesus who ascends the mountain in the first Gospel and declares the will of God which is henceforth binding on the disciples

---

[44]Cited are G. Barth, "Matthew's Understanding of the Law," 157-59; Davies, *Setting*, 92-93; W. Trilling, *Das wahre Israel* (SANT 10; 3rd ed.; München: Kösel, 1964), 38, 186, 217.

[45]Kingsbury (p. 84) acknolwedges that the distinction is for convenience alone and is not "absolute."

is the Son of God and not, strictly speaking a new Moses. To refer to Jesus as a 'new Moses' is to import into Matthean christology a category Matthew himself repeatedly refused to make" (p. 91).

Given the endorsement of Kingsbury's work in many quarters, his arguments must be carefully considered. What then, to begin with, of his evaluation of "(the) prophet"? Should we be content to describe it as having "only negative value"? The title is, no doubt, inadequate; but in this connection inadequate can mean either wrong (= "only negative") or—and the difference is considerable—insufficient of itself. Jesus, according to 11:9, informed the crowd that it went out to see a prophet (= John the Baptist). Jesus then added that John the Baptist was "more than a prophet." There is not, against the impression left by Kingsbury,[46] any antithesis here. "What then did you go out to see? A prophet? Yes [nai—note bene], I tell you, and more than a prophet." John—who, after all, is implicitly and explicitly identified with the eschatological prophet Elijah: 3:4; 11:14—was both a prophet *and* more than a prophet. In like manner, and like another evangelist, Luke, Matthew could have simultaneously regarded Jesus as a prophet and as the eschatological Mosaic prophet and as much else besides, including Son of God.[47] In line with this, there is no good reason— quite the opposite—to categorize the crowds' confession of Jesus as "(the) prophet" in 21:11 and 46 as "only negative." In 21:9 the crowds shout: "Hosanna to the Son of David! Blessed in the name of the Lord is he who comes. Hosanna in the highest heaven!" This at least is not "only negative." The positive value of "the Son of David" for our evangelist cannot be gainsaid.[48] So is it not natural to see the crowds' subsequent confession, just a few verses later, as also something other than "only negative"? Observe that the crowds which go before Jesus at the entry are contrasted with the people in Jerusalem: "And when

[46]P. 89: "The Jewish 'crowd' may well think of John as a prophet (14:5; 21:26), but Jesus, on the other hand, declares to them that John is 'more than a prophet' (11:7, 9)."

[47]Contrast E. P. Blair, *Jesus in the Gospel of Matthew* (New York: Abingdon, 1960), 131: although Matthew did wish "to represent Jesus, the second Deliverer, as in many respects like the First," he did not regard Jesus as the eschatological prophet like Moses: Jesus was more than a prophet. (Pp. 124-37 of *Jesus in the Gospel of Matthew* are on "Jesus as the second Moses;" they do not, however, offer any new insights. Rather, casting his vote for or against, Blair simply notes where others have discovered the new Moses motif.)

[48]See esp. B. M. Nolan, *The Royal Son of God: The Christology of Matthew 1-2 in the Setting of the Gospel* (OBO 20; Göttingen: Vandenhoeck & Ruprecht, 1979), and the review of this by David Hill, in *JSNT* 9 (1980):66-69. Quite unpersuasive is Kingsbury's claim that Matthew's church had "outgrown" the title, Son of David (*Structure, Christology, Kingdom*, 102).

he entered Jerusalem, all the city was stirred, saying, 'Who is this?' But the crowds (*hoi de ochloi*) said, 'This is the prophet Jesus (*ho prophētēs Iēsous*) from Nazareth of Galilee'" (21:10-11). I have urged that here "the prophet" does likely allude to Deut. 18:15, 18. For present purposes, however, all that need be said is that the crowds which hail Jesus as the Son of David speak the truth while those in the guilty capital hold no opinion. This interpretation and the positive nature of the crowds' speech are confirmed by 21:15-16, where "the children" repeat part of the earlier confession ("Hosanna to the Son of David"). This, as Jesus himself makes perfectly plain, is inspired utterance: "Have you never read, 'Out of the mouth of babes and sucklings thou has brought perfect praise'?"

There is further nothing negative about "prophet" in 13:57. Here Jesus, adopting a proverb, declares that a prophet is not without honor save in his own country and his own house. According to Kingsbury, once one takes into account the antithesis between "prophet" and "Son of God" in 16:14-16, "we can begin to appreciate the scorn with which Matthew imbues the comment of Jesus to the Jews of Nazareth, who take offense at him (13:57): his former neighbors, like his worst enemies but unlike even the crowds, will not afford him so much as the honor due a prophet" (p. 89). This appears to mean that Jesus, although more than a prophet, does not obtain even a prophet's reward. But this is not what the text literally says, and Kingsbury's subtle interpretation is not required. It hinges upon an antithesis allegedly established in another place. If one begins to doubt the antithesis,[49] 13:57 stands as Jesus' indirect confession of himself as "prophet."

Before proceeding further, a few comments concerning the significance of titles for Matthean Christology are in order. Even if "(the) prophet" were a wholly negative appellation, or even if it failed to occur at all, what would be implied? Kingsbury was wont to approach Christology through the titles given to Jesus. But great caution is required. Jesus is called "rabbi" twice, both times by Judas (26:25, 49).

[49] 16:13ff. does not oppose "prophet" to "Son of God." It rather opposes "Son of God" to the identification of Jesus with any particular prophet now dead—John the Baptist, Elijah, Jeremiah, or "one of the prophets." The status of Jesus as a prophet or as "the prophet" is not disputed. On the contrary, it is presupposed. The people think Jesus might be one of the prophets of old precisely because his ministry is truly prophetic. For the proposal that Matthew inserted "Jeremiah" in order to hint at the parallelism between Jesus and the biblical prophet see M. J. J. Menken, "The References to Jeremiah in the Gospel according to Matthew (Mt 2,17; 16,14; 17,9)," *ETL* 60 (1984):5-24.

He is called "teacher" by a scribe who fails to become a disciple (8:19),[50] the Pharisees (9:ll), scribes and Pharisees (12:38), Jewish tax collectors (17:24), a rich man who decides not to follow Jesus (19:16), the disciples of the Pharisees and Herodians (22:15-16), the Sadducees (22:23-24), and a lawyer of the Pharisees (22:36). One might suppose that "rabbi" and "teacher" are only negative titles, or nothing more than Jewish terms of respect, and that their content made them inappropriate for true disciples to employ. And yet in 10:24-25; 23:8-10; and 26:18 Jesus refers to himself as "teacher." More importantly, his status as teacher is one of the dominating features of the First Gospel. There are five great discourses, and in every narrative section Jesus teaches. In fact, what Jesus does more than anything else is deliver instruction and issue commands. It is telling that the conclusion, 28:16-20, in looking back upon the earthly ministry now completed, does not mention Jesus' miracles or sacrificial death or resurrection. The stress is rather upon "all that I have commanded you." This concluding emphasis upon Jesus as teacher does not, however, have its correlate in any one christological expression: although their content is fundamental, "rabbi" and "teacher" remain relatively minor titles never used by any disciple except Judas. Which is to say: the christological titles are scantily indicative of the fundamental theme of Jesus as teacher. One wonders: could it not be the same with other christological themes? Could it not be the same with Matthew's Moses Christology? Even if "(the) prophet" is not a major title, and even if it is, in itself, inadequate, and even if "the prophet like Moses" does not appear at all, the significance for Matthean theology of Jesus' likeness to Moses is not thereby settled.

It has been said that "concentrating on titles does not lead one into Paul's christology but right past it."[51] There is some truth to this, and so too for Matthew. Christology is more than titles, and there is a difference between words and concepts. As David Hill, with Kingsbury in mind, has well said, Matthew's "Christology is in the whole story," and "because he [Matthew] portrays Jesus by means of a story no one category—teacher, healer, Wisdom incarnate, triumphant Son of man, not even Kyrios or Son of God—is adequate to contain that Jesus

---

[50]See J. D. Kingsbury, "On Following Jesus: the 'Eager' Scribe and 'Reluctant' Disciple (Matthew 8.18-22)," *NTS* 34 (1988):45-59.

[51]L. E. Keck, "Toward the Renewal of New Testament Christology," *NTS* 32 (l986):362-77.

reverenced by the church, the Jesus on whom Matthew then reflects in his book."[52]

Returning again the Kingsbury, what of his argument that the "allusions [to Moses] have all been drawn from portions of the Gospel in which Matthew is at pains to develop his Son-of-God christology"? An adequate reply to this would involve a critique of Kingsbury's method and so take us beyond the bounds of our immediate concerns. But one may well wonder whether the SM or Matthew 8-9 should be especially associated with the title, "Son of God." Concerning the SM, the truth is that (a) the speaker is literally just "he" (5:1-2) or "Jesus" (7:28); (b) the only christological title in the entire discourse is "Lord" (7:21-22); and (c) in Matthew 1-4, which introduces the SM, Jesus is "the Messiah" (1:1, 18; 2:4), the "Son of David" (l:l), "Emmanuel" (1:23), "king of the Jews" (2:2), "the coming one" (3:11), as well as "Son (of God)" (2:15; 3:17; 4:3, 6), and there is no hint, *pace* Kingsbury, that this last should subordinate all others to it. One may accordingly doubt that "Jesus, ascending the mountain to teach his disciples and the crowds, occupies a setting that in itself alludes to him as the Son of God" (p. 91).[53]

Also problematic is the surmise that the ten mighty works of Matthew 8-9 are to be especially linked to a Son of God Christology. "Son of God" occurs only once in those chapters (8:29). Also occurring are "Lord" (8:8, 21, 25), "Son of man" (8:20; 9:6), and "Son of David" (9:27); and, once more, how Kingsbury was able to determine that Matthew sought to subordinate or subsume all these titles under "Son of God" is lost on me. In sum, if there be a new Moses theme in Matthew 5:1-2 or 8-9, it is far from obvious that it is directly related to or muted by a Son of God Christology.

Let us look further at chapters 1-7. Here Jesus is called the Son of God three times (3:17; 4:3, 6), "Son" once (2:15). Of the three instances of "Son of God," two are in the same pericope and on the lips of Satan, and all three were taken over from the tradition (Mark and Q; cf. Mark 1:11; Luke 4:3, 9). None was first generated by special Matthean concern. As for "my Son" in 2:15, it is indeed redactional; but it is part

---

[52]D. Hill, "In Quest of Matthean Christology," *IBS* 9 (l986):140.

[53]Even if, for the sake of argument, it is by design that "Son (of God)" is associated with a mountain in 17:5 and 28:19 (so Kingsbury), that does not make up the lack in 5:1. Further, "Son of God" is used in the first two temptations, not the third, and it is the third that takes place on a mountain, so the link between "Son of God" and "mountain" which Kingsbury perceives in chapter 4 is problematic. Finally, against Kingsbury, *Structure, Christology, Kingdom,* 57, the confession of Jesus as the Son of God in 14:23 is not clearly associated with the mountain in 14:33.

of a quotation which in the Hebrew Bible refers to Israel and the exodus from Egypt. Its main function in its present context is to further a new exodus theme, a theme intimately bound up with the Jesus/Moses parallelism. In my judgment, Matthew was no less "at pains" in his first few chapters to summon a vision of a Jesus with Mosaic qualities than he was to label Jesus God's Son. We have already seen that there is in Matthew 1-8 a confluence of Mosaic traits and exodus-like events; they in fact abound prodigiously (pp. 140-207). Here I observe only that the following verses, so often thought of as making Jesus in the image of Moses, are generally taken to be redactional: 2:15 (the quotation from Hos. 11:1); 4:2 ("and forty nights" is editorial; cf. Exod. 34:28; Deut. 9:9); 5:1-2 (Jesus sits on a mountain and utters his demands; see pp. 170-80); 7:28-29 (cf. LXX Deut. 31:1, 24; 32:45); 8:1 (Jesus descends the mountain; cf. Exod. 19:14; 32:1, 15; 34:29). There is an obvious pattern here, a fixity of purpose, a consistent attempt to insert items in the Gospel from the Exodus history. Such elements may, without the key, seem divers or obscure; but, as Gerhard von Rad remarked, "very often it is merely a matter of fairly trivial reference to attendant circumstance, by means of which the connexion between the New Testament saving events and prototypes in the Old become clear for those who understand ('And he gave him to his mother,' Lk. vii. 15b = 1 Kings xvii. 23)."[54] I have argued above not only that many items in chapters 1-8 recall the story of Moses but that the structure of the entire section was shaped by a desire to make the new exodus and new redeemer resemble the first exodus and first redeemer. If so, the Moses Christology was very much near the center of Matthew's concern.

Similar results attend examination of 17:1-8, the transfiguration, where Jesus is both "Son of God" and, as urged by Davies and others, a new Moses. Are Kingsbury's words, "Matthew is at pains to develop his Son-of-God christology," apt here? "My Son" was taken from Mark 9:7; and as one fails to see any other feature in this story which highlights Jesus' filial relation to God,[55] Kingsbury's assertion is

---

[54]G. von Rad, *Old Testament Theology*, vol. II (New York: Harper & Row, 1965), 365.

[55]If Kingsbury's remarks on p. 68 of *Structure, Christology, Kingdom* ("In speaking of his face as shining 'like the sun' and of his garments as being white 'like the light' (vs. 2), Matthew, to a greater degree even than Mark (cf. 9:3), pictures the transfigured Jesus in the full radiance of heavenly splendor (cf., e.g. 13:43; Ps. 104:2). This, in turn, serves to reinforce the cardinal Matthean dogma that it is in the person of his Son Jesus that God is present") are meant to be argument to the contrary, they do not achieve their intended effect.

inappropriate. On the other hand, there are, as we have seen, at least five redactional changes that may plausibly be claimed to reflect Matthew's interest in Jesus as one like Moses. One is thus tempted to turn the tables: in 17:1-8 Matthew enhanced the new Moses theme at the expense of the Son of God theme. Such a contention, however, would be alien to the text: its Christology is paratactic, not hypotactic.

Kingsbury's third point is no more compelling than the first two. It comes down to this, that Matthew was "intent upon following the thrust of a passage such as Exod. 20:1 (the one who 'spoke' atop Mt. Sinai was 'God') at the expense of other pentateuchal passages which stress the mediating role of Moses" (p. 9l). But if that were really so, then why did the evangelist allow Mark 1:44 = Matt. 8:4 ("the gift that Moses commanded") and Mark 10:3 = Matt. 19:7 ("Why then did Moses command...?") to remain unaltered?[56] And regarding the changes from "Moses" to "God" in Mark 7:10 = Matt. 15:4 and Mark 12:26 = Matt. 22:31, Kastner is right: if one should recognize in them any deep sense is difficult to say.[57] The alterations might simply be stylistic (cf. 1:22; 2:15). If not, the first should perhaps be explained as reflecting a desire "to sharpen and reiterate the opposition between 'the commandments of God' and 'your tradition.'"[58] The second may be explained similarly: the contrast between God and the Sadducees is more rhetorically effective. Nothing mandates Kingsbury's explanation.

One final comment. Kingsbury wrote: "however many of the aforementioned allusions to Moses one may finally decide are legitimate [he leaves the question open], Matthew's position is clear: it is not with a new Moses that the reader has to do in these portions of the first Gospel, but with the Son of God" (pp. 91-92). The antithesis in this last line—"not with a new Moses... but with the Son of God"—invites scrutiny. What is its textual justification? Why not say, which is surely more natural, that the new Moses is the Son of God, or *vice versa*, or that Jesus is both the Son of God and a new Moses? Why the disjunction? Kingsbury conjured an antithesis and subordinated one christological

---

[56] According to Kingsbury, *Structure, Christology, Kingdom*, 9l, "in debate with the 'Pharisees' on divorce Matthew redacts Mark's pericope in order to emphasize more strongly than the latter the supersession of the will of Moses by the will of God (cf. 19:4b, 7-8 with Mark 10:3b-6)." On the contrary, it is the Pharisees who see a contradiction between Jesus' position and what Moses taught while Matthew's Jesus explains why God allowed Moses to permit (not command) divorce.

[57] *Moses*, 141.

[58] Gundry, *Matthew*, 304.

title to another. Thus his discussion of the new Moses motif is primarily an act of sublimation, and it is incurious concerning which suggested parallels with Moses are clear to demonstration and which are not. But again, what is the textual justification? Even if one title is most important, or most appropriate confessionally, why should that diminish other titles or christological themes? The reasoning seems to be: A is greater than B, so B need not be pursued further—hardly a procedure that recommends itself. Further, the many names of Jesus in the First Gospel have their unity in a person, not in one of the titles. That is, the titles refer to Jesus, so what is gained by instead relating them to each other? We should remember that *poluōnumos* was often used of the gods in Greek literature,[59] and that the hymn in *Apocalypse of Abraham* 17 lists over three dozen names and attributes for God, and that *Memar Marqah* 5:4 refers to the "twenty names" of Moses. It is a general rule in ancient texts: the more titles, the more honor—and the more understanding, because each title makes it own unique contribution. So too with the titles of Jesus in Matthew. "Lord" and "Son of man" and "Son of David" all carried connotations "Son of God" did not. This is why they all appear. That some, to use Kingsbury's terminology, are major, others minor, may be conceded. Still, each christological title or motif should first be considered in itself. Matthew's Moses Christology and the title "the prophet" are not exceptions. We should not impede their impact by artificially subordinating them, or imposing between them and Jesus, some other motif or theme. They are themselves, not something else. In conclusion, then, Kingsbury's approach, which suffers the Mosaic parallels to fly away without leaving any trace upon interpretation, amounts to obfuscation, for it reduces to practical insignificance too much redactional activity.

[59]E. R. Goodenough, *By Light, Light* (New Haven: Yale, 1935), 227, n. 193; cf. Cleanthes, *Hymn to Zeus*, beginning; Diogenes Laertius 7:135; LSJ, s.v. Philo used the word of the *Logos* (*apud* Eusebius, *Praep. ev.* 11:15 [533C]), as did Gregory of Nyssa after him: *C. Eun* 10 (= PG 45:832A). Note Martin Hengel, "Christology and New Testament Chronology," in *From Jesus to Paul* (Philadelphia: Fortress, 1983), 41: "The earliest community made christological 'experiments,' if one likes to put it that way, but not in sectarian exclusiveness; they had a readiness to accept new elements and thus 'enrich' the worth of Christ. The multiplicity of christological titles does not mean a multiplicity of exclusive 'christologies' but an accumulative glorification of Jesus. The titles must be considered from the perspective of a 'multiplicity of approaches' of the kind that is typical of mythical thought." These lines apply equally, *mutatis mutandis*, to Matthew.

APPENDIX V

R. Mohrlang and the Messianic Torah

Given the conclusions reached on pp. 182-90 herein, attention needs to be directed towards R. Mohrlang's *Matthew and Paul: A Comparison of Ethical Perspectives*.[60] Only three pages of this concern our theme (pp. 23-25). These, however, merit careful consideration, for they come close to expunging altogether from Matthew the motif of Jesus as a new lawgiver like Moses.

Mohrlang's first main point is formulated in this fashion: "Various attempts have been made to trace to motifs of a 'new Moses' and a 'new law' in Jewish messianic expectation of the time, and to relate these to the Gospel; but there appears to be no conclusive evidence that such a belief [*sic*] was ever prominent or widespread at the time" (p. 23).[61] He continues: "such expectations as there were appear to be rather late and quite varied, and often represent little more than the esoteric speculations of small but learned minorities" (p. 23).[62] These comments scarcely compel. Why imagine that the presence or absence of a motif in Matthew in any way depends upon its being "prominent" or "widespread" or not "varied" in Judaism? The canonical gospels overflow with items that were peripheral to or ill-defined by Judaism or even foreign to it (for instance, a virginal conception, a command to love enemies, a rejected and crucified Messiah, two messianic advents). Despite continuity with the past, Christianity brought new things into the world, and what was cynosure for it had not always been such for Judaism. This is what gives the following remark of Davies its force: "there were elements inchoate in the Messianic hope of Judaism, which could make it possible for some to regard the Messianic Age as marked by a New Torah."[63] Why deny Christianity's power to precipitate? Beyond that there is an additional difficulty. The use of "rather late" in connection with the new Moses and new Torah themes is exceedingly odd. The Dead Sea Scrolls plainly show that Deut. 18:15 and 18 were taken to foretell an eschatological figure like Moses; and there are in addition the eschatological prophets in Josephus, some of

---

[60]SNTSMS 48; Cambridge: University Press, 1984.
[61]He here cites R. Banks, "The Eschatological Role of the Law in Pre- and Post-Christian Jewish Thought," in *Reconciliation and Hope*, ed. R. Banks (Grand Rapids: Eerdmans, 1974), 173-85.
[62]His support for this statement includes Davies, *Setting*, 109-90.
[63]*Setting*, 184.

whom were clearly imitators of Moses (see above, pp. 78-84). Moreover, the new Moses motif appears already in Joshua, and it is after that not infrequent in Jewish tradition, as pp. 23-95 herein attest. Even if all eschatological speculation about another Moses were post-Talmudic, that would not determine our reading of Matthew: it would still have been altogether natural for Christians to liken their teacher to Moses. Jewish testimony aside, Acts 3 and 7, taken with the Gospel of John, blast any doubt that early Christians could have seriously concerned themselves with depicting Jesus as one like Moses. As for the expectation of a "new law," it is already present, in some sense, in Jeremiah 31.

Mohrlang's second observation also invites dissent: "When we turn to the Gospel, though we find a number of parallels between the lives of Jesus and Moses, the motif is certainly not a dominant or exclusive one; and nowhere does the evangelist even refer to Jesus explicitly in Mosaic terms" (p. 23). "Exclusive" is a strange word in this context.[64] What Matthean motif is "exclusive," if by that is meant, what my dictionary says, "single, sole"? As for "dominant," that is correct usage; but to deny dominance is not to gauge importance, and many scholars have thought the new Moses theme to be an important facet of Matthew's Christology. What then of the appeal to a lack of explicitness? What is its force? Does explicitness equal importance, inexplicitness unimportance? Consider Matthew's opening verse (which I take to be the book's title): *biblos geneseōs Iēsou Christou huios Dauid huios Abraam*. The interpretation of this line can be nothing other than the unfolding of what is not stated. For all the words in 1:1 derive from tradition, and to understand them aright we must know their

[64] But cf. the similar remark of Hahn, *Titles*, p 386: the Moses Christology "is only a single element of his [Matthew's] Christology; it is interwoven with many other motifs and is not the sole key [*der alleinige Schlüssel*] to the explanation of the Gospel" (p. 386). The truth of these strange words (which have, oddly enough, been quoted by others; see e.g. Kastner, *Moses*, 171) is beyond cavil. Indeed, the comment is banal, so manifestly indisputable that one wonders what called it forth. Where is the commentary, where is the article which urges that a Moses Christology is the only Christology in Matthew, or that such a Christology is the "sole key" to the book? No one, to my knowledge, has ever made such vast claims for any christological element of Matthew, including "(the) Son of God," the title so many today think most prominent. Hahn's affirmation could not in fact have been directed against anything other than a figment of his imagination. Do we have here just careless overstatement (aimed perhaps at Bacon?) or the sound of theological axe grinding? Although I do not presume to divine Hahn's motives, a dichotomy between law and grace is so axiomatic for many, especially Lutherans, that the positive association of Jesus with Moses or the characterization of Jesus' teaching as a *nova lex* or some kind of Torah must seem to them a sin against the Holy Ghost of Protestantism.

itinerary. *Biblos geneseōs* occurs in LXX Gen. 2:4 and 5:1 while "Genesis" came to be, in the Greek-speaking world, the title for the first book of Moses. As for *Christos*, it was firmly associated with Jewish eschatological expectation. So too *huios Dauid*. And *huios Abraam*, likewise a fixed expression, also had its own special connotations. Now all this, which was undoubtedly known to Matthew's Jewish-Christian audience, is fundamental for interpretation. But Matt. 1:1 directly conveys none of this information. Rather it assumes that the requisite sensibility will pass from the explicit to the implicit, that it will go beyond what the words directly denote to what they connote—which is why the more Matt. 1:1 is engaged, the more it evokes. Words and phrases (such as "Son of David" and "son of Abraham") are not simple things; nor is language ever born anew: it is always old.[65] A combination of words is like a moving trawler, whose dragnet, below the surface and out of sight, has taken catch and now pulls along so much. Just as it would be erroneous to equate the function of the fishing vessel with what goes on in plain sight, so similarly can focus on what is explicit in a literary text lead one right past much meaning—above all in a book such as Matthew, beneath whose literary surface is the Jewish Bible, which is alluded to far more often than expressly cited. Mohrlang's argument places a disproportionate emphasis upon the explicit and underestimates the informed imaginations of Matthew's first hearers or readers as well as the evangelist's ability to access a common universe of meaning through connotative speech; and thus Mohrlang wrings from the text far too little: he sees the light but not the shadows it casts. The truth is, our evangelist had no need to trumpet the manifest, and the allusions to Moses were, I have argued, manifest enough to those who lived and moved and had their being in the Jewish tradition.[66]

How do we evaluate Mohrlang's next argument, that Jesus' teaching is not a *nova lex*, "at least in the strict sense," because it is not, in form or content, "a collection of legal regulations" (pp. 23-24)? With very few exceptions (5:31-32; 18:15-18; 19:3-9), casuistic or legalistic formulations are, most assuredly, missing from Matthew; and rabbinic *halakoth* are rather different from the commandments of the

---

[65]On this see Greene, *Light in Troy*, 4-27. He has much of interest to say regarding the purposes of literary alluding.

[66]The obvious often goes unmentioned in literature. Thus Joseph Conrad's *Heart of Darkness* never names the Congo River. One thinks too of the sacramental references in John 6 (although here the lack of explicitness has moved some to deny presence).

Matthean Jesus. But what follows? Could not our evangelist still have considered the sayings of Jesus to be eschatological Torah, perhaps in accordance with Jeremiah 31, interpreted as foretelling an internalization of the Mosaic law (cf. p. 189)? Whence the notion that a messianic Torah—which earlier Mohrlang spoke of as a concept "quite varied"—must resemble Deuteronomy or the Mishnah?[67] The Torah of Moses, if by that is meant the Pentateuch, itself contains much besides legal principles. Moreover, when Paul spoke of the *nomos tou Christou* (Gal. 6:2) and John of an *entolē kainē* (John 13:34), they did not, although they must have been thinking of something somehow analogous to the law of Moses, have in mind legal minutiae. Consider also 4 *Ezra* 14, where Ezra composes anew the Torah once given to Moses (is this not literally a "new Torah"?). Here "the law of life" (v. 30) give to the scribe contains not just *halakoth* but also history and apocalyptic visions and much else (cf. vv. 5-6, 22, 45-47).

Lastly, Mohrlang affirms that for Matthew the law of Moses is still valid, that Jesus only interprets that law, and that "to claim for Jesus' teachings the status of 'new law' would be to deny his assertion of the validity of the old (5.17ff.)" (p. 24). The first assertion is sound. The second is doubtful, for Jesus does more than just interpret Moses. Neither the prohibition of divorce save for *porneia* nor the demand to love the enemy is exegetical product: these imperatives go Moses one better. The third assertion, that a new law would necessarily contradict the old law (= Moses), which Jesus, on the contrary, upholds, is, as far as I can determine, empty of justification (unless it be patristic opinion; cf. Justin, *Dial.* ll). Would Mohrlang so simply dismiss Ben Zion Wachholder's thesis, that *llQTemple* was new or eschatological Torah for the Qumran sectarians, by observing that those sectarians accepted the authority of the Pentateuch and so could not have had a second Torah? One is at a loss to see why, if the Matthean Messiah not only interprets the old law but brings additional commandments of his own, his words cannot be construed as "new Torah." Are we to suppose that any Jew who entertained thoughts of a "new Torah" thereby must have contemplated the end of Moses? Surely that was not the case with the Jewish-Christian editor of *T. Levi* 16, who referred to a man (= Jesus) renewing the law (*anakainopiōn ton nomon*, v. 3).

---

[67]Does not variety in the concept make it easier to interpret the SM as eschatological Torah? Cf. Hahn, *Titles*, 385.

APPENDIX VI

T. L. Donaldson on Sinai and Zion

T. L. Donaldson's *Jesus on the Mountain: A Study in Matthean Theology*[68] is an interesting and fresh exploration of the mountain motif in the First Gospel. The texts examined in minute detail are 4:8-10; 5:1-2; 15:29-31; 17:1-9; 24:3; and 28:16-20—each of which has been thought by at least some to echo Sinai. Donaldson's thesis, seemingly novel, is that the mountains in Matthew "function not primarily as places of revelation or isolation, but as eschatological sites where Jesus enters into the full authority of Sonship, where the eschatological community is gathered, and where the age of fulfilment is inaugurated" (p. 197). So it is not the memory of Moses on Sinai that first informs (*to*) *oros* but expectations concerning Zion, the eschatological mountain of gathering, pilgrimage, new Torah, and enthronement. This is not to say that Donaldson altogether eliminates the presence of Sinai in the various mountain scenes. He considers such "certain" in 4:8-10 (p. 98) and "likely" in 5:1-2 (p. 112). Further, in 17:1-8 "Mount Sinai plays a major typological role" (p. 143), and in 28:16-20 "Sinai overtones may be detected" (p. 179). In each case, however, Sinai is not "dominant" or "the controlling factor." Rather, the primary background of (*to*) *oros* is in each instance Zion.

It is beyond the present investigation to review in any depth Donaldson's exegetical work or his major thesis. Luz, in the second volume of his commentary on Matthew, finds the hypothesis of a Zion typology wanting. Professor Davies and myself, in the second volume of our commentary, have found it compelling only for 15:29-31. But even if a more favorable verdict is justified, two points should be made. First, Donaldson relies heavily upon the conclusions of Davies and Kingsbury. For instance, in the section on 4:8-10 there is this: "Davies and Kingsbury demonstrate that although Mosaic typology is present, it is a secondary theme that has been caught up into the larger pattern of Son-christology" (pp. 98-99); and on p. 113: "of more weight... is Davies' demonstration that wherever Mosaic typology is present in Matthew, it is not dominant, but is transcended and absorbed by a higher Son-christology."[69] As we have seen, however,

[68]JSNTSS 8; Sheffield: JSOT, 1985.
[69]On my reading, *The Setting of the Sermon on the Mount* demonstrates no such thing. I believe Donaldson has read Kingsbury into Davies.

reservations may be harbored about Kingsbury's whole approach to the issue of Moses in Matthew; and Davies' position on the matter has undergone a significant change in recent years. Donaldson's appeals to the authority of Davies and Kingsbury consequently do not secure him as solid a foundation for his exegetical edifice as he supposes.

Secondly, Donaldson's case for Zion is often made by pruning back as much as possible the Sinai motif. (One is reminded of those who set Sinai and Zion, and the covenants they represent, against each other.) Is this necessary? Already in the Hebrew Bible Sinai and Zion are closely associated,[70] as in Psalm 89 and Ezekiel 40 (see pp. 50-53); and this is also true in later Jewish tradition.[71] A key text in this regard is Isa. 2:2-3: "out of Zion shall come forth Torah." Here Mount Zion functions as the eschatological Sinai, the mountain of the law. Compare Isa. 4:3-6, where Zion is cleansed by "a spirit of judgment burning like fire" and has over it "a cloud of smoke by day and a bright flame of fire by night" (cf. Exod. 19:16, 18; 20:18; Deut. 5:4, 20-23). The typological equation of one mountain with another, a thing easily demonstrated in extra-canonical Jewish sources,[72] is, as Michael Fishbane has recently shown, also readily found in the Tanak (note especially 2 Chron. 3:1: Solomon built the temple on Mount Moriah).[73] In view of this, if there is Zion imagery in Matthew it can only compliment the Sinai theme.

APPENDIX VII

Otto Betz's "Bergpredigt und Sinaitradition"[74]

The Matthean texts discussed in most of the books and articles which address the new Moses theme are almost always the same. From Dabeck (1948) on, and whether the object is to behold Moses or to exorcise him, the same passages have been commented on, sometimes in passing, sometimes at great length; but there is always a weary feeling of *déjà vu*. With Betz, however, we have a truly fresh proposal,

---

[70]See further J. D. Levenson, *Sinai and Zion* (Minneapolis: Seabury, 1985).
[71]E.g. *Liv. Proph. Jer.* 11-19; *Tg. Neofiti* on Exod. 4:27; *Midr. Rab.* on Ps. 68:9.
[72]See Donaldson, *Mountain*, 55-59, 77-78.
[73]*Interpretation*, 368-72.
[74]"Bergpredigt und Sinaitradition. Zur Gliederung und zum Hintergrund von Matthäus 5-7," in *Jesus: Der Messias Israels* (WUNT 42; Tübingen: J. C. B. Mohr (Pl Siebeck), 1987), 333-84.

to wit: the structure of the SM is partly patterned on Exodus 19-24, which tells of Moses receiving the law on Sinai and delivering commandments to the people. According to Betz, the SM, whose major theme is righteousness (5:20; see pp. 336-54), is not gospel but the "law of the new covenant," and it is not addressed primarily to the disciples but to "the representatives of the new Israel" (p. 333; cf. p. 335). He proposes these parallels with Exodus 19-24:

Exodus	Matthew
19:1-3: Israel is before "the mountain" (Sinai); God tells Moses what to say to Israel	5:1-2: Jesus goes up on "the mountain;" he speaks to Israel
19:4: this recites God's saving acts in the exodus	5:3-12: the beatitudes foretell God's future saving acts
19:4, 5: "you have seen what I did;" "you shall be my own possession;" "the children of God"	5:8, 9: "shall see God," "the sons of God"
19:5-6: the calling of the people of God in the world: "you shall be my own possession among all peoples; for all the earth is mine, and you shall be to me a kingdom of priests and a holy nation"	5:13-16: the calling of the people of God in the world: "you are the salt of the earth," "you are the light of the world"
19:7-8: the doing of the commandments: "So Moses came and called the elders of the people, and set before them all these words which the Lord had commanded him. And all the people answered together and said: 'All that the Lord has spoken we will do'"	5:17-20: the doing of the commandments: "whoever then relaxes one of the least of peo- of these commandments and teaches others so, shall be called least in the kingdom of heaven; but the one who does them shall be called great in the kingdom of heaven"
20-23: various laws, including	5:21-48: six paragraphs on the law:

prohibition of murder, 20:13	on murder
prohibition of adultery, 20:14	on adultery
	on divorce
prohibition of taking God's name in vain, 20:7	on oaths
eye for eye, tooth for tooth, 21:24	on turning the other cheek instead of taking an eye for an eye
	on loving neighbor and enemy

Betz further contends that Matt. 7:13-14 has been influenced by the two-way theme of Deuteronomy 28-30 (cf. 28:8-9; 30:16) and that the emphasis upon hearing "my word" in Matt. 7:21-27 puts one in mind of Deut. 18:15-22 and the promise of a prophet like Moses ("him you shall hear," pp. 352-53).

That Matt. 5:1 recalls Sinai is a sentiment which Betz, for good reason, shares with others, myself included. And he is justified also in directing attention to 26:28 ("this is my blood of the covenant"). This verse proves that the new covenant theme was not foreign to Matthew and encourages one to consider the possibility of interpreting the SM as the "Torah of the new covenant" (p. 334). For the rest, however, doubts are to be expressed.

(i) Neither the content nor vocabulary shared by Exod. 19:4-8 and Matt. 5:3-20 is at all impressive. As for the few words that are common, does coincidence not here hold sufficient explanatory power?

(ii) The parallels Betz draws between Exodus 20-23 and Matt. 5:21-48 do not occur in the same order: if Matthew's sequence is 1, 2, 3, 4, 5, 6, that of Exodus is 4, 1, 2, 5. Would not the prohibition against oaths come first if Matthew had been following Exodus?

(iii) The prohibition of murder and adultery are also found in Deuteronomy, in 5:17 and 18; and reasons perhaps exist for supposing that Matthew had those verses (and not Exod. 20:13 and 14) is mind.[75] Certainly the third paragraph in Matt. 5:21-48, which follows those on murder and adultery, treats of a passage in Deuteronomy, not Exodus (Deut. 24:1-4). Furthermore, the prohibition of oaths is no more tied to Exod. 20:7 than to Lev. 19:12; Num. 30:3-15; Deut. 23:21-23; Zech. 8:17; or Wisd. 14:48. In fact, Ps. 50:14 is the best candidate if there is a particular text in the background (see the commentaries). In addition,

---

[75]Davies and Allison, *Matthew*, 1:504.

the eye for eye text also appears in Lev. 24:20 and Deut. 19:21, which last could be most pertinent for interpreting Matt. 5:33-37.[76]

(iv) While the two-way theme appears in Deuteronomy, it appears also in numerous other texts, within and without the Bible;[77] so although Betz could be right to associate Matt. 7:13-14 with Deuteronomy 28-30, his reasons are inadequate.

If Betz's major thesis, for the reasons just given, fails to command allegiance, it cannot, let me add, be dismissed as nugatory. 5:1-2 does have close verbal links to LXX Exod. 19:3, 12, 13; and Jesus does, in 5:21-48, refer to precepts mediated by Moses, in Exodus and elsewhere. Surely the informed reader must ponder the relationship between Jesus and Moses and indeed, given the Matthean themes of a new exodus, a new covenant (26:28), and eschatological fulfilment in Jesus Christ, wonder whether the SM is not after all eschatological Torah, or Torah of a new covenant. It is certainly suggestive that Jer. 31:31-34, which may be alluded to in Matt. 26:28, foresees, in connection with a new covenant, the interiorization of the Torah, and that the SM is partly about the interiorization of the commandments (5:21-30). Betz's error, then, is the old one of multiplying assumptions beyond necessity and so pressing the evidence too far. There is assuredly a connection between the SM and the revelation of the law on Sinai. But that in Exodus 19-23 we find the SM's conceptual skeleton is a proposition which will, if I may play the prophet, not collect many adherents.

[76]R. A. Guelich, *The Sermon on the Mount* (Waco: Word, 1982), 219.
[77]Davies and Allison, *Matthew*, 1:695-96.

BIBLIOGRAPHY

Abrams, M. H, "History and Criticism and the Plurality of Histories," in Wayne C. Booth, *Critical Understanding: The Powers and Limits of Pluralism* (Chicago: University Press, 1979).

Achtemeier, Paul J., "*Omne verbum sonat*: The New Testament and the Oral Environment of Late Western Antiquity," *JBL* 109 (1990):3-27.

J. S. Ackerman, "The Literary Context of the Moses Birth Story (Exodus 1-2)," in *Literary Interpretations of Biblical Narratives*, Gros Louis, K. R. R. et al. (Nashville: Abingdon, 1974).

Ackroyd, P. R., *Exile and Restoration* (London: SCM, 1968).

Allen, W. C., *A Critical and Exegetical Commentary on the Gospel according to St. Matthew* (3rd ed.; ICC; Edinburgh: T. & T. Clark, 1912).

Allison, Dale C., Jr., "The Baptism of Jesus and a New Dead Sea Scroll," *BAR* 18 (1992), pp. 58-60.

idem, *The End of the Ages has Come* (Philadelphia: Fortress, 1985).

idem, "Jesus and Moses (Mt 5:1-2)," *ExpT* 98 (1987):203-205.

idem, "Matthew: Structure, Biographical Impulse, and the *Imitatio Christi*," in *The Four Gospels 1992*, ed. C. M. Tuckett et al. (BETL 100; Leuven: Leuven University Press, 1992), vol. 2, pp. 1203-1221.

idem, "Psalm 23 in Early Christianity: A Suggestion," *IBS* 5 (1983):132-37.

idem, "The Son of God as Israel: A Note on Matthean Christology," *IBS* 9 (1987):74-81.

idem, "The Structure of the Sermon on the Mount," *JBL* 106 (1987):423-45.

idem, "Two Notes on a Key Text: Matthew 11:25-30," *JTS* 39 (1988):472-80.

idem, "Who will come from East and West? Observations on Matt. 8.11-12 = Luke 13.28-29," *IBS* 11 (1989):158-70.

Alter, Robert, *The Pleasures of Reading in an Ideological Age* (New York: Simon and Schuster, 1989).

Anderson, B., "The Exodus Typology in Second Isaiah," in *Israel's Prophetic Heritage*, ed. B. Anderson and W. Harrelson (New York: Harper & Row, 1962), 177-95.

Auerbach, E., *Mimesis* (Princeton: University Press, 1953).

Auld, A. Graeme, "Gideon: Hacking at the Heart of the Old Testament," *VT* 39 (1989):257-67.

Aurelius, E., *Der Fürbitter Israels: Eine Studie zum Mosebild im Alten Testament* (CBOT; Stockholm: Almquist & Wicksell, 1988).

Aus, R. D., *Weihnachtsgeschichte, Barmherziger Samariter, Verlorener Sohn* (Berlin: Institut Kirche und Judentum, 1988).

Bacon, B. W., *Studies in Matthew* (New York: Henry Holt, 1930).

idem, "The 'Five Books' of Matthew against the Jews," *Expositor* 15, series 8 (1918):56-66.

Balch, David L., "Backgrounds of 1 Cor. VII: Sayings of the Lord in Q; Moses as an Ascetic *Theios Anēr* in II Cor. III," *NTS* 18 (1972):351-64.

Bammel, Ernst, "The Feeding of the Multitude," in *Jesus and the Politics of His Day*, ed. Ernst Bammel and C. F. D. Moule (Cambridge: University Press, 1984), 211-40.

Banks, R., "The Eschatological Role of the Law in Pre- and Post-Christian Jewish Thought," in *Reconciliation and Hope*, ed. R. Banks (Grand Rapids: Eerdmans, 1974), 173-85.

idem, *Jesus and the Law in the Synoptic Tradition*, SNTSMS 28 (Cambridge: University Press, 1975).

Barnett, P. W., "The Jewish Sign Prophets—A.D. 40-70," *NTS* 27 (1981):679-97.

Barth, G., "Matthew's Understanding of the Law," in G. Bornkamm, G. Barth, and H. J. Held, *Tradition and Interpretation in Matthew* (London: SCM, 1963), 58-164.

Batto, B. F., "The Reed Sea: *Requiescat in Pace*," *JBL* 102 (1983):27-35.

Baumgarten, J. M., "The Duodecimal Courts of Qumran, Revelation, and the Sanhedrin," *JBL* 95 (1976):59-78.

Beare, F. W., *The Gospel according to Matthew* (New York: Harper & Row, 1981).

Becker, E., "Konstantin der Grosse, der 'neue Moses.' Die Schlact am Pons Milvius und die Katastrophe am Schilfmeer," *Zeitschrift für Kirchengeschichte* 31 (1910):162-175.

idem, "Protest gegen den Kaiserkult und Verherrlichung des Sieges am Pons Milvius in der christlichen Kunst der Konstantinischen Zeit," in *Konstantin der Grosse und seine Zeit*, ed. F. J. Dölger (Freiburg i. Br.: Herders, 1913), 155-90.

idem, *Das Quellwunder des Moses in der altchristlichen Kunst* (Strassburg: Heitz und Mündel, 1909).

Begg, C., "'Josephus's Portrayal of the Disappearance of Enoch, Elijah, and Moses': Some Observations," *JBL* 109 (1990):691-93.

Belleville, Linda L., *Reflections of Glory: Paul's Use of the Moses-Doxa Tradition in 2 Corinthians 3.1-18* (JSNTSS 52; Sheffield: JSOT, 1991).

Bentzen, E., *King and Messiah* (London: Lutterworth, 1956).

Bercovitch, S., ed., *Typology and Early American Literature* (Amherst: University of Massachusetts, 1972).

idem, "Typology in Puritan New England," in *Typology and Early American Literature*, 179-81.

Bergen, T. A., "The 'People coming from the East' in 5 Ezra 1.38," *JBL* 108 (1989):675-83.

Berger, Peter L. and Luckmann, Thomas, *The Social Construction of Reality* (New York: Doubleday, 1966).

Betz, O., "Bergpredigt und Sinaitradition. Zur Gliederung und zum Hintergrund von Matthäus 5-7," in *Jesus: Der Messias Israels* (WUNT 42; Tübingen: J. C. B. Mohr (Paul Siebeck), 1987), 333-84.

idem, "Miracles in the Writings of Flavius Josephus," in *Josephus, Judaism, and Christianity*, ed. L. H. Feldman and Goher Hata (Detroit: Wayne State University, 1987), 212-35.

Beyerlin, W., "Geschichte und heilsgeschichte Traditionsbildung im Alten Testament: ein Beitrag zur Traditionsgeschichte von Richter vi-viii," *VT* 13 (1963):1-25.

Bikerman, Élie, "La chaîne de la tradition pharisienne," *RB* 59 (1952):44-54.

Blair, E. P., *Jesus in the Gospel of Matthew* (New York: Abingdon, 1960).

Blenkinsopp, J., *Prophecy and Canon: A Contribution to the Study of Jewish Origins* (Notre Dame: University Press, 1977).

Bloch, R., "A Methodological Note for the Study of Rabbinic Literature," in *Approaches to Ancient Judaism: Theory and Practice*, ed. William Scott Green (Chico: Scholars Press, 1978), 66-67.

Boilng, R. G., *Judges* (AB; Garden City: Doubleday, 1975).

idem, "Solomon, the Chosen Temple Builder," *JBL* 95 (1976):581-90.

Boismard, M.-E., *Moise ou Jesus. Essai de christologie johannique* (BETL 84; Leuven: Leuven University, 1988).

Box, G. H., "The Gospel Narratives of the Nativity and the alleged influence of Heathen Ideas," *ZNW* 6 (1905):80-101.

idem, *The Virgin Birth of Jesus Christ* (London: Sir Isaac Pitman and Sons, Ltd., 1916).

du Bourguet, Pierre, *Early Christian Painting* (New York: Viking, 1966).

Braun, Roddy, *1 Chronicles* (WBC 14; Waco: Word, 1986).

Bright, John, *Covenant and Promise* (Philadelphia: Westminster, 1976).

idem, *A History of Israel* (3rd ed.; Philadelphia: Westminster, 1981).

Brock, S., *The Luminous Eye: The Spiritual World of St. Ephrem* (Rome: C.I.I.S. Rome, 1985).

Brongers, H. A., "Die Zehnzahl in der Bibel und in ihrer Umwelt," in *Studia Biblica et Semitica Theodoro Christiano Vriezen*, ed. W. C. van Unnik and A. S. van der Woude (Wageningen: H. Veenman en Zonen, 1966), 30-45.

Broughton, P. E., 'The Call of Jeremiah," *AusBR* 6 (1958):37-46.

Brown, Peter, "The Saint as Exemplar in Antiquity," in *Saints and Virtues*, ed. John Stratton Hawley (Berkeley: University of California, 1987), 3-14.

Brown, Raymond E., *The Birth of the Messiah* (Garden City: Doubleday, 1977).

idem, *The Gospel according to John (i-xii)*, 2 vols. (AB 29; Garden City: Doubleday, 1966, 1970).

idem, "Jesus and Elisha," *Perspective* 12 (1971):85-104.

idem, "The Messianism of Qumran," *CBQ* 19 (1957):53-82.

idem, *A Risen Christ in Eastertime* (Collegeville: The Liturgical Press, 1991).

idem, *The Semitic Background of the Term "Mystery" in the New Testament* (FBBS; Philadelphia: Fortress, 1968).

Brownlee, W. H., *The Meaning of the Qumran Scrolls for the Bible* (New York: Oxford, 1964).

idem, "Messianic Motifs of Qumran and the New Testament," *NTS* 3 (1956-57):12-30, 195-210.

Bruns, J. E., "The 'Agreement of Moses and Jesus' in Eusebius," *VC* 31 (1977), pp. 117-25.

Büchler, *Types of Jewish-Palestinian Piety from 70 B.C.E. to 70 C.E.* (New York: KTAV, 1968).

Bultmann, R. *History of the Synoptic Tradition* (rev. ed.; Oxford: Basil Blackwell, 1963).

Carlson, R. A., "Élie à 1 Horeb," *VT* 19 (1969):416-39.

Carroll, R. P., "The Elijah-Elisha Sagas," *VT* 19 (1969):400-15.

idem, *Jeremiah* (Philadelphia: Westminster, 1986).

Cassuto, U., *A Commentary on the Book of Exodus*, 2 vols. (Jerusalem: Magnes, 1961, 1964).

idem, *A Commentary on the Book of Genesis*, Part I (Jerusalem: Magnes, 1978).

Chavasse, C., "Jesus: Christ and Moses," *Theology* 54 (1951):244-50, 289-96.

idem, "The Suffering Servant and Moses," *Church Quarterly Review* 165 (1964):152-63.

Charlesworth, J. H., "The Portrayal of the Righteous as an Angel," in *Ideal Figures in Ancient Judaism*, ed. George W. Nickelsburg and John J. Collins (Chico: Scholars Press, 1980), 135-51.

idem, *The Pseudepigrapha and Modern Research* (Missoula: Scholars Press, 1976).

Chernus, R., *Mysticism in Rabbinic Judaism* (SJ 11; Berlin: de Gruyter, 1982).

idem, *Redemption and Chaos: A Study in the Symbolism of the Rabbinic Aggada* (Ann Arbor: University Microfilms, 1978).

Chestnut, Glen F., *The First Christian Historians* (2nd ed.; Macon: Mercer, 1986).

Childs, B. S., *The Book of Exodus* (Philadelphia: Westminster, 1974).

Chilton, Bruce, "The Transfiguration: Dominical Assurance and Apostolic Vision," *NTS* 27 (1980):121-22.

Coats, G. W., "Healing and the Moses Traditions," in *Canon, Theology, and Old Testament Interpretation*, ed. G. M. Tucker et al. (Philadelphia: Fortress, 1988), pp. 131-46.

Cohn, R. L., "The Literary Logic of 1 Kings 17-19," *JBL* 101 (1982):333-50.

Collins, M. F., "The Hidden Vessels in Samaritan Traditions,' *JJS* 3 (1972):97-116.

Collins, R. F., *These Things have been written* (Louvain Theological and Pastoral Monographs 2; Louvain: Peeters, 1990).

Coote, R. B., "Yahweh recalls Elijah," in *Traditions in Transformation*, ed. B. Halpern and J. D. Levenson (Winona Lake: Eisenbrauns, 1981), 115-20.

Cope, O. L., *Matthew: A Scribe Trained for the Kingdom of Heaven* (CBQMS 5; Washington: Catholic Biblical Association of America, 1976).

Coppens, J., *Le Messianisme et sa rèleve prophétique* (BETL 34; Gembloux: Duculot, 1974).

Cox, P., *Biography in Late Antiquity* (Berkeley: University of California Press, 1983).

Cranfield, C. E. B., *A Critical and Exegetical Commentary on the Epistle to the Romans*, 2 vols. (ICC; Edinburgh: T. & T. Clark, 1975, 1979).

idem, *The Gospel according to Mark* (rev. ed.; Cambridge: University Press, 1977).

Cross, F. M., Jr., *The Ancient Library of Qumran and Modern Biblical Studies* (Garden City: Doubleday, 1961).

idem, *Canaanite Myth and Hebrew Epoch* (Cambridge, Mass.: Harvard, 1973).

Crossan, J. D., "From Moses to Jesus: Parallel Themes," *BibRev* II/2 (1986):18-27.

Cullmann, Oscar, *The Christology of the New Testament* (2nd ed.; Philadelphia: Westminster, 1963).

Curtis, John B., "An Investigation of the Mount of Olives in the Judaeo-Christian Tradition," *HUCA* 28 (1957):137-80.

P. Dabeck, "'Siehe, es erscheinen Moses und Elias' (Mt 17,3)," *Bib* 23 (1947):175-89.

Dahl, N. A., "Christ, Creation, and the Church," in *Jesus in the Memory of the Early Church* (Minneapolis: Augsburg, 1976), 120-40.

Dahood, M., *Psalms I. 1-50* (AB 16; New York: Doubleday, 1965).

Daniélou, J., *The Bible and the Liturgy* (Notre Dame: University Press, 1956).

idem, *From Shadow to Reality* (London: Burnes & Oates, 1960).

D'Angelo, Mary Rose, *Moses in the Letter to the Hebrews* (SBLDS 42; Missoula: Scholars Press, 1979).

Daube, David, *The New Testament and Rabbinic Judaism* (London: Athlone, 1956).

idem, *Studies on Biblical Law* (Cambridge: University Press, 1947).

idem, "Typology in Josephus," *JJS* 31 (1980):18-36.

Davies, P. R., *The Damascus Covenant* (Sheffield: JSOT, 1983).

idem, "The Teacher of Righteousness and the 'End of Days,'" *RevQ* 49-52 (1988):313-17.

Davies, W. D., *Paul and Rabbinic Judaism* (rev. ed.; Philadelphia: Fortress, 1980).

idem, *The Setting of the Sermon on the Mount* (Cambridge: University Press, 1963).

Davies, W. D. and Allison, Dale C., Jr., *A Critical and Exegetical Commentary on the Gospel according to Matthew*, 2 vols. (ICC; Edinburgh: T. & T. Clark, 1988, 1991).

idem, "Matt. 28:16-20: Texts Behind the Text," *RHPR* 72 (1992):89-98.

idem, "Reflections on the Sermon on the Mount," *SJT* 44 (1991), pp. 283-310.

De Vries, Simon J., *1 Kings* (WBC 12; Waco: Word, 1985).

idem, "Moses and David as Cult Founders in Chronicles," *JBL* 107 (1988):119-39.

Dillard, R. B., *2 Chronicles* (WBC 15; Waco: Word, 1987).

Dobschütz, E. von, "Matthäus als Rabbi und Katechet," *ZNW* 27 (1928):338-48.

Dodd, C. H., *According to the Scriptures* (London: Fontana, 1965).

idem, *The Interpretation of the Fourth Gospel* (Cambridge: University Press, 1953).

Donaldson, T. L., *Jesus on the Mountain: A Study in Matthean Theology* (JSNTSS 8; Sheffield: JSOT, 1985).

idem, "Moses Typology and the Sectarian Nature of Early Christian Anti-Judaism: A Study of Acts 7," *JSNT* 12 (1981):27-52.

Driver, S. R., *The Book of Genesis* (3rd ed.; London: Methuen, 1904).

idem, *A Critical and Exegetical Commentary on Deuteronomy* (ICC; Edinburgh: T. & T. Clark, 1916).

Dunn, J. D. G., *Romans 9-16* (WBC; Waco: Word, 1988).

Dupont, J., *ΣΥΝ ΧΡΙΣΩΤΙ* (Bruges: Editiones de l Abbaye de Saint-Andre, 1952).

Dutton, Denis, "Why Intentionalism Won't Go Away," in *Literature and the Question of Philosophy*, ed. Anthony J. Cascardi (Baltimore: Johns Hopkins, 1987), 194-209.

Dvornik, F., *Early Christian and Byzantine Political Philosophy*, vol. 2 (Washington: Dunbarton Oaks Center for Byzantine Studies, 1966).

Eichrodt, W., *Ezekiel: A Commentary* (Philadelphia: Westminster, 1970).

Eliot, T. S., "Tradition and Individual Talent," in *Selected Essays 1917-1932* (New York: HBJ, 1932).

Empson, William, *Seven Types of Ambiguity* (3rd ed.; Norfolk: New Directions, 1953).

Evans, C. F., "The Central Section of St. Luke's Gospel," in *Studies in the Gospels*, ed. D. Nineham (Oxford: Basil Blackwell, 1955), 37-53.

Farley, F. A., "Jeremiah and 'The Suffering Servant of Jehovah' in Deutero-Isaiah," *ExpT* 38 (1927):521-24.

Farmer, W. R., *Maccabees, Zealots, and Josephus* (New York: Columbia, 1956).

Farrer, A., *St. Matthew and St. Mark* (Westminster: Dacre, 1954).

idem, *The Triple Victory: Christ's Temptation according to St. Matthew* (Cambridge, Mass.: Cowley, 1990).

Fascher, E., ΠΡΟΦΗΤΗΣ (Giessen: Alfred Töpelmann, 1927).

Feilchenfelt, W., "Die Entpersönhohung Moses in der Bible," *ZAW* 64 (1952):156-78.

Fenton, J. C., *Saint Matthew* (Baltimore: Penguin, 1963).

Fiebig, P., *Jüdische Wundergeschichten des neutestamesntlichen Zeitalters* (Tübingen: J. C. B. Mohr, 1911).

Fishbane, Michael, *Biblical Interpretation in Ancient Israel* (Oxford: University Press, 1985).

idem, *Text and Texture* (New York: Schocken, 1979).

Fischer, J., "Das Problem des neuen Exodus in Isaias c. 40-55," *TQ* 110 (1979):111-20.

Fitzmyer, J. A., "Glory Reflected on the Face of Christ (2 Cor 3:7-4:6) and a Palestinian Jewish Motif," *TS* 42 (1981):630-44.

Fohrer, G., *Elia* (ATANT 53; Zürich: Zwingli, 1957).

Fox, E., *Genesis and Exodus: A New English Rendition* (New York: Schocken, 1991).

France, R. T., *Jesus and the Old Testament* (London: Tyndale, 1971), 38-82.

idem, *Matthew* (Tyndale New Testament Commentaries; Grand Rapids: Inter-Varsity, 1985).

Frankemölle, H., *Jahwebund und Kirche Christi* (NTAbh, n.F. 10, 2nd ed.; Münster: Aschendorf, 1984).

Frankfurter, D. M., "The Origin of the Miracle-List Tradition and Its Medium of Circulation," in *Society of Biblical Literature 1990 Seminar Papers*, ed. D. J. Lull (Atlanta: Scholars Press, 1990), pp. 344-74.

Fridrichsen, A., "The New Exodus of Salvation according to St. Paul," in *The Root of the Vine*, by A. Fridrichsen et al. (New York: Philosophical Library, 1953).

Fretheim, T. E., "The Plagues as Ecological Signs of Historical Disaster," *JBL* 110 (1991): 385-96.

Friedman, R.E., *Who Wrote the Bible?* (New York: Summit, 1987).

Frye, N., *The Great Code: The Bible and Literature* (San Diego: HBJ, 1981).

Fuller, R. H., *The Foundations of New Testament Christology* (London: Lutterworth, 1965).

Fuller, R. H., and Perkins, P., *Who Is This Christ?* (Philadelphia: Fortress, 1983).

Gager, J. G., *Moses in Greco-Roman Paganism* (SBLMS 16; Nashville: Abingdon, 1972).

Garland, D. E., *The Intention of Matthew 23* (NovTSup 52; Leiden: E. J. Brill, 1979).

Garrett, Susan R., "Exodus from Bondage: Luke 9:31 and Acts 12:1-24," *CBQ* 52 (1990):656-80.

Genovese, E. D., *Roll, Jordan, Roll: The World the Slaves Made* (New York: Random House, 1974).

Georgi, Dieter, *The Opponents of Paul in Second Corinthians* (Philadelphia: Fortress, 1976).

Gerhardsson, B., *Memory and Manuscript: Oral Tradition and Written Transmission in Rabbinic Judaism and Early Christianity* (2nd ed.; Uppsala and Lund: Gleerup, 1964).

idem, *The Testing of God's Son (Matt 4:1-11 & Par.)* (CB,NT 2/1; Lund: Gleerup, 1966).

Giblet, M., "Prophétisme et attente d'un messie-prophète dans l'ancien Judaïsme," in *L'Venue du Messie*, ed. E. Massaux et al. (Bruges: Desclée, 1962), 85-130.

Ginzberg, L., *The Legends of the Jews*, 7 vols. (Philadelphia: Jewish Publication Society, 1942).

Glasson, T. F., *Moses in the Fourth Gospel* (SBT 40; London: SCM, 1963).

Glazier-McDonald, B., *Malachi* (SBLDS 98; Atlanta: Scholars Press, 1987).

Gnilka, J., *Das Matthäusevangelium*, 2 vols. (HTKNT; Freiburg: Herder, 1986, 1989).

Godet, F., *Introduction to the New Testament: The Collection of the Four Gospels and the Gospel of St. Matthew* (Edinburgh: T. & T. Clark, 1899).

Goldberg, M., *Jews and Christians: Getting Our Stories Straight* (Nashville: Abingdon, 1985).

Goodenough, Erwin R., *By Light, Light* (New Haven: Yale, 1935).

idem, "Kingship in Early Israel," *JBL* 48 (1929):169-205.

idem, "The Political Philosophy of Hellenistic Kingship," in *Yale Classical Studies*, vol. 1, ed. A. H. Harman (New Haven: Yale, 1928), 55-102.

Gorday, Peter J., "Moses and Jesus in *Contra Celsum* 7:1-25," in *Origen of Alexandria*, ed. C. Kannengiesser and W. L. Petersen (Notre Dame: University Press, 1988), 313-36.

Goulder, M., *Midrash and Lection in Matthew* (London: SPCK, 1974).

idem, *Type and History in Acts* (London: S.P.C.K., 1964).

Grabar, A., *Christian Iconography* (Princeton: University Press, 1968).

Gray, J., *I and II Kings* (2nd ed.; Philadelphia: Westminster, 1970).

Greene, T. M., *The Light in Troy: Imitation and Discovery in Renaissance Poetry* (New Haven: Yale, 1982).

Grelot, P., "La naissance d'Isaac et celle je Jésus: Sur une interprétation 'mythologique' de la conception virginale," *NRT* 94 (1972):462-87, 561-85.

Grözinger, K.-E., *Ich bin der Herr, dein Gott!* (Bern: Herber Lang, 1976).

Grubbe, G. M. A., *The Greek and Latin Critics* (London: Methuen, 1965).

Guelich, R. A., *The Sermon on the Mount* (Waco: Word, 1982).

✓ Gundry, R. H., *Matthew: A Commentary on His Literary and Theological Art* (Grand Rapids: Eerdmans, 1982).

✓ idem, *The Use of the Old Testament in St. Matthew's Gospel* (NovTSup 18; Leiden: E. J. Brill, 1967).

Hahn, F., "Das Problem alter christologischer Überlieferungen in der Apostelgeschichte unter besonderer Berücksichtigung von Act 3.19-21," in *Les Actes des Apôtres*, ed. J. Kremer (BETL 48; Gembloux/Leuven: J. Duculot/Leuven, 1979), 129-54.

idem, *The Titles of Jesus in Christology* (London: Lutterworth, 1969).

Halperin, D. J., *The Merkabah in Rabbinic Literature* (American Oriental Series 62; New Haven: American Oriental Society, 1980).

Hanson, A. T., "The Midrash in II Corinthians 3: A Reconsideration," *JSNT* 9 (1980):2-28.

Harl, M., "Moïse figure de l'évêque dans l'Eloge de Basile de Grégoire de Nyssa (381)," in *The Biographical Works of Gregory of Nyssa*, ed. Andreas Spira (Philadelphia: Philadelphia Patristic Society, 1984), 71-119.

Harris, J. Rendall, *Testimonies*, Part I (Cambridge: University Press, 1916); Part II (Cambridge: University Press, 1920).

Harvey, S. Ashbrook, "The Sense of a Stylite. Perspectives on Simeon the Elder," *VC* 66 (1986):376-94.

Hawkins, J. C., *Horae Synopticae* (rev. ed.; Oxford: University Press, 1909).

Hay, D. M., "Moses through New Testament Spectacles," *Int* 44 (1990):240-52.

Hegermann, H., *Jesaja 53 in Hexapla, Targum und Peschitta* (Gütersloh: Bertelsmann, 1954).

Hengel, M., *From Jesus to Paul* (Philadelphia: Fortress, 1983).

idem, *The Son of God* (Philadelphia: Fortress, 1976).

Henry, Matthew, *Matthew Henry's Commentary on the Whole Bible* (Peabody: Hendrickson, 1991).

Hill, D., "In Quest of Matthean Christology," *IBS* 9 (1986):135-42.

idem, "Son and Servant: An Essay on Matthean Christology," *JSNT* 6 (1980):2-16.

Holladay, William L., "The Background of Jeremiah's Self-Understanding," *JBL* 83 (1964):153-64.

idem, *Jeremiah*, 2 vols. (Hermeneia; Philadelphia: Fortress, 1986, 1989).

Holladay, C. R., "The Portrait of Moses in Ezekiel the Tragedian," in *Society of Biblical Literature 1976 Seminar Papers*, ed. George MacRae (Missoula: Scholars Press, 1976), 447-52.

idem, *THEIOS ANER in Hellenistic Judaism* (SBLDS 40; Missoula: Scholars Press, 1977).

Hollander, John, *The Figure of an Echo: A Mode of Allusion in Milton and After* (Berkeley: University of California, 1981).

idem, *Melodious Guile: Fictive Pattern in Poetic Language* (New Haven: Yale, 1988).

Hollerich, M. J., "Myth and History in Eusebius' *De Vita Constantini*: *Vit. Const.* 1:12 in Its Contemporary Setting," *HTR* 82 (1989):421-45.

Holt, E. K., "The Chicken or the Egg—Or: Was Jeremiah a Member of the Deuteronomist Party?," *JSOT* 44 (1989):109-22.

Holtzmann, H. J., *Lehrbuch der historisch-kritischen Einleitung in das Neue Testament* (3rd ed.; Freiburg im Breslau: J. C. B. Mohr (Paul Siebeck), 1892).

Hooke, S. H., *Middle Eastern Mythology* (Baltimore: Penguin, 1963).

Horbury, W., "The Messianic Associations of 'The Son of Man,'" *JTS* 36 (1985):34-55.

idem, "The Twelve and the Phylarchs," *NTS* 32 (1986):503-27.

Horsley, R. A., "'Like One of the Prophets of Old,'" *CBQ* 47 (1985):435-63.

Hubbard, B. J., *The Matthean Redaction of a Primitive Apostolic Commissioning* (SBLDS 19; Missoula: Society of Biblical Literature, 1974).

Hull, J., *Hellenistic Magic and the Synoptic Tradition* (SBT 28; London: SCM, 1974).

Hunter, A. M., "Crux Criticorum—Matt. 11.25-30," *NTS* 8 (1962):241-9.

Hurtado, L. W., *One God, One Lord: Early Christian Devotion and Ancient Jewish Monotheism* (Philadelphia: Fortress, 1988).

Jacob, E., "Prophètes et Intercessors," in *De la Tôrah au Messie: Mélanges Henri Cazelles*, ed. M. Carrez, J. Doré, and P. Grelot (Paris: Desclée, 1981), 205-17.

Jeremias, Gert, *Der Lehrer der Gerechtigkeit* (SUNT 2; Göttingen: Vandenhoeck & Ruprecht, 1963).

Johnson, M. D., "Reflections on a Wisdom Approach to Matthew's Christology," *CBQ* 36 (1974):44-64.

Jones, P., "L Apôtre Paul: Un second Moïse par là Communaté de la nouvelle Alliance: Une Étude sur l'Autoritié apostolique paulinienne," *Foi et Vie* 75 (1976):36-58.

Jonge, M. de, *Jesus: Stranger from Heaven* (Missoula: Scholars Press, 1977).

Juhl, P. D., *Interpretation: An Essay in the Philosophy of Literary Criticism*

(Princeton: Princeton University Press, 1980).

Kaminka, A., "Hillel's Life and Work," *JQR* 30 (1939):107-22.

J. M. Kastner, *Moses im Neuen Testament* (München: Ludwig-Maximillians-Universität [diss.], 1967).

Keck, L. E., "Toward the Renewal of New Testament Christology," *NTS* 32 (1986):362-77.

Kee, Howard Clark, *Knowing the Truth: A Sociological Approach to New Testament Interpretation* (Minneapolis: Fortress, 1989).

Kikawada, I. M., and Quinn, A., *Before Abraham was* (Nashville: Abingdon, 1985).

Kingsbury, J. D., *Matthew: Structure, Christology, Kingdom* (Philadelphia: Fortress, 1975).

idem, "On Following Jesus: the 'Eager' Scribe and 'Reluctant' Disciple (Matthew 8.18-22)," *NTS* 34 (1988):45-59.

Knight, G. A. F., *Isaiah 40-55* (Edinburgh: Handsel, 1984).

Knowles, M. P. "Moses, the Law, and the Unity of IV Ezra," *NovT* 31 (1989):257-74.

Koch, K., "Ezra and the Origis of Judaism," *JSS* 19 (1974): 173-97.

Koestler, A., *The Act of Creation* (London: Hutchinson, 1964).

Kraus, H.-J., *Worship in Israel* (Oxford: Basil Blackwell, 1966).

Kretschmar, G., "Himmelfahrt und Pfingsten," *ZKG* 66 (1954/55):217-22.

Krieller, C. A., "Moses und Petros," *Stimmen aus Maria Laach* 60 (1901):237-57.

Kugel, James L., *In Potiphar's House: The Interpretive Life of Biblical Texts* (San Francisco: Harper & Row, 1990).

Kysar, Robert, *The Fourth Evangelist and His Gospel* (Minneapolis: Augsburg, 1975).

Lacomara, Aelred, "Deuteronomy and the Farewell Discourse (Jn 13:31-16:33)," *CBQ* 36 (1974):65-84.

Lafargue, M., "The Jewish Orpheus," in *Society of Biblical Literature 1978 Seminar Papers*, ed. P. J. Achtemeier (Missoula: Scholars Press, 1978), vol. 2:137-43.

Lagrange, M.-J., *Evangile selon saint Matthieu*, 7th ed. (Paris: J. Gabalda, 1948).

Leaney, A. R. C., *The Rule of Qumran and Its Meaning* (Philadelphia: Westminster, 1966).

Leclercq, J., *The Love of Learning and the Desire for God: A Study of Monastic Culture* (New York: Fordham, 1982).

Le Déaut, R., *La Nuit Pascale* (AB 22; Rome: Pontificial Biblical Institute, 1963).

Levenson, J. D., *Sinai and Zion* (Minneapolis: Seabury, 1985).

idem, *Theology of the Program of Restoration of Ezekiel 40-48* (HSM 10; Missoula: Scholars Press, 1976).

Levertoff, P. P., "The Gospel according to St. Matthew," in *A New Catholic Commentary on Holy Scripture*, ed. C. Gore et al. (New York: Macmillan, 1928).

Levi, P., "The Podgoritza Cup," *HeyJ* 4 (1963):55-60.

Lindars, B., "The Image of Moses in the Synoptic Gospels," *Theology* 58 (1955):78-83.

idem, *New Testament Apologetic* (London: SCM, 1961).

Loewenstamm, S. E., "The Death of Moses," in *Studies on the Testament of Abraham*, ed. G. W. E. Nickelsburg (Missoula: Scholars Press, 1976), 185-217.

idem, "The Testament of Abraham and Texts concerning Moses' Death," in
    ibid., pp. 219-25.

Lohfink, G., "Die deuteronomistische Darstellung des Übergangs der Führung
    Israels von Moses auf Josue," *Scholastik* 37 (1962):32-44.

Lövestam, E. "The Eschatology in Mk 13.30 parr.," in *L'Apocalypse johannique
    et l'Apocalyptique dans le Nouveau Testament*, ed. J. Lambrecht (BETL 53;
    Gembloux: J. Duculot; Leuven: Unviersity Press), pp. 403-13.

Lüdemann, Gerd, *Early Christianity according to the Traditions in Acts*
    (Philadelphia: Fortress, 1989).

Luz, Ulrich, *Matthew 1-7* (Minneapolis: Augsburg, 1989).

McBride, S. D., "Polity of the Covenant People: The Book of Deuteronomy,"
    Int. 41 (1987):229-44.

McCarthy, D. J., "An Installation Genre?," *JBL* 90 (1971):31-41.

Macdonald, J. *The Theology of the Samaritans* (Philadelphia: Westminster, 1964).

Mähler, M., "Évocations bibliques et hagiographiques dans la vie de saint
    Benoît par saint Grégorie," *RBén* 83 (1973):145-84.

Mailloux, Steven, *Interpretive Conventions: The Reader in the Study of American
    Fiction* (Ithaca: Cornell, 1982).

Mánek, J., "The New Exodus in the Books of Luke," *NovT* 2 (1955):8-23.

Mann, Thomas W., "Theological Reflections on the Denial of Moses," *JBL* 98
    (1979):481-94.

Manson, T. W., *The Teaching of Jesus* (Cambridge: University Press, 1935).

Martin, R. P., *2 Corinthians* (WBC; Waco: Word, 1986).

Martyn, J. Louis, *History and Theology in the Fourth Gospel* (rev. ed.; Nashville:
    Abingdon, 1979).

idem, "We have found Elijah," in *Jews, Greeks and Christians*, ed. R. Hamerton-
    Kelly and Robin Scroggs (SJLA 21; Leiden: Brill, 1976), pp. 181-219.

Meeks, W. A., "Moses as God and King," in *Religions in Antiquity: Essays in
    Memory of Erwin Ramsdell Goodenough*, ed. J. Neusner (Leiden: E. J. Brill,
    1970), 354-71.

idem, *The Prophet-King: Moses Traditions and the Johannine Christology* (NovTSup
    14; Leiden: E. J. Brill, 1967).

Menken, M. J. J., "The References to Jeremiah in the Gospel according to
    Matthew (Mt 2,17; 16,14; 17,9)," *ETL* 60 (1984):5-24.

Mettinger, T. N. D., *A Farewell to the Servant Songs* (Lund: Gleerup, 1983).

Meier, John P., "John the Baptist in Matthew's Gospel," *JBL* 99 (1980):383-405.

idem, *Law and History in Matthew's Gospel* (AnBib 71; Rome: Biblical Institute,
    1976).

idem, *Matthew* (Wilmington: Michael Glazier, 1980).

idem, "Two Disputed Questions in Matt 28:16-20," *JBL* 96 (1977):407-24.

Meyer, Ben F., *The Church in Three Tenses* (Garden City: Doubleday, 1971).

Michel, O., *Der Brief an die Hebräer* (6th ed.; Göttingen: Vandenhocek and
    Ruprecht, 1966).

Milburn, R., *Early Christian Art and Architecture* (Berkeley: University of
    California, 1988).

Miner, E., ed., *Literary Uses of Typology*, Miner (Princeton: University Press, 1977).

Miscall, P. D., *1 Samuel: A Literary Reading* (Bloomington: Indiana University
    Press, 1986).

Moessner, D. P., *The Lord of the Banquet: The Literary and Theological Significance
    of the Lukan Travel Narrative* (Minneapolis: Fortress, 1989).

Mohrlang, R., *Matthew and Paul* (SNTSMS 48; Cambridge: University Press, 1984).

Moïse: *L'Homme de L Alliance* (Paris: Desclée, 1955).

Morgenstern, J., "Moses with the Shining Face," HUCA 2 (1925):1-27.

Morosco, R. E., "Matthew's Formation of a Commissioning Type-Scene," *JBL* 103 (1984):539-56.

Mortley, R., "The Past in Clement of Alexandria," in *Jewish and Christian Self-Definition*, vol. 1, ed. E. P. Sanders (Philadelphia: Fortress, 1980), 186-200.

Moulder, W. J., "The Old Testament Background of Mark x. 45," *NTS* 24 (1977), 120-27.

Mowinckel, S., *He That Cometh* (New York: Abingdon, n.d.).

Moye, R. H., "In the Beginning: Myth and History in Genesis and Exodus," *JBL* 109 (1990):596-97.

Moynahan, J., "The Mayor of Casterbridge and the Old Testament's First Book of Samuel: A Study of Some Literary Relationships," *Publications of the Modern Language Association* 71 (1956):118-30.

Muilenburg, James, "Baruch the Scribe," in *Proclamation and Presence*, ed. J. I. Durham and J. R. Porter (London: SCM, 1970), 215-38.

idem, "The 'Office' of Prophet in Ancient Israel," in *The Bible and Modern Scholarship*, ed. J. Philip Hyatt (Nashville: Abingdon, 1965), 74-97.

Munck, Johannes, *Paul and the Salvation of Mankind* (London: SCM, 1959).

Murdoch, K. B., "Clio in the Wilderness: History and Biography in Puritan New England," *CH* 24 (1955):221-38

Murphy, F. J., *The Religious World of Jesus* (Nashville: Abingdon, 1991).

Myers, J. M., *I and II Esdras* (AB 42; Garden City: Doubleday, 1974).

Nelson, R. D., *First and Second Kings* (Atlanta: John Knox, 1987).

idem, "Josiah in the Book of Joshua," *JBL* 100 (1981):531-40.

Nepper-Christensen, P., *Das Matthäusevangelium* (Aahrus: Universitets-forlaget, 1958).

Nestle, E., "Die Fünfteilung im Werk des Papias und im ersten Evangelium," *ZNW* 1 (1900):252-54.

Nickelsburg, G. W. E., *Jewish Literature between the Bible and the Mishnah* (Philadelphia: Fortress, 1981).

Niditch, S., "Ezekiel 40-48 in a Visionary Context," *CBQ* 48 (1986):208-24.

Nolan, B. M., *The Royal Son of God: The Christology of Matthew 1-2 in the Setting of the Gospel* (OBO 20; Göttingen: Vandenhoeck & Ruprecht, 1979).

North, C. R., *The Suffering Servant in Deutero-Isaiah* (2nd ed.; Oxford: University Press, 1956).

O'Connor, J. Murphy, "Le genese litteraire de la Regle de la Communaute," *RB* 76 (1969):528-49.

idem, *The Theology of the Second Letter to the Corinthians* (Cambridge: University Press, 1991).

O'Connor, K. M. *The Confessions of Jeremiah* (SBLDS 94; Atlanta: Scholars Press, 1988).

Oded, B., "Judah and the Exile," in *Israelite and Judaean History*, ed. John H. Hayes and J. Maxwell Miller (Philadelphia: Westminster, 1977), pp. 435-88.

Ogawa, A., *L'histoire de Jesus chez Matthieu* (Europäische Hochschulschriften 23/116; Frankfurt am Main: Lang, 1979).

Ogden, G. S., "Moses and Cyrus," *VT* 28 (1978):195-203.

Olsen, H., *The End of Literary Theory* (Cambridge: University Press, 1987).

Olyan, S. M., "The Israelites Debate their Options at the Sea of Reeds," *JBL* 110 (1991):75-91.

O'Toole, R. T., "The Parallels between Jesus and Moses," *BTB* 20 (1990):22-29.

Overman, J. A., *Matthew's Gospel and Formative Judaism* (Minneapolis: Fortress, 1990).

Page, S. H. T., "The Suffering Servant between the Testaments," *NTS* 31 (1985):481-97.

Peckham, B., "The Composition of Joshua 3-4," *CBQ* 46 (1984):413-31.

Perrot, C., "Les récits d'enfance dans la haggada antérieure au II siècle de notre ère," *RSR* 55 (1967):481-518.

idem, "'Un prophète comme l'un des Prophètes' (Mc 6.15)," in *De la Tôrah au Messie: Mélanges Henri Cazelles*, ed. M. Carrez, J. Doré, and P. Grelot (Paris: Desclée, 1981), 417-23.

Pesch, R., *Das Abendmahl und Jesu Todesverständnis* (QD 80; Freiburg: Herder, 1978).

Petersen, J. M., *The "Dialogues" of Gregory the Great in their Late Antique Cultural Background* (Rome: Pontifical Institute of Mediaeval Studies, 1984).

Plumpe, J. C., "Some Little-Known Early Witnesses to Mary's *Virginitas in Partu*," *TS* 9 (1948):567-77.

Pokorny, P., *The Genesis of Christology* (Edinburgh: T. & T. Clark, 1987).

Polzin, R., *Moses and the Deuteronomist* (New York: Seabury, 1980).

Porter, J.R., *Moses and Monarchy* (Oxford: Basil Blackwell, 1963).

idem, "The Succession of Joshua," in *Proclamation and Presence*, ed. J. I. Durham and J. R. Porter (London: SPCK, 1970), 102-32.

Prabhu, G. M. Soares, *The Formula Quotations in the Infancy Narrative of Matthew* (AnBib 63; Rome: Biblical Institute Press, 1976).

Preiss, T., "Étude sur le chapitre 6 de l'Évangile de Jean," *ETR* 46 (1971):144-56.

Propp, W. H., "The Skin of Moses' Face—Transfigured or Disfigured?," *CBQ* 49 (1987):376-77.

Rad, G. von, *Old Testament Theology*, 2 vols. (New York: Harper & Row, 1962, 1965).

Rajan, B., *Paradise Lost and the 17th Century Reader* (London: Chatto and Windus, 1962).

Ramsey, A. M., *The Glory of God and the Transfiguration of Christ* (Philadelphia: Westminster, 1946).

Rawlinson, A. E. J., *The New Testament Doctrine of the Christ* (London: Longmans, Green, and Co., Ltd., 1926).

Réau, Louis, *Iconographie de l'art chrétien*, vol. 2, part 2 (Paris: Presses Universitaires de France, 1957).

Renov, I., "The Seat of Moses," in *The Synagogue*, ed. J. Gutman (New York: KTAV, 1975), 233-38.

Riaud, J., "La figure de Jérémie dans les Paralipomena Jeremiae," in *Mélanges bibliques et orinetaux en l'honneur de M. Henri Cazelles*, ed. A. Caquot and M. Delcor (Neukirchen-Vluyn: Neukirchener, 1981), 373-85.

Richards, I. A., *The Philosophy of Rhetoric* (London: Oxford, 1976).

idem, *Principles of Literary Criticism* (reprint ed.; San Diego: HBJ, 1985).

Richards, Jeffrey, *The Popes and the Papacy in the Early Middle Ages, 476-752* (London: Routledge and Kegan Paul, 1979).

Richardson, Alan, *An Introduction to the Theology of the New Testament* (London: SCM, 1958).

Robinson, B. P., "Elijah at Horeb, 1 Kings 19:1-18," *RB* 98 (1991):513-36.

Rosenberg, H., *Arshile Gorky: The Man, the Time, the Idea* (New York: Grove, 1962).

Rousseau, O., "Saint Benoît et le prophète Élisee," *Revue du moyen-âge latin* 144 (1956):103-14.

Rowley, H. H., *The Servant of the Lord and Other Essays on the Old Testament* (Oxford: Basil Blackwell, 1965).

Sahlin, H., "The New Exodus of Salvation," in *Root of the Vine*, 81-95.

Saito, T., *Die Mosevorstellungen im Neuen Testament* (Europäische Hochschulschriften Series 23, Theology, vol. 100; Bern: Peter Lang, 1977).

Sand, A., *Das Evangelium nach Matthäus* (Regensburger Neues Testament; Regensburg: Friedrich Pustet, 1986).

idem, *Das Gesetz und Propheten, Untersuchungen zur Theologie des Evangeliums nach Matthäus* (Regensburg: Friedrich Pustet, 1974).

Sarna, M. N., *Exploring Exodus* (New York: Schocken, 1986).

Schaberg, J., *The Father, the Son, and the Holy Spirit* (SBLDS 61; Chico: Scholars Press, 1982).

Schapiro, Meyer, *Late Antique, Early Christian and Mediaeval Art* (New York: George Braziller, 1979).

Schiller, G., *Iconography of Christian Art*, 2 vols. (Greenwich, Conn.: New York Graphics Society, 1968).

Schlatter, A., *Der Evangelist Matthäus* (3rd ed.; Stuttgart: Calwer, 1948).

Schoeps, H. J., *Theologie und Geschichte des Judenchristentums* (Tübingen: J. C. B. Mohr (Paul Siebeck), 1949).

Schökel, Alonso, 'Jeremías como anti-Moses," in *De la Tôrah au Messie*, ed. M. Carrez et al. (Paris: Desclée, 1981), 245-54.

Scholem, G., *Sabbatai Sevi* (Princeton: University Press, 1973).

Schulz, J. P., "Angelic Opposition to the Ascension of Moses and the Revelation of the Law," *JQR* 61 (1971):282-307.

Schulz, P., *Der Autoritätsanspruch des Lehrers der Gerechtigkeit in Qumran* (Meisenheim am Glan: Anton Hein, 1974).

Schürmann, H., "'Das Gesetz des Christus' (Gal 6,2)," in *Neues Testament und Kirche*, ed. Joachim Gnilka (Freiburg: Herder, 1974), 282-300.

Scobie, Charles H. H., "The Use of Source Material in the Speeches of Acts III and VII," *NTS* 25 (1979):399-421.

Selwyn, E. G., *The First Epistle of St. Peter* (London: Macmillan, 1947).

Silver, D. J., *Images of Moses* (New York: Basic Books, 1982).

idem, "Moses and the Hungry Birds," *JQR* 64 (1973):124-53.

Simon, Marcel, *Verus Israel* (Paris: E. de Boccard, 1964).

Smyth, K., "Matthew 28: Resurrection as Theophany," *ITQ* 42 (1975), 259-71.

Smith, M., "Ascent to the Heavens and Deification in 4QMa," in *Archaeology and the Dead Sea Scrolls*, ed. L. H. Schiffmann (JSPSS 8; Sheffield: JSOT, 1990), 181-88.

idem, "Helios in Palestine," *Eretz Israel* 16 (1982):199-214.

Snaith, N. H., *Five Psalms (1; 27; 51; 107; 134)* (London: Epworth, 1938).

Spicq, C., *L'Épître aux Hébreux*, vol. 2 (EB; Paris: J. Gabalda, 1953).

Stegner, W. R., *Narrative Theology in Early Jewish Christianity* (Louisville: Westminster/John Knox, 1989).

Steidle, B., "Homo Dei Antonius: zum Bild des 'Mannes Gottes' im alten Mönchtum," *Studia Anselmiana* 38 (1956):148-200.

Steiner, G., *In Bluebeard's Castle* (New Haven: Yale, 1971).

Stockhausen, C. K., *Moses' Veil and the Glory of the New Covenant. The Exegetical Substructure of II Cor 3,1-4,6* (AnBib 116; Rome: Pontifical Biblical Institute, 1988).

Stone, M. E., "Apocalyptic Literature," in *Jewish Writings of the Second Temple Period: Apocrypha, Pseudepigrapha, Qumran Sectarian Writings, Philo, Josephus*, ed. M. E. Stone (Compendia Rerum Iudaicarum ad Novum Testamentum; Assen/Philadelphia: Van Gorcum and Fortress, 1984), 383-441.

idem, "The Apocryphal Literature in the Armenian Tradition," *Proceedings of the Israel Academy of Sciences and Humanities* 4 (1971):59-77.

idem, "Three Armenian Accounts of the Death of Moses," in *Studies on the Testament of Moses*, ed. G. W. E. Nickelsburg (Cambridge, Mass.: Society of Biblical Literature, 1973), 118-21.

idem, *Fourth Ezra* (Hermeneia; Minneapolis: Fortress, 1991).

Strauss, D. F., *The Life of Jesus Critically Examined*, ed. P. C. Hodgson (Philadelphia: Fortress, 1972).

Straw, Carole, *Gregory the Great: Perfection in Imperfection* (Berkeley: University of California, 1988).

Strugnell, John, "Moses-Pseudepigrapha at Qumran," in *Archaeology and History in the Dead Sea Scrolls*, ed. L. Schiffmann (JSOT/ASOR Monographs 2; Sheffield: JSOT, 1990):221-56.

Stuhlfauth, G., *Die apokryphen Petrusgeschichten in der altchristlichen Kirche* (Berlin: de Gruyter, 1925).

Suggs, J. M., *Wisdom, Christology, and Law in Matthew's Gospel* (Cambridge: Harvard, 1970).

Sweet, J. P. M., *Revelation* (Philadelphia: Westminster, 1979).

Talbert, C. H., *Literary Patterns, Theological Themes, and the Genre of Luke-Acts* (Missoula: Scholars Press, 1974).

Tanselle, G. Thomas, *A Rationale of Textual Criticism* (Philadelphia: University of Pennsylvania, 1989).

Tcherikover, V., *Hellenistic Civilization and the Jews* (New York: Atheneum, 1970).

idem, "Jewish Apologetic Literature Reconsidered," *Eos* 48 (1956):169-93.

Teeple, H. M., *The Mosaic Eschatological Prophet* (SBLMS 10; Philadelphia: Society of Biblical Literature, 1957).

Theil, W., *Die deuteronomistische Redaktion von Jeremia 1-25* (WMANT 41; Neukirchen-Vluyn, 1973).

Trilling, W., *Das wahre Israel* (SANT 10; 3rd ed.; München: Kösel, 1964).

van der Horst, P. W., "Moses' Throne Vision in Ezekiel the Dramatist," *JJS* 34 (1983):21-29.

idem, "Seven Months' Children in Jewish and Christian Literature from Antiquity," *ETL* 54 (1978):346-60.

van der Woude, A. S., *Die Messianischen Vorstellungen der Gemeinde von Qumran* (Assen: Van Gorcum & Co., 1957).

idem, "11QMelchizedek and the New Testament," *NTS* 12 (1966):301-26.

Vermes, G., *Jesus the Jew* (London: William Collins Sons, 1973).

idem, *Scripture and Tradition in Judaism* (Leiden: Brill, 1961).

Vögtle, A., "Die matthäische Kindheitsgeschichte," in *L'Évangile selon Matthieu: Rédaction et Théologie*, ed. M. Didier (BETL 29: Gembloux: Leuven University, 1972), 153-83.

Wacholder, B. Z., *The Dawn of Qumran* (Cincinnati: Hebrew Union College Press, 1983).

Watts, John D. W., *Isaiah 34-66* (WBC; Waco: Word, 1987).

Webb, B. G., *The Book of Judges: An Integrated Reading* (JSOTSS 46; Sheffield: JSOT, 1987).

Weinfeld, M., "Sabbath, Temple, and the Enthronement of the Lord: The Problem of the Sitz im Leben of Genesis 1:1-2:3," in *Mélanges bibliques et orientaux en l'honneur de M. Henri Cazelles*, ed. A. Caquot and M. Delcor (AOAT 212; Neukirchen-Vluyn: Neukirchen; Kevelaer: Butzon and Bercker, 1981), 501-12.

Weingreen, J., " '*hws' tyk* in Genesis 15.7," in *Words and Meanings*, ed. P. R. Ackroyd and B. Lindars (Cambridge: Unviersity Press, 1968), 209-15.

Wenham, G. J., *Genesis 1-15* (WBC; Waco: Word, 1987).

Westcott, B. F., *The Epistle to the Hebrews* (2nd ed.; London: Macmillan, 1892).

Westermann, C., *Isaiah 40-66* (London: SCM, 1969).

idem, *Sprache und Struktur der Prophetie Deuterojesajas* (CTM; Stuttgart: Calwer, 1981).

Widengren, G., *The Ascension of the Apostle and the Heavenly Book* (Uppsala: A. B. Lundeqvistska, 1950).

idem, "King and Covenant," *JSS* 2 (1957):1-32.

Wieder, N., "The 'Law-Interpreter' of the Sect of the Dead Sea Scrolls: The Second Moses," *JJS* 4 (1953):158-75.

Wilkens, J., *Der König Israels*, vol. 1 (Berlin: Furche, 1934).

Wilkens, W., "Die Versuchung Jesu nach Matthäus," *NTS* 28 (1982):479-89.

Williamson, H. G. M., "The Accession of Solomon in the Books of Chronicles," *VT* 26 (1976):351-61.

idem, *Israel in the Book of Chronicles* (Cambridge: University Press, 1977).

Wilshire, L. W., "The Servant-City," *JBL* 94 (1975):356-67.

Windisch, H., *The Meaning of the Sermon on the Mount* (Philadelphia: Westminster, 1951).

Winter, P., "Jewish Folklore in the Matthean Birth Story," *HeyJ* 53 (1954):34-42.

Wise, M. O., *A Critical Study of the Temple Scroll from Qumran Cave II* (Studies in Ancient Oriental Civilization 49; Chicago: Oriental Institute, 1990).

idem, "The Eschatological Vision of the Temple Scroll," *JENS* 49 (1990):155-72.

Wolff, C., *Jeremia im Frühjudentum und Urchristentum* (Berlin: Akademie-Verlag, 1976).

Zakovitch, Y., "Assimilation in Biblical Narratives," in *Empirical Models for Biblical Criticism*, ed. J. H. Tigay (Philadelphia: University of Pennsylvania, 1985), 176-96.

Zehnle, R. F., *Peter's Pentecost Discourse* (SBLMS 15; Nashville: Abingdon, 1971).

Zeron, A., "Einige Bemerkungen zu M. F. Collilns 'The Hidden Vessels in Samaritan Tradition,'" *JSJ* 4 (1974):165-68.

idem, "The Martyrdom of Phineas-Elijah," *JBL* 98 (1979):99-100.

Zevit, Z., "The Priestly Redaction and Interpretation of the Plague Narrative in Exodus," *JQR* 66 (1976):193-211.

Idem, "Three Ways to look at the Ten Plagues," *BibRev* VI/3 (1990):16-23, 42.

Zimmerli, W., *Ezekiel*, 2 vols. (Hermeneia; Philadelphia: Fortress, 1979, 1983).

INDEX OF NAMES

INDEX OF SUBJECTS ————————

INDEX OF PASSAGES ────────────

Other Midrashim

Tanhuma